# The Perpetual Enterprise Machine

# The Perpetual Enterprise Machine

## Seven Keys to Corporate Renewal Through Successful Product and Process Development

Editors

**H. Kent Bowen**
**Kim B. Clark**
**Charles A. Holloway**
**Steven C. Wheelwright**

New York   Oxford    Oxford University Press   1994

Oxford University Press

Oxford   New York   Toronto
Delhi   Bombay   Calcutta   Madras   Karachi
Kuala Lumpur   Singapore   Hong Kong   Tokyo
Nairobi   Dar es Salaam   Cape Town
Melbourne   Auckland   Madrid

and associated companies in
Berlin   Ibadan

Published by Oxford University Press, Inc.
200 Madison Avenue, New York, New York 10016

Library of Congress Cataloging-in-Publication Data
The Perpetual enterprise machine : seven keys to corporate
renewal through successful product and process
development / H. Kent Bowen . . . [et al.].
p. cm.   Includes bibliographical references and index.
ISBN 0-19-508052-1
1. Industrial project management—United States.
2. New products—United States—Management.
3. Production management—United States.
4. United States—Manufactures—Case studies.
I. Bowen, H. Kent.
HD69.P75P47 1994
658.4′04—dc20   93-43172

2 4 6 8 9 7 5 3 1

Printed in the United States of America
on acid-free paper

# Preface

*The Perpetual Enterprise Machine* is the product of a unique collaborative research effort between five companies—Chaparral Steel, Digital Equipment Corporation, Ford Motor Company, Hewlett-Packard, and Eastman Kodak—and four universities—Harvard University, Massachusetts Institute of Technology, Purdue University, and Stanford University. The book is about the principles that drive outstanding development of new products and processes. But at a deeper level, it is a book about creating the future. It is about the kind of enterprise that will thrive and prosper in the years ahead: an enterprise that perpetually builds and renews itself because of its superior capabilities in creating new products and processes.

This book got its start on a fall evening in a Boston hotel room in the late 1980s. In the room were senior executives from three companies (the other two joined soon thereafter) and engineering and business academics from four universities. We were there to talk about the future of manufacturing enterprises: how we might work together to understand better what was going on and what we might do about it. The wind rattling the windows that night was the perfect background for our meeting, because winds of change were blowing in the companies and universities represented. In some the winds were at gale force, while others could see but the first rustling of the leaves. But all of us were convinced that what we taught and what we practiced had to change. Each company had its own reasons for joining the group. Chaparral, as a small but growing company that had been very successful in developing a spirit of entrepreneurship among its employees, was worried about how to keep this spirit alive as it grew. The large companies sought to understand how to revitalize their manufacturing enterprises and to relearn from Chaparral how to operate small organizational units. All of us were convinced we could learn from each other.

What came out of that meeting and many others that followed was a commitment to collaborate in creating new understanding about the future of the manufacturing enterprise. We chose to focus on the development of new products and processes, both because development is a critical process in the enterprise, but also because development is in many respects a microcosm of the larger enterprise. And we decided to practice what we intended to preach. We all believed that creating new understanding in manufacturing would require fundamental changes in the way companies and universities worked together. Moreover, we believed that within the university itself, progress would require closer relationships between schools of engineering and business. Thus, we decided that our approach must be representative of a broad, integrated effort. We formed collaborative teams, dubbed ourselves the Manufacturing Vision Group, and set to work.

In the following chapters we lay out the central themes to emerge from our study of twenty product and process development projects. We provide substantial background information on the companies and the specific projects we studied within them. The theme chapters cut across the projects and draw from them evidence and insight about the character and impact of that theme on development performance. Readers who desire to pursue further a particular illustration of a line of argument or a particular aspect of the practical realities of a discussion will find the company descriptions and the project descriptions a useful source of rich insight.

The ideas, thoughts, and words in these chapters are the result of many hours of discussion and collaboration among Vision Group members; in the end, however, particular members of the group took responsibility for the chapter drafts. While we celebrate the contributions of all members of the Vision Group, we give special mention to those who captured ideas in these drafts and then worked with the editors to yield this volume:

"The Manufacturer's Perpetual Enterprise Machine"—H. Kent Bowen
"Core Capabilities and Core Rigidities"—Dorothy Leonard-Barton, H. Kent Bowen, William Hanson, Douglas Braithwaite, Michael Titelbaum, and Gil Preuss
"Guiding Visions"—Dorothy Leonard-Barton, Douglas Braithwaite, H. Kent Bowen, William Hanson, Michael Titelbaum, and Gil Preuss
"Pushing the Performance Envelope"—Charles Holloway, James Solberg, Harold Edmondson, and Sara Beckman
"Project Leadership and Organization"—Kim Clark, Marco Iansiti, and Richard Billington
"Ownership and Commitment"—Steven Wheelwright, Thomas Eagar, and Gordon Forward
"Prototyping: Rapid Learning and Early Testing"—Philip Barkan and Marco Iansiti
"Integration within Projects"—Carolyn Woo, Steven Wheelwright, C. (Robin) Farran, David Groff, and Jack Rittler

Mark Fischetti served as rapporteur for "An Opportunity for Leadership in Learning" and, early in the writing process, helped synthesize the disparate styles, voices, and drafts of the entire manuscript.

Finally, the editors express appreciation to the numerous assistants and colleagues who aided this long process; in particular, we thank Jean Smith, who managed the manuscript generation process. The nearly impossible task of coordinating the Manufacturing Vision Group meetings at sites across the country was directed by Douglas Braithwaite, who served both as colleague and executive secretary to the group.

*Boston*                                                    H.K.B.
*December 1993*                                             K.B.C.
                                                           C.A.H.
                                                           S.C.W.

# Contents

# The Perpetual Enterprise Machine

# INTRODUCTION

# The Manufacturing
# Vision Group

This book is one of several products to come out of the Manufacturing Vision Group (MVG), an organization of like-minded academics and company executives who were motivated by the competitive pressures of the late 1980s to share experiences and knowledge with the hope of making sense of the transformations taking place in the U.S. manufacturing industry. In particular, members shared a common interest in (1) analyzing and exploring how manufacturing firms learn, and (2) determining the impact of trends and dislocations awaiting firms as new business and manufacturing paradigms evolved.

The group members' diverse backgrounds and experiences provided a unique perspective on the probable changes manufacturing firms would undergo as a consequence of new competitors, global markets, changes in technologies, and significant shifts in national priorities. The members of the MVG agreed that the world in which manufacturers exist had changed in such profound ways that most of the accepted wisdom and operating models needed to be questioned. Yet what seemed clear to this group was transparent to many middle and senior managers: ''They just don't get it!'' was an oft-repeated statement. Thus, the overarching theme was learning to adjust to and even anticipate change and new paradigms.

**Table 1**  Manufacturing Vision Group Members

| *Digital Equipment Corporation* | *Purdue University* | *Hewlett-Packard Corporation* |
|---|---|---|
| William Hanson | James Solberg | Harold Edmondson |
| Douglas Braithwaite | Carolyn Woo | Sara Beckman |
| Michael Titelbaum | Ferdinand Leimkuhler | |
| | | |
| *MIT* | *Chaparral Steel Company* | *Stanford University* |
| H. Kent Bowen | Gordon Forward | Charles Holloway |
| Thomas W. Eagar | David Fornie | Philip Barkan |
| George Stephanopoulos | | |
| | | |
| *Eastman Kodak Company* | *Harvard University* | *Ford Motor Company* |
| C. (Robin) Farran | Dorothy Leonard-Barton | Richard Billington |
| David Groff | Kim B. Clark | Max Jurosek |
| Jack Rittler | Marco Iansiti | |
| Rohn Harmer | Steven Wheelwright | |
| John Owen | Gil Preuss | |

From its inception the MVG project demonstrated an innovative cross-institutional model for research and learning. The academics came from management and engineering disciplines and represented Stanford University, Purdue University, Harvard University, and the Massachusetts Institute of Technology (MIT). Industry leaders were from Chaparral Steel Company, Digital Equipment Corporation, Eastman Kodak Company, Ford Motor Company, and Hewlett-Packard Corporation (HP). (**Table 1** lists the members and their affiliation.) The firms, which represented different industrial sectors with very different cultures and markets, varied on many dimensions, including revenues (from $500 million to $90 billion per year), number of employees, union representation for employees, and age of the corporation.

The company executives all had extensive experience heading organizations and careers that involved developing and implementing new product and process concepts. Their experience bases, however, had been developed through exposure to disparate situations; length of company product life cycles, maturity of the technology, and vintage of key competitors were a few of the many variations the MVG members and their companies brought to the project landscape. Similar discipline and cultural chasms existed between the academics. For example, Harvard and MIT could not be more different in their culture and style. The power of the MVG—the energy and light to examine critical issues through a new lens—was derived from the disparity at these institutional, disciplinary, and professional boundaries.

After approximately 18 months and a number of seminar-style discussions, a more formal research project was organized with the goal of creating an exercise from which all the institutions could learn. The MVG members selected development projects as the most interesting unit of analysis and as a means to gain insight into how companies change their product and process capabilities (and, as a result, create the capacity for further change).

The group sought to address a number of fundamental questions, including:

- How do companies carry out development projects?
- What are the company's policies, procedures, and practices?
- Are particular structures and processes commonly used?
- What are the roles of individuals and functions?
- What characteristics make development projects successful beyond the targeted project outcome of a new product or process?

It is hard to describe the electricity generated as group members toiled over this difficult territory, investing time and energy—not because of duty, but because of a desire to tackle these questions. The MVG project was outside everyone's job description. What could Chaparral Steel have in common with HP or Ford? How could a mechanical engineering design professor discuss new product development with a social science professor? How could the megaprojects be compared to projects involving only a few dozen people?

To facilitate analysis and provide "live data," the five member companies proposed several development projects for review. The MVG subsequently chose four recently completed projects from each company for a total of 20 projects. (A summary of the 20 projects, by company, is given in the Appendix to this chapter. Further descriptions of the companies and projects are given in Chapters 10 through 14.)

This final set of development projects was intended to be far-ranging in markets served and technologies incorporated. More significant, the set of projects had met with varying degrees of success. To allow the necessary breadth and depth of investigation, the group agreed to prioritize the goal of learning (rather than cataloguing successful projects) and to subjugate any potential risk of embarrassment.

The MVG project went through a project definition phase not unlike that of a corporate procedure. The group had postulated that the business paradigm was changing for manufacturing firms and wanted to measure representative characteristics within firms that might be used as a barometer of the organization's capacity for change.

The study was structured with a prescribed framework: rather than collect a large statistical sample on development projects, the MVG opted for a smaller data set where each datum was thoroughly understood—a methodology that allowed for rich debate about individual projects as well as across the set of projects. Group members presumed that this approach would help them acquire insights not readily determined through survey questions or broader interviews.

The company study teams typically included a management professor, an engineering professor, and one or two corporate managers. Each team was responsible for gathering raw data and providing preliminary analyses. The interviews with senior executives and members of the development project teams were usually conducted by the academics because they were viewed as impartial observers. After a single project in each company was studied, the data-gathering process was refined. The vision group members convened on multiple occasions to analyze preliminary observations and to fine-tune the project's structure and direction.

The group members discovered that despite the size of the company, a common set of themes existed, and that if these themes were further developed and articulated into prescriptive policies and practices within the proper context for the firm and market, the development projects would have a higher probability of success. Furthermore, the MVG concluded that successful development projects were the key to the perpetual enterprise machine.

In an important sense, this book is the product of our own development process. But the Manufacturing Vision Group has had an impact on the companies and the universities far beyond the creation of these pages. The concepts, principles, and tools discussed here have found application in many different projects across the companies; their impact has been felt in measurable improvements in lead time, productivity, and design quality. Creating an outstanding development process is a never-ending challenge, and the Vision Group companies continue to face that challenge in the markets they serve.

The universities, too, have felt the impact of the Manufacturing Vision Group. In both engineering and business, group members have launched new initiatives in research and course development intended to deepen our understanding of the manufacturing enterprise and push forward our ability to educate a new generation of leaders far more effectively than in the past. In keeping with the spirit of collaboration that guided the Manufacturing Vision Group, new programs that link engineering and business in study and teaching about manufacturing are now an important feature of the landscape.

## Appendix—Project Summaries

### Chaparral Steel

1. *Horizontal Caster.* This project was begun to develop a new casting process for high-grade steel. At the time, all carbon-steel makers were using a so-called vertical casting process. A horizontal caster would enable Chaparral, a minimill, to compete with the large integrated steel conglomerates in the manufacture of carbon steels and low-alloy forging-quality steels. The project resulted in the first horizontal steel caster in the world.

2. *Pulpit Controls.* This project was initiated to upgrade furnace control systems. The electric arc furnaces used by Chaparral to melt scrap were all controlled with analog instrumentation. To improve efficiency, the project team decided to develop digital controls, and despite some resistance from within the company, ended up developing the world's first digital furnace control system.

3. *Microtuff 10 Steel.* This project was intended to move Chaparral into a new market—the highest quality alloy steels, called "special

bar'' steels. Though sales never amounted to much, the new steel met all the strict quality standards and in so doing established Chaparral as a high-tech innovator, an image it had not had before.

4. *Arc Saw.* This was an attempt to develop the industry's first electric-arc saw for cutting volumes of steel. The huge saw was to use intense electrical arcs instead of saw blades to cut steel, which had never been done on the scale or throughput required for mass production. The project failed, but brought to light two important lessons about project development, one negative and one positive.

## Digital Equipment Corp.

1. *RA90 Disk Drive.* This project was undertaken to develop a high-density disk drive for computers. It was divided into three subprojects that progressed in parallel but without coordination, which in the end proved troublesome. It represented the kinds of integration problems that could arise at DEC and other companies organized by function. In part due to this project, DEC began to develop a standard process that would help development teams better integrate their work.

2. *LANbridge 200.* This product, a communications network that would link several computer networks, was a follow-on to an earlier product. Because the team consisted of many of the same people who had developed the first product, work proceeded in an integrated fashion, pointing to the benefits that better integration could bring to other projects.

3. *DECstation 3100.* Facing competitive pressure, DEC launched this project to develop a new workstation based on a UNIX operating system, instead of the company's standard VMS system. It was a technical success completed in record time, but sold less than intended because of a lack of software.

4. *CDA Software.* As DEC's line of office workstations expanded, the company perceived a need to develop an overreaching computer architecture to link its desktop publishing products. The compound

document architecture (CDA) software was the solution, and it was pursued with the idea that it would become a standard for desktop publishing. The project offers insights into how DEC overcame integration difficulties.

## Eastman Kodak Co.

1. *Factory of the Future.* This project was initiated to upgrade and expand the capacity of Kodak's factories that cut, spooled, and packaged 35-mm consumer films. It was begun early in Kodak's conversion from a functional structure to a line-of-business structure, and illustrated the lack of shared vision that could sometimes crop up in the old organization.

2. *Antistatic Film Coating.* To improve sales, this project was undertaken to develop a new, clear, antistatic coating for microfilm, to prevent the film from attracting dust while maximizing the perceived sharpness of the images on the film as seen by the end-user. It made use of off-the-shelf but state-of-the-art technology. The project was fully executed under Kodak's new company-wide system for managing development projects, called MAP.

3. *FunSaver Camera.* This project was begun to design and produce the world's first "single-use" camera. In this scheme the film was packaged in a simple, inexpensive plastic camera body. Once pictures were taken, the consumer handed the whole assembly to a photofinisher. The film was processed and the body was discarded or recycled. The design was based in part on existing design knowledge but was done on a unique CAD/CAM system that greatly helped integration and shortened the lead time from design to production.

4. *Panda Printer.* Panda was to be a thermal printer that could output large-format, color images of extremely high quality from digital data. Such a product was needed by the U.S. Department of Defense and top-of-the-line industrial and professional concerns. It was one of Kodak's first attempts to integrate divisions from different lines of business, and to merge both government and consumer product

specifications. As such, the project was tugged in different directions and suffered substantial cost and schedule problems, but the final product succeeded in both markets.

## Ford Motor Co.

1. *1988 Lincoln Continental (FN9)*. This was Ford's first attempt to build a luxury car on the new Taurus platform. It required major suspension system modifications, and was the first implementation of a 3.8-liter engine in a transverse configuration. The Continental was begun in the "old Ford," in which projects were organized by function, but by the time it was completed a new company-wide system, called C-to-C (Concept-to-Customer), for developing projects had been initiated. Spanning the transition caused some difficulties, but the car was successful.

2. *1989 Thunderbird/Cougar (MN12)*. This generation of the Thunderbird was built on a new car platform that including a novel supercharged engine. It was the first project begun as lessons from the Taurus program were codified, and Ford tried to complete it under the new C-to-C system. It suffered from growing pains experienced within the C-to-C scheme.

3. *1991.5 Crown Victoria/Grand Marquis (EN53)*. The Crown Victoria was a new car built on an existing platform. It was the second vehicle to use a new modular engine. The project was the first to be launched under the full C-to-C system, and showed the great benefits of the approach.

4. *FX15 Air-Conditioning Compressor*. This project represented the first time Ford tried to design in-house a compressor for automobile air-conditioning systems. The compressor was developed by Ford's Climate Control Division, which was run as a separate company and did not use the C-to-C system. However, the division did try several new methods for product development, including concurrent engineering. The compressor was a success and so were many of the new techniques.

## Hewlett-Packard Co.

1. *DeskJet Printer.* This was a rush project to design a new class of low-cost computer printers based on ink-jet print technology. The development effort put forth to get it to market in nine months and at low cost was unprecedented at HP. It illustrated the company's early attempts to integrate manufacturing, marketing, and R&D. The DeskJet sold extremely well, and saved the printer division from extinction.

2. *HP150 Computer.* The HP150 was the company's first formal attempt to enter the personal computer market. Unfortunately the strategy was not fully developed, and the development team tried to design a machine that would function as both a stand-alone PC as well as a terminal for a central computer. This project made clear the difficulties in integrating development across a diverse set of autonomous corporate divisions.

3. *Logic Analyzer.* This was an attempt by HP to beat out a competitor in the newly emerging "digital oscilloscope" market. The instrument was developed in the early 1970s in HP's traditional development setting, which, like most engineering companies of the day, was organized along functional lines. It provided some interesting insights into the "old HP."

4. *Hornet Spectrum Analyzer.* This was a classic project undertaken to develop a more inexpensive version of a standard instrument, in this case a spectrum analyzer. The Hornet was targeted to reduce encroachment by competitors at the low end of the market. The project required breaking some well-entrenched product development concepts. The effort, undertaken in the "new HP," provided good contrast to the Logic Analyzer project.

**Table A.1**  Performance of Projects Studied

| Company and project | Project date | Met schedule | Initial market acceptance | Met technical objectives | Met business objectives |
|---|---|---|---|---|---|
| | | Degree of success in meeting objectives | | | |
| **Chaparral Steel** | | | | | |
| *Horizontal Caster* for high grade steel | Q2 1984–Q3 1990 | 3 | 4 | 5 | 4 |
| *Digital Pulpit Controls* for arc furnace | Q1 1987–Q3 1988 | 2 | 5 | 5 | 5 |
| *Microtuff 10*—New alloy steel | Q1 1987–Q2 1988 | 4 | 4 | 4 | 5 |
| *Electric Arc Saw* | Q2 1985–Q3 1987 | 2 | NA | 1 | 1 |
| **Digital Equipment Corp.** | | | | | |
| *DECstation 3100*–UNIX workstation | Q3 1988–Q2 1989 | 5 | 2 | 5 | 3 |
| *LANbridge 200* local area network | Q3 1987–Q3 1989 | 2 | 4 | 3 | 4 |
| *RA90*—High-density disk drive | Q3 1981–Q4 1987 | 2 | 3 | 3 | 4 |
| *CDA*—Desktop publishing software | Q4 1986–Q4 1989 | 3 | 4 | 4 | 4 |
| **Eastman Kodak** | | | | | |
| *Factory of the Future*— 35mm film | Q4 1986–Q1 1988 | 1 | NA | 2 | 2 |
| *FunSaver*—Single-use camera | Q2 1987–Q3 1988 | 5 | 4 | 5 | 4 |
| *Chom 181*—Antistatic coating | Q4 1985–Q1 1987 | 5 | 5 | 5 | 5 |
| *Panda*—Large format printer | Q4 1988–Q4 1989 | 1 | 4 | 4 | 3 |
| **Ford Motor** | | | | | |
| *EN53*—1991 Crown Victoria | Q1 1987–Q3 1991 | 2 | 3 | 5 | 4 |
| *MN12*—1989 Thunderbird/Cougar | Q2 1984–Q1 1989 | 4 | 3 | 4 | 2 |
| *FN9*—1988 Lincoln Continental | Q4 1981–Q3 1987 | 2 | 4 | 4 | 2 |
| *FX15*—Air conditioner compressor | Q1 1986–Q1 1988 | 4 | 2 | 3 | 3 |
| **Hewlett-Packard** | | | | | |
| *Logic Analyzer*—Digital oscilloscope | 1972 | 3 | 4 | 4 | 5 |
| *Hornet*—Spectrum analyzer | Q1 1985–Q3 1988 | 4 | 5 | 5 | 5 |
| *HP 150*—Computer to use as a: | Q4 1981–Q4 1983 | | | | |
| terminal | | 4 | 4 | 4 | 2 |
| personal computer | | 4 | 2 | 4 | 2 |
| *DeskJet*—Inkjet printer | Q4 1986–Q3 1987 | 4 | 5 | 5 | 5 |

Note: 5 = very high; 4 = high; 3 = medium; 2 = low; 1 = very low; NA = not applicable

# The Manufacturer's Perpetual Enterprise Machine

## THE QUESTION

The survival of U.S. manufacturers has become a critical issue in the 1990s as the nation emerges from the major industrial transformations of the 1970s and the global competitiveness wars of the 1980s. These historical changes, which have motivated an *ad hoc* group of academics and industry leaders—the Manufacturing Vision Group (MVG)—to meet over a period of five years, are propelling the U.S. into the future along with a new twist: successful companies have been required to transform their organizations into much leaner and more dynamic enterprises that are constantly searching for sustainable competitive advantage, increasingly driven by continually improved levels of product quality and performance at low costs. The MVG itself was driven by a strong sense of concern for their companies and their fields, asking themselves the question: How can manufacturing companies continue this breathless process, meeting customer's latent needs; maintain a competitive advantage; and sustain profitability while achieving a constant state of evolution and self-renewal?

# RENEWING THE ENTERPRISE

A vision of the future is an important aspect of the dream shared by many inventors and entrepreneurs who, in their quest for a better life, have long sought to create valuable products or processes. Successful inventors and innovators view the physical world quite differently from others. They use their creativity and resourcefulness to interpret the needs of people and markets and explore possibilities, utilizing available resources, for satisfying those needs. Inventors and innovators never seem content with their surroundings or environment; they always question the current state of affairs. Inventive and innovative processes are carried out both in their minds and in the physical world. But they are not just dreamers; they are dream actuators. Inventors and entrepreneurs have the imaginative powers not only to define a future state, but to conceive of pathways to bring themselves from the present to the future. Throughout history, entrepreneurial political leaders have attempted to harness combinations of mass human will into eternal empires and inventors have envisioned the penultimate perpetual motion machine that, once put in action, would continue its motion infinitely.

The leaders of successful manufacturing firms have their own dreams of creating and maintaining ownership of an equivalent of the perpetual motion machine—something we might call the perpetual enterprise machine. But these leaders know that their companies cannot simply perpetuate the past; they know that their organization must perpetually evolve, or it risks extinction. Successful firms have mastered the art of melding the power of human will and organization. But the key to their vitality is their world-class capabilities in selecting, guiding, and completing **development projects,** which are the building blocks of renewal and change. The companies that can repeat this process again and again have discovered the manufacturer's perpetual motion machine.

Today's manufacturing world is dynamic: customer needs and the competitive environment are constantly changing as new technologies and knowledge become available at an ever-increasing rate. Since the perpetual enterprise machine is powered by a system that creates and brings new products and processes to the marketplace, the system must, like the inventive entrepreneur, continually recognize and meet customers' needs. These needs are often difficult to understand or predict, but as the system operates through successive cycles, it actually transforms the perpetual enterprise machine so that it becomes even more adept at sensing and responding to future needs.

If a particular product or process fails or if the available knowledge, skills, or organizational structure are inadequate for present or future needs, the perpetual enterprise machine learns from the failure and redirects physical and human resources. To achieve this end, the perpetual enterprise machine relies on internal and external sources of knowledge and experimentation. It must literally project itself into the future based on its acquired knowledge and by developing its own best practices and operating rules. To be perpetual, this total product, process, and service delivery system must be flexible enough to function well under conditions when markets are quasi-predictive or stable as well as when there are major disruptions or transformations in the markets and business environment. Thus, the enterprise is capable of sustaining itself through this bootstrapping and probing of the future and initiating requisite changes of the machine itself. The owners of the enterprise, as well as its employees and customers, can depend on the long term because the perpetual enterprise machine succeeds in delivering timely, high quality, cost-effective new products, processes, and services on a reliable, recurring basis.

This idealized, organic notion of the enterprise—requiring constant rejuvenation, recalibration, and redirection—encompasses elements that are driven by the dynamics of competition and the unending evolutions and revolutions occurring in science and technology. In the world of manufacturing of the 1990s, the only strategy for corporate success is to learn more rapidly than competitors and to convert that learning into commercialized products, processes, and services. Thus, the knowledge-based company capitalizes on its knowledge and redefines itself through its successful use of development projects.

# DEVELOPMENT PROJECTS: THE PERPETUAL MACHINE

Development projects are a concrete way to envision the perpetual enterprise machine. The ultimate source of power derived from development projects comes from a company's discovery and systematic application of unique principles and procedures. Development projects are defined and organized, first and foremost, to create a particular new product, service, or process, but, in addition, they can be used to develop less tangible assets. These assets might include new tools or methodologies for inventing and designing products or new machines and systems for producing them. On a more subtle level, assets might also include the development of new individual skills and organizational capabilities.

The development project (or especially a set of projects) has many characteristics that render it a microcosm of the company or business unit: the project team is composed of members from many functional areas within the business unit; the success of the project is determined by the integrated outcome of many individuals' work, and not by the achievements of a single individual, function, or discipline; and many of the business systems and organizational structures that support the success of the enterprise will generally be expressed in the work of a series of development projects. Thus, the development project becomes a convenient tool for experimentation and learning about the business unit.

Like the business unit, development projects have customers and suppliers, interact with physical and social systems, involve technology and people, are aided or inhibited by organizational structures and incentives, and must be tracked on quantifiable and nonquantifiable measures. The workings of development projects provide a much more comprehensive, real-time assessment of the values, systems, and structures of the whole firm or business unit than do assessments of individual functional organizations or representations in organizational charts.

Except in very small companies, a development project includes people who depend on their functional groups for support in addition to using the established corporate systems and structures. By its nature the development project will often amplify and highlight existing problems at the interfaces and boundaries of different groups in an organization. Thus, the workings of a project capture much of the essence of the firm's integrated workings.

Because the development project is a small but representative piece of the larger entity, it is also an appropriate unit with which to try out new ideas and a place where new capabilities can be developed and nurtured. Here again, the project objectives can be directed to achieve outcomes fundamental to the perpetual enterprise machine: not only the primary goal of a new product, process, or service, but also less tangible goals, such as an atmosphere that fosters understanding, learning, improvement, and rejuvenation of the business unit's assets.

If a manufacturing firm is to accrue sustainable advantage, it must create a unique version of the perpetual enterprise machine that will enable it to meet future needs. Because sustainable advantage is determined by what an organization can do, not what it can buy, world-class development projects provide benefits that can never be acquired simply by the direct purchase of assets, such as buying patents, technology, plants, or even a complete business unit.

## Seven Critical Elements of Outstanding Development Projects

The MVG gained an understanding of the role of development projects in renewing a company's assets by carefully studying 20 individual development projects. To gain this insight, the MVG established that the unit of analysis, the development project, would need to have specific characteristics (both by itself and as part of a set of projects). The projects studied were central to each company's business success—none of them was off the main track or a "sandbox" project. The MVG knew that these projects had experienced varying degrees of internal success, and had, in fact, provided mixed contributions to the overall success of the business.

Understanding development projects in general required the MVG's commitment to broad, in-depth analysis and examination of varying project elements: for example, the intricacies of thin film process technology, the synthesis skills of an individual project contributor, or the project management tools used in different divisions of the same company. The MVG realized that it could only recognize important trends or unifying concepts through analyses at multiple levels using data from many sources and perspectives.

Although each of the 20 projects had its own story to tell, the MVG found that the greatest learning came from integrating the experience and lessons from all the projects. The common challenges and patterns, despite their diversity, created the basis for identifying shared themes and distilling translatable concepts.

This book focuses on (1) what makes development projects successful, (2) what causes projects to achieve (or fall short of) their market and technology goals, and (3) how projects can be mechanisms for growth and learning for the firm given the challenges facing world-class manufacturers in a dynamic, competitive environment. In the chapters that follow, we diverge from the topics traditionally addressed in discussions of new product development, manufacturing, and competitiveness; many of these topics, important as they are, are considered in other works. Instead, we focus on the factors that help development projects succeed and the factors that inhibit the kinds of sustained learning necessary for a perpetual enterprise machine. The participants in the MVG examined or took part in hundreds of development projects, but it was through a systematic analysis of projects in five companies, as well as years of experience in industry and academia, that this diverse group reached its conclusions and consensus. To us the evidence is compelling. We hope that the readers—whether technical or management leaders in business or academia, in both small groups and large organizations—will recognize and embrace the key concepts we have identified for making development projects successful.

Given a good development project concept, a team, and the necessary resources as a starting point, what other inherent elements improve the likelihood of a project's success and create long-term benefits for the organization? The MVG found seven key elements or themes in the 20 development projects they examined **(Table 1.1)** that, when integrated into a holistic approach, become critical ele-

**Table 1.1**  Seven Key Elements for Outstanding Development Projects

1. **Core Capabilities and Core Rigidities**   New product/process development projects should be conducted with full recognition of their interaction with core capabilities (i.e., strategically important capabilities) that are multi-dimensional and include the dimension of value. Core rigidities—the flip side of core capabilities—inhibit innovation, but new product and process development projects can act as agents of both short- and long-term change to ameliorate core rigidities in an organization.

2. **Guiding Visions**   Three interlocking visions for the development project—the *product concept,* the *project vision,* and the *business unit vision*—provide the link between specific design decisions and the growth of strategic capabilities within the firm by identifying the project's learning goals, including what the product means to its users. Guiding visions are fed from many information sources, including critical market information not accessible through traditional market research.

3. **Pushing the Envelope**   Understanding and managing the interrelation of performance envelopes will determine a firm's competitive position. The proper role of management and the mechanisms and needs for pushing performance envelopes are different for product envelopes, process envelopes, and envelopes associated with the firm's other internal capabilities. The degree to which performance envelopes are pushed and the perceived consequences of potential failure will influence the most effective organization, the behavior of those involved in the project, and the likelihood of project success.

4. **Project Leadership and Organization**   Achieving functional or disciplinary excellence and internal/external system integrity in development projects requires innovative and appropriate project leadership and management within the organizational structure. The development of people and organizational skills and procedures for high-performance projects requires time, and the firm gains experience from systematic learning across projects.

5. **Ownership and Commitment**   Challenging development projects require strong ownership and commitment from three levels: (1) the *individual project team members* gauge project ownership by their ability to make a difference and the degree to which they identify and associate their personal success with the project's success; (2) the *project team,* a central organizing unit, derives its identity from the project and its goals; and (3) *senior management* demonstrates its commitment by a clear recognition that corporate success depends on achieving project goals.

6. **Prototyping—Rapid Learning and Early Testing**   Prototyping is, in its broadest sense, largely underutilized and is often misconstrued as a project hurdle or an activity to answer phase review questions. In fact, prototyping is a process for facilitating structuring and systematic learning throughout the project and builds integrity into the product/process. The practice of using more prototypes early in the project and more prototypes that represent system interactions reduces the risks of failure and increases the payoffs for improved product/process performance and project success.

7. **Integration Within a Development Project**   Integration of people and visions within a development project is a process—not an event or a state—and formal, bureaucratic, or procedure-driven systems alone won't guarantee integration. Integration requires new skills for people and organizations and requires changing the way work gets done.

19

ments for success. The seven themes are discussed individually in Chapters 2 through 8, but here we wish to indicate their scope and range and suggest why collectively they are so powerful—why these elements, together with good project concepts, create the perpetual enterprise machine. Outstanding development projects are those that have achieved the appropriate mix and balance of (1) core capabilities, (2) guiding visions, (3) pushing the envelope, (4) leadership and organization, (5) ownership and commitment, (6) prototyping, and (7) integration.

Our study of the vision projects, as well as research in a variety of industries, underscores the importance of laying the foundation for product development projects. Projects that achieve high performance are inevitably associated with senior management processes that provide both clarity in their missions and the requisite base of capability in their execution. Two of our themes—core capabilities and guiding visions—capture the fundamental importance of the front end of the development process. The importance of that foundation lies not only in getting off to a good start; a strong foundation facilitates the attitudes, behavior, and action that are critical to successful development.

The notion of *core capabilities* is a familiar catch phrase often associated with the development of a corporate or business strategy. For development projects, the power of distinctive capabilities arises from the ability to work across functions, to integrate disciplines and organizations, and to bring together institutions critical to the success of the program. A core capability might be reflected as much in innovative and creative approaches to structuring project tasks and chartering projects as it is in a unique technology. There is a dark side to a core capability, however: firms that consistently over-rely on a perceived core capability as "the right answer" or fail to recognize that its advantages have been displaced by a new environment risk engendering a *core rigidity.*

The right capabilities give development teams the wherewithal to succeed. But those means must be applied with direction and focus. In a world of uncertainty, a willingness to take risks, the ability to sort out competing demands, and the capacity to cut through confusion and noise to find excellent solutions depend heavily on *guiding visions* that operate at multiple levels of the organization. Outlining these visions is the task of management. Guiding visions have the clear objective of creating boundaries for the project team so it is not continually redefining its direction and goals. An effective guiding vision provides a sense of direction and creates power by providing focus without inhibiting initiative and innovation. With no guiding vision, management is inclined to be either too specific in commissioning a project team or too broad in setting objectives, which leads to floundering from lack of focus.

Core capabilities and guiding visions provide a foundation for a development project. A third theme, *pushing the envelope,* also addresses a fundamental organizational capability: the ability to drive renewal across the entire organization. Performance envelopes must be pushed for processes and less tangible internal capabilities as well as for products. Each type of envelope has characteristics that require different organizational responses. Projects must push these envelopes on critical dimensions. But this entails significant risk. How soon does one dare to use a new technology in a product or process? Who makes the ultimate decision that considers the risk and the opportunity to reposition the business unit? Where is the leverage across products and processes? How does one delineate the opportunities for pushing in the direction of product features as opposed to using resources to push the process envelope and change the production capability? Making those trade-offs effectively, creating processes that identify risks, putting in place approaches to managing them, and tying those choices to the project strategy and its guiding visions are the essence of pushing the envelope.

With a strong foundation, the work of the project itself can be more focused and can bring to bear the right kinds of skills, tools, and methods. But an outstanding development project is far more than the simple execution of a well-guided plan or the application of established skills. When products are complex—involving many components and parts as well as different technologies—and customer demands are sophisticated and changing, an effective development project requires leadership. It requires an organization that facilitates integration across functions and brings the voice of the customer to bear on the detailed engineering and design decisions that define the product. Thus, a critical theme in our study was *leadership and organization* of a type far different from the traditional hierarchical models so prevalent in modern business. Development projects create temporary organizations and require unique leadership and team skills from their members. Successful development projects seek to build a microcosm of the organization where the key members have not only a working knowledge of their function and discipline, but also the broad thinking, networking, and leadership skills usually associated with senior people in the traditional organization. Like the breadth of talent of technical and business leaders in the permanent organization, the talent of development project members increases as they progress to more senior levels of responsibility. In outstanding firms, the preparation and training processes (and the supporting organizational structures) for staffing development projects are very nontraditional and distinctly different from less successful firms.

A structure of organization and a pattern of leadership that fosters excellence in teamwork and integration are thus essential to outstanding development. But unless that organization and those who lead it create an environment in which not only individual team members, but also individuals involved in supporting the team, feel personal identification and an allegiance to the success of the total program, the development project is unlikely to achieve its potential. The alignment of the team members' personal interests with the project's objectives and interests is largely determined by the company's procedures for establishing and bolstering *ownership and commitment.* High levels of ownership and commitment lead to members developing a personal identity with the success of the project and the company that goes well beyond a "what's-in-it-for-me" attitude. The devotion shown by inspired development project members is comparable to that usually reserved for an avocation—for example, the after-work inventor who spends hours each week over a period of years working in the garage on a new device.

From the standpoint of the project, an effective team and strong leadership embedded in an organization that fosters ownership and commitment has a high probability of success. But there is more. Within such teams there still remains the detailed work of design, testing, and making trade-offs—the action that defines the product, develops the process, and implements an integrated system in the marketplace.

No matter what level of change and innovation a project intends, if it is to be successful, the team carrying it out must create effective processes for learning. We talk not of learning in the abstract, but in the day-to-day detailed work that ultimately defines the success of the project. In that context, the outstanding projects that we studied use *prototyping* as a fundamental learning strategy. Prototyping is commonly viewed as a secondary activity at the end of a set of tasks, but we believe it occupies a central role. It is an integral part of the design-build-test cycle of learning and has an almost magical effect in bringing parts of the organization together and solving problems that are difficult, even with traditional project management methods. Prototyping has leverage in its effect on the rate of learning and its usefulness as a measure of how the project is progressing and how the elements are integrated.

Where it works effectively, prototyping is a way to bring all the elements of the product and process system together to learn about its ultimate performance. At the end of the day, when all is said and done, what really matters is how that system performs—the ownership experience it delivers to customers, its cost performance in manufacturing, the excellence of its design, its time to market, and its fit with the strategy of the business. The theme that seems to differentiate those projects that achieve outstanding performance is *integration*. Whether we find it across functional units, disciplines, regions, or even organizations, these instances of integration share common characteristics. Perhaps most important, integration occurs at a deep level. It is not mere coordination but instead a very different pattern of framing and solving problems. Traditionally, project management has been viewed as a process of coordination for alleviating problems at the boundaries or interfaces of activities. Integration is a broader concept: it redefines the work content in the function and changes processes, both within the boundaries and at the interfaces. Effective integration ultimately leads to a complete rethinking of individual tasks in the project. Value is created because the development project is not suboptimized. By moving beyond a focus on mere coordination and the summation of locally optimized tasks, integration allows the efficiency and speed of a development project to be maximized.

Pulling these seven themes out of the richness of the project histories and the analysis that underlies their interpretation has helped us to structure our thinking and identify critical sources of difference in performance. But it is important to understand that these seven themes do not stand alone—in fact, they are closely connected. Indeed, the truly outstanding firms we have studied (both in this project and in extensive work on product development) achieve excellence because of the pattern of their total approach to development. In a fundamental sense, it is the pattern that matters.

Thus, taken together, linked in critical ways, and reinforced and understood as a whole, these seven themes underlie outstanding development projects and build a foundation for a perpetual enterprise. We wish to reemphasize that these conclusions have been derived from careful analysis of the details of how new product and process development projects work—what causes, and what inhibits, their optimal success. We believe that these seven themes are necessary foundation concepts for building successful projects, but do not claim that they are the sole factors for success. We do claim that development projects with customized versions of these seven concepts are well on their way to building a perpetual enterprise machine. But a word of caution is called for. We have also discovered that the practice of these concepts is very difficult in small and midsize organizations and extremely difficult in large organizations. Indeed, it was the search for ways to formulate and resolve some of these difficulties that led to the formation of the MVG in the fall of 1987.


## THE REALITY

We began this chapter with a difficult, multidimensional question, and we end with a reminder of the reality. The MVG started as an experiment in cross-institutional learning with a focus on perhaps the most critical problem facing manufacturing firms in the 1990s: fast-paced, competitive challenges with concomitant evolution and renewal of the company. During its exploration process the MVG discovered the power of development projects—which function as the engine for the perpetual enterprise machine—and it quickly recognized the difficulties inherent in keeping that engine primed for both today's and tomorrow's needs.

In many ways, the group as a whole relearned and synthesized what each member had already experienced firsthand within his or her own organization. The five companies had all witnessed, and continue to witness, dramatic changes in their markets, and most have begun substantial initiatives to create more responsive organizations and systems. The four universities had experienced, and continue to experience, parallel challenges to their status quo: job markets, course content, and curricula are changing to accommodate the transformations in industry and the economy. Whether our institutions, corporate or academic, are renewed and become perpetual enterprises will largely be determined by our practice of the principles described in the following seven theme chapters.

## CHAPTER 2

# Core Capabilities and Core Rigidities

By now you've heard it countless times—that American companies are strong in design but weak in manufacturing. This imbalance, industry soothsayers have said over and over, must be rectified if the United States is to become a stronger competitor in the international marketplace.

Indeed the observation is a tired one. And it may seem remote, even untrue, to a particular manager in a particular company. But there is a message at the core of the comment for every manager in every industry—that companies all too often rely passively on traditional strengths and assume that these strengths continue to be competitively advantageous. Electronics companies pride themselves on strong engineering, but often find themselves lacking in marketing. Auto makers are masters at marketing, but often have trouble integrating with precision the thousands of parts needed for assembly of a new car. The leaders of the very best companies in the 1990s, however, are not content to rest on tradition or tolerate mediocrity. They realize that no matter how capable their firm may be in certain disciplines, it is the weak links that will put them at a competitive disadvantage.

In the last few years urgency in this effort has been added for American firms due to assertions that Japanese companies understand, nurture, and exploit their core capabilities better than their U.S.-based competitors.[1] Increasingly, leveraging the core capabilities of an organization is being suggested as the way to gain advantage in a marketplace. In fact, the terms "core competence" and "core capability" are bandied about rather loosely. The concepts are in danger of becoming so broad as to be meaningless cliches. Yet many companies are finding the process of identifying core competencies a fruitful exercise in self-examination.

Moreover, core capabilities are fundamental to the success of new development projects that companies depend on to advance a market. Core capabilities in the best companies grow stronger with each development project. Knowledge begets more knowledge, and skills more skills.[2] Furthermore, because a company becomes known for its particular strengths, it attracts the best people in those disciplines. This cycle supports itself; a company's core capabilities tend to dominate product and process development projects.

However, in this chapter, we take a hard look at the concept of core capabilities and expose a perspective too often overlooked. Few companies recognize that their basic strengths can have dysfunctional effects. Because new development projects represent a firm's response to market changes, they are the focal point for the tension between innovation and organizational status quo. They quickly become the center of a firm's struggle to maintain certain strengths and renew or even replace others. Therefore, development projects expose the down side of core capabilities: core rigidities. The same capabilities that a constitute a strength also comprise a vulnerability. Projects that go awry often do so because they do not overcome core rigidities.

Say, for example, that a computer company traditionally strong in making mainframes decides to develop a personal computer and staffs its project team with its best designers. Even though these people know they are trying to create something different, they may well set up the design process in the same manner in which they would for a mainframe. When this falls flat, the company may then try to bring in consultants to help rework the project, but will likely still run into problems because the mindset of their people is too far afield from the one needed. A core capability has become a rigidity.

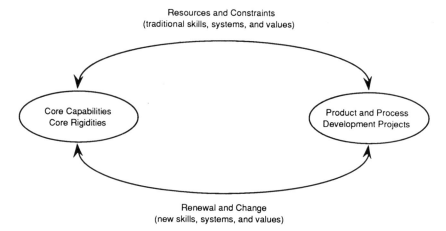

Resources and Constraints
(traditional skills, systems, and values)

Core Capabilities
Core Rigidities

Product and Process
Development Projects

Renewal and Change
(new skills, systems, and values)

**Figure 2.1.** A company's strengths—its core capabilities—drive new product and process development. However, these same attributes, if not properly aligned with a project, can constrain its progress; the capabilities become rigidities. The pursuit of development projects, in turn, can improve or renew a company's capabilities, and even initiate new ones. The cycle feeds on itself and therefore must be consciously managed for the best results.

The paradoxical nature of core capabilities can pose severe challenges to management, because failure to recognize and consciously manage core rigidities can hamper project performance, compromising the company's future. Therefore, all players in a development project—the project manager, members of the project team, and others in the company who support the effort—will be more successful if they understand the multi-dimensional, systemic nature of core capabilities. They must recognize when the down side of a core capability threatens to reduce project effectiveness, and must manage development projects for their potential to aid organizational learning about capabilities as well as for the immediate project results needed (see **Figure 2.1**).

To understand how core capabilities and rigidities affect product and process development, and how they can be managed to improve the chances for project success, we examine in this chapter the basic composition of core capabilities, first through a brief example and then by dissecting capabilities into their four dimensions. Next we consider how projects are influenced by core capabilities and rigidities. Then, by dissecting actual projects from the companies studied by the Manufacturing Vision Group, we take a close-up look at how the individual dimensions of core capabilities and rigidities interact, enhancing or inhibiting development. Finally, we return to the managerial level to show how core rigidities, not always obvious, can be recognized, and how projects can be picked for the express purpose of overcoming a rigidity or turning a mediocre capability into a strong one.

## DIMENSIONS OF CORE CAPABILITIES

Networking is a core capability of Digital Equipment Corporation. To be sure, networking here means a workstation or terminal on the desk of almost every Digital employee. The term also implies extensive, sophisticated software (local area and wide area networks) connecting these pieces of hardware around the globe so that any employee can reach another electronically. However, the physical systems mirror and also support a very horizontal, networked style of management. Everyone working at Digital knows that because of the high level of computer literacy and use, an electronic message is more likely to reach a fellow employee and stimulate a response than even the telephone. Moreover, extending requests for information or action through horizontal chains of informal networks is as likely to yield results as working through vertical, formal hierarchical channels. In fact, the networked approach is often *more* effective, since individual freedom and responsibility are highly prized and power is exercised through informal relations. Therefore, Digital's networking capability derives not only from the highly linked physical hardware and software systems and from the employees' skills in using those systems, but also from management practices and preferences that foster the networked task-force approach to most issues. That is, the networking capability permeates routine and culture.

### The Four Critical Dimensions

Core capabilities are sometimes referred to as distinctive competences, core or organizational competencies, or firm-specific competence.[3] Discussion of their strategic importance has increased because research on diversification shows there is a positive relationship between strategies that complement and build on an existing skill or resource base in the firm and high overall corporate performance.[4] Recent research, including that of our group, continues to confirm this dynamic.

One of the key issues underlying the interest in core capabilities is finding ways to manage the tension between new technological directions and current corporate strengths. Managers are advised to build capabilities and then encourage the development of plans for exploiting them, that is, to "stick to the knitting."[5] Yet they also know that to stand still is to fall behind; therefore they must innovate. Innovation necessarily involves some degree of "creative destruction"; even seemingly minor innovations that alter the architecture of a product can undermine the usefulness of deeply embedded knowledge. Hence the development of any new product or process interacts with core capabilities, and managers need to understand that interaction. To do so, they must understand the various dimensions of a core capability.

Descriptors of core capabilities such as "unique," "distinctive," "difficult to imitate," or "superior to our competition" might seem to render the concept self-explanatory. However, these terms convey little understanding of the nature of core capabilities. Capabilities are composed of four interdependent dimensions, each described in the ensuing paragraphs: knowledge and skills, managerial systems, physical systems, and values. The last dimension—values—plays a crucial but often subtle role, and one that many people fail to recognize or address.

*Knowledge and skills* embodied in company employees is the dimension of core capabilities most often recognized.[6] Technical expertise, for example, constitutes a major resource that is both mined and cultivated. Other types of knowledge include methodological know-how, scientific know-why, and even interpersonal know-who—ties into critical communities such as regulatory bodies.

*Managerial systems* can consist of unique incentive programs, internal educational systems, or methodologies that embody procedural knowledge. As such, they can contribute importantly to a capability, and should be managed with that potential contribution in mind, not simply left to evolve on their own.

*Physical systems*—production lines or information systems that constitute compilations of knowledge—usually derive from many individuals, and become greater than the sum of their parts. Several of the firms our group studied considered their proprietary software simulation and test systems to be significant parts of the corporate brain, constituting a real advantage over competitors.

The fourth dimension of core capabilities is *values,* which are reflected in attitudes, behaviors, and norms that dominate in a corporation.[7] Values and norms are most often overlooked, but as we shall see they exhibit subtle yet very powerful forces on the other three dimensions. Even physical systems may embody cultural values. At Digital, for example, the computer architecture of the internal networks the company uses reflects a strong tradition of individual control versus centralized control over information. This value shows up in the way information within the company is formatted and the communication protocols that exist between individual computers. For example, DEC's landmark Ethernet system, which connects workstations and minicomputers, reflects the needs of DEC's own employees and customers in similar types of companies, many of whom are design engineers. Ethernet differs from the networking systems of the more mainframe-minded companies, such as IBM, in that if one node fails on Ethernet the whole system does not go down. This robustness may come at the cost of more standardized operating protocols, but DEC is willing to make that trade-off because, as indicated above, it places high value on enabling every employee to reach any information or any other person through the network.

There are several reasons why recognition of the values dimension of core capabilities is critical to understanding the effect of those capabilities on development projects. First, like the other three dimensions of a core capability, values operate paradoxically; the very same values, norms, and attitudes can both enable and constrain new product and process development. Second, even if the dark side of a core capability is recognized as inhibiting the development process, managers who try to alter it are unlikely to succeed if they do not recognize and address the values dimension. And third, the value embodied in a particular core capability is the dimension of that capability that takes the most managerial attention and effort to change.

## Interaction Among the Four Dimensions

The major reason for emphasizing that core capabilities can be thought of as four conceptually distinct but interrelated dimensions is that all four come into play to differing degrees during a development project. Success or failure is often driven by the interplay between the dimensions. Furthermore, managers should recognize that the four dimensions may be present in very different proportions in various core capabilities, and therefore the leverage point for improving the development process differs among projects.

The four dimensions of a core capability interact to create a self-reinforcing system that enables new product and process development (see **Figure 2.2**). For example, the physical systems of a company cannot be fully utilized without a properly skilled workforce, and skills unrewarded by managerial systems or undervalued will atrophy or flee the company. Managers at Chaparral Steel are very conscious of building each dimension of a core capability as they build their products, and are aware of how building one dimension affects the

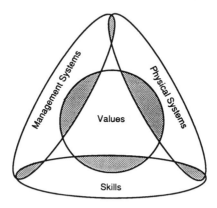

**Figure 2.2.** Core capabilities are composed of four dimensions. Though separate in nature, they constantly interact with each other in development projects. For example, the technical systems of a company could not be utilized without a properly skilled workforce. At the center are a company's values, which are infused through all capabilities.

others. Thus, proposals for changes of all types, from a new furnace to a profit-sharing scheme, are scrutinized for potential to enhance or disrupt the total system.

This attention to interrelationships is somewhat easier for a company like Chaparral, which is still relatively small (930 employees) and young (17 years old). Managers will have to guard that the company does not fail to evolve as it grows; they believe the flexibility to alter projects so as to keep the dimensions of core capabilities strong and integrated gets harder as companies get bigger.

## Aligning Core Capabilities with Development Projects

The interaction between development projects and core capabilities differs according to how well the requirements of the project align with the core capabilities currently held by the firm (see **Figure 2.3**). Within large firms with multiple core capabilities, it is possible for a given project to be well aligned with the capabilities of one division and incompatible with those of another.

Among the 20 development projects studied by the Vision Group, for example, Hewlett-Packard's HP150 project encountered such misalignment. The HP150 was originally conceived as a terminal for use with the HP3000, an industrial computer already on the market. Development of this terminal was closely aligned with HP's traditional capabilities. As work progressed, however, senior management expanded the project's goal, to create a version that would function as a stand-alone personal computer. The attempted transformation was not completely successful because it required both new technical capabilities (e.g., a low-cost monitor) and new marketing capabilities (e.g., selling to individuals). Moreover, the project challenged traditional HP values and managerial systems. The increased system complexity represented by a stand-alone computer, such as the need for disk drives, required that the development team procure components from other divisions, each of which, true to HP tradition, was independent and entrepreneurial. Since the project was not directly aligned with the priorities and capabilities of these other divisions, and because HP as a company was not strong at that time in interdivi-

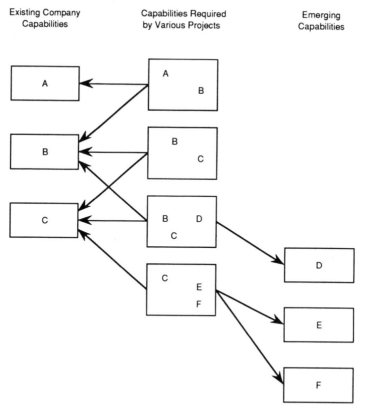

Existing Company Capabilities     Capabilities Required by Various Projects     Emerging Capabilities

**Figure 2.3.** All development projects require certain core capabilities. The needs of some projects match well with the existing capabilities of a company (left). But others require new capabilities (right). If the second case is not foreseen, the project will probably fall short of its objectives. However, if recognized and planned for, the project can serve as a vehicle to develop the new capability, leading to a successful new product and a new strength for the company.

sional cooperation, the division managers had no incentive to cooperate for the greater corporate good.

The projects we studied ranged across the spectrum, from those well-aligned with traditional core capabilities to those that were not aligned—sometimes deliberately so. The latter were sometimes projects designed to launch the corporation toward a new capability. Companies were asked to identify one highly traditional core capability they strongly identified with. **Table 2.1** presents these, along with an example of one project that was highly congruent with that capa-

**Table 2.1** Relationship of Selected Projects with a Traditional Core Capability

| Company | Traditional Core Capability | Highly Aligned | Not Aligned | Additional Capability Required for Success |
|---|---|---|---|---|
| Ford Motor Co. | Total vehicle architecture | 1988 Lincoln Continental | FX15 compressor for air conditioner | Testing requirements for aggressive compressor technology |
| Chaparral Steel | Science of casting molds | Horizontal caster | Arc saw | Magnetics and electrical arcs |
| Hewlett-Packard | "Next-bench design" | Hornet spectrum analyzer | HP150 as a personal computer | Cross-division integration |
| Eastman Kodak | Silver halide technology | Chem 181 film coating | Panda printer | Factory and distribution led development project |
| Digital Equipment Corp. | Networking | LANbridge 200 | DECstation 3100 | Software applications development |

bility, and one that was not. For example, the successful horizontal caster project at Chaparral pushed the science of molds, a corporate strength, to new heights; the failed arc saw project required capabilities in magnetics that turned out to be inaccessible. The successful LANbridge 200 local area network developed at DEC grew directly out of the company's considerable expertise in networking; the new UNIX operating system for the DECstation 3100 challenged the domain of the dominant proprietary VMS technology, and initial sales were poor because there were only 20 compatible software programs at the time of launch compared with 500 for a similar workstation from Sun Microsystems, a major competitor. Similarly, Kodak's highly successful Chem 181 project drew heavily on traditional film-related values, skills, and systems, whereas the somewhat less successful Panda printer project required expertise and capabilities in electronics, mechanical engineering, and software.

The nonaligned projects shown in **Table 2.1** did not necessarily involve "radical" innovations; rather, they were untraditional for the organization along several of the four dimensions of the core capability, and were hence likely to experience one (or more) traditional capability as a rigidity rather than a benefit. DEC's deep appreciation of VMS users' needs and awareness of those customers' large pools of VMS-compatible software led DEC managers to underestimate the importance of involving third-party software developers in the launch of the totally new workstation. Similarly, Chaparral managers had so much confidence in their traditional strengths in experimentation and problem solving of metallurgical problems that they did not recognize for some time that implementing an arc saw required totally different knowledge sets. Though many of the projects with less-than-successful outcomes were not aligned with core capabilities, this does not suggest that low alignment inevitably leads to failure. However, low alignment does make project management more difficult. Unless such projects are physically separated from the rest of the organization in a self-sufficient capsule, they operate in the same environment that nurtures aligned projects, and the misalignment may not receive the attention it needs.

## THE UP SIDE: CAPABILITIES ENHANCE DEVELOPMENT

In order to better understand how the four dimensions of core capabilities can affect project development, it is necessary to examine them at greater depth. In this section we place projects under the microscope, looking for the dimensions of core capabilities that enhance product and process development. In the subsequent section we look for the inhibiting down side. We then turn to the topic of how these attributes can be managed to achieve the best project results.

### Values Dimension

Broad-based values, constantly reinforced by corporate leaders and embodied in management practices, affect all the development projects in a company. Two values particularly influence the development process: empowerment of employees, and the status of certain groups of employees within their company and their industry.

*Empowerment of project members.* The degree of empowerment invested in the members of a project team affects all development projects. Managers in companies that foster empowerment believe that each individual has the potential to make significant contributions to a project and place the responsibility on each employee to try to do so. The benefit of this is to create an atmosphere in which innovation and problem solving excel. As explained further in the chapter on guiding visions, empowerment does not mean lack of leadership—just a different kind.

At Hewlett-Packard, Digital Equipment, and Chaparral, empowerment is an especially strong element of their core capabilities. At HP and DEC, project ideas often come up from the ranks, instead of down from senior management. Often teams are authorized to initiate projects off-line, and they are given enough rope to hang themselves. In this way the companies move into the future through multiple experiments; the strategy of the entire corporation evolves as much from the projects undertaken as from direction by top management. At Chaparral Steel, strategy is jointly determined by executives, foremen, and the many line operators who run melting, casting, and rolling mill processes. This is possible because the relatively small number of people in the company and its extremely flat organization enable swift communication between top management and team members. The assumption at all three of these companies is that empowered employees will create multiple strategic options, and the company selects from and executes these as needed to improve its competitive position. The future of the corporation rests on the ability of such individuals to create and champion new products and processes that may grow into whole new businesses.

For their part, project team members in these companies believe in their ability to influence the future of the company by creating a viable product or process. They often convey a sense of exhilaration derived from a challenge they perceive to be largely of their own making. The HP team developing the DeskJet printer and the DEC team working on the RA-90 disk drive felt that they had turned the course of their mammoth corporate ship a critical degree or two. Such empowerment engenders a tremendous sense of ownership over projects, spurring team members to remarkable achievements—often in the face of great odds. The HP DeskJet team invented some technical show-stoppers; they estimated that 75 percent of the effort expended on the printing head was devoted to invention, rather than development.

*High status for the dominant discipline.* For historical and cultural reasons, individuals based in certain disciplines and functions within each company we examined felt more empowered than their colleagues. Each company displayed a cultural bias toward the technical base in which it has its roots. For Kodak, that base is chemistry, chemical engineering, and design of process equipment; for HP and DEC, it is electronics and computer engineering. A history of high status for the dominant discipline enables the corporation and the projects to attract, hold, and motivate talented people who join up for the challenges, the camaraderie with competent peers, and the status associated with the skills of the dominant discipline or function. Once these people are in the company, they perform as expected—excellently. At Kodak, for example, the 5 percent of engineers who design premier film products constitute the professional elite within the company and the industry, and chemical engineers there aspire to reach that level.

A natural outgrowth of the high status accorded a particular discipline is its predominance in product design. High-status members dominate development teams (see **Figure 2.4A**). In many manufacturing firms, for example, the design engineer naturally leads, as a logical outgrowth of design being the traditional source of innovation. A reinforcing cycle of values and managerial systems lends power and authority to this engineer, who in turn is usually accorded primary responsibility for project success or failure. This cycle can also prove to be a trap, as we will see when we look at the down side of core capabilities.

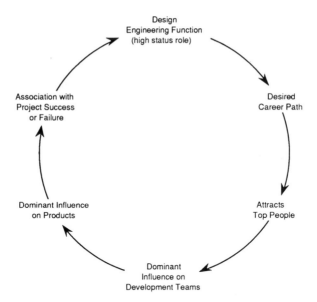

**Figure 2.4A.** In many companies, one discipline dominates. In high-tech firms, design engineering often enjoys the highest status, as shown at the top of this diagram. The dominant discipline reinforces itself over time; design engineering becomes the most desired career path, which attracts top outside people. These people tend to lead development projects, and have the most influence over success (or failure). Because their role is so visible, their performance is most strongly linked with the project's outcome, increasing the perception of the dominance of their function. If properly meshed with other disciplines, the dominant role can be positive; if allowed to overshadow other roles, it will lead to imbalance in projects.

## Knowledge and Skills Dimension

The right knowledge and skills obviously are basic requirements for the success of any development project. This knowledge usually accumulates both within the dominant disciplines and as a general reservoir of relevant knowledge within a company.

*Excellence in the dominant discipline.* One of the most necessary elements in a core capability is excellence in the technical and professional knowledge and skills base underlying major products. The elite in many companies earn their status by demonstrating remarkable skills in every project. They expect to "achieve the impossible," and

Core Capabilities and Core Rigidities ▪ 39

Marketing
Manufacturing
(low status role)

Less Experienced
People Hired

Lower Pay

Low Expectations
from Rest of
Development Team

Team Discounts
Advice

Weak Influence
on Products

**Figure 2.4B.** The perceived low status of nondominant disciplines is often reflected in a negative reinforcing cycle. In many high tech companies, marketing and manufacturing are seen as subservient to design engineering. Because of this perception, less experienced people are hired at lower salaries for these positions, and development teams hold low expectations of them. The input of these people is then discounted, and they have less influence on a project, reinforcing the perception that their functions are less important.

it is often asked of them. Managers of development projects that draw on acknowledged core capabilities have rich resources. We saw numerous cases in which seemingly intractable technical problems were solved through engineering excellence, leading to successful project results.

One DEC project provides a good example. Although the engineers working in the thin-film media group within the company's RA-90 disk drive project had little or no prior experience with the thin-film media that would constitute the drive's memory (because the company had always used ferrite-based media), they were able to invent their way out of difficulties. Before this project was over, the geographically dispersed team had invented not only new media and new heads to read data off the media, but also the software and hardware necessary to integrate these components in the new device.

*Pervasive technical competence.* Besides attracting a cadre of superbly qualified people to work in the dominant discipline, time-honored core capabilities create a reservoir of complementary skills and interests. This reservoir is composed of people who have absorbed technical knowledge from the daily milieu in which they work or who have expertise in complementary technical areas. In several projects, managers tapped the technical competence of colleagues outside the project team to test products under development. The feedback they received integrated reaction from a prospective user with insight from a technician, and constituted a real advantage over projects relying on disparate sources for such information.

For example, in DEC's CDA software project, the developers persuaded other employees to field test their emerging products. The employees tried out the software, sent to them over the company computer network, and reported all reactions back to a "Notes" file kept on the system. This internal field testing relied on not only willing and technically able employees but on a computer system set up for easy worldwide networking. Similarly, the company's DECstation 3100 workstation team recruited an internal "wrecking crew" to evaluate the new product. Employees who found the most "bugs" were rewarded by getting to keep a prototype workstation. At Kodak, engineers developing the FunSaver camera loaded down a colleague who was going on a weekend trip with as many of the single-use cameras as he could carry. With his highly developed eye for subtleties of color and resolution, he could report back on the camera's performance in terms of desired technical changes.

In these companies internal testing is so commonplace that it is taken for granted as a logical step in the creation of a new product. However, it represents a significant advantage over competitors who either lack such technically sophisticated personnel or whose personnel are technically astute but in irrelevant disciplines. The internal field testing of products not only provides reactions from individuals able to relate their findings in technical terms, but feedback is faster, helping development teams hit market windows.

The point is that core capabilities are woven into the fabric of a company. They support all activities. They grow over time and are not confined to a few elite employees or groups.

## Management Systems Dimension

Far-reaching managerial systems affect all development projects. Such systems constitute part of a core capability when they incorporate unusual blends of skills, or foster beneficial behaviors not observed in competing firms. They vary widely, from incentive systems that encourage certain kinds of innovation, to unusual in-house educational systems.

An example of the former exists at Chaparral. Almost all employees at Chaparral are shareholders, and feel that every project they work on is an effort to improve a process they own. Consequently, even line operators and maintenance personnel are tenacious champions for innovative projects. Chaparral's Pulpit Controls project, to upgrade furnace control systems from analog instrumentation to digital, was initiated by a maintenance person; his initial proposal met with opposition from his nominal superior, but he was convinced of the project's merit and persevered. In the end, the project was sanctioned and succeeded. It not only increased furnace operations efficiency, but laid the foundation for digital controls to become a new area of competence for Chaparral, contributing to the technical dimension of their core capability in steel casting.

Another example of a managerial system that supports the growth of a core capability is Chaparral's unique apprenticeship program for the entire production staff, involving both classroom education and on-the-job training. This program is unusual in at least two respects: it is a general rather than trade-specific apprenticeship (unlike those sponsored by trade unions), and the classes are taught by mill foremen on a rotating basis. Thanks to the combination of mill-specific practices grounded in the real-world experiences of the foremen, and general workplace education (including such topics as interpersonal skills), "graduating" students become increasingly skilled and self-confident problem-solvers. The foremen have their own incentive to do a good job, because they must live on the factory floor with people applying the skills and solutions they have taught. For Chaparral, the system creates a staff more proficient than that of competitors. The unusual education program is difficult for competitors to imitate, if only because of the diversity of abilities required of the foremen who teach the classes. This managerial system, tightly integrating technical theory and practice, is reflected in every development project undertaken at Chaparral.

## Physical Systems Dimension

Just as pervasive technical competence among employees can constitute a corporate resource, so do all the systems, procedures, and tools that have been created by talented individuals over the years in support of a core capability. Current project teams tap into these mechanisms, giving them an edge in efficiency, quality, depth of detail, and other competitive factors.

In several of Ford's projects, for example, models that simulate noise inside a car allowed engineers to identify the root causes of unwanted noise that they were finding in prototype vehicles. Some of the causes were far from obvious, since they resulted from the interaction of physically separated components. A noise apparently located in a floor panel, for example, turned out to be caused by the acoustical interaction of sound waves reverberating between the roof and floor, something neither a human ear nor an examination of the parts would have identified. Similarly, the effects of various types of crashes on the structure of a bumper could be simulated by computer rather than by crashing real cars. Such simulations, representing thousands of hours of experience, cut development time as well as costs. They both build on and enhance the skills of the engineers. As such, they constitute a dimension of a core capability that can be leveraged during development.

## THE DOWN SIDE: RIGIDITIES INHIBIT DEVELOPMENT

The same core capabilities that enhance product and process development can also inhibit it, that is, can constitute core rigidities. Even in projects that eventually succeed, problems often surface as the time for product launch approaches. In response to gaps between product specifications and market information, or problems in manufacturing, project managers face unpalatable choices. They can recycle back to some prior phase in the design process, but that route almost certainly necessitates a schedule slippage. Or they may ship a product that in some way falls short of the desired one.

While some of these problems are idiosyncratic to a particular project, others occur repeatedly in multiple projects and therefore are so pervasive as to constitute core rigidities. Core rigidities can affect all projects, even those that are reasonably congruent with current core capabilities. To the degree that such rigidities hamper effective coordination among functions represented on the development team, the establishment of new skills, or the acceptance of new technical systems, they can cripple or at least slow the development process.

In order to avoid rigidities, managers must realize at the outset of a project which rigidities may be present, and then plan ways to confront them. As was the case in looking for the up side of core capabilities, understanding the down side depends on recognizing how the four dimensions of capabilities can affect development projects, but this time in a negative way.

## Values Dimension

While it may well be the greatest single value that can be leveraged to improve development projects, empowerment also has a potential down side: empowerment as entitlement. This down side shows up when individuals construe their empowerment as an implicit "psychological contract" with the corporation, yet the boundaries of their responsibilities and freedom are not clear. Because individuals undertake heroic tasks for the corporation, they expect rewards, recognition, and freedom to act. When in their view the corporation abrogates the "contract," either because the corporation rejects their ideas, or pays too little recognition for all their self-sacrifice, or cuts into their freedoms when those are seen as exceeding certain boundaries, employees often leave the company—sometimes with a deep sense of betrayal. The problem also occurs at finer degrees of distinction; if a person's heroic efforts lead to success for his or her part of a project, but the project as a whole fails, the same feelings can arise if the individual effort is not recognized.

In finding the right balance of empowerment and limitation, managers have to realize that employees who put it all on the line for a critical project feel a real sense of personal risk, and rely on the unspoken contract for support. One project manager described the beginning of a demanding project as "going into the tunnel," from which the team would emerge only when the job was done. She further verbalized the sense of commitment required of her by saying "You either do it or you don't . . . You don't have any other life."

The project went through months of harrowing difficulties and, like most project managers, this one paid a high personal price for progress. Yet at that point, she recalled, "It was the best role I ever played." Entrepreneurs like this woman seem to enjoy the stress—as long as the psychological contract they feel they have with the company remains intact. At the outset of the project, senior management told this project manager that "sometimes you have to break the rules," meaning they would tolerate the departure from traditional product development approaches that she had proposed. But interpreting the comment to extend to her personal management style, she felt she must navigate free from corporate interference. When she pushed her personal sense of empowerment further than the corporation could allow by refusing, among other things, to meet with senior corporate managers during the height of the project press, corporate management drew boundaries within which she was ordered to function. She felt her contract was abrogated, and left both the project and the company just two months before the scheduled product launch. Her abrupt departure deprived the project of some continuity in guiding vision, especially since she had articulated the vision for an entire stream of products.

Because development projects require enormous initiative and yet great discipline in fulfilling the corporate mission, management faces a significant challenge in channeling individual energy toward corporate aims without destroying creativity. Empowerment as a value and practice greatly aids in development projects, until it conflicts with the greater corporate good. Unless this clash is foreseen and prevented, highly valued people may drop a project or even leave the company. Many of the projects we studied had lost members. Some went on to succeed, but could have reached the same end without the loss of sometimes critical knowledge en route had the value of empowerment been managed more effectively.

*Lower status for nondominant disciplines.* There is a clear flip side to the advantages of having a dominant discipline; those employees who aren't part of it tend to be viewed as less important, even if only subconsciously. As noted earlier, chemical engineers and related scientists at Kodak are more highly regarded than mechanical engineers and manufacturing engineers. Therefore, projects involving polymers or film are perceived as more prestigious than equipment projects. There was a clear hierarchy of status at the other companies we studied as well.

A pervasive bias in four of the five companies we studied (Chaparral being the exception) was the reluctance of top engineers to tackle manufacturing issues because of the perceived lower status assigned to those tasks. In this way, a negative cycle evolves; the fewer skilled people who choose to work in manufacturing, the less able manufacturing is to solve difficult problems, and the more convinced everyone is that the lower status is deserved. The lower status of nondominant disciplines was manifested in some rather subtle ways, which constrained how much members of the subordinate disciplines could contribute to a development project and therefore limited the cross-functional integration so necessary to innovation (see **Figure 2.4A**). A few of these negative influences are discussed below.

*Who travels to whom.* One seemingly minor yet important manifestation of unequal status is that the lower status individuals usually traveled to the physical location of the higher status people, because of the implicit hierarchy of functions in the company. Manufacturing engineers were far more likely to go to design sites than vice versa. This was true for short, one-day visits of manufacturing engineers to the offices of the development engineers to discuss design, for temporary postings of several months, and even for permanent assignments. In several projects, the necessity for manufacturing engineers to spend time and effort proving themselves to other team members slowed development.

Some companies rationalized this by maintaining that design precedes manufacturing in the development process, and therefore managers of downstream activities should travel to managers of upstream activities. However, as the recent emphasis on the cost-effectiveness of design-for-manufacturing and simultaneous engineering suggests, not only does such one-way travel reinforce the lower status of the manufacturing engineers, but it slows critical learning by design engineers, reinforcing their isolation from the factory floor. The exceptions to the rule that we saw, when design engineers traveled to manufacturing sites, not only aided in cross-functional coordination by fostering more effective personal relationships, but also educated the design engineers about some of the rationale behind design for manufacturing. A design engineer in one project commented on the understanding he gained of "what [manufacturing] is up against" when he visited the factory floor. At DEC, the team producing follow-on products to the DECstation 3100 workstation commented on how much faster the new development process went, in part because more equality and respect among team members had been generated during the course of the 3100 project.

*Self-fulfilling expectations.* Even if a bias is unspoken and largely ignored, it will affect the performance of the people who are discriminated against. Dozens of experiments with the effects of unconscious interpersonal expectations have demonstrated that person A's expectations about the behavior of person B will significantly increase the probability that B will behave as expected. Psychologists maintain this "Pygmalion effect" results from various cues such as body language, inferences in voice, and predisposed reactions.[8]

Experiments have shown, for example, that randomly chosen students in a new class performed better if teachers were told before the class started that the selected students would excel or were more intellectually capable than others. The interactions that supported this outcome took various forms; teachers unwittingly listened longer or paid more attention to what was said by the prejudged top achievers.

The same kind of interaction can take place between managers and development team members; employees expected to be intrinsically better performers often get more encouragement, and their contribution is often judged more charitably.

Expectations about *roles* can be self-fulfilling prophecies too. The expectation that marketing can provide no insight into product definition will cause a development team to discount marketing's input, even if it is insightful. In the engineering-driven companies we monitored, the marketing personnel assigned to projects tended to be young and relatively inexperienced. In some cases, their role was more to take information from the project to the sales department than to provide information from the field that would aid the product design process. Their skills were not perceived as part of any core capability—often to the detriment of the project.

In the DEC LANbridge 200 project, the marketing people discovered early on that users wanted several important features in the network. However, they lacked the experience to evaluate the importance of that information and the self-confidence to push for inclusion of the features. Not until that same basic information was gathered later on directly from customers by two of the much more credible and experienced consulting engineers was it actually used. Precious time was lost, as the schedule slipped four months to allow the "new" customer information to be incorporated. So it is that expectations born of core rigidities affect the creation of a project team, and the roles team members play.

*Unequal credibility.* Yet another result of the status hierarchy is the dominance of the information originating in the higher status function. For instance, in the HP DeskJet printer project, marketing people conducted studies in shopping malls to discover what potential customers thought about a proposed printer. When marketing brought back 20 "show-stoppers"—suggestions for important changes that would be necessary to ensure marketplace success—the product designers heeded only four. Marketing became insistent that the design engineers go to the mall to hear from the future customers' own lips what was wanted. After direct exposure to the same information they had rejected before, the designers made the other 16 changes originally requested. The point is that history often confers greater credibility on information originating in the dominant function and other sources have to earn their credibility; they start at a disadvantage.

*The "wrong" language.* Even if lower status groups present smart information, it may be discounted if it is not presented in the language of the dominant function. For example, the customer service representatives in the DEC LANbridge 200 project were unable to convince engineering to design the computer boards for field repair as opposed to the traditional approach of replacing the whole system with a new box and conducting the repairs back at the service center. The service representatives failed to get their point across because they did not present their argument in cost-based figures that engineering could believe. In such a case, a visit to a couple of customers might have established the real value of the information, but instead the engineers assumed that an argument that could not be presented in the form of compelling arithmetic was unimportant and could be safely ignored.

## Knowledge and Skills Dimension

Any corporation's resources are limited. Heavily emphasizing a given discipline naturally makes the company somewhat less attractive for top people in a nondominant discipline. A very skilled marketing person knows that she will represent a minority discipline in an engineering-driven firm. Similarly, engineering graduates from top schools generally find the prospects of working for the manufacturing department in a fabrication-based company less attractive than working for design. Not only are manufacturing salaries usually noncompetitive, but the level of existing engineering expertise is often lower in manufacturing. Just as one improves one's tennis game by playing with more skilled rather than less skilled players, so one improves one's mental skills by seeking expert colleagues who will coach, challenge, and inspire one to learn. Therefore, in general, we observed that the need for manufacturing engineering expertise in fabrication, which has finally been recognized in U.S. industry, constituted a challenge in a number of the projects we studied. For example, many of the system problems that caused considerable delay in DEC's RA-90 disk drive project were a result of insufficient and only late involvement of mechanical and manufacturing engineering.

In each of the less successful projects, specific nontraditional types of knowledge were missing. For instance, at Chaparral Steel the arc saw project required a deep understanding of how electromagnetic fields interacted for a variety of metal alloys, a very different knowledge set than the usual metallurgical expertise required in casting. The Hewlett-Packard HP150 project suffered from a lack of knowledge about personal computer design and manufacturing. The company had a long history of successful instrument development using "next bench" design; designers based new product decisions on the needs of engineers working at the next bench within the company. However, such engineers were not representative of personal computer users. The traditional sources of information and design feedback were not applicable for this project.

DEC's new 3100 workstation project met with less than optimal market acceptance because the traditional focus on producing a "hot box" of excellent hardware resulted in less attention to developing software applications for the machine. The knowledge relevant to hardware development flowed through well-established channels, but there was much less knowledge about the need for and how to create applications software. Therefore, the first few working prototypes were shipped for evaluation to customers rather than to third-party software developers. Though this practice had worked well to stimulate interest in the company's well-established lines of hardware, for which much software was available, it was not appropriate for the new workstation, which could not be fully used and evaluated until more software was generated.

## Management Systems Dimension

Management systems can grow just as intractable as physical ones—perhaps more so, because one cannot just plug in a new career path when a new project requires strong leadership.

In several companies, the role of a project leader was not a strong one, partly because there was no career path for such individuals. In such companies, the more likely road to the top is through individual technical contribution. For instance, the hardware engineering manager of one project considered his contribution as an engineer to be much more important than his simultaneous role as project manager, which he said was "not my real job." His unfortunate perception of the relative unimportance of the leadership task not only weakened the power of the role but reinforced the view held by some that the problem solving in project management requires less intelligence than technical problem solving.

## Physical Systems Dimension

Physical systems can embody rigidities also. The skills and processes captured in a technical system, such as software or hardware, may live long beyond their usefulness and resist change. Sometimes it is not obvious to new product designers exactly how many such systems they are affecting. For example, in DEC's 3100 workstation project, the new software base posed an extreme challenge to the site where it was to be manufactured because all the diagnostic and test systems in the factory were based on an entirely different software. Project members commented that the impact of this incompatibility had been underestimated, given the tight nine-month time line for product delivery. The product designers, from their vantage point over a thousand miles away, had not foreseen the amount of change the switch to the UNIX architecture represented in hundreds of systems throughout the plant.

## MANAGERIAL IMPLICATIONS: PROJECTS AS AGENTS OF RENEWAL

To the degree that new product and process development is managed as a series of stand-alone projects focused on localized output, the interaction of development projects with core capabilities and rigidities can be overlooked, and the corporate effects of the interaction can be underestimated and unmanaged. One of the major conclusions the Vision Group drew from its study is that companies should manage development projects for their potential to enhance, redefine, and alter core capabilities in the organization. Development projects can serve a dual purpose: they can produce the desired new product or process, and they can also contribute to a company's knowledge base by strengthening traditional core capabilities, sparking new ones, and overcoming core rigidities.

Experts who study how organizations can be changed maintain that the first step is to "unfreeze" current routines. For this to happen, there must be some dissatisfaction with the status quo. However, a manager cannot simply create a state of dissatisfaction; he or she must convince people that something is broken before they'll let it be fixed. The second step in managing change is to provide a vision of what can be accomplished—a model of the desired future state. Then people asked to alter the practices in their work life will understand why they must do so. Finally, managers need to provide mechanisms to reach the new operational state.[9]

Development projects can aid in all three of these activities. First, they can create dissatisfaction by revealing gaps in current capabilities, either by bringing to the fore the down side of core capabilities, or by highlighting friction between current capabilities and the ones needed for the future. Second, projects can provide models of future capabilities. For instance, a project can serve as a pilot demonstration of new cross-functional cooperation, of new strategies for sourcing technology, or of a new role for a project manager. Finally, projects can be chosen to serve as mechanisms of transition from old capabilities to the new.

Of the companies studied, Chaparral made the most extensive use of development projects as agents of renewal and organization-wide learning. The philosophy at Chaparral turns an old axiom on its head: if it ain't being continuously fixed (improved), it's broke. Projects at Chaparral simultaneously create dissatisfaction with the status quo and provide mechanisms to create future capabilities, through such activities as benchmarking against best-in-the-world capabilities. For example, the model for the new horizontal caster that Chaparral wanted to make was generated after personnel from vice-presidents to line operators spent months visiting all the horizontal casters in operation around the world (there were only a handful at the time), even though the casters were much smaller and were optimized for different products or markets. Three years into development, team members revisited some of these sites, because they felt they still needed to learn more. The project resulted in much more than a new machine; it brought an entire new manufacturing capability to the company.

Chaparral makes line managers in the factory the technical gate-keepers who are supposed to keep the company at the cutting edge of technology. This requires an extensive, worldwide network of con-tacts at the best laboratories, so that the company will know about advanced technology even before scientific or engineering papers are presented at conferences. In one case, they used a development proj-ect to move themselves to the technological forefront. After deciding to begin the Microtuff 10 project to develop new alloy steels of the highest quality, Chaparral initiated and cosponsored with leading aca-demics a conference to learn about the state of the art. This kind of outreach raises consciousness of what is possible—one way to create dissatisfaction with status quo—and also provides a concrete model of future capability. Chaparral's mechanism for getting to this future capability is through rapid iterations of new product and process de-velopment projects. Each development project boosts the company another step up the ladder of renewal.

However, all the companies undertook projects that did more than renew—they challenged the old way of organizing.[10] They directly confronted one or more core rigidities. In several projects the usual negative cycle that reinforced the lower status of manufacturing or marketing was broken—to the benefit of the corporation. For in-stance, in the DEC 3100 workstation project, the manufacturing engi-neers eventually earned the respect of the design engineers by demon-strating that their knowledge could improve design. At the beginning of the project, manufacturing representatives on the team believed that perhaps only 20 percent of their comments were even listened to, much less acted on. However, by the end of the project, they said as much as 80 percent of their remarks at least received a fair hear-ing, and they felt they were influencing and adding value to design.

Even more important were those cases in which the projects were being consciously used as wedges to interrupt the self-reinforcing cycle of a core rigidity, in hopes that the new model seen in the project would spread across the whole company. In an effort to raise manufacturing engineering skills to equal status with that of the more prestigious development engineering skills, Hewlett-Packard's Vancouver Division created a manufacturing engineering group within R&D that would work on the DeskJet printer project. Once the group was well established, management moved it to manufacturing. A rotation plan between manufacturing and R&D was then set up; engineers who left research to work in manufacturing were given a guaranteed "return ticket." The same offer was made to manufacturing engineers if they transferred to research, although there was little movement in that direction. These changes were made to benefit the immediate project, to avoid delays that the inequality between design and manufacturing had always created during development. The project interrupted the traditional negative cycle for manufacturing depicted in **Figure 2.4B**; it signaled a change in status, and attracted more senior, experienced people to manufacturing. Furthermore, the project proved to be a model for teamwork, and has been used as such in the company.

The change at HP shows that it is possible and beneficial to interrupt the negative cycle that constitutes a core rigidity. Development projects can be used in a less dramatic way to improve a core capability, or regain an edge a company has lost. Kodak achieved each of these goals. By employing the newly developed project management system (MAP), the Chem 181 antistatic film project demonstrated the benefits of leveraging each subgroup's contributions. The resulting gains in speed, product integrity, and lower costs strengthened the company's entire development process. Similarly, part of the reason for the FunSaver camera development project was to renew Kodak's market position as a leading manufacturer of 35-mm cameras, a position Kodak once enjoyed but had let slip dramatically.

## MANAGING FOR THE FUTURE

The Vision Group's study led to one overarching conclusion about core capabilities: they are not something that simply exist; they can be consciously created or destroyed. Development projects are not at the mercy of a company's core capabilities and rigidities; if properly managed, the projects can make great use of capabilities and can avoid rigidities. Furthermore, development projects themselves can be used to alter core capabilities and rigidities. Although some project managers are intuitively aware of the interaction of their projects with core capabilities, that interaction is rarely consciously considered or managed. It is especially important to recognize the core capabilities that are required for the success of a project, and to align the project with the right mix of old and new core capabilities.

Most development projects have the potential to enhance core capabilities. Therefore they should be strategically positioned to accomplish that end and should be mined for knowledge. However, the very capabilities that have ensured past successes in product and process development are barriers to nontraditional projects. Such development projects can serve as diagnostics, revealing important dysfunctional patterns in attitude, behavior, or physical systems that hamper the development process. Development projects can thus serve as agents of change and renewal.

Increasingly, the core capabilities of an organization are being recognized as the basis for competitive strategy. But to use them in the ways just described, managers have to examine two aspects of core capabilities that are not usually recognized. The first is that there are four subdimensions to capabilities. Of these, the cultural component—the values dimension—is extremely critical (see **Figure 2.5**). The second point is that core capabilities should be seen as two-sided with respect to their interaction with the development process. At the same time that they enable innovation, they hinder it, and they are not easy to change because of this pervasive dimension of values. It is important to recognize this duality, because core capabilities cannot be managed from a single point of control. Their very nature as a collection of knowledge means that they are distributed and are being constantly enhanced from multiple sources. Once a core capability is established, the enhancement proceeds automatically through organizational routines and programs that are likely to go largely unchallenged.

Yet organizations have no choice but to challenge their current

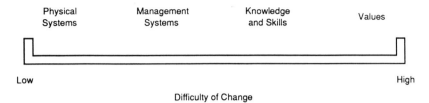

| Physical Systems | Management Systems | Knowledge and Skills | Values |

Low                                                                High

Difficulty of Change

**Figure 2.5.** While all four dimensions of core capabilities can contribute to success or failure, some are easier to change than others in established firms. Though it may involve significant work, changing technical systems is easiest. Managerial systems are tougher because they usually span large segments of a company and have been built up over time, meaning considerable inertia must be overcome. Company-specific skills have also built up over time; critical knowledge is often tacit, so this deeply embedded dimension is difficult to alter. Values, though, are the most nebulous and systemic, and involve those most difficult of hurdles to cross—personal and psychological issues.

paradigms. The swift-moving environment in which they function makes it imperative that the smoothly rolling wheels be consciously disturbed. Development projects provide opportunities for such disturbances.

Even within the lifetime of the single projects studied by the Vision Group, which ranged from more than eight years to less than one, projects highlighted core rigidities. To counter these, development projects can act as small perturbations that aggregate to cause very large changes. Thus project managers who deliberately and constructively "discredit" the systems, skills, or values traditionally revered by their company may cause a complete redefinition of core capabilities or initiate new ones. The need for this kind of organizational learning is a critical element in competitiveness.

## CHAPTER 3

# Guiding Visions

The forward momentum of innovative companies is driven by the creative power of thousands of employees. A company's future success depends in particular on the contributions of individuals working on development teams, the focus of this book. Each day team members in the laboratory, at the workbench, and in meeting rooms face dozens of seemingly small decisions that collectively determine whether a product or process will succeed or fail. Every time a person makes a decision about a material, a color, the location of a switch, the functionality of a component, or the importance of a software subroutine, the project as a whole moves closer or farther away from the targeted product and the expected contribution to corporate capabilities.

Too often the developers making such decisions have two major sources of guidance, neither of which helps much. The first possibility is the traditional corporate strategic plan that was evolved in a process several organizational levels removed from the design bench. If the developers have ever seen the plan (which in our experience is not likely), they will need to make many assumptions about how their own design decisions relate to it. The other source of guidance is much closer to hand—the product definition or specifications. However, if those specifications were detailed enough to guide every possible contingency or decision, they would be far too lengthy and constricting. Even for the most traditional products, for which the technical specifications, cost, and price range are quite clear, critical uncertainties emerge throughout development. New functionalities may be more difficult to build than anticipated, requiring trade-offs. Customers may change their minds about desired features, and competitors may introduce products with characteristics that must be met or bettered. Team members are buffeted from all sides with information that can either help focus their efforts or derail them.

In making their many independent choices, development team members often look in vain for guidance. They fall back on their personal concept of what the new product or process is to mean to the user, and of how their development project fits with the strategy and capabilities of the firm. The problem is that personal concepts can differ radically.

Consequently, hundreds of decisions are made on an ad hoc basis, resulting in products that reach the market late, products that miss some vital functionality, and internal corporate capabilities that are developed too slowly or not at all. Individuals in subprojects unwittingly make incompatible choices that render integration into the final product difficult, and opportunities are missed for using common components in multiple products or for other types of continuity across projects. Even if, at some level in the company, there is a clear idea of what a given product and project is to accomplish, that idea may be obscured from the view of the people in the trenches making daily decisions.

Moreover, as suggested in the prior chapter, every development has no single outcome, but in fact two: not only the product itself, but the contribution the project makes to corporate learning—to corporate capabilities. Product specifications do not address what is to be learned from the project or what new capabilities may be implied by design decisions. For instance, if a design for a circuit board calls for computer chips to be secured using a new surface-mount process rather than the traditional through-hole wiring, or if it requires new types of software skills, then the product design decision in effect commits the corporation to sizeable investments in equipment and human resources. The decision to outsource a critical component can mean relinquishing leadership in a particular technology. Therefore, even apparently minor design decisions can imply enormous changes in facilities use, training, hiring practices, distribution, or marketing.

Although project managers need to steer their teams toward the desired objectives, no manager could make every design and procedure decision personally—or would want to. Managers need ways to ensure that all team members make compatible individual design decisions, without micromanaging the development process. As suggested in the prior chapter, empowered team members can make all the difference in getting a product to market. However, it is a management paradox that the more one wishes to delegate decision making downward, the clearer must be the goals.

A powerful solution for new product development teams, we have observed from our study, is a hierarchy of guiding visions that function at multiple levels throughout a company and guide the numerous microdecisions made during product development. The visibility, quality, and acceptability of these visions affect both the efficiency and the effectiveness of the development process. As we will explain, such visions serve competitive—not merely symbolic—purposes. Their presence or absence importantly affects each project outcome: the success of the product and the contribution of the project to the corporate capabilities.

## What Is a Guiding Vision?

In the context of new product and new process development, a guiding vision is a clear picture of an operational future, an organizational or project destination that serves as a referent and focal point for current decision making. As we discuss later, we do not believe such visions need to originate at the top of the corporate hierarchy, but can spring from creative minds anywhere in the organization. Whatever their origins, however, such visions are truly useful only if they are shared by all the people working on a team and in support of the team.

Guiding visions are adaptable in that they emphasize what must be accomplished and why, but leave much room for individuals to pragmatically determine the details of how the vision is to be realized. Although managers certainly need to put mechanisms in place to achieve the visions, the visions themselves are not detailed strategic plans. However, guiding visions are rich enough to inspire ownership across disciplines and functions. Finally, effective guiding visions promote learning and organizational "reach." They stretch the boundaries of today, rather than draw a complacent line around existing capabilities. They invite revisiting, reevaluation, and reinterpretation, particularly at the line-of-business level. Otherwise they become a recipe for stagnation.

In this chapter we examine three guiding visions that are critically important to new product development: the line-of-business vision, the project vision, and the product concept. A few of the development efforts we studied had strong visions of all three types. More commonly, however, a project had one or two types of vision but not the full complement. It is our thesis that having all three visions, linking them together, and communicating them continuously to the development team increase the probability that the resulting product or process will meet both schedule and market targets. Furthermore, as shown in **Figure 3.1**, it is the product concept and the project vision that provide the necessary links between line-of-business visions and the particular specifications that define new products and processes.

We begin by explaining each of the three visions—what they should be and shouldn't be, and how to characterize them. We then show how the visions must be linked together. Finally, we uncover how managers create successful visions, by weaving together all kinds of information from within and outside the company.

## LINE-OF-BUSINESS GUIDING VISION

Whereas a project manager in the bowels of a company worries about some apparently minor design decisions, general managers at the division level are concerned with the future of the entire line of business. For the two to work in concert, they must share the same line-of-business guiding visions.

In a walk around the Chaparral Steel plant in Midlothian, Texas,

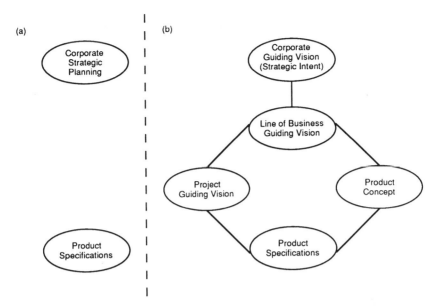

(a)

Corporate
Strategic
Planning

Product
Specifications

(b)

Corporate
Guiding Vision
(Strategic Intent)

Line of Business
Guiding Vision

Project
Guiding Vision

Product
Concept

Product
Specifications

**Figure 3.1.** Using visions to link corporate strategy with product specifications. (a) In many companies, a vacuum exists between the strategic business planning process and the product design decisions being made many organizational levels below by a development team in response to specifications. (b) To ensure that a proposed product or process fits in with corporate strategy, that it meets both customer needs and internal demands, and that the development project proceeds on course, three types of guiding visions are necessary. The line-of-business vision relates corporate strategy to the local part of the company pursuing the development. The project vision guides the work of the team by suggesting what capabilities need to be enhanced, what learning must take place, and what functions must be integrated. The product concept guides the team by capturing their perception of what a new product should mean to its eventual users. Together, the project vision and product concept provide the necessary links between line-of-business visions and the particular specifications that define the new product or process.

visitors hear the same phrases and statements cropping up in conversations being held by everyone from the CEO to line operators: "Rock the boat—continuously . . . To stand still is to fall behind . . . International low-cost supplier of high quality steel products." Are these just part of the party line? Yes—but not in the sense of a mindless catechism. The business vision behind the words, guiding hundreds of decisions and acts daily, is very clear to everyone in this relatively compact organization. The guiding vision at Chaparral is of a continuously growing organization that will stay ahead of the competition by being fleeter, leaner, and more innovative. Chaparral people articulate this by describing their company as a steel "market mill" rather than a minimill. The performance criteria for every employee and every project are tied to continuously increasing the number of tons of steel produced per employee and per time period. While it is important to all employees that the firm be profitable, since they all share in profits, the vision is operations rather than finance based.

A guiding vision is most useful when it is defined in operational terms rather than as static goals. Despite the apparent precision introduced by a specific numeric goal, profit-based objectives such as "15 percent return to stockholders" are vague in terms of the guidance they provide development teams, and they are too far removed from the creative process to be meaningful. Profit-based goals do not translate readily into innovation in the laboratory or on the factory floor. Goals based on competitive issues or internal capabilities do. A line-of-business guiding vision must help facilitate a stream of projects to achieve the stated objective. An appropriate end-point could either describe a future organic system or an external standard toward which the company can strive.

Such conceptual leadership is difficult and rare enough in smaller companies like Chaparral, which has some 930 employees. Providing it in the context of a large, multidivisional company is a significant management challenge.

Conceptual leadership can flow either from the top of the organization down through the ranks, or, in cultures that encourage it, from the bottom and all around. Chaparral is small enough that new ideas and concepts flow rapidly from all sources; there is not a predominant direction. However, conceptual leadership at the other companies we studied springs from differing quarters depending in part on long-standing traditions. At Ford and Kodak, creative ideas indeed bubble up from project managers, but the job of integrating these ideas into a strategic thrust for a line of business rests with upper management.[1] At these companies guiding visions for the lines of business are owned by the managers at the top of each line. The visions are interpreted, sometimes quite liberally, by managers deep in the organization, and are legitimized by the projects they manage.

Hewlett-Packard and DEC constitute somewhat of a contrast in that explorations of future directions often originate very low in the organizational hierarchy and constitute a rich source of new businesses. Managers in both companies have traditionally emphasized the importance of empowering employees, since the future of the corporation is assumed to rest on the ability of such individuals to create and champion new products and processes that grow into whole new businesses. The cultures of these companies are rife with corporate lore about the successes of strategic improvisation, of engineers feeling their way into the future through exploratory thrusts.[2]

In HP's Logic Analyzer Division a significant change in the business vision was precipitated by the work of a few engineers who verified the capabilities of digital technology in logic analyzers by successfully completing several projects pursued in a skunkworks environment. Similarly, DEC's line of UNIX/RISC workstations grew from one project championed by several engineers and sold directly to the CEO and founder. The key element of the line-of-business vision guiding the DECstation 3100 project was a direct challenge to Sun Microsystems, a major competitor. To be effective, the challenge would have to be swift, and the machine would have to be powerful, with a UNIX operating system, instead of DEC's standard VMS system. These implications of the central challenge to Sun were clear to the development team; in fact, the team members laid out the vision themselves when they proposed the project.

Visions such as this, that bubble up from the bottom, must be legitimized by top management at Digital and Hewlett-Packard. However, responsibility for articulating the future into which these projects fit and for understanding the critical linkage between the visions guiding the project and the ones guiding the line of business rests with project managers. Project managers understand that they are empowered to lead the company's charge—and to succeed or fail. They own the vision and most of the risk.

Although the traditions and cultures of the companies examined by our group led to different mechanisms for creating guiding visions, we found examples of bottom-up improvisation and top-down direction in all five companies. The difference between the bottom-up and the top-down momentum is one of degree, and it is important for project development, because it impacts the extent of ownership that project managers feel over their own destiny. Regardless of how the line-of-business vision originates, the issue for development team members is that the vision be accessible to them, so it helps guide them in their daily decisions. There must be a connection between the direction in which the business seems to be headed and the detailed product specifications each team is working on. The challenge is how to make that connection. In the following pages we look first at the project-level guiding vision, and then at the product concept, as the two critical links between a line-of-business's guiding vision and product specifications.

## PROJECT GUIDING VISION

The most important link between a line-of-business vision and a product definition is the vision that guides the development project. A project guiding vision captures the developers' understanding of what the line-of-business experience with the product should be. It guides team members in understanding what learning must take place in order to successfully complete the project, what they in turn need to learn from the project so follow-on projects will run more smoothly, and what the company must learn from the project to enhance its own internal capabilities so it will be more competitive in the future. The project vision integrates across functions and across time. It provides an understanding of the context in which a project is conducted, both in terms of all the knowledge and services that surround a product when it finally comes to market and, most important, in terms of the capabilities that the company is building over time in a particular technology or process.

An example may help place this idea. As noted above, the line-of-business vision for the DECstation 3100 was to become more competitive in the modern workstation market, and specifically to challenge Sun Microsystems. In support of this line-of-business vision, the project's guiding vision contained three critical components: that the new line of DEC workstations be developed based on UNIX language software rather than DEC's proprietary VMS, that to keep up with competitors, the new product had to be to market in nine months, and that the architecture be based on a very fast chip. To provide the speed and performance desired in the engineering workstation market, the central processing unit would use a relatively new design, known as RISC (Reduced Instruction Set Computing). The aggressive nine months development deadline dictated that the workstation could contain only off-the-shelf components. Since there was no time to perfect the new processor chip being designed internally, the RISC chip would be purchased. This decision led in turn to the suspension of the internal RISC chip development efforts.

The decision to use UNIX software instead of the proprietary VMS software on which Digital's mainstream of minicomputers was based forced a recognition that the company would need to develop as substantial a competence in UNIX software as the company had in VMS software architecture. This recognition represented a substantial departure from past policies and affected product design, testing, and manufacture for multitudinous peripherals as well as the workstation itself. Thus the project vision included understanding where this project fit into a proposed stream of products built on UNIX and RISC. Moreover, the nine-month market window required that this project pioneer a new capability in Digital in assembling state-of-the-shelf (purchased) components into a world-class product. Future products designed around this capability would learn from what went well or what went poorly in this project.

This three-part project vision of bringing a UNIX/RISC machine to market within nine months drove substantive decisions, such as the choice to limit peripherals and to use a single circuit board with existing chips. Because of the very clear project vision, the team was able to launch a competitive new line of workstations in record time. The vision also was the basis for physical and personnel decisions; recognizing the need for very tight integration across functions, team management insisted on locating all designers in one place in Palo Alto. Even DEC's world-class capacity for "virtual co-location" of all its people at various sites, through extensive computer networking, teleconferencing, and so on, would have been insufficient to meet the demands for daily and immediate contact among team members. Eventually 35 software engineers and several manufacturing engineers were temporarily transferred to Palo Alto to accelerate product development. To satisfy the aggressive time-to-market schedule, DEC also modified its policies and decision-making conventions that related to project reviews, parts qualification, and testing processes.

In many development projects we studied, the guiding vision at the project level included a recognition of the complexities manufacturing would face. The more subunits that were involved, the more difficult it was to reach and maintain agreement on the nature of the project-level guiding vision. There was a natural tendency for subunits of the project to be influenced by their local environment, to follow their own interpretations of the project vision, including its link with business or corporate strategy. In larger companies, subunits often have somewhat separate agendas, different priorities, and varied incentives. In several projects team members even went to lengths such as purposely missing meetings to guarantee that their own agenda would not be altered.

The more complex a project is to manage (complexity usually increased directly with the number of subunits and work sites), the greater the need for strong conceptual leadership. Without a strong, commonly held vision combating the centrifugal force of such projects it is very easy for subgroups to become misaligned with each other and with the business vision and the product concept. Procedures are needed to quickly recognize and resolve such divergences before they lead to costly and often incompatible investments. Predictably, the manager of one project at DEC, the CDA software project that involved three subprojects, was forced to create a separate technical team that bridged the three groups, after each of them had interpreted the given specifications according to their own needs. Different views of a project-level vision are significantly more difficult to resolve once groups have become firmly invested in their particular views.

Like those visions guiding businesses, project-level guiding visions must be rich enough to be ''owned'' by team members from multiple functions. To motivate behavior, a shared vision also must be simple enough to be understood by all team people who most likely have different professional "languages." And talented project managers must nurture the incorporation of contributions from team members who may be perceived by some as representing less "prestigious" functions.

In studying a wide variety of development projects we found several characteristics that were key to the success of a project vision. In turn, the lack of any of these caused problems as a project proceeded. The three features—alignment with the business guiding vision, integrativeness across function, and visibility to the development team—are examined below.

## Alignment with the Business Guiding Vision

A project vision positions a given project on a technology development trajectory necessitated by the line-of-business vision. The project vision makes it clear for team members if their particular project will result in a new platform or if it is related to an already established one. The DEC workstation project vision included a clear perception of desired market position, not only for the product at hand but for two follow-on products. The project manager knew she was building toward not just the current DECstation 3100 but a machine that would deliver similar performance at a lower cost and one that would provide greater performance at the same price.

Thus a project vision provides a view into the future. Each time a team member chooses the placement of a switch, the substitution of one component for another, even the color of a cabinet, he will know what he is building toward and from. In most cases, a project should not be seen as a "one-shot deal." It has ancestors and will have progeny. The project vision provides a degree of consistency over time, helping integrate a product or process into the stream of projects that are creating new markets and new capabilities for the company.

Excellent guiding visions at the project level, like ones at the business level, also promote organizational learning—which is needed to achieve the desired output of a new product or process and contributes to an important core capability of the firm. The project-level guiding vision must be able to focus energy and behavior toward the proliferation of ideas, the linking of old and new ideas, and the solving of unpredictable setbacks and surprises. To achieve rapid product development the project vision also creates a framework in which individuals can make good decisions quickly and integrate their actions with one another.

Most project managers we talked with agreed with the axiom that during the time spanning the first 15 percent of a development project, 85 percent of the funds to be spent on the rest of the development effort will be committed. Paradoxically, they found the graph depicting this relationship to be surprising, because they had not consciously managed with that apportionment in mind (see **Figure 3.2**). Given this relationship, upper management should work hard to help establish the project vision during this initial 15 percent of the project duration, so funds and time are not improperly committed. Moreover, upper management bears a good bit of the responsibility for forcing attention on solving identifiable technical and market problems before the project is launched, so that during the project resources can be devoted to the inevitable unforeseen problems.

Many of the development team members we interviewed reported that they wished they had spent more time in pre-project planning and ironing out problems during that first 15 percent of the formal project schedule. In several projects, development involved invention. In those cases the extent of the technical uncertainty was inadequately addressed at the outset, both by project managers and upper management. However, once the project vision was established and the project launched, top management interest then often became counterproductive, especially if it resulted in preempting project manager control over development details.

The project-level guiding vision helps to obviate the tendency of upper managers to micromanage projects by linking the business vision to the product definition, since in the final analysis specific details on how to reach line-of-business goals must be delegated to project managers and developers.

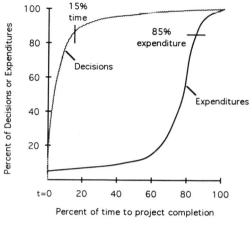

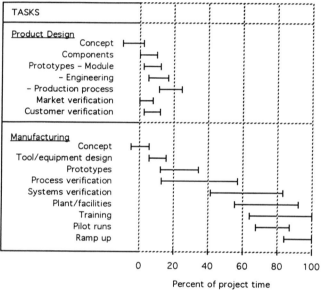

**Figure 3.2.** Schematic representation of the relationship between the timing of project expenditures and the decisions that eventually trigger those expenditures. It is commonly observed that on completion of about 15% of the project time, most (85%) key expenditure decisions have been implicitly or explicitly determined. Representative tasks and their timing are shown below the timing curves. In addition to the general 15/85 rule observed in the Vision Group projects, we have seen analogous presentations from other companies including Boeing, Westinghouse, Motorola, and BMW.

## Integrativeness Across Functions

Strong project visions also place the project in the context of total company capabilities—in customer service, manufacturing, marketing, and finance. The project vision provides for progress on the agendas of all the relevant functions as the company moves in new directions. Inevitable conflicts of interest, priority, and agenda that arise among team member who retain some loyalty and perspective to their particular function—be it manufacturing, customer service, or marketing—have to be resolved. Lack of a strong project vision leaves individuals to make decisions in a vacuum. An example is provided in the project building DEC's LANbridge 200, a communications network that links several computer networks. Engineers on the team assumed that in keeping with prior practice, faulty units would be repaired in the field. Customer service people, however, wanted to be able to pull a malfunctioning unit, replace it with a functioning unit, and take the faulty one back to DEC to repair. They saw this immediate replacement as a logical next step in improving customer service. The engineers believed that strategy would be too costly. The choice of strategy would affect design. When the conflict arose, the project manager had nowhere to turn for guidance. It was not clear what the future repair strategy was of the line of business under which the product fell, nor how this project was intended to further that strategy.

While a strong vision is required for integration, balance within the vision is also important. For example, the vision guiding Hewlett-Packard's DeskJet project, undertaken to develop a new class of low-cost computer printers, heavily emphasized manufacturability. A new manufacturing engineering capability was created by R&D people and then transferred to manufacturing. In this case, the zeal to optimize manufacturability actually led to an overemphasis on reducing the number of parts in the printer cabinet. The final cabinet was a single piece of molded plastic so complicated to make that it was difficult to test, increasing labor costs to beyond what would have been incurred had the cabinet been assembled from a number of pieces. The trade-off between assembly and test labor was not analyzed. However, the division learned much about the true meaning of manufacturability from this project and succeeded in integrating design and manufacturing to a degree formerly unreached.

## Visibility to the Team

The project guiding vision provides a critical link between line-of-business strategy and the product definition. However, if the project vision is not visible, it does no good. In making their design and development decisions, team members must have two objectives in mind: the product that will be delivered to a particular set of customers, and the company capability to which they are contributing. The output of the project development process is twofold, and a strong project vision helps keep the dual purpose in plain view. To be sure, we found pockets of exceptional clarity throughout the companies we examined; usually it was senior architects who knew exactly where a development trajectory was pointed and how each project or subproject fit into the objectives. These individuals almost always felt that they had communicated their vision to their subordinates. Yet, while there were some notable exceptions, subordinates on most teams did not see the vision with anything approximating the same clarity. Consequently, they neither "owned" the vision nor used it to aid them in making efficient decisions. The more a leader wishes to delegate, the more the team must share the goal; the more team members are to be empowered, the clearer must be the project vision and the product concept.

Another problem was that guiding visions were not always articulated in language equally understandable to all those on the team. When technically proficient managers constructed their visions they tended to think of a product or process in technical terms, and of the product-line trajectory in terms of the performance criteria guiding the development efforts. A line of printers might be described in terms of density of ink on paper; a product line of disks in terms of formatted capacity. However, marketing people need to think in terms of segments served, customer service personnel in terms of hours of flawless operation, manufacturing engineers in terms of cost per unit, and so on. The vision has to be expressed in terms common enough to aid the efforts of all the actors.

## PRODUCT CONCEPT

As in the case of the project vision, the product concept links the business vision to the daily decisions made by developers. The product concept is a construct that captures the developers' perception of what a new product should mean to its eventual users. It is therefore a view into the marketplace. A product concept provides critical information by clarifying to each developer how his or her component interacts with others to create a coherent product unit.[3]

Sometimes these constructs can be disarmingly simple; for example, the product concept for a new car could be expressed as a "pocket rocket." Immediately, an auto industry employee would understand that the car will be both small and fast. The concept helps clarify the transmission type, the handling, and maybe even the appropriate advertising campaign. Team members would be aware that such a car should sell at a premium compared with the base model, but should still be affordable. And the driving experience should be fun: quick at the getaway, nimble in the turns, and very fast at the straightaways. This product concept frames the future customers' experience with the car. Obviously, many details would have to be defined, but this product concept sets a framework against which later decisions can be focused and aligned. It also provides a significantly clearer picture of the future vehicle than a traditional, humdrum description would; compare in your own mind the mental image of "a pocket rocket" with that of "a sports car in the mid-price range."

The product concept, while clarifying the future product, is open to specific interpretation by the developers. It must provide different but consistent information about the market to a varied group of people, each of whom focuses on a different aspect, subsystem, or component of the future product. Some people on the development team will use the concept to determine what the product does, while others will understand from it what the product is. Still others may derive from it a sense of whom the product serves or what the product means to the customer. A powerful product concept evokes all these responses within people and results in a coherent perspective that determines the product's ultimate definition.

Coming up with a product concept that hits the bull's-eye is not easy, and entails much more than coining appropriate phrase. In the projects we monitored, we found three chief characteristics of product concepts that were important in guiding the fulfillment of product definition: completeness, constancy during the life of the project, and visibility to the development team. Understanding these will help leaders of future projects develop useful product concepts with their own development teams.

## Completeness

To truly guide a product definition, a product concept (and the statement embodying it) must be complete. It must reflect all the essential ingredients of a successful user experience with the new product. This is asking a lot. As explained in the chapter on core capabilities and core rigidities, even projects that depart from the traditional strength of a company sometimes remain shackled to the past. Traditional ways of thinking, the prevalence of certain disciplines on a project team, and the embedded technical infrastructure of a company often influence the product concept. For example, as suggested earlier, Digital Equipment's relatively successful DECstation 3100 project arose out of the passion of a few engineers to enter the UNIX/RISC market with a competitive workstation as quickly as possible. The development team was confident of its ability to build a "hot box." The "hot box" image conveyed a sense of power, performance, and functionality. In capturing the potential user's experience in such a phrase, the developers were reflecting both their own predilections and the long history of preferences of DEC's engineering customers. Armed with a good deal of computer expertise, engineering customers of DEC's VMS line had long appreciated the power and performance of the DEC machines. Each new machine built on the applications of earlier machines. Applications software was therefore traditionally less important than the operating system of the machine itself.

However, in moving to the new UNIX platform the DECstation 3100 developers launched into unknown territory. While they achieved their very ambitious goals of bringing out a fast, powerful machine for the price desired, in an astonishing eight months, the team had developed only 20 software applications, while the competitor that they hoped to outdistance had 500. Had DEC's product concept included a clearer understanding of users' needs for applications, the first prototypes might have been deployed differently. The first machines were distributed, in time-honored tradition, to key customer accounts. In the past, when promoting the VMS line, this kind of deployment served the company well. VMS customers, who already possessed plenty of software, could try out the new machine, see its speed and agility, and testify to that on behalf of the company. However, in the case of the DECstation, had the first machine been sent instead to third-party software developers it is likely that much more software could have been made available at the time of product launch. A product concept that was somewhat more complete than the traditional "hot box" could have helped. Perhaps if the concept had been a "hot tool," effort would have been expended to not only create powerful hardware but to draft a host of software applications that would have been available when the "box" was ready.

The project at Ford that resulted in the 1988 Lincoln Continental benefited greatly from focus on a product concept articulated only late in the project as developers recognized the importance of explicitly capturing in a succinct phrase the vision that had guided the project. Team members wanted to create a product with the traditional look and feel of a luxury car, but that also had contemporary flair. The term "luxury" conjured up the large, boxy styles of the past in addition to the sense of soft contours and quality interiors. Adding the word "contemporary" tempered that outdated vision, suggesting more modest proportions, rounded lines, but still the ride and feel of an expensive car. The concept "contemporary luxury" evolved to depict the vision guiding the decisions of the development team. When making small but vital decisions about everything from the design of the suspension system to the contour of the dashboard, the developers were guided by the product concept they all had in common. "Contemporary luxury" clearly described a car that would look, handle, and drive far differently from a traditional "luxury" car, and certainly from a "pocket rocket," and captured the essence of the desired customer experience.

## Constancy

The second characteristic important to a product concept is constancy during the life of the project. Though, as the preceding chapter suggests, the ability of a company to steadily alter time-honored practices and develop flexibility in its development process is fundamental to competitiveness, shifts in product concept and management during the life of a single project only serve to lengthen its duration. A good example of this was Kodak's Panda printer project, initiated to develop a large-format computer printer that converted digital input into color images. The product was originally undertaken to fill a need expressed by the U.S. Department of Defense, and Kodak's Federal Systems division, experienced in filling Defense Department needs, formed a well-focused product concept and went about its work. A year into the project managers in one of Kodak's consumer products divisions convinced corporate management that there was great potential to sell the printer to commercial markets also. The corporate managers charged the project team with developing the product for both markets.

This decision implied a shift in product concept, since the needs of the users in the two markets, and consequently their desired experience, were quite different. However, the product concept was never expressly changed and work took off in various directions. Although the final product was a technical success, total project costs and schedules missed their targets by substantial amounts. In such cases, until shifting product goals are resolved in a new, sound concept, development team members will likely pursue incompatible objectives. Projects in our study that were guided by clear, specific, complete, and constant product concepts therefore had an advantage. The product concept was an important coordinating mechanism.

## Visibility

Even if a product concept is complete and remains constant, it is of little use if it is not well articulated. Facile wording cannot save a flawed concept. However, an excellent concept is only powerful if it is well communicated. Team members must understand it and get behind it 100 percent. When Ford's Lincoln Continental team hit on the concept of "contemporary luxury" and communicated this vision throughout the community, it caused the large number of diverse people involved with the project to finally coalesce and unify. The challenge to project managers is to establish this critical link between the line-of-business guiding vision and the product definition and communicate it regularly.

## LINKING THE VISIONS

The two visions we have been discussing—the project vision and the product concept—provide the necessary link between a line-of-business strategy and the definition of a specific new product or process. As noted, all three visions must work together, and we have explained the reasons why.

It is not possible to draw up rules for ways to make sure all three visions work together. Constructing the visions, and seeing that they mesh, is the job of the development team and the senior management overseeing it. What is important here is to appreciate how the visions can be linked, and why they need to be. To see the linkage in action, let us revisit the DEC workstation project for a moment.

The DECstation 3100 project arose from the passion of a few managers whose business vision was to initiate a new line of DEC workstations as quickly as possible. The project's guiding vision, developed by the managers and accepted by upper management, contained three critical components: UNIX, RISC, and a nine-month window. From this project vision, together with market and technical information, the team developed a particular product concept that answered the questions: Who would the customers be? What would these customers want? What type of interaction would the users want to have with the workstation?

The product concept theorized that the target customer would be an engineer desiring a low-cost "hot box," who was experienced with UNIX, capable of personalizing the system to meet his or her needs, and for whom the performance advantages offered by RISC would be critical. While this concept was somewhat incomplete, it

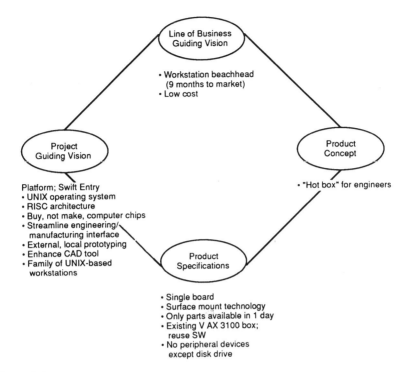

**Figure 3.3.** Visions for the DECstation 3100. An example of how the linking of visions drives critical decisions that define a new product and its development is shown here for Digital Equipment Corp.'s DECstation 3100 workstation. The line-of-business guiding vision contained two key components: the need to initiate a new line of DEC workstations for the engineering community, and the need to build a competitive machine in nine months. These components both required breaking from traditional DEC development approaches and learning new ones. The team developed a particular product concept—a low cost "hot box" for engineers experienced with the UNIX operating system and RISC computer architecture. The project guiding vision translated those two visions into operational terms, dictating what would be bought and what made, how much innovation would be attempted in this first project in the anticipated stream of UNIX/RISC workstations, and how the work would be coordinated.

provided focus for the project. The project vision and the product concept led to the product definition that spelled out all the necessary specifications (see **Figure 3.3**).

The project vision required that the team break from traditional DEC development approaches to meet the aggressive time-to-market objective. These included new part-qualification methods and radical product management techniques, as well as, for the first time at DEC, the external purchase of a microprocessor and state-of-the-shelf technology instead of internal innovation. The line-of-business vision established that the DECstation 3100 would be only the first of a stream of UNIX/RISC workstations. Therefore, the development team not only had to produce the ultimate workstation in at least nine months but also had to create a solid foundation for future products.

As these visions coalesced the product concept was further refined. The workstation would have only a single computer board and minimal peripherals, and it would have to provide enough performance to break what was known as the $1000/MIPs barrier, at the time a state-of-the-art measure of computing bang per buck. This refined product concept, plus the ongoing project vision, contributed critical pieces of information used to drive the ultimate product specifications and to link them to both the business vision and the customer's needs.

## CREATING EFFECTIVE VISIONS

The creators of all three kinds of guiding visions—the business vision, the product concept, and the project vision—do not conjure them up from pure imagination. They create visions by accessing all kinds of market and technical information. Part of the reason that project visions and product concepts varied in strength from project to project and from company to company we looked at was that managers varied in their ability to access different information. In part, company traditions tend to emphasize certain sources over others. Companies strong in engineering tend to have relatively clearer project visions, and a sense of technological progress along some known dimension (say, cost per 1000 megabytes of computer memory). Companies strong in marketing tend to have clearer product concepts because they more actively seek information about targeted users.

As a consequence, project managers we spoke with did not always have a full range of sources from which to select information. Moreover, some potentially important sources of market and technical information were underutilized in almost all the projects, regardless of the company, or they were accessed so late in a project that costly last-minute revisions were required. One of the challenges to managers in creating guiding visions is to nurture the company's ability to access useful information. While not all sources may be relevant in any single project, we believe all should be available for exploitation. One the following pages, we present a host of sources and the roles they can play in helping managers create successful visions.

## Market Information and Sources

Sources of market information range from the exploration of known needs and markets to the creation of new markets. As shown in **Figure 3.4**, the sources range from very reactive influences (on the far left of the diagram) to very pro-active influences (on the far right). We explain each of the sources below.

*Customer specifications.* Sometimes customers know their needs so exactly that they can provide designers with the precise specifications for the desired product or proess. None of the companies studied received such requests. However, Chaparral Steel frequently gives its vendors detailed designs for equipment such as molds, thus retaining design knowledge in-house.

*Voice of the current customer.* Seeking input from current customers begins with such steps as interviews, surveys, and focus groups but extends to much more sophisticated techniques. The customers' voice reflects immediate and known market needs. In the projects we studied at Ford, extensive market research played an important role in establishing the characteristics desired in a car by specific market segments. For example, research showed that older buyers, who accounted for most sales of the Lincoln Continental, almost exclusively preferred one type of seat. Of course, this design was chosen for the "contemporary luxury" version of the car released in 1988, not only pleasing buyers but making them feel comfortable as they test drove cars before making their purchasing decision.

*Competitive benchmarking.* Most of the projects we studied involved some form of competitive benchmarking, but it was often an evaluation of one specific competitor. For instance, managers of soft-

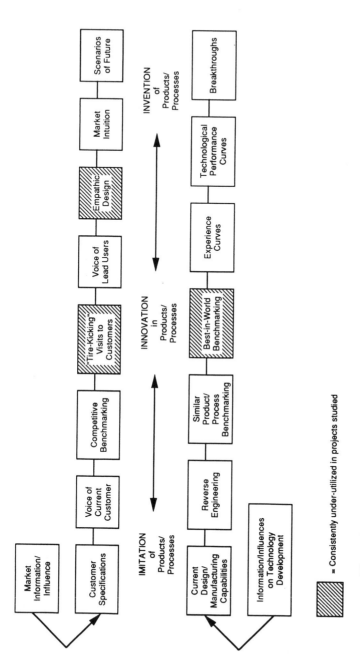

**Figure 3.4.** Sources of information for guiding visions. Managers create guiding visions by accessing all kinds of market and technical information, which range from very reactive influences (at left) to very pro-active influences (right). Some important sources (shaded) are routinely underutilized. Any one project is not likely to require equal access to the entire range of sources, but a successful corporate product and process development system should provide capabilities to access all of them, so that project managers are aware of the possibilities and can call on the sources they need.

80

ware projects at DEC were sensitive to how their products compared to those of Apple. Wider comparisons will yield greater insight.

*Tire-kicking.* A few projects involved visits by engineers to customer sites, in order to see firsthand how prior generations of their products or processes were functioning in the customer or manufacturing environment. Information gathered during such tire-kicking visits can greatly supplement market research for several reasons. First, product engineers are likely to react more strongly to customer desires when they hear them directly. Even more important is that developers may obtain ideas about product enhancements and additional features from seeing how their customers actually use the products, by observing the often quite creative "work-arounds" that customers invent to deal with shortcomings in the product for particular applications and from the problems encountered in particular environments.

*Voice of lead users.* Those customers whose needs, interests, and capabilities drive them to seek the most advanced technology, and therefore whose desires may foreshadow the needs of the majority of users in the near future, were tapped in a few projects.[4] Lead users are critical for Ford because of the lengthy development cycle in the automobile industry. Ford has identified a distinct market category of car buyers who are called "style progressives," people who have a craving for the latest advances in automobiles. Their desires tend to foreshadow those of the general market and are explored and used to guide the company's direction.

*Empathic design.* In many cases customers are unable to clearly articulate their future needs, not only because the future in their own organization is uncertain but because they have little idea of what is technically feasible and what opportunities might be offered by a nascent technology.[5] Projects that involve invention rather than adaptive innovation or competent imitation do not merely react to the customer environment; they shape it. Developers who actually live in or visit the user environment so extensively that they *develop a strong empathy* for user concerns and a full understanding of the users' business can visualize future possibilities. They then can design a new product or process based on their capability to integrate known technological potential with anticipated need. Empathic design is technology "push," but with a heart and a brain, not obsessive concentration on the technology to the exclusion of relevance.

One of the most famous industrial designers, Henry Dreyfus, trained his students to spend time engaged in the activity for which they were designing tools. They spent hours using machinery as far afield as corn pickers and vacuum cleaners. They were trying to get inside the work environment of the user. Chaparral Steel sometimes utilized empathic design to stay ahead of its competitors. For example, the new Microtuff 10 steel it developed was not invented in response to any stated need of customers, yet Chaparral employees concluded from listening to a range of customers that there seemed to be a niche for significantly tougher, high-quality alloy steels. To fully utilize this new material, however, the customers needed to alter their fabrication processes. As is usually the case when technology requires changes in current practice, Chaparral's customers had to be educated about Microtuff's benefits.

Another form of empathic design is found in large engineering organizations, where engineers in one area design new equipment for the "next bench," meaning their fellow employees or even themselves. The developers of the DEC workstation said they built the machine they had always wanted themselves. While effective, the danger in this approach is also obvious: that the empathy is myopic. However, there are times when the knowledge of technological potential and future user desires must come together in one head or be synthesized by a very small group, and such convergence can propel the development process way beyond concepts derived from even the best of lead users. Successful empathic designs create new markets.

*Market intuition.* Market intuition is by its nature difficult to define. Rather than providing guidance for a specific product, market intuition conveys a general sense of market trends, of kinds of functionality that may be desired in the future. This intuition can support the empathic design of products for a particular market segment. Nonetheless, it was cited by several project leaders as an important influence on the development process, derived from deep experience in the market. Engineers on the DECstation team built heavily on their personal sense of the workstation market, built up through prior development projects as well as prior work experience, to envision the entire line of workstations of which their creation was but the first. Managers at Chaparral sensed the potential for the Microtuff alloy because of intricate experience in their market. When an R&D team at Hewlett-Packard first started experimenting with digital oscilloscopes, neither the market nor HP management yet recognized the coming need for those products. Customers' requests and management attention were focused on the immediate market for analog technology. It took two years for management to catch up with the researchers' market intuition and sanction a formal development project. However, HP was still able to bring out a digital product four to five years ahead of the competition.

*Scenarios of the future.* Brainstorming over possible future scenarios extends the view of the market out beyond any sense of certainty. None of the projects we studied involved such exercises, but many companies find them useful for constructing sensitivity analyses about current and proposed product lines. Therefore the category is mentioned here for completeness.[6]

## Technical Information and Sources

Sources of technical information, as portrayed in Figure 3.4, constitute an equally important continuum of influences ranging from the constraints of technologies embedded in current products and production facilities to the very uncertain potential of breakthrough inventions. As we did in the last section for market sources, we will examine the range of technical sources here.

*Current capabilities.* Current testing and manufacturing capabilities can influence the design process, and developers must often debate the trade-off between new features and the cost of changing production processes to enable them. Capital-intensive processes influence design even more profoundly than assembly-type production, particularly in larger, older companies. However, at Chaparral, where product and process are extremely intertwined and where changes in product often imply very large capital investments, current capabilities are regarded only as temporary place-holders in a constantly changing process. While it can be difficult to overcome the inertia of changing a process, the success of Chaparral points to the value of such an investment.

*Reverse engineering.* Taking apart competitor's products to help set goals and decide what features to emulate is a common source of information in most companies, including those we studied. Software as well as hardware can be reverse-engineered if the source code is accessible.

*Product or process benchmarking.* Benchmarking is slightly more future-oriented, since it is possible to benchmark against product performance characteristics that have been announced but are not yet available on the market. For example, after visiting Japan, the team carrying out DEC's RA90 to develop a high-density disk drive for computers reset performance goals. They decided to try for 45 million bits of data storage per square inch instead of 30 million, to achieve parity with Fujitsu's highly ambitious targets. The goal turned out to be unreachable for both companies in the given time frame, but DEC's project manager noted that if one aims only for parity, one is sure to fall behind. Therefore the competitive information spurred the team to higher achievements than would have otherwise been likely.

*Best-in-world benchmarking.* This is a strategy that was underutilized in most of the projects we studied. Unlike market benchmarking, which identifies features in competitors' products, best-in-world benchmarking requires that a team seek the very best practices associated with the technology they are working with, in whatever industry they may occur. For example, several companies used surface-mount technology in their manufacturing of circuit boards. While they benchmarked their products against direct competitors, they didn't think to open up VCRs or other consumer products in which such technology had been used for a longer time and where, as a consequence, techniques were highly developed and manufacturing knowledge was at the leading edge. Best-in-world benchmarking often requires exploration far away from the home industry, as, for example, when ceramicists seek to understand rheology from paint manufacturers, when the makers of steel cabinets borrow concepts in computer-aided cutting from the garment industry, and when customer service operations examine the best mail-order houses.

*Experience and performance curves.* Several projects we studied were guided by technical experts' understanding of industry experience curves, which lie along certain performance dimensions such as gigabytes of memory per dollar of disk cost, and their knowledge of curves indicating the theoretical level of possible performance. Though some project managers used known curves to set reasonable project goals, others pushed beyond current experience to test the bounds of the curves. Chaparral succeeded in doing this when it took on a very new alloy in the Microtuff project; it failed when it attempted unsuccessfully to design a revolutionary electric-arc saw for cutting steel. Members of the DEC RA90 project had cost-versus-performance curves clearly in mind as they developed the requisite thin-film technology, and knowledge of these curves dictated product definition.

*Technological breakthroughs.* Of course, breakthroughs cannot be planned, but they do offer opportunities for new products and processes. In a few projects breakthrough inventions were required for success. The RA90 team, for example, succeeded in inventing the necessary thin-film media for their product. Chaparral's arc saw team was unable to achieve the needed breakthroughs, and the project simply could not be done any other way. A critical management decision is whether a development project that depends on breakthrough innovation should be launched. (For more on this topic, see Chapter 4.)

Any one project is not likely to require equal access to the entire range of market and technical information sources discussed here. Our contention is that a successful corporate product and process development *system* should provide capabilities and access to all of them, so that project managers are aware of the possibilities and can call on those sources they need. Systematic processes to capture and codify market and technical knowledge are key to creating effective visions and realizing high performance project teams.

The guiding visions featured in this chapter are likely to draw on these sources to varying degrees. A *product concept* draws more on market information than on technical sources, since it is intended to exemplify the users' experience. In fact, it is possible to derive a successful product concept solely from information concentrated at the left-hand side of the market information spectrum featured in **Figure 3.4**. However, a successful *project vision* must elicit information from across the spectrum, since it must include an understanding of the capabilities a company is developing. A *line-of-business* vision not only draws on the full complement of sources but is likely to access all the sources in **Figure 3.4**, since its scope is far-reaching.

## CREATING AND COMUNICATING A VISION

Guiding visions are the tangible output of conceptual leadership. They must be visible and continuously communicated during development projects. The most successful guiding visions that we observed were promoted by articulate leaders who understood the need of the team for this "soft" management mechanism. However, the visions themselves were not the sole creation of those leaders. They integrated technical and market information from multiple sources.

In all the companies we studied, we were more likely to find visionary leaders for new products than for new processes, with the possible exception of Chaparral, where product and process are almost indistinguishable. New production processes were in general regarded by team members more as means to an end, namely a particular product, than as capabilities to be developed that would support many different products. Project guiding visions helped to counter the dominance of the highly visible product development priorities over the accumulation of knowledge in the form of production capabilities.

For most of the projects we studied all three kinds of guiding visions tended to be developed reactively, in response to competitive moves, rather than proactively. There were a few exceptions, in which the project's objective was to define the market, rather than respond to it, as, for example, the Chaparral Microtuff project. The typically reactionary mode had a number of effects, some beneficial and some potentially disadvantageous. On the up side, development team members had a clearer target at which to shoot when they knew they were trying to go the competition one better. The DECstation team knew its hot box needed to compete with those from Sun Microsystems; the Kodak team developing the single-use FunSaver camera was clearly racing against a similar effort from Fuji. The clarity of such goals helped team coordination. On the down side, reactionary moves tended to reinforce the perceived importance of product over process, since the latter are a less visible form of competition. They also worked to shorten everyone's horizon; the obvious near-term goal was pursued, sometimes to the detriment of longer-term visions. Visions were also more easily constructed if a project was closely aligned with current corporate strategy rather than with a new thrust.

As the examples in this chapter illustrate, guiding visions are communication vehicles, serving to help coordinate and steer the development effort of people with very different agendas, skills, and priorities. The more parties involved in a project, the greater the need for a clear vision at multiple levels. However, the larger the project the more difficult it is to construct a vision that has meaning for everyone. Kodak's ambitious Factory of the Future project foundered not because of a lack of skill or dedication, but in part because there were conflicting visions that were not resolved in time for everyone to be assured they would reap benefits from the project. In order to benefit all the stakeholders the project would have had to grow even larger; when the vision was pared back to the most obviously attainable goals it no longer held out promise of payback for everyone involved.

Guiding visions, especially the project and line-of-business visions, include a recognition of the capabilities a company needs to nurture or build. Visions drive companies to expand current capabilities and create new ones. Therefore these visions must be realistic as well as challenging. One of the most difficult questions posed by any new development project is just how far to stretch current capabilities in search of new ones. The next chapter addresses this issue.

# Pushing the
# Performance Envelope

In the decades following World War II, stable markets and well-established patterns of competition allowed leading companies to maintain competitive positions with a relatively relaxed approach to product and process development. Substantial innovations in products or technology were the exception not the rule. Product life cycles were measured in years if not decades. For the most part companies turned out familiar products using well-known technologies. But in the early 1980s all this changed. No longer was it possible for companies to approach product and process development in this manner. The cliche about the explosion of knowledge and technology is in fact evident on numerous fronts including the proliferation of new and innovative products, the availability of highly educated and experienced scientists, engineers, and managers to enterprises located almost anywhere on the globe, and the rapid dissemination of newly generated and codified knowledge to any company interested in using it to create new products, services, or processes. The contemporary business environment, characterized by competitive stresses and rapid change, demands that a company work constantly to improve its products, manufacturing processes, and internal capabilities. A company that hopes to prosper must uncover and remedy its own weaknesses before the competition can gain advantage. This chapter addresses the problems of making the constant improvements—pushing the performance envelope—needed to cope with this rapidly changing, turbulent environment, and discusses some mechanisms used by companies in our study for dealing with them. We found that in the most successful projects, the environment, an understanding of future customers' needs, and resourceful leaders created forces that "pulled the performance envelope," thus creating a more fertile implementation foundation. The subtle yet critical difference is an atmosphere of problems and opportunities looking for solutions, not solutions looking for problems; the net effect is the pushing of boundaries.

A performance envelope conceptually expresses what is possible with the current state of capabilities. At any point, a company's performance envelopes will determine how competitive the company's products and processes are compared with other players in the market. Advances in technology and other capabilities over time move these envelopes. Performance envelopes can be represented graphically; the curve in **Figure 4.1** illustrates the trade-off possibilities between speed and cost for an imaginary product. In the development of any product, service, or process there are many such curves that designers and project managers must consider.

"Pushing the envelope" describes the process of moving an envelope over time. We use the phrase to capture the idea of advancing one's own capabilities by deliberate action. The envelopes of capabilities for an entire firm involve many dimensions, including technologies, skills, methods, and organization. There will be many envelopes to push and the accelerating pace of change in technology and product markets makes this activity both difficult and critical for a firm. The accumulation of the decisions on which envelopes to push, when, and how far will determine a firm's future competitive position. Because of the speed of these changes, a company that does not aggressively pursue improvements will quickly find itself uncompetitive; competitive advantages can be wiped out literally overnight. Even firms that are technological followers must be agile and fast just to keep up. A well-managed effort to push the envelopes is no longer optional. **Figure 4.2** depicts the context and the consequences of the decisions on pushing the envelope.

The most obvious performance envelopes are those related to prod-

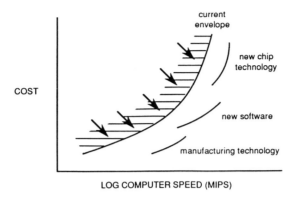

Cost-Speed Envelope for
Computer Workstations

current
envelope

new chip
technology

new software

manufacturing technology

COST

LOG COMPUTER SPEED (MIPS)

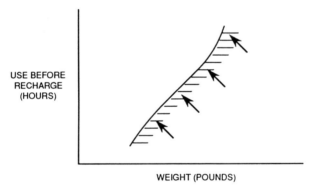

Use Time-Weight Envelope for Laptop
Computers

USE BEFORE
RECHARGE
(HOURS)

WEIGHT (POUNDS)

**Figure 4.1.** A ''performance envelope'' defines how competitive a company's products and processes are compared with other players in a market. Performance envelopes can be thought of graphically as curves; this curve shows the trade-off between speed and cost, two basic parameters that define the performance of a product. There are many such performance curves that managers must regularly consider. Some, like speed versus cost, relate to products; others, such as the yield of a manufacturing line, or the ability to get information about competitors' strategies, relate to the performance of processes or of organizational capabilities. As a company progresses, it moves these curves in advantageous directions.

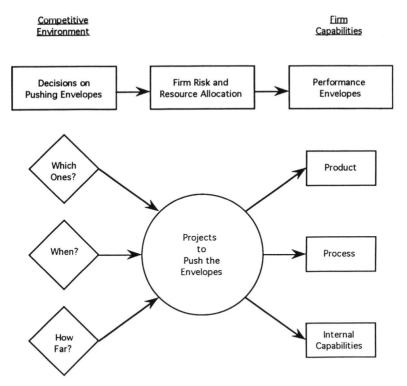

**Figure 4.2.** Analysis of the competitive environment and the risks accompanying alternative project plans and objectives are critical elements for determining which performance envelopes to push.

uct functionality. Bringing to market a product that is cheaper, faster, lighter, or stronger has clear competitive advantages, and most companies understand these issues. But there are also performance envelopes related to other capabilities, such as the yield of a manufacturing line, that are often neglected. Many companies do not seem to include these capabilities in their efforts to sustain a competitive edge and therefore make little effort to push the envelopes in these dimensions. We have found it useful to divide the envelopes associated with these other capabilities into two groups: process envelopes, by which we mean the manufacturing or product realization process used by the firm; and internal capabilities envelopes, by which we mean the firm's technological and organizational capabilities. An example of an internal capability is a firm's marketing capacity: is the market-

| Stage I | Reactive | No program to monitor the competitive environment and anticipate or define the state-of-the-art on products, processes, or internal capabilities |
|---------|----------|------------------------------------------------------------------------------------------------------------------------------------------------------|
| Stage II | Competitive on Products | Programs in place to meet and/or lead the state-of-the-art on products; processes and internal capabilities are reactive |
| Stage III | Competitive on Processes | Programs in place to meet and/or lead the state-of-the art on products and processes; internal capabilities are reactive |
| Stage IV | Competitive on Internal Capabilities | Program in place to meet and/or lead the state-of-the-art on products, processes, and internal capabilities |

**Figure 4.3.** Stages in pushing the envelope.

ing function able to monitor, understand, and communicate to product development teams the needs of current and potential customers?
Closely related is the product definition process. Core technological
and engineering capabilities, such as the inkjet technology at HP and
the engineering design capability Kodak developed using CAD systems during the FunSaver project, must be continually enhanced.
Chaparral will have special expertise in the chemistry of metals. An
essential and underdeveloped capability in most firms is the ability to
translate a firm's experience into useful and lasting learning. These
broader internal capability envelopes must be pushed if a firm is to
enhance and maintain its competitive position.

Our experience is that almost without exception firms are clear on
the need for pushing product envelopes and organized in some way
to accomplish this. However, there is a significant fall off in both
understanding the need and developing projects for pushing process
and internal capabilities envelopes. **Figure 4.3** defines four stages of
organization for pushing performance envelopes. Most U.S. compa-

nies, including those in our study, would be classified in Stage II. We discuss some of the reasons for this in the next section.

In competitive markets, it is generally necessary to maintain equality or superiority with competitors along many fronts, such as product performance, cost, ease of use, and even service. Straying too far from state of the art in any one category leaves a company vulnerable. There seems to be a region of acceptable practice; if a company stays "close enough" to best practice in most performance dimensions and becomes the leader in a few critical areas, the company will stay competitive (see **Figure 4.4**). Therefore, in some cases a firm will be pushing state-of-the-art envelopes (which means improving on the best that anyone else can do) and in other cases it will be catching up to what others can already do. There is growing evidence that for many industries the band of acceptable practice is narrowing. Hence "pushing the envelopes" is becoming more critical from a competitive standpoint and more difficult to manage.

For companies that want to conquer this challenge, it is helpful to break it down into three pieces: managing performance envelopes, maintaining balance between them, and managing the risks inherent in pushing the envelopes. These three aspects are explained briefly, and will be dealt with extensively in the rest of the chapter.

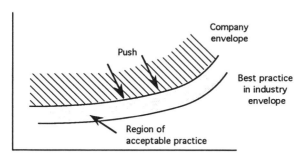

**Figure 4.4.** "Pushing" an envelope is the deliberate action taken to advance a performance curve over time. In competitive markets, it is necessary to maintain equality or superiority with competitors along many fronts. While it is unnecessary to push every performance envelope along every dimension, straying too far from the state of the art in any one category leaves a company vulnerable. There is a region of acceptable practice; if a company stays "close enough" to best practice in most performance dimensions, and pushes the envelope so it becomes the leader in a few critical areas, the company will stay competitive.

## Managing Performance Envelopes

Different approaches are required for managing product, process, and internal capabilities envelopes. A key difference among them is the role played by markets in defining what is acceptable. A second difference is the degree to which envelopes for a given company (internal envelopes) and state-of-the-art envelopes are observable. These distinctions seem to be important in explaining why some companies are very aggressive in product design but lag in process technology, for example. Later in the chapter we develop a framework for understanding these differences, discuss their implications for managing envelopes, and suggest methods for pushing different envelopes.

In several of the development projects examined by the Manufacturing Vision Group, we found that managers did not understand where their company's current envelopes were positioned. Part of the problem was poor knowledge of the location of the state-of-the-art envelopes. For example, the arc saw project at Chaparral Steel, an attempt to develop the industry's first electric-arc saw for cutting volumes of steel, was hindered from the beginning by poor knowledge of the state of the art. Early on, when prototype tests were run, knowledge of the use of electric arcs to rapidly cut large sections of steel was not sufficient to understand that the tests were inappropriate. Eventually the project was terminated because Chaparral was unable to solve technical problems that no one else had been able to solve.

Hewlett-Packard's Signal Analyzer project provided an example of underestimating the performance dimensions needed to produce a competitive product—misreading the state of the art. The development team continued to work on enhancing functionality, which added cost, when the push required by the market was to maintain functionality and lower cost. Even after several people in the company recognized the need to develop a less expensive product, it took an extraordinary effort to change the basic mentality of R&D engineers so they would focus on cost first and functionality second.

The FunSaver project at Kodak, undertaken to produce a single-use camera, demonstrated an internal state-of-the-art design capability that was hampered by marketing's ability to push beyond its traditional role and recognize new niche market opportunities. In this case, development had done the research to be confident that a single-use camera would sell, but it was not able to get marketing's approval until after a competitor, Fuji, announced a similar product. Marketing's lack of confidence in development's ability to produce a camera in a high-quality, low-cost market was evident right up to the point of introduction. It was only after sales far exceeded expectations that marketing became fully supportive and gave more credibility to development's input. In this case, marketing's lack of understanding of development's state-of-the-art internal capabilities led to a missed early entry opportunity for a highly successful product.

## Maintaining Balance

The second piece of the envelope challenge is maintaining a balance among envelopes. If an organization gets too far in front on one dimension while neglecting others, it may be unable to capitalize on the new capability; advanced design with primitive manufacturing can result in an uncompetitive product, for example. In some of the 20 cases studied we observed that the three domains of product, process, and internal capabilities performance envelopes were not sufficiently balanced. In others, there was a mismatch within one of these domains.

For example, in Hewlett-Packard's HP150 project, its first entry into the personal computer market, there was an initial failure to recognize the number of different dimensions along which envelopes needed to be pushed. The project clearly pushed the state of the art on several technical fronts. In addition, manufacturing, marketing and supplier distribution networks were not at the level required to compete—they were out of balance. When this was discovered, initiatives were started to implement just-in-time (JIT) manufacturing and install automatic insertion equipment, and to create a new distribution network. The magnitude and extent of these pushes made it difficult to focus the development effort. The manufacturing system suffered from major downtime because of the new machines. JIT could only partially be introduced. The distribution network was not effective. While each of these pushes was potentially important for the product and the company, the total effort overwhelmed the team, and made it difficult to reach its goals. Had the manufacturing, marketing, and supplier envelopes been in balance with the technical design envelopes, the resulting product likely would have been more successful.

## Managing Risk

A third piece of the envelope challenge is managing the risk associated with pushing envelopes. The extent to which a development project will push various envelopes determines the work necessary for successfully completing the project. This combined with the actions of competitors, markets, and the internal capabilities of the company determines the degree of risk associated with a project and influences the way in which it is organized and managed. Further, the perceptions of risk by the involved parties, the consequences of failure, and the size and complexity of the project all combine to influence the behavior of the team and the likelihood of meeting its objectives.

Digital Equipment Corp.'s RA90 project, undertaken to develop a high-density disk drive for computers, provided an example of attempting to push too many elements too far. The initial specifications for the product were so aggressive in comparison to the technologies that were available to make the disk drive that the project became substantially more risky than initially understood. The product was introduced more than a year late and cost much more than anticipated.

The three pieces of the envelope challenge define the organization of this chapter. The first two sections discuss the management of envelopes; they identify the different characteristics of product envelopes and how these must be taken into account when pushing one type of envelope versus another, and present some mechanisms that can be used to determine how far to push a given envelope at a given time. The third section addresses the general problem of how to maintain balance among all the capabilities of a company as particular envelopes are advanced. The last two sections discuss managing risks associated with pushing envelopes.

## MANAGING PERFORMANCE ENVELOPES

Mechanisms for deciding which envelopes to push and how far differ with the characteristics of the envelopes. In this section we describe the characteristics of the three types of envelopes—product, process, and internal capability—and discuss how they affect the way these envelopes are managed.

### Product Envelopes

As a general rule product envelopes are more easily controlled than process envelopes. Product features such as costs and quality are often easily determined; if nothing else, products can be purchased and "reverse engineered." In addition, products and therefore product envelopes must stand the test of the marketplace. There is no way a firm can avoid this test of how competitive its product envelope is. The market will discipline the firm to create a product envelope that meets the market test. The length of the product development cycle will affect the degree to which a market will provide guidance for managing the product performance envelope; short cycles will result in timely feedback about the state of the art of a product envelope. Long cycles will reduce the timeliness of market feedback.

### Process Envelopes

The competitiveness of processes is more difficult to observe, and there is often no direct market feedback to signal that a process envelope is falling short. The market might indicate that a product's features perform poorly, but it will be up to the company to trace the reason for this, and to understand that it might be due to a lagging production process. The market might determine that a product costs too much; it will be the company that has to determine whether the excessive cost is due to inadequacies in the design or the manufacturing process or both. In any case, market feedback is not as timely or effective in providing guidance on process envelopes as it is for product envelopes.

A few of the companies we studied, such as Chaparral and in some cases Kodak, maintained good intelligence about their competitors' process capabilities. In some industries it is even common to share such information freely. It is also common for such information to flow by way of suppliers; for example, a machine tool salesman may carry the information from one customer to another. In general, however, it is more difficult to benchmark what competitors are doing inside their factories, particularly if they wish to conceal their work, than to benchmark products that are available on the open market.

Most U.S. producers in nonprocess industries have traditionally relied on suppliers to provide new generations of process equipment. The principle of "sticking to your main business," which is interpreted as designing and selling products, generally discourages forays into the development of new machines, control equipment, and so forth. While there is obviously some merit to this view, it can also lead to competitive losses. In contrast, some companies, including many of those in Japan, employ large numbers of engineers to provide factory innovations that no supplier could or would offer.

It follows that competitive process envelopes are more difficult to assess and maintain than product envelopes. While it is harder to gain access to information on a competitor's process, the success of Chaparral and Kodak make it clear that this information can be had. For instance, new methods are evolving by which teardown examination of a product allows insights into the process used to manufacture it. The acquisition of this information, however, requires a concerted effort by management.

## Internal Capabilities Envelopes

The problems of lack of observability, lack of market feedback, unclear relationships, and inherent time lags are even greater for internal capabilities than for process envelopes. Most firms monitor technological and organizational developments and have active programs to "keep up to date," but by the time the lack of capability shows up in a product's market performance a company will likely find itself far behind.

For example, if Hewlett-Packard had not been developing ink-jet printing technology when Japanese firms gained dominance in the small-printer market, it would not have been able to launch its Desk-Jet ink-jet printer in a timely manner. The degree to which a firm can be a technological follower and look to the product market to signal new technologies depends on the product, the technology, and the degree of competition, but it is risky at best to rely on the product market to signal that an internal capability envelope is falling behind the band of acceptable practice. Actively assessing and pushing internal capabilities is the responsibility of company management.

## Implications for Management

Clearly the challenges faced by managers in trying to assess and push product, process, and internal capabilities envelopes can be quite different. We found aspects of these differences in a number of the projects we studied. Many firms focus more directly on product envelopes, which create a set of expectations and demands that are immediate. Pushing process and internal capabilities envelopes often is not seen as an immediate need. It requires a longer-term perspective and willingness to invest in the face of substantial uncertainty. This makes it harder for managers to commit, and they tend instead to look for tangible vehicles, such as product development projects, which can be used to justify the required investments. However, the characteristics that make these investments difficult to justify—lack of observability and market feedback—also make competitive advantages based on them more long-lasting. **Figure 4.5** depicts how effective management control approaches are driven by the degree of market feedback.

These observations, based on our study of the 20 Vision projects, lead us to three hypotheses about the effect of market conditions on envelopes and the degree to which internal initiatives are needed within companies to push various envelopes.

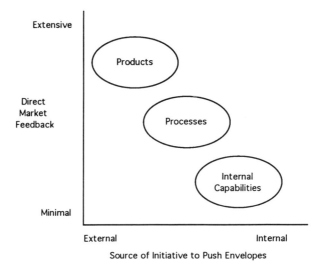

**Figure 4.5.** The pushing of envelopes is driven to varying degrees by market feedback. There is extensive market feedback on products, and this feedback usually initiates pushing the product envelope. There is less direct feedback with respect to a company's processes, and less still for its internal capabilities; for these envelopes initiatives for advancement must come more from internal sources.

*Hypothesis.* The ease and frequent availability of market feedback on products results in a narrow band of "acceptable practice." To stay competitive, companies will have to make frequent and incremental pushes of product envelopes.

*Example.* In the case of Hewlett-Packard's DeskJet printer, the design of a second-generation product was well on its way to completion before the first version had been completely ramped up. The follow-on product was then put into production using the same manufacturing process as the first product.

Several derivative workstations quickly followed the original Digital PMAX workstation based on market inputs from the first product. All used the manufacturing processes and new internal capabilities set up for the original workstation.

*Hypothesis.* The lack of immediate, market-based feedback applicable to process and internal capabilities envelopes results in less frequent efforts to push these envelopes, large sometimes unintentional leaps when pushes are made, and a tendency to push these envelopes only when a new product development project demands it.

*Example.* In the DeskJet project the groundwork for ink-jet technology had been laid for several years, and the internal capability for integrating manufacturing and marketing had been advanced prior to the project's start. However, the design-for-manufacturability (DFM) effort was undertaken only in conjunction with the development of the new product and the magnitude of the effort required was significant. While the DeskJet product was very successful in terms of sales, technological leadership, and the integration of manufacturing and marketing, a major part of the DFM effort was not. The focus on reducing the number of parts to make manufacturing easier went too far, resulting in a one-piece molded cabinet that was very difficult and time-consuming to design and to manufacture meeting specified tolerances. The team acknowledged later that it would have been faster and less expensive to have used more parts.

Kodak's Factory of the Future project grew out of a perceived need for additional spooling capacity for 35-mm film. Since such upgrades occurred infrequently and in major chunks, it was the view of people in manufacturing and technical engineering that if their new ideas weren't put into the Factory of the Future project they would not have another chance for at least a decade to do so. So they pulled in concepts they knew were not yet proven or ready for a commercial development project because they were afraid of missing the opportunity. As a result the effort became much larger than expected and in time was cancelled for lack of results. Looking back, they admit that they should not have tried to put so much into a single project.

The development of the high-density storage system at Digital, the RA90 thin-film disk drive system, was a rich example of the co-invention of product and process that placed meeting market timing requirements at risk. Major process technology inventions for fabricating thin-film read/write heads, for producing thin-film media disks, and for final drive-system assembly were abnormal stretches for an organization also inventing the product.

*Hypothesis.* When companies understand the importance of their processes and internal capabilities, in addition to product attributes, they can and will develop internal initiatives for managing and controlling these envelopes.

*Example.* As a firm in a "process industry," Chaparral naturally focuses on its production process. But it has gone beyond that to develop an internal capability that allows it to obtain feedback on processes from its customers, suppliers, and competitors, and to continually revise processes in almost real time. A specific example of a substantial payoff from this capability is the horizontal caster project, to develop a new casting process for high-grade steel. Early in the project the team visited every horizontal casting operation in the world (about half a dozen existed). While those casters were used for different purposes and in different ways from those the team had in mind, it did give them extensive information on the position of the state-of-the-art envelope. A few years later, after they had gotten substantial internal experience, the team went back and revisited all the same sites. This time they had a much better perspective from which to ask questions and interpret responses. Indeed, they came back from the second set of visits and quickly resolved several remaining major problems that had been hindering them. By the project's end, Chaparral had a process that clearly exemplified "best practice" in the industry.

## MECHANISMS FOR DETERMINING HOW FAR TO PUSH THE ENVELOPE

Managers in the firms we studied dealt with the problem of how far to push envelopes in a variety of ways. As a general rule, systematic planning that encompassed the spectrum from design to delivery was key. At Digital the combination of business unit leaders and corporate engineers (the technical gurus of the company) provide the long-range planning direction. At Kodak and Ford the processes are more formal and include more people and multiple organizations.

The decision on how far to push an envelope relies on information about a company's current position and the state-of-the-art envelope. How to get this information, and how to use it to determine when and how far to push, depends on whether you are pushing a product, process, or internal capabilities envelope.

## Product Envelopes

In all the cases we studied, companies were actively involved in gathering information on competitors' products. This was done through reverse engineering and talking to users, suppliers, and others who had contact with competitive products. In addition, the companies used several means to understand customer requirements. These on-going information-gathering activities on competitors' products (determining the state-of-the-art product envelope) and customer requirements provided the basis for launching new product development teams. When launched, the teams usually assumed responsibility for the continuing effort to determine how far and along which dimensions to push the product envelope. Below we discuss four mechanisms we found in use at the companies in our study to help them understand competitor and customer requirements.

*Next bench*. At HP and to some extent DEC a traditional way of understanding what customers might want is called the "next bench" approach. The idea is that for products or processes that are being built for customers who are very much like the employees working inside the company, it is efficient and effective to push the envelope to the point that is attractive to a set of leading-edge, in-house users. Many of HP's products, for example, are aimed at development engineers, which HP itself employs in large numbers.

This approach works well when functionality and reliability are the main determinants of a product's acceptance, and not ease of use or cost. It also works better when the marketplace is relatively stable so that the need for innovation can be adequately stimulated within a single firm. This method would not work well when external market information is important, since it is not likely to be available at the next bench. When price competition is key, when technological and functional requirements are changing rapidly, or when cultural differences among users are considerable, the next bench approach is too narrow.

*Customer's bench.* Putting design engineers in direct contact with technically literate customers is one step up from the next bench approach. It relies on the customer's "bench" for information. This approach worked well for HP on its Logic Analyzer project; even though sales and marketing people were asking potential customers "what" they wanted, it took an engineering person to ask "why" and interpret the answer. The answers to "what" led HP to continue their analog approach while the answer to "why" suggested a shift to digital technology.

This approach works well when technical requirements override cost concerns and when technical people are the ones making the buying decisions. It may not be adequate if cost is a strong factor and customers are not technically oriented.

*Traditional market research.* One of the problems that plagues market research is the unpredictability of consumers. They may respond to surveys in one way but act in another. And if there is a long development time, customers can completely change their views. The U.S. automobile industry, which engages in a great deal of sophisticated market research, has been caught in this trap several times in the past two decades. Ford has learned that the likes and dislikes of the average car owner are rather poor indicators of what the market will value five years in the future, the typical development time for new vehicles. Consequently, it has developed a way to identify a subset of customers, whom it calls "progressives," that seems to provide truer indications of future market trends. The problem is especially difficult when completely new products are introduced with capabilities that consumers do not fully appreciate. Manufacturers of computer hardware and software, for example, find it very difficult to use survey techniques.

Traditional market research works well when target consumers can be identified with certainty and products can be described in terms that are easily understandable. It does not work well when products are so new that consumers cannot evaluate their needs or preferences.

*Joint engineering and marketing research.* This combines traditional marketing, market research, and engineering in defining products. This was the approach used for HP's DeskJet, though only after some friction between team members. The engineering group initially set product parameters based on overall strategic positioning. The marketing group then took prototypes into the field, and returned with a list of 20 "show-stoppers"—concerns of potential customers that were considered so serious that failure to overcome them would prevent acceptance. Engineering rejected 16 of them. But marketing insisted that engineers accompany them to shopping malls for a series of tests, during which the engineers heard for themselves how important the show-stoppers were. In the end, all 20 items were addressed. Pushing the product envelope not only involves the engineer's perception of function and features, but also those of end-users, which often can be subtle and hard to describe in technical terms.

There is growing evidence that getting engineers out into the field is fundamental to responsive product design. This scheme requires close teamwork between engineering and marketing, and thus the development of mutual respect and reliance between these traditionally separated groups. For this approach to work, management must make a concerted effort to bring the two groups together.

## Process and Internal Capabilities Envelopes

Gathering information and deciding on when and how far to push on processes and internal capabilities are just as important, and even more difficult, than with products. As technologies (e.g., CAD/CAE) and methodologies (e.g., QFD) for product development push the time-to-market envelope, the availability of state-of-the-art fabrication and assembly processes becomes crucial. More often than not, debugging new production equipment and systems is on the critical path for the introduction of a new product. We previously discussed the difficulty of gathering information on competitors' processes and internal capabilities. We also found that companies typically lacked well-organized procedures for determining the needs of internal customers (product designers and those who run the current manufacturing processes). In addition, even when it was clear that process envelopes should be pushed, the mechanism for pushing them was not always evident. Examples of how these issues were dealt with by companies in our study are discussed below.

*Using product development teams.* In many cases we found that pushing process and internal capabilities envelopes ended up in the hands of product development teams, challenging the teams to understand competitors' processes as well as the current state of internal processes. While adding another dimension to the project, there was an advantage to this arrangement: these teams, as the internal customers for the new process, ensured a strong linkage between process developers and customers. Although these projects can be used as effective levers to focus an organization's attention on the need to push nonproduct envelopes, this mechanism can also lead to a number of problems. These go beyond difficulties in gathering information; they can affect the ultimate outcome of a project and a company's competitive position:

- If nothing else, the project content is increased, which increases the project's duration and the risk of market failure.
- Projects will be undertaken in the crisis atmosphere that often surrounds product development. The rush will limit the creativity, quality, and quantity of effort directed toward the process or capability.
- If the work is simply grafted onto a project, it is unlikely that comprehensive analysis of what really is needed in processes or internal capabilities will be undertaken. Big opportunities for developing competitive advantages may be missed.
- Finally, using product development as the means for pushing process and capabilities increases the chance that no effort will be made until product market requirements cannot be met; this may well put the company at a competitive disadvantage from which it is difficult to recover.

Nonetheless, there is one sometimes overriding benefit to using the product development process to push process and internal capabilities envelopes: it may be the only way in which work toward new processes and capabilities can be justified given financial control procedures used by a company. In addition, it may provide a very fruitful setting for those involved in pushing process and internal capabilities. Many have championed the need for product designers to understand the requirements for manufacturing. It is equally true that those who are pushing process and capability envelopes need to be current on the requirements of product designers. The key is to have the information gathering controlled and work well planned so that both efforts contribute to an overall build-up of the capabilities and do not weigh down the product development projects so that they fail to meet their own objectives.

*Placing manufacturing personnel in the field.* When firms must obtain information on competitive processes, the key is to get the people who will design and use the new process into the field so they can understand what is possible. Unlike gathering information on competitors' products, we found that this is seldom an ongoing effort. Chaparral is an exception. Management arranges for manufacturing personnel to visit other plants on a regular basis to benchmark their process envelopes. Everyone is involved in benchmarking competitors, customers, and suppliers. As a result, the company's assessments of what is needed and what is possible are much better calibrated and are done in a much richer context than were those we found at other companies.

*Doing R&D on the line.* The problem of understanding the internal customer's need is solved at Chaparral by giving line managers responsibility for the process development projects. This provided a very powerful confluence of interests. A single person is the end-user, the process specifications writer, and the project manager.

Concentrating responsibility in one person, however, means that he or she must be capable of operating effectively at many levels. The person is more likely to succeed if the amount of new technology is limited and improvements in technology are incremental rather than breakthroughs. When new technologies requiring specialized knowledge are an important part of the development effort, line personnel who are selected for their general capabilities as opposed to deep technical knowledge may not be effective leaders of the project. Ideally an organization would like to "cross" those who are narrow but deep with those who have broad understanding of process specifications. It is also important to match the project size with the ability of a line person to take on added responsibility. One could not expect a line manager to properly lead a large and complex project if the demands of the line job were too great. The measures and perceived rewards of the organization must be supportive if line managers are to effectively function in these multiple roles.

*The laboratory solution.* A contrasting approach to using the line organization for developing new processes is using an in-house laboratory or outside supplier. This is usually done by establishing process development projects. The separation from the internal customer means there is a need for line managers to provide inputs on the specifications. The actual process development is done by specialists in a lab setting. Kodak like Chaparral is a process-oriented company. In addition to manufacturing research capability at Kodak Park, there is also a broadly based capability in design and engineering. These groups have recently been consolidated into the Manufacturing Research and Engineering (MRE) organization. The 1800-plus engineers and technicians have strong functional bases in traditional engineering disciplines such as chemical or mechanical engineering as well as machine design and systems engineering. The MRE organization is able to develop new processes, machines, and facilities for future products and by and large develops close working relationships with operating units. The challenge is to keep it able and motivated. If it becomes too closely linked to business units, it narrows its views and could become less driven to push the envelope on internal capabilities.

The conditions under which the lab approach works well mirror those where R&D on the line works well. The largest challenge is to devise a mechanism to connect lab units with the product and process people who will ultimately be served by the labs. One way is to move people across boundaries, for example, to have the internal "end-users" participate on the lab's development projects. Just as it is important to have manufacturing (a downstream activity) involved in design, it is important for the lab staff (an upstream activity) to have downstream users involved. It will help them understand the product and process needs that should guide decisions on investment in new technologies and organizational forms.

## MAINTAINING BALANCED CAPABILITIES

It is likely that over time a company will use some mix of methods to push envelopes. As this occurs, typically in fits and starts, management must maintain some perspective on how the company is advancing as a whole. As noted, there is a danger in being too far from the best practice in any category. And it may not even be enough to be within the band of acceptable practice if a company does not excel in at least a few endeavors. What is needed is to keep a balance among envelopes.

The idea is a simple one: great expertise in one area without the capability to match it in others will be wasted. A firm cannot operate for long without having product, process, and internal capability envelopes that are each competitive, mutually supportive, and integrated. Although some organizations like to maintain the pretense of pushing envelopes in all dimensions, as a practical matter that is usually impossible. Whether by choice or by accident, every company will be more advanced relative to competitors in some areas than in others. The best companies, however, choose these positions consciously and strategically. Any organization that leaves its pursuit of excellence to natural evolution is likely to find itself uniformly mediocre, a fatal course in these competitive times. On the other hand, a choice of emphasis should not become an excuse for neglecting other areas. For example, a company like HP or DEC may choose, for very good reasons, to emphasize the necessity of staying at the cutting edge in product design. Chaparral or Kodak may benefit more from superiority in process technology. But if any of the vital capabilities of the company are neglected, a competitor may eventually win over the market with lower cost or higher quality products.

Managers must also realize that the appropriate balance is likely to change dynamically. The most critical need at one time might be in pushing product design envelopes, because the market is demanding a whole new product line, while at another time new process technology will need to be installed to achieve necessary quality levels. This is especially difficult for a company like Ford whose major products contain so many complex systems and subsystems with wide-ranging technology content. Pushing the envelope at Ford means potentially thousands of discrete products and processes. One of the difficulties in managing the balance is that individuals, and sometimes whole organizations, tend to be biased in their perspectives. Accomplishments in one area may lead to a belief that that one area is all that really matters. Slogans such as "build on our strengths" can easily lead to neglect of weak areas that eventually can become fatal flaws. As discussed in the Core Competencies chapter, strengths can become rigidities as the organization holds onto old processes and methods. Below we discuss levels at which imbalances occur and some mechanisms for managing them.

## Balance at the Product, Process, and Internal Capability Levels

In the Digital and HP projects we found an imbalance between product development and the internal capabilities of marketing. In these two technology- and engineering-driven companies, we observed the same imbalance to a lesser extent between engineering and manufacturing. In each of the HP cases the product envelope was significantly more advanced than either the marketing (an "internal capability") envelope or the process envelope. Moreover, each division in which the HP projects resided continued to push the product envelopes at a faster rate than the process and marketing envelopes. In two cases this resulted in products that never reached their sales or profit potential, and in another case it resulted in a significant delay in meeting the competition. In the fourth case, a rapid change within the project allowed the product to be launched on time and be competitive.

HP's logic analyzer project provides a good example of how a weak capability, in this case marketing and sales, can negate the effort of advancing a product envelope. For years Tektronix had been the leading producer in this category, with HP a distant and unprofitable second. In various projects, including the logic analyzer, HP's strategy was to push the product envelope by inventing more advanced products with added features. The self-reporting was that HP did in fact out-invent Tektronix. However, HP was never able to capitalize on the "newer" products because Tektronix would match them before experiencing any erosion in the marketplace. Tektronix had superior marketing and sales capabilities and used them to keep their customers with such devices as new product announcements and sales policies. Without penetrating Tektronix's customer base HP could not take advantage of its technological breakthroughs.

In HP's Hornet project, to develop an inexpensive spectrum analyzer instrument, manufacturing was not an equal player and the process envelope lagged behind the product envelope. The manufacturing staff assigned to the project was heavily involved with the production of other products, plus they were not made to feel an integral part of the design team. As a result the ramp-up was difficult. There was no significant effort to design the product for manufacturability. In contrast, manufacturing was represented strongly from the beginning in HP's DeskJet project. Manufacturing team members were fully consulted in the design and forced the designers to take "design for manufacturability" seriously. They became such valuable members of the team that the designers even lobbied management for more manufacturing people.


## Balance at the Technological Capabilities Level

Not only do product, process, and internal capabilities envelopes have to be balanced, technological capabilities must be balanced as well. This is an obvious point, but it is not always heeded. The RA90 project at DEC provides an example. The project required investment in material sciences, thin-film processing, and mechanical engineering. But because of DEC's culture and historical perspective, management presumed that the joining of advanced component technologies into a new electro-mechanical design using automated assembly would be rather straightforward, and they underinvested in early prototypes to validate component and systems integrity. Best estimates are that the project was 10 to 12 months late because of technical challenges unmitigated by earlier investment in pushing process capabilities.

Other projects proved the value of balancing capabilities. In the horizontal caster project at Chaparral, balance between equipment technology, mold technology, digital control technology, and basic metallurgy was maintained by staffing the project with skilled people from all four areas, by giving the team full responsibility for the project, and by then providing the supporting resources so that each function could not only push its envelope but also transfer learning back to other parts of the company so they could benefit from it.

## Mechanisms for Managing Balance

The challenge for managers is to discover imbalances early and correct them before they endanger the success of a project or even the company. As competition intensifies, companies will not have the luxury of discovering imbalances and correcting them on the fly. Delays of only six months can put a product out of its market window altogether. Balance is needed at both the project and corporate levels.

*Systematic and comprehensive planning.* At both levels systematic planning is fundamental to effective projects and for learning. Such planning led to the success of the DeskJet. HP's Vancouver division was making investments to develop manufacturing engineering capabilities several years before it launched the DeskJet project. Lack of planning for the marketing function was evident in the other HP product groups, however. When HP did a systematic and comprehensive evaluation of their capabilities, it did see that its marketing envelope was well behind the band of acceptable practice. The lesson is that a relatively straightforward planning process, if done systematically and comprehensively, will uncover imbalances that can block successful product and process development.

Prior to Kodak's transition from a functional to a line-of-business organization, a business plan for its Factory of the Future project, heavily biased by the functional organization, had been initiated. Its emphasis did not fully reflect line-of-business priorities, and over 100 people were working on the project before the final consolidated business plan was completed. When the technical team saw the line-of-business plan and realized what was now desired, they knew the project was in trouble. The project reassessment based on the consolidated business plan caused the initial project to be canceled and a new one defined. Had more thought by the initial project managers been given to the impending change from functional to line-of-business organization, much time and effort would have been saved, and the project would have had a better chance of success.

*Project organization.* At the project level imbalances can be amplified or reduced by the type of organization used. Organizing work by function ties the project to the internal capabilities envelopes of the company, which may be imbalanced. An independent project organization, on the other hand, can work to balance envelopes. At HP the best example was the DeskJet project, in which the final responsibilities and duties of the marketing and manufacturing groups went beyond those existing in other divisions or even in other parts of the same division.

There are many variables that affect the type of organization used in the development of new products and processes but the ability to create the proper balance among envelopes is important. Projects that require a different balance of capabilities than exists in the rest of the company can only succeed if the team is allowed to organize in whatever way, conventional or unconventional, that will help them achieve balance.

*Ongoing and incremental pushes in technology and organizational capabilities.* We would expect that companies in which envelopes are routinely pushed would do better at maintaining balance, since they regularly face the question of where to push. This leads them to develop a planning process and to think comprehensively about the envelopes. The best example among our companies is Chaparral, which undertakes development projects on a continuing basis. Pushing envelopes is part of the culture and management has become very good at identifying when to push an envelope and what kind of effort it will require. As a consequence, Chaparral is comprehensive in its approach and ends up with a high degree of balance.

## MANAGING AND CONTROLLING RISK

Behind every decision made in trying to balance envelopes, and in deciding which envelope to push when and how far, are the questions: How likely is the effort to succeed? How much risk are we taking? There is a natural tension between control and freedom in the development process. We want control for efficiency, economy, conformance to standards, and broad directions (i.e., make sure products are aimed at a useful market segment). We want freedom in order to promote creativity, innovation, etc. Walking this line can be one of the most difficult tasks for an organization or a project manager. Companies do not want to become so regimented that they hurt the creative "magic" that is an essential part of developing new capabilities. But, the more freedom provided, the more opportunities there are for pushing envelopes, which in turn can increase the risk to the company.

Vocabulary is significant here. Some people attach a negative connotation to the word "risk," suggesting reckless gambling or taking chances unnecessarily. Our use of the term is broader and not tied to a wholly negative connotation. Risk and innovation go hand-in-hand. Organizations involved in product or process development must take and even encourage risks in at least some dimensions. In speaking of risk, we are merely acknowledging that companies must act with imperfect, incomplete knowledge. They cannot know in advance that everything will work out as well as hoped. There is a possibility, for whatever reasons, of failure. The assessment of this possibility will affect how far one is willing to reach beyond the safe limits of certain knowledge and practices, and hence where and how far the envelopes will be pushed. Once the scope of the project is set, the development process itself can be viewed as a period of risk reduction. That is, development proceeds in a manner that reduces uncertainty until it is eliminated.

It is of course true that failure to achieve all that one hopes for does not doom a project to failure. It is possible to fall back to more familiar ground and retrieve some value from the effort. Digital Equipment uses the terminology "failing forward" to suggest that you can gain ground even when failing to achieve all that you had hoped.

It is also true that some development projects tolerate only very limited amounts of risk. At Ford (and other auto makers) the standard practice in developing a new car is that anything not "implementation ready" by a certain cutoff date will be eschewed. If in the planning for a new Thunderbird, for example, Ford decides to develop a new transmission, work progresses under the assumption that either the new or an already proven transmission will be used. If the new transmission can actually be developed and tested in time, it can be used; if not, the old one is used. Considering the complexity of an automobile and the consequences of the failure of even one component, such a policy would seem to be prudent. On the other hand, a company like Digital Equipment or HP would have to be somewhat more aggressive about innovations to remain competitive.

We found that some managers tended to think differently about technical, market, and managerial risk. Consequently, their approach to dealing with each was somewhat different. These managers were more comfortable with accepting technical and market than managerial risk. Their reasoning went something like this.

*Technical Risk.* In describing technical risk they point out that technology development always has unknowns. The entire development effort is aimed at overcoming this lack of knowledge. Everyone, from the engineer on the bench to the general manager, knows that there is risk associated with technical advancement.

*Market Risk.* The difficulty of predicting customer tastes and reactions to new products is well established in the minds of technical and nontechnical business people alike. Markets are notoriously uncertain and fickle. Engineers and managers are willing to believe that it is impossible to predict what customers will want and what competitors will do, and therefore there is a natural and understandable risk in marketing new products.

*Managerial Risk.* In the case of both technical and market risk, it is difficult to assign cause and effect for a bad outcome. In addition, a feeling exists that technical and marketing risks associated with development projects are a necessary part of doing business. Therefore they feel it is unlikely that an individual project member will be penalized for a bad outcome. However, the same people consider the personal risk for project managers to be substantially greater.

There appears to be a belief that managers should be held responsible for bad outcomes. Managers should be able to control costs, schedules, and the revenue stream, even though they are directly impacted by technical and market uncertainty. It is the managers' job, they feel, to make sure that things turn out all right in the end. For example, if there is uncertainty about a delivery date, the manager should allocate more resources to ensure that the activity is completed on time. Likewise, if there is technical uncertainty, a manager should provide alternative solutions through a portfolio of different approaches.

This differential assessment of technical, market, and managerial risk can create a problem for companies and will affect the ways in which incentives are provided to ensure that the organization undertakes the right amount of risk. No general rules are available, but based on our observations companies such as HP should be careful to monitor their technical and marketing teams to prevent taking on too much risk, and should work to provide incentives for project managers that encourage them to make decisions in the best interest of the company even in the face of personal risk.

## MECHANISMS FOR MANAGING RISK

Managing the risk associated with pushing envelopes is a difficult but necessary task for companies. In some cases incentives must be provided for individuals to encourage them to take appropriate risk. In others the amount of risk needs to be limited. In many cases the acceptance of risk in one area will lessen it in another; for example, market risk may be lessened by taking on more technological and managerial risk. But, if carried too far, this will increase project content to the point that development time will increase, which may increase the risk of being late to market. Managing risk requires analysis, judgment, and balance. Yet in the projects we studied, we found few cases where a systematic assessment of risk was undertaken.

In this section we discuss some of the mechanisms available for managing risk. These include creating incentives, sharing risk, distributing risk, and running development projects in ways that help reduce risk from the outset.

## Individual Incentives for Pushing the Envelope

There are several ways a company can provide incentives for individuals to push an envelope in an innovative way by creating an environment in which individuals and groups are encouraged to accept appropriate risk. The use of incentives depends mainly on the setting. For instance, a plan that will induce people to sign up for a risky project may need to differ from one that provides an incentive to work hard after joining a project.

*Convey clear economic and organizational threats.* Individuals become more willing to accept risk in order to avoid undesirable consequences, but purposely creating an economic threat hardly seems a desirable mechanism for a manager to use. On the other hand, forthright communication of real-world economic threats can be used to create an environment in which individuals will take appropriate risks.

An example where this approach was used effectively was in the HP DeskJet project. The team was given clear signals that the division's continued existence was tied to the successful completion of the project. The seriousness of the problem was advanced by the division general manager, who routinely stated that ''If you are not working on the DeskJet, you are just rearranging chairs on the Titanic.'' Team members responded by making a significant push in the state-of-the-art printer market that involved both new technologies and new methods of project management.

*Set targets "high" enough so that significant risk is evident.* If project goals are seen as a stretch by a team and its supporters in the company, then accepting the risk of pushing for them becomes easier. It provides an atmosphere in which risks of failure are accepted as necessary to reach lofty goals. In particular the risk must be understood by top management. A number of researchers of Japanese practices have noted that this is a key feature of their product development strategy. We found the most consistent use of this strategy at Chaparral. In every case stretch targets were set and top management clearly recognized the magnitude of the stretch.

*Establish rewards for good outcomes.* We found that individuals involved in development projects responded to a variety of different rewards. If these rewards are tied to good outcomes, they will induce the individuals to accept the risk of pushing the envelope. Some rewards mentioned by project managers were high visibility within the company, access to the next "good" project, professional recognition based on seeing a product in the market and the pride of invention, and financial rewards such as salary increases, bonuses, and stock options.

Of these, nonfinancial rewards were the most powerful incentives in the minds of engineers at the companies we studied. In one case, a very creative engineer almost left the company to pursue a career in an entirely unrelated field over frustration that "his" product concept was going to be supervised by someone else.

*Limited penalties for failure.* The other side of the coin is limiting the penalties for failure. If individuals fear that failure on a risky project will result in a severe penalty to their job or career, they will understandably avoid risk. Management must provide some protection against bad outcomes. Most important in the minds of the engineers with whom we talked was continued access to interesting new projects. They did not want to be taken off the "fast track" on the basis of a bad outcome with a risky project.

## Risk Sharing

An important means for controlling the amount of risk imposed on a single individual or team is risk sharing. The idea is to reduce the risk on any individual by getting others in the organization to "sign up" for the project, in particular senior managers. Not only can the senior-level manager take some responsibility for the possibility of a bad outcome, but he or she can provide encouragement and guidance throughout the project when questions arise about the amount of risk to take.

We observed several ways in which this sharing can be accomplished. In some cases, team members and their supporters declared they were "betting the badge" on the project. Taken literally the phrase suggests that if things did not work out successfully, the employees would be fired. At first we thought this was a way for people to express the risk they were taking. But it became less clear that the individuals had thought about it that way. There seemed to be no fear that they would really lose their job. Stating that they were betting the badge was a means of signaling that they had signed up for the project. They were making a public commitment to join the team and share the risk.

We saw another example of risk sharing in the RA90 project. DEC made sure there were two senior managers, one technical and one business, who could champion the cause of the project and re-energize it when required. This spread risk and helped employees from different groups sign up for it. Unfortunately, when the project did get into some technical difficulties, it happened at a time when the senior managers were absorbed elsewhere, and there were delays in getting them to refocus on the project and help manage the risks. The RA90 project could have used more consistent hours of senior management attention.

At Chaparral the bigger the project risk the more senior managers get involved. In the case of the horizontal caster and the arc saw, senior managers not only got involved in the review process but also became champions to help keep the ball rolling and refocus the project when needed. The risk sharing between the team and senior management was clearly important for both the company and the team.

The way in which a project is staffed and organized will affect the degree of risk sharing too. A traditional functional organization will provide the least amount of risk sharing; a Project Execution Team will provide the most. More about the way in which teams can be formed and led appears in Chapter 5.

## Distributing Risk

Another way to control risk is to distribute it across projects, organizations, or approaches so that all "the eggs are not in one basket." The HP DeskJet provides an effective example. Early in the project the R&D manager identified the development of the ink-jet nozzle as requiring the largest push (highest risk) for the project. To reduce the risk it posed, he modified the tasks of those involved in designing the subsystems that interfaced with the nozzle, giving them the responsibility to lessen demands on the nozzle to as much a degree as possible. For instance, the nozzle team ran into problems meeting the specifications on ink drying. The manager assigned another group the responsibility of adapting other parts of the printer to work around the "wet" ink.

A good example of distributing risk throughout an organization was found in Kodak's Chem181 project, undertaken to develop a new antistatic coating for microfilm. Kodak formed a senior management guidance team and a health and safety team to augment the development team. Key business and toxicology risks were assessed by these teams, which took some of the burden off the project team, which may not have been as qualified to assess these special kinds of risks. Other companies also distribute risk by placing some development demands on suppliers.

Risks can also be distributed across projects. For example, one development project may be charged with reaching as far as it can in product performance while employing a conservative approach to process technology, another project could emphasize advancing the process technology using a mature product design, and a third project could emphasize the improvement of worker skills. Within a product line this might be done over time by staggering the various pushes (see **Figure 4.6**). For example, a first-generation product within a

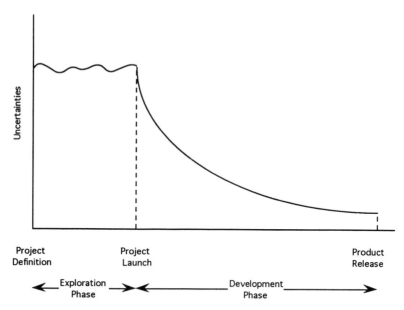

**Figure 4.6.** In the early definition of a development project—the exploration phase—uncertainties run high, yet little can be done to reduce them as multiple options are explored. But once actual development is begun the project team must try to reduce uncertainty as much as possible. While the actual work done in carrying out development generates information that by its nature is used to reduce uncertainty, the degree to which it is reduced will be much greater if managers make explicit plans for reducing uncertainty in a timely manner and get appropriate efforts underway.

product line could push the envelopes in design, the second generation could emphasize process improvements for cost reduction or quality improvement, and the third could emphasize worker training to raise the efficiency of manufacturing. This approach meshes well with the notion of product life cycles. Furthermore, in a sizeable company with many product lines, one can picture overlapping cycles in different product lines, with beneficial crossover effects.

The lesson here is to manage the process consciously and in a manner that everyone understands. It may mean, for example, telling people who want to improve their manufacturing process that "This time, take the safe approach; next time, we will want you to take some risks."

Ford has learned to cycle pushes even within the product design

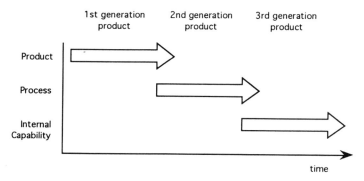

**Figure 4.7.** One way to distribute risk over time is to stagger the pushing of various envelopes. A first generation product within a product line could push the envelopes in design, the second generation could emphasize process improvements for cost reduction or quality improvement, and the third generation could focus on improving internal capabilities, such as worker skills. This approach meshes well with the notion of product life cycles.

category. For example, management will introduce a new engine into a production car that otherwise remains the same. Six months later they may introduce a new transmission, and so on. They have learned *not* to attempt more than one major change at a time.

## Reducing or Eliminating Risk

The actual carrying out of a development process is by its nature a period of risk reduction. In the early definition of a project—the exploration phase—uncertainties run high, but once actual development is begun the team tries to reduce uncertainty as rapidly as possible (see **Figure 4.7**). A problem observed in several projects was that the team did not make a clear distinction between the exploratory and development phases, and as a result did not focus on eliminating uncertainties as soon as they should have. When the exploration phase is over, the task is to focus on eliminating uncertainty and hence risk. The chapter on prototyping addresses important parts of this process (see Chapter 7).

It is useful to distinguish between innovation and invention, particularly during the middle stages of a project. It may be possible to make improvements (innovations), but you do not want to have to come up with and depend on entirely new concepts (inventions) once you are in the "delivery chute." Some companies use the concept of a "wall of invention," which refers to a point in time beyond which any new concepts are forbidden. Ford insists that innovations be "implementation ready" at the wall of invention. Kodak uses the term "capital project" to designate one that has reached the point of firm commitment. Once a project is designated a capital project, it must be implementation ready. The term does not relate to either the amount of capital at risk or even whether there is a significant financial investment. It has to do with the commitment to deliver. Both approaches, while useful, must be managed carefully, because it is counterproductive to stifle inventiveness too early in a project. One part of the resolution of the conflict between freedom, exploration, and creativity versus discipline, schedule, and elimination of risk lies in the timing. If everyone understands that there are at least two phases to a project, during which risk behavior is entirely different, it can go a long way toward resolving this problem.

## A STRATEGY FOR COMPETING

Thinking about performance envelopes for products, processes, and internal capabilities raises important questions. How far should any particular envelope be pushed? Is there a need for balance among them, and how can that be achieved? How can the right amount of risk taking be undertaken?

The answers to each of these questions have operational and strategic implications for managers and their companies. They are strategic because the answers will determine the competitive position of the firm. The competition faced by companies studied by the Vision Group, indeed by most companies, is intensifying and changing from the traditional emphasis on cost to quality and cycle times. New ways of managing development projects will be required to keep pace.

The lessons from our study make it clear that gains can be made if companies consciously plan for ways to push envelopes and manage those pushes once they are begun. The results of the projects we studied also make it clear that pushing process and internal capabilities as well as product envelopes is increasingly important for companies that want to be able to respond to ever more rapidly changing market conditions. Companies that neglect to systematically manage efforts to change will find it increasingly difficult to compete.

## CHAPTER 5

# Project Leadership
# and Organization

$\mathbf{D}$eveloping a new product or process is much like setting off on a journey into territory only partially mapped. For example, the product under development will be introduced into the market sometime in the future, and that future, at least for most businesses today, is fraught with uncertainty. Where technologies are changing and evolving, customer demands are dynamic, and competition is intense, it is difficult to predict with certainty which design concepts will dominate the market, which product features and attributes customers will find most attractive, and what competitors are likely to do. But there may be another challenge as well. Not only is the future customer and technical environment uncertain, but the product itself may be quite complex. Development will thus involve many different people, bringing different kinds of expertise, working together over an extended period of time.

A product or process development team faced with uncertainty and complexity requires leadership. To be effective, the development team needs a leader with a clear concept of what the product should be and a vision of the project's mission. It needs someone in charge who can offer direction and focus on the substantive issues the team will confront. The team itself provides leadership to the organization as a whole and in the functional groups. But the team must have someone with the ability to navigate uncertain terrain; someone who sees the project's essential elements and how they fit together into a coherent whole.

In the development of new products and processes, effective leadership has a particular character derived from the basic mission of the development team. In general, the product development team focuses on three objectives:

1. Achieving basic functionality in the components and subsystems of the product—in an automobile, this means brakes that brake, cooling systems that cool, and transmissions that shift gears effectively.
2. Integrating the systems and components into a coherent unit. The excellence of the product as a system depends not only on the functionality of the components and subsystems, but also on the way they interact in creating overall system performance. In our automobile example, the brake system may brake well, but be too bulky and heavy to accommodate the desired level of system performance in terms of weight and overall vehicle packaging.
3. Achieving a fit between the experience the product creates and the customers' expectations of what an outstanding product should be. An automobile may achieve excellent functionality in its components and tight integration into an effective system, but create an experience that customers find unattractive.

Leadership is important in each of these dimensions. Our focus in this chapter is to explore the nature of that leadership and its impact in terms of functionality, coherence, and fit.

Although we will focus on the behavior of project leaders who have achieved significant levels of performance, the effectiveness of leadership is not only a matter of individual talent and initiative. We also recognize that the effectiveness of leadership and the overall project depends on the way development is organized. Leaders need a structure, a framework, and a process that supports and encourages initiative, focus, and vision. Furthermore, leaders do not operate alone. They need people working in an organization with processes that effectively deliver functionality, coherence, and fit.

The interaction between leadership and organization is well illustrated in the history of Chaparral Steel. Many of Chaparral's leaders came from large steel companies, where their talents found far less scope for expression and application. People like Ron Lincoln, who, until he passed away in 1989, was the leader of Chaparral's melt shop, were mavericks in the environment of big steel companies. They had ideas and a natural capacity for leadership, and wanted to change things, but they found themselves restricted and undercut at traditional companies like the old U.S. Steel. At Chaparral, with a structure and process that valued and supported leadership, people like Lincoln flourished. Whether he worked at U.S. Steel or Chaparral, Ron Lincoln was Ron Lincoln—aggressive, skillful, irreverent, and dedicated. But at Chaparral, Lincoln was a leader with a mandate. The performance of Chaparral's development projects, not only in the melt shop but throughout the mill, reflected that leadership.

This strong link between project leadership and organization, and project performance, is something we have found throughout the projects studied by the Manufacturing Vision Group. As described in detail in this chapter, we maintain that a specific pattern of leadership and organization that we call "heavyweight project management" is particularly effective in balancing the requirements of specialization and integration in the growing number of markets where speed and efficiency is key. Implementation of the heavyweight model leads to superior achievement of high-quality products in a timely fashion.

We begin this chapter by framing the analysis of project leadership and organization in terms of the development process's three basic objectives: functionality, coherence, and fit. We develop a framework for thinking about the choices firms make in the way they organize to achieve these objectives.

In the following section we use the framework to define four stylized patterns of project leadership and organization: (1) a functional system, where the basic work gets done within, and leadership occurs through, the functional organizations; (2) a lightweight project team system, where a project manager coordinates and schedules activities through liaison representatives, but the basic work and much of the substantive leadership occur through the functions; (3) a heavyweight project team system, where the work is done in the functions, but a project leader and a core team of functional leaders take responsibility for all aspects of the project; and (4) a dedicated project team system, where the people working on the project are pulled out of their functional organizations and dedicated to a team led by a strong and empowered project leader.

We then examine the patterns of leadership associated with these modes of organization, with particular emphasis on the role of the heavyweight project leader. Leadership is important in any project, large or small, and in any mode of development organization, whether it be functional or a dedicated team. But we have found that the heavyweight system is particularly effective for large projects in turbulent, highly competitive environments, and yet is quite difficult to make work. It thus deserves special attention.

In the last section of the chapter we look at the role of senior management. Much of the chapter focuses on the project level, but senior management has a crucial role to play in creating effective leadership and organization in development projects. Although the concepts and practices identified here seem powerful in their impact on performance, making them work and instituting essential, fundamental change in structure, processes, attitudes, and behavior is no small challenge. Indeed, we argue that creating effective patterns of leadership and organization at the project level is every bit as difficult (perhaps more) as creating an outstanding new product or manufacturing process, and requires every bit as much leadership. That is the role of senior management. To illustrate the impact of these ideas and the challenge of implementation, the chapter concludes with the story of how one company—Ford—managed to make a radical break with its past and evolve an approach to heavyweight project leadership that has led to notable successes in recent years.

## THE THREE OBJECTIVES OF
## DEVELOPMENT ORGANIZATIONS

How a firm organizes for development and the pattern of leadership it seeks to create defines its approach to three basic objectives of the development process: functionality, coherence, and fit.[1] Each of these dimensions is essential to success in the market, and each grows out of different aspects of the way projects are led and organized. For simplicity we will use product development as the example, but analogous logic applies to process development.

*Functionality* is a basic requirement for market introduction. To be viable in the market a new product must achieve a minimum level of function; in most markets, it must meet high standards of functional performance. Functionality is rooted in the performance of specific components and subsystems. In a hard disk drive for workstations and PCs, for example, the "head" that reads and writes information off of and onto the disk must move across the disk at high speed while maintaining a small distance between itself and the surface. It must never touch the sensitive magnetic media on the spinning disk, but must be close enough to read and write the information. Disk head design engineers have likened their challenge to designing a 747 that could fly one meter from the ground without ever hitting anything on the surface. Achieving that level of functionality requires depth of expertise in materials science, magnetics, aerodynamics, and mechanical design.

*Coherence* is a property of the product as a technical system and measures the extent to which the functional components and subsystems work well together. Achieving coherence is a matter of integrating the functional elements, taking into account critical interactions, and making adjustments and modifications that enhance the product's overall behavior as a system. In the case of disk drives, for example, a development team may have an exceptional read/write head, but achieve slower access times (how long it takes to read a bit of data) than a team whose head design, while somewhat less advanced, is nonetheless better integrated with the actuator, disk, and electronics. Coherence also applies to the interaction between the design of the product and the design of the process to make the product.

*Fit* is a property of the relationship between the customer and the product. Functionality and coherence are essential, but not sufficient, for development success. A development team may create a product with good functionality that operates as a technically coherent system yet fails to attract customers. Products that attract, satisfy, and even delight customers create an experience that "fits" their expectations of what a great product should be. In a disk drive, for example, several drives may have good read/write heads, and some may achieve general technical coherence, but the drives that attract the customer (in this case, the computer company) achieve excellent performance in the customer's system—they are well matched to the system's specific characteristics, easy to use and install, and have self-diagnostics and automatic error recovery. Or, fit may include simply the dimensions of the disk drive and thus the volume it requires in the overall system package.

In our study of development projects in the Vision Group companies we have found specific organizational processes and choices, and specific patterns of leadership, associated with each of these dimensions of development performance. How the firm combines its choices in achieving these three objectives establishes its overall approach to project leadership and organization. Thus, before we look at the overall approach, we examine the specific organizational issues connected to functionality, coherence, and fit.


## Functionality

Throughout the projects studied by the Vision Group we encountered countless problems with functionality whose solutions required extensive in-house expertise. Given the complexity of most products and projects we studied, that expertise is delivered by specialists who have developed deep knowledge about a particular aspect of the product. However, we also encountered a wide difference in the degree and depth of specialization required for a particular project.

The variance in demand for specialized knowledge was well illustrated by two projects at Kodak. The Chem 181 project was aimed at deepening and refining established techniques and concepts needed to develop an antistatic coating for microfilm. The substantial depth of knowledge of a few project members was essential in achieving the degree of technical advance required. In this case project members were assigned very specific tasks that closely matched their areas of expertise. However, in Kodak's FunSaver project, an attempt to produce the world's first single-use camera, engineering tasks were more broadly defined, and individuals took responsibility for an entire component or subsystem. Extensive specialization was not necessary; the emphasis was not on the refinement of a fundamental technical base but on the execution of relatively well-defined and less technically challenging project tasks.

Companies have traditionally organized along lines of specialization in order to accumulate and preserve the technical expertise essential to functionality.[2] The rapidly changing competitive and technological environment that characterized the 1980s has added a twist to this problem, however. While the accumulation of knowledge is indeed made easier by the existence of a highly specialized organization, the existence of a rigid organizational structure for storing technical knowledge may hinder the responsiveness of that organization to market-driven and technological changes. Both the requirements for functionality and the technical basis for it may change. Indeed, given the blinding speed of recent technological change, many companies have found themselves in a position where much of their specialized expertise and established technical approaches have been rendered obsolete.

While a degree of specialization among engineers and others is still required to compete, some corporations have developed broader roles for some of their most senior and successful technical people, and have allowed project development programs to be organized around them. The organization at DEC is an interesting example of this new thinking. Future development centers around "consulting engineers," chosen from among the most prestigious engineers in the company, who are given powers comparable to a corporate vice-president. DEC consulting engineers and associated staff keep watch over families of related technologies critical to one or more of the company's product lines and help forecast technological shifts needed to meet emerging product requirements. Consulting engineers are expected to become gurus in their areas of focus, and DEC gives them the resources they need to achieve this. Consulting engineers become drivers of the company as they take on extensive responsibilities to choose and implement new technologies in new generations of DEC products. While they will tend to specialize in technologies and subsystems that are critical to the long-term competitiveness of the company, consulting engineers are also forecasters and integrators. They become acquainted with a broad set of new and old techniques and technical developments and will integrate them into effective solutions that will satisfy future development requirements.

As the above description of DEC illustrates, specialization can be an essential, even powerful source of advantage in product functionality. And leadership—in the DEC case, technical leadership—is an important part of making specialized expertise and deep knowledge effective in influencing the focus of its application and the direction of the company's efforts. But the evidence on overall development performance in our study suggests that specialists and technical leaders need to be developed and focused with some care. The problem is that people can specialize in a manner that pulls them away from the central mission of the project and even the overall organization. Moreover, specialization sometimes goes so far (e.g., the automobile left-rear tail-light engineer) that the problem of achieving coherence is much more difficult. Thus the issue is not whether a company should strive for expertise and technical leadership in its development organization, but rather how to define specialization and combine it with the right degree of breadth.

The key to achieving the right kind of expertise and specialization is to combine depth in a particular area with a breadth of experience and knowledge that brings a broader perspective to the specialized work. This is particularly critical in markets and technologies where change is rapid, where time is critical, and where customers demand increasing performance in cost and quality. In computers, for example, it is important to have experts in packaging and components integration techniques like surface-mount technology. But instead of creating a highly specialized individual who just knows a narrow aspect of the technology (e.g., bonding), the company will be better served with somewhat more broadly gauged interconnection engineers who have expertise in surface mount but also are knowledgeable about packaging in general, including the electrical, mechanical, and thermal aspects related to design and manufacturing as well as alternative packaging technologies. The evidence suggests that such "T-shaped" (deep in one area, broad in many) engineers not only deliver expertise to the project, but do so in a way that allows for more effective linkage with the work of other people on the project.

And such linkage is crucial to achieving an effective, integrated product.

While the breadth and depth T-model has general applicability to most fast-paced projects, where there is significant change from past product or process capabilities, one can also reflect on projects of a scope that requires only engineers with functional depth because the integration procedures have been well established and are readily operational. There is another clear message from our study: there are few "no brainer" projects, and thus engineers with no disciplinary depth lack the rigor to be valued contributors.

## Coherence

The challenges of coherence have been described by one of the managers interviewed in our study as similar to that of getting several high-speed trains, running fast on different tracks (perhaps slightly out of control), to converge in one station all at the same time. The Vision Group witnessed many examples of the difficulties involved in achieving coherence. All of them seek to integrate activities and approaches in different functional areas (addressing the problem is dealt with in depth in Chapter 8).[3] Many approaches have been taken that differ in strength and effectiveness. They range from lists of rules and procedures, to task forces and committees, to partially and fully dedicated development teams.

The use of highly focused teams with strong leadership may be very effective. Consider, for example, the FX15, an air-conditioner compressor developed by Ford's Climate Control Division (CCD). The FX15 project was driven by intense competitive pressure, great enthusiasm from within the company, and strong management support. The project objectives were very aggressive, both in product design and in the design process. The product was engineered by a co-located group of design and manufacturing engineers, and it achieved aggressive goals in cost, size, and performance. The overall project leader had worked as a design engineer and then as a production manager at the plant on CCD's previous generation compressor. While others on the team led the technical effort (particularly one of the design engineers), the team leader was instrumental in creating a focus on coherence, especially in the connections between design and manufacturing. The goal of the team (a goal shared by all) was not just a great design, but a great design that could be made at low cost with high reliability. The team leader reinforced that objective in all the interactions with the rest of the 15 members: two designers, five engineers, three machining specialists, one quality control specialist, two assembly specialists, one plant engineer, and a materials handling specialist. The structure of the team brought to one place individuals combining extensive manufacturing and design experience under the leadership of someone who understood the issues in both areas and led to a design that incorporated aggressive performance and packaging goals as well as extensive design for manufacturability.

Many aspects of the FX15 project were impressive: the aggressive targets were met due to the daily face-to-face interaction of everyone on the team. Competitive products and alternate processes were benchmarked. Vendors were carefully selected for their capabilities and cost. And design improvements reflected close attention to manufacturability issues. In the basic product and process design work on the project, the members of the team brought a measure of expertise to their work, but the solutions they developed to specific problems were not developed in isolation. Not only did the members of the team share common objectives; they also created processes for problem solving that integrated issues and concerns in different areas such as design and manufacturing and led to superior overall results.

### Fit

The FX15 project cannot be deemed a complete success, however. It suffered from a lack of input from its "customer," Ford's Car Product Development organization. Failure to integrate the customer in the process caused the FX15 to fall short in system performance when integrated with the rest of the automobile, resulting in serious noise and vibration problems in the car's interior. Though the project was a fine example of strong leadership and a dedicated team approach to technical coherence and integration within the team, it also illustrates the dangers of not fully addressing fit and integration with the customer.

In achieving integration, most organizational mechanisms and most project managers tend to focus on technical coherence and interactions within the team. For the most part, that means coordination. In the literature on organizations and in our experience with a wide range of companies, we have found coordination to be the primary objective of most project managers, committees, and liaison groups. Most are trying to get the functional groups to work together better. Integration with the customer has received much less attention.[4] Achieving a match between the product and the customer has either simply been assumed in the objectives of traditional integration activities or made the focus of one particular functional group such as product planning or product testing.

If customer expectations are relatively clear and widely known, as when matching a competitor's product, or if they are defined by component functions, a good fit with the customer may be achieved as a by-product of achieving functionality and product coherence. But in markets in which customer requirements are changing and firms have achieved functional parity—more and more the case in the 1990s—beating the competition relies on perfecting the "total product experience." This entails developing a distinctive product concept that matches future customer expectations and user environments, and infusing this concept into basic and detailed product designs. To accomplish this, the product concept must be communicated to the entire engineering and manufacturing organization at each step of the development process. Achieving such a good "fit" with customer expectations is a substantial challenge (see **Figure 3.4** for the multiple sources of early customer input). Integration requires a conscious organizational effort to enhance the integrity of the development process by matching the philosophy and details of product design to the expectations of target customers (see **Table 5.1**). This is partly a matter of organizational processes, such as making customer requirements an explicit focus of milestone reviews in the development process. But it is also a matter of leadership. Particularly when customer requirements are ambiguous, the project team needs leader-

**Table 5.1** The Three Dimensions of Organizing Product Development

| Dimension | Objectives |
|---|---|
| Functionality | • Accumulation and preservation of technological expertise at the level of individual components or activities<br>• Speed and efficiency for executing narrowly-defined tasks |
| Coherence | • Fast product development through better coordination across functional or departmental boundaries<br>• High coherence of total product<br>• Contribution to total product integrity |
| Fit | • Matching of product concept, design, and customer expectations<br>• Contribution to total product integrity |

ship in creating a compelling guiding vision for the product concept and communicating that concept throughout the organization down into the details of the design.

Throughout the projects we studied, we identified several approaches to leading and organizing the integration of customer expectations into the development process. A firm may create an explicit role for what might be called an "external integrator" and assign people to that role in each functional unit (e.g., engineers who test the prototypes against customer performance features or product planners in marketing who are intimately familiar with customer needs). Alternatively, a firm might assign all its external integrators to a single, specialized unit, which may be organized along product lines or be product independent. Similarly, the functions of concept creation and concept realization might be either assigned to different groups or consolidated under one leader. The influence, power, and strength of the individuals charged with the task of integrating the customer with the process vary with the different schemes as shown below.[5]

## Achieving Fit and Adherence with the Customer at Hewlett-Packard

Hewlett-Packard's HP150 and DeskJet projects provide contrasting approaches to achieving a fit with customer expectations. At the outset, the two projects had a lot in common. Both were considered major efforts and had very aggressive goals. Both involved significant design challenges. Both were consumer products, aimed at opening up a new segment of a marketplace for HP. But while the objectives were similar, the execution of customer integration was profoundly different.

Born as an effort to design a terminal for the HP3000 minicomputer, the HP150 project quickly expanded to include development of a personal computer in response to IBM's introduction of the PC in 1981. The HP150, it was determined, would function as both a terminal and a personal computer, and thus represented HP's first entry into the consumer market. It was a revolutionary project for HP. The company's prior products were all oriented toward engineers. The new customer base required very different types of product features and attributes. However, the HP150 lacked any comprehensive marketing plan. When the product concept changed from terminal to terminal/PC, few changes were made in the marketing strategy. The decision to distribute the HP150 through dealer channels, for example, was made only six months before product introduction, and it was the first time HP would use dealers.

As a result of these and other similar problems, the HP150 never became profitable as a personal computer and was unable to significantly challenge the IBM PC. It did sell well as a terminal, however, as its concept apparently satisfied its old engineering customer base. The consumer failure of the HP150 can be attributed at least in part to problems with fit. Customer expectations for the HP150 were clearly uncertain and ambiguous, as the PC market was quite undeveloped at the time. However, the project lacked a substantial and focused effort to understand what for HP was a new customer. Moreover, the project lacked any clear and explicit mechanism to translate any understanding there might have been into information that would focus the efforts of the engineers on the project.

Effective integration with the customer was not achieved on the HP150 because of a lack of leadership. The project had no focused vision, charter, and mission from top management; some on the project viewed it first and foremost as a terminal, others as a PC. There was a project manager, but little project leadership. The project manager tried but failed to exercise leadership, primarily because the organization, especially senior management, did not support the project manager in playing that role. As a result, the project manager was unable to establish a common vision of what the project should be; his efforts were overridden by senior managers who would provide intermittent and often contrasting inputs. The senior managers were not involved enough to understand the project's intricacies, yet they felt free to interfere. As a result of both factors, the project lacked coherence and customer fit. The many design, manufacturing, and marketing issues necessary to develop a successful personal computer were not resolved in a coherent fashion, and did not fit with the future customer's expectation of the product.

The DeskJet project provides a startling contrast to the HP150. Identified as an absolutely critical project by HP's Vancouver Division, the project benefited from clear senior management direction. The project also had a clear leader, the division R&D manager, who was deeply involved in the details of the project and also provided guidance as to its objectives and concept. While he was not formally appointed as project leader, he played that role throughout the entire project.

Great effort was put into pre-project planning and product definition for the DeskJet. Early in the process, the team developed extensive data on user preferences. Systematic marketing steps were undertaken to provide crucial input to the product's definition and detailed design. Prototype products were even placed in shopping malls to elicit customer reactions, which affected the design process in substantial ways.

While effort was focused on developing a detailed vision of future customer preferences, there was also a clear process by which this vision evolved and was implemented. Once the product concept was fully developed, the project leader and the team had clear authority to make almost all decisions. The project leader was a highly respected figure in the organization, and had formal and informal authority over a great part of the team.

The HP DeskJet was a success, establishing HP as a major player in the PC printer market. The product was delivered on time and exceeded shipping rate expectations by a factor of three.

# THE FOUR SYSTEMS OF ORGANIZING DEVELOPMENT

While we can analyze a development organization by describing how it approaches functionality, coherence, and fit, the approaches to these three dimensions are not independent. The elements of organization we observed fall naturally into patterns. For example, certain approaches that a firm may use to integrate customers into the process, such as a clear concept champion, will affect its approach to achieving coherence, or technical integration. Likewise, an organization with individual engineers who are very highly specialized will need different mechanisms for achieving coherence than an organization with less specialized people.

The project leadership and organization in the companies can be analyzed as four different structures for carrying out development projects. The structures vary in the degree to which they make use of specialization, teamwork to achieve coherence, and integration with the customer. The structures, depicted in **Figure 5.1**, are stylized representations meant to provide a framework that captures the essential features of the many different kinds of leadership and organization we have seen. Though they differ to some extent in their approach to the degree of functionality, especially specialization, the major differences lie in how they achieve coherence and fit. In **Figure 5.1**, the vertical boxes represent functional subunits, such as engineering or manufacturing, each of which is supervised by a manager. In all but the first structure, a project leader (PL) for a particular project orchestrates the work of the functional units; the shaded region represents the area in which the project leader exercises influence. Weak influence is shown in a light shade, strong influence in dark. The area of influence may be limited to engineering, or it may extend to production, marketing, and even to the market itself through customer integration. An intersection between the market and the project leader's zone of influence indicates that the leader is also in charge of concept creation and maintains direct contact with customers.

In the traditional functional structure, depicted in the upper left

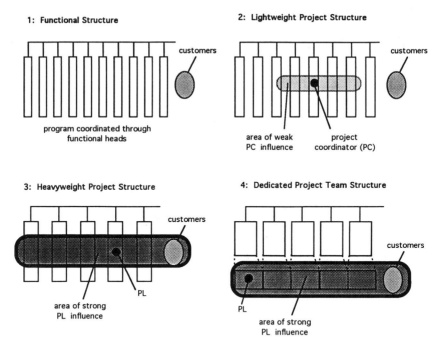

**Figure 5.1.** Development projects tent to be organized in four ways. In each, functional units such as engineering or marketing are shown as vertical boxes. The width of the functional chimney indicates the level of specialization; a broader chimney implies larger breadth of expertise. In the functional structure, there is no project leader; no one person has overall responsibility for the total project. The lightweight mode is similar, but there is a project coordinator who keeps the functional groups informed, organizes meetings, and facilitates decisions. In the heavyweight system, the project leader has broad responsibility and clout over working-level people within functions. In the dedicated team approach, people are removed from their functional groups and are dedicated to the project full-time. They report directly to the project leader and do the detailed work.

quadrant of **Figure 5.1**, development is organized by functional discipline and engineers are relatively specialized. No individual has overall responsibility for the total product or process. Leadership occurs within specialized groups and generally takes the form of technical direction and application of expertise in solving difficult problems. Senior functional managers are responsible for allocating resources within their function and for the performance of their people. Coordination occurs through rules and procedures, detailed specifications, shared traditions among engineers, occasional direct con-tacts, and meetings. Kodak's Chem 181 project is a good example of this mode (see **Table 5.2**).

In the lightweight project system, depicted in the upper right quadrant of **Figure 5.1**, the basic organization and level of specialization remain comparable. What is different is the existence of a project coordinator who keeps track of development activities through representatives from each function. Project coordinators in this mode have no direct access to working-level people, and compared to the functional managers, have much less status or power in the organization. They usually have little influence over the substance of the work, and they have neither direct market contact nor concept responsibility. Like the project coordinator, the members of the project team have little influence in their respective functions. They are liaisons who transmit information, but they do not make decisions, are not involved in, and are not responsible for the work in the functions. Together with the project coordinator they make a team, but it is a

**Table 5.2**  Characteristics of Projects Organized Along Various Development Modes

|  | Functional Mode | Lightweight Mode | Heavyweight Mode | Project Team |
|---|---|---|---|---|
| *Project* | Kodak Chem 181 | HP HP150 | HP DeskJet | Ford FX15 |
| *Characteristic* | | | | |
| Project leader's influence on engineering | Weak | Medium | Strong | Strong |
| Project leader's influence on marketing, manufacturing | Weak | Weak | Strong | Strong |
| Responsibility for coordination | Dispersed | Focused | Focused | Focused |
| Responsibility for continuity of concept | Dispersed | Dispersed | Focused | Focused |
| Location of team members | Dispersed | Dispersed | Dispersed or partially co-located | Fully co-located |
| Team members' link to function | Very strong | Strong | Medium | Weak |
| Direct link to market/customers | Strong | Weak | Initially weak, then strong | Weak |

lightweight team from the perspective of the project's substantive issues. Its main purpose, and therefore the main purpose of the project coordinator, is to coordinate—to collect information on the status of work, to help the functional groups resolve conflicts, and to facilitate the project so as to achieve its overall objectives.

A lightweight project coordinator thus does not exercise substantive leadership in the project. Where it exists in the lightweight setup, leadership of that kind occurs within the functions. But project coordinators and lightweight teams can play their role more or less well. A coordinator that pulls together information effectively, spots emerging problems of coherence, and facilitates interaction and problem resolution can have an important impact on the coherence of the product or process and the speed and efficiency of the project, particularly compared to the pure functional system. In that sense, "lightweight" does not necessarily mean "ineffective." Indeed, in playing the coordinating role exceptionally well, a project coordinator can exercise leadership in making the process of integration work within the constraints established by the way development is organized. Of course, where the organization works against that kind of leadership—where the project coordinator becomes a clerk (e.g., tracks events, schedules meetings, and publishes minutes) but no more—then "lightweight" can truly mean "ineffective."

The heavyweight system depicted in the lower left quadrant of **Figure 5.1** stands in sharp contrast to the lightweight structure. Although the formal business unit organization is still largely functional, there is now a project leader with broad responsibility and influence. Leaders of heavyweight projects are usually senior in the organization, often at the same or higher rank as the heads of the functional organizations. The R&D manager in HP's DeskJet project is a good example (see **Table 5.2**). In the heavyweight system, some of the work occurs in the functional areas and team representatives serve as local project leaders within their functional groups. Thus the team provides leadership within the functions as well as across the entire project effort. It combines overall concept and integrative leadership in the form of the project leader, and functional expertise and technical leadership in the form of the functional representatives. Moreover, the organizational setup facilitates the exercise of that leadership. The team and the project leader have direct access to working-level people. Though heavyweight project leaders may lack formal authority over working-level people, they exercise strong direct and indirect influence across all activities. They are responsible not only for internal coordination, but also for product and process planning, concept development, and integration of the customer into the process. The heavyweight project leader functions much as a general manager of the project.

Although the heavyweight system works within a functionally organized company, the strong product or process focus of the project leader may extend into the functional groups, to the point of reorganizing the structure within functions. In a car company, for example, body engineers may be grouped by type of body (e.g., large cars, small cars, or utility vehicles) instead of by the kind of engineering they perform (such as interior trim versus body panels). Employees still work within a functional area and may work on more than one project at a time, but they have a stronger systems orientation than those in the purely functional or lightweight systems.

The focused, singular-purpose team, shown in the lower right quadrant of **Figure 5.1**, takes the project orientation quite a bit further. In the dedicated team setup, a project leader works with a team of people who are devoted to the effort full time. This is not the same as a team of functional leaders; the people on the team do all the functional work required by the project. They leave their functional groups and report directly to the project manager, as was the case in the FX15 project described earlier. These individuals are not necessarily as specialized as those in the functional structure, and they assume broader responsibilities in their tasks as members of the team. Functional managers retain responsibility for personnel development and overall resource allocation for specific support work. But a project leader's influence on project issues is greater than in the heavyweight mode because they oversee a group of people subscribed to the project.

The four systems of leadership and organization laid out in **Figure 5.1** provide managers with a framework for thinking about organizing development projects. Such a framework seems crucial. In the popular press the phrases "cross-functional team" and "multi-functional team'' almost have become cliches. They are touted as the solution for many a product development ill. But it is sobering to realize that in the Vision projects we found managers applying these phrases to all of the forms of organization depicted in **Figure 5.1**, except the functional structure. Managers described all the rest as "teams." Yet each of these modes is quite different in its basic structure and process, and each has distinctive strengths and weakness. Getting at the real value of each mode, therefore, requires understanding at a deeper level the differences among them.

The challenge is to recognize these differences and match the requirements of the projects one undertakes with the appropriate pattern of organization and leadership. We examine this issue in more depth below, but it will be useful at this point to note that a well-run lightweight system with effective coordination seems to work where technical solutions are critical, customer requirements relatively well defined and stable, and time pressures not so intense as to require a highly integrated process. The tighter the time pressure, the more significant the project, the higher the degree of uncertainty, and the more important an overall system solution is in the market, the more crucial a heavyweight system will be.

The dedicated team is effective under these conditions as well, but its special strength is in breaking new ground. Thus, an autonomous team is likely to work well where the firm is entering a new market, introducing a breakthrough technology, or in other ways departing from established practice. Despite the fact that the dedicated team appears to have all the trappings of the popular "cross-functional team," it is not an effective approach to every development situation. The critical issue is to find the structure and process that matches the needs of the project.


## PROJECT LEADERSHIP

Once companies understand that development projects can be organized in various ways, they can select a structure at the outset of a new project that they believe will be the most effective given the project's requirements. Once that is done, the challenge is to then effectively manage the project within the chosen mode. This section proposes a paradigm for effective project management and crystallizes a few of the essential features that distinguish effective project leaders. In thinking about leadership and the challenge of managing projects it is useful to distinguish between two separate tasks, both of which are necessary for ensuring the proper convergence of complex projects. The first task is aimed at coordinating—essentially, ensuring the smoothest possible flow of information between the various parties involved in the project and the creation of a shared understanding of the issues. The second task is aimed at championing—providing a constantly reinforced vision for the project, involving substantial conceptual guidance. Both keep integrity in process and outputs and empower contributors to make day-to-day decisions.

## The Traits of Leadership

Ensuring effective coordination is a basic requirement for all project managers, regardless of the mode in which they are working. What stands out in achieving integration are sharp differences in the strength of leadership. We have classified the problem in terms of the ''weight'' of the organization; in our scheme, the leader of a heavyweight system is most able to champion a project.

The type of project organization is determined by the responsibility of the organization. The coordinator of a lightweight organization can have a significant rank or title. The leader of a heavyweight project possesses professional stature as well as specific skills and experience, and uses them in a very different role. It may be difficult to tell a heavyweight organization from a lightweight organization by looking at an organization chart; both show up as project teams with managers, but the leaders have different roles to play.

We compiled a set of characteristics observed in leaders of heavyweight projects who had outstanding qualities. The following list summarizes some of the most critical behavioral patterns and skills for new product development.

- Heavyweight project leaders have coordination responsibility in wide areas, including production and sales as well as engineering.

- They have coordination responsibility for the entire project period from concept to market.
- They are responsible for concept creation and championing as well as cross-functional coordination.
- They have responsibility for and authority over product specifications, cost targets, and major component choices.
- They ensure that the product concept is accurately translated into technical details.
- They have frequent and direct communication with designers and engineers at the working level.
- They have direct contact with customers (e.g., the project manager's office conducts market research independent of any marketing group).
- They have skills in the various functions that must be integrated, and speak the language of each functional group, so they can communicate effectively with each group and translate between them.
- They are more than neutral referees or passive conflict managers; they initiate conflicts to prevent designs or plans from deviating from the original product concept.
- They possess market imagination and the ability to forecast future customer expectations based on ambiguous and equivocal clues in the present market.
- They circulate among project people and strongly advocate the product concept rather than do paperwork and conduct formal meetings.
- They are mostly engineers by training, possessing broad if not deep knowledge of total product engineering and process engineering.

## Creating Effective Heavyweight Leaders

As evidenced in the foregoing list, heavyweight project leaders behave differently from lightweight coordinators. The difference is more than a matter of doing what coordinators do, but with more influence. It relies on specific approaches to a different, broader set of activities. The heavyweight project leader plays different roles, summarized in **Table 5.3**.

The role and behavior of the project leader are inextricably linked

**Table 5.3**  The Numerous Roles of the Heavyweight Project Leader

| Role | Action |
|---|---|
| Direct market observer | First-hand contact with customers. |
| Multilingual translator | Communication in the proper language of the designers, assemblers, marketers, and other groups relevant to a project. |
| Direct engineering manager | Direct contact with development team, directly involved in critical elements of the project. |
| Program manager in motion | Continuous, informal face-to-face communication with all members of the development team. |
| Concept infuser | Guardian and preacher of product or process concept and project objectives. |

to the way development is organized; while a heavyweight team cannot operate effectively without powerful leadership, leadership cannot function without an organizational context that empowers it. However, to lead effectively, the surrounding organization will need to train, support, and empower those characteristics. An organization cannot create heavyweight project leaders by placing a corporate vice-president in charge of each major project. Rather, an organization must have a system for creating effective project leaders, and a development process that specifically supports and encourages them to carry out their leadership task.

To function properly, a project leader must have a clear charter from senior management. The leader must be able to extract his or her interpretation of the project objectives from a guiding vision that derives from the company's strategic intent. This vision must thus be thorough enough to provide guidance for project leadership (see Chapter 3), but must also leave room for the interpretation of the product or process if the project leader is to be a true champion. This can be accomplished through extensive interactions between the project leader and top management and with the different functions, channeling the inevitable diversity and resolving key issues before the project begins. Once the project starts, the project leader must be able to implement the guiding vision throughout the development process within the framework established by the project's charter. (**Figure 2.2** suggests that senior management's role is helpful only at the beginning of the project; later intervention verges on Monday-morning quarterbacking and meddling.)

The overall culture of the organization must be supportive of project leadership. Project leaders must be respected and have acquired the status their roles demand. Without this understanding, a development effort will suffer from lack of support. For example, when Kodak initiated its Factory of the Future project, to upgrade the capability of the manufacturing system to finish, cut, and package 35-mm film, the project management structure had barely been implemented. The job of a project manager in Kodak was not perceived as a credible one, and the chosen project leader was not able to win support within the business-unit structure. As a result, the project lacked coherence and focus.

Finally, the company must develop career paths that encourage employees to take on the role of project leader. Individuals who pursue this track need experiences that build on a solid base of expertise and also allow them to broaden their roles in a gradual and consistent fashion, developing the extensive skills described above. Some organizations have found ways to groom individuals for project leadership. The details differ, but the broad pattern of individual development is similar. During their careers these individuals acquire expertise in the design and engineering of subsystems that are particularly critical to the company's products and take on assignments that put them in direct touch with customers. Through these experiences, they develop engineering knowledge, customer insight, and acquire the respect of peers. These individuals also gradually acquire organizational responsibilities as project leader assistants, project coordinators, and finally true project leaders.


## DEC's Battle to Muster Support for Project Leadership

A study of the way in which DEC organizes development projects crystallizes the challenges of achieving a supportive organizational context for project leadership. Throughout its history, DEC has been an engineering-driven company that lives and dies as a function of its excellence in electrical and computer engineering and more recently in software and systems/network engineering. In particular, it has emphasized the development of superior computer hardware. DEC has actively sought to eliminate any overhead and bureaucracy that might hinder the creative pursuit of technical excellence. In this setup, engineers work on very few projects at a time and derive professional fulfillment from peer recognition and association with technically outstanding products. This focus has clearly attracted some of the best people in the industry, and the company capitalized on it in the past.

However, the dominance of hardware engineering has created problems in achieving coherence in the total system and integration with the customer in more recent development projects. Both formally and informally, hardware engineering always oversaw projects. Thus, the leadership on projects was rooted in technical experts. Although software engineering, manufacturing, customer service, and marketing all had official roles on development teams, the individuals fulfilling those roles had comparatively little power and influence on product design. Ironically, although project managers were almost always chosen from the ranks of hardware engineers, the project manager position suffered from the same cultural bias. There was little recognition at DEC that project managers added any value to the development process. Moreover, the project manager role was seen by engineers as a less attractive or even nonexistent career path. One hardware engineering manager, for example, spoke disdainfully of his simultaneous role as project manager as "not my real job"; he derived satisfaction and respect only from his engineering tasks.

DEC project managers were not empowered to take on the leadership required in a heavyweight organization. Because of the organizational context, their role was restricted to one of coordinator, rather than one of leader. While they were seen as liaisons between functions, and took ownership of a product after it was designed, they were not usually seen as the main conceptual drivers behind products. Conceptual guidance and leadership was instead usually provided by a few highly skilled and creative engineers who evolved into powerful technical "gurus." Highly respected and influential, they informally steered multiple projects from their own vision of the future of technology. These gurus often became *de facto* project leaders, providing the conceptual guidance that the coordinators sometimes lacked. While occasionally effective, this process had drawbacks, because technical gurus tended to be involved in many projects at once, and their attention may have been drawn away from critical issues in any single project.

The increasingly competitive marketplace that demands quicker responsiveness to a dynamic customer base has challenged DEC's approach to development. As a result, the company is moving toward heavyweight project organizations and the old role of project coordinator is changing to project leader and increasing in scope, sometimes clashing with the surrounding culture. The challenge for companies like DEC is to implement a form of strong project leadership, with more responsibility for coherence and fit with customers, without at the same time damaging the culture of engineering excellence that has been critical to its achievements.

The DECstation 3100 project, begun in early 1988, was an interesting example of the challenges DEC faced in making the shift to stronger project leadership. DEC was under great pressure to not only deliver higher performance workstations, but also respond to the RISC architecture and UNIX operating systems not used in the standard DEC hardware. The vision for the DECstation 3100 workstation was developed primarily by a senior sales manager, a very dynamic and eloquent individual, who persuaded corporate management to adopt a new approach to workstation development. The project vision involved the integration of state-of-the-art, off-the-shelf components into an advanced workstation that delivered substantially more computing power for much less money than others before it. The development time was particularly aggressive—less than nine months from concept development to customer introduction.

To achieve these challenging goals, the project leader adopted very clear and evocative design guidelines. These guidelines, for example, restricted the system from using more than one circuit board, and limited the development of unnecessary features that might hurt time-to-market, cost, or functional performance goals.

The project achieved the remarkable performance goals within the required time. While the product did not sell well at first, due to the limited software available, it enabled DEC to enter the workstation marketplace in a very short period of time. Software applications were subsequently developed and DEC has become a successful player in the new workstation market.

The DECstation 3100 project demonstrates that factors critical for heavyweight project leadership are not necessarily inconsistent with DEC's corporate culture. Yet the organization needs to develop a far more supportive structure. The 3100's aggressive goals and operating burden within the company, for example, resulted in "burnout" of the project leader. The future challenge in project development will be to create a stable, consistent process approach to project management that is appropriate for the challenges of a dynamic market.

## CHOOSING THE APPROPRIATE ORGANIZATION

### Matching Organizational Structures to Development Demands

All projects need leadership. But the appropriate type of leadership and the organizational structure to support it will be determined by the type of project and its context. For some kinds of projects, particularly major projects to develop a complex product requiring significant integration with a dynamic customer environment, a heavyweight team with appropriate leadership has significant advantages. Indeed, the projects we studied provided data with which to examine the crucial conjecture presented in this chapter. For major projects in dynamic environments, there is a positive relationship between the "weight" of the project organization and the success of a project. This relationship is examined in **Figure 5.2**.

In the figure, the character of the organization is assessed by the extent to which it matched a number of indicators typical of heavyweight organizations. The success of the project was characterized by the extent to which it met its business and technical objectives. Out of our sample of 20 projects, 17 fell into the category of major projects in dynamic markets.

Despite the wide differences in project scope, content, and envi-

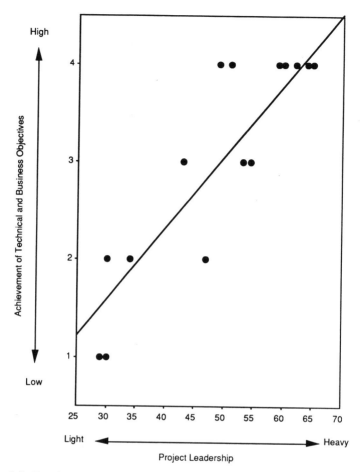

**Figure 5.2.** Despite the wide variety of differences in scope, content, and environment of the projects studied by the Vision Group, those that were most successful had heavyweight leaders. We rated each project in terms of 16 indicators characteristic of a heavyweight project organization. Total rating appears on the horizontal axis. The extent to which each project met its business and technical objectives was then rated from 1 to 4 (the higher the better). What resulted was a strong correlation between the weight of the project leader and the success achieved; the ''heavier'' the leader, the greater the success. (Three of the 20 projects were inappropriate for this analysis.)

ronment we found a strong correlation between the ''heaviness'' of the organization and the project leader and the level of success achieved. We thus see that for major projects in most current competitive environments a heavyweight team will tend to outperform other systems in speed, efficiency, and the achievement of a distinctive

152 ▪ The Perpetual Enterprise Machine

product or process. The structure is particularly effective in environments that are highly dynamic and require achievement of impressive system-level functional performance and integration of complex customer preferences into product design. Heavyweight teams will combine a well-developed knowledge base with a focused project and customer orientation, ensuring that the desired technological developments will be effectively integrated into the desired product/process concepts and architectures.

For less demanding environments, and for projects that may be less complex or less urgent, such as extensions of product lines or product refinements, for example, a full-blown heavyweight team with a heavyweight project leader may not be necessary. To take an extreme case, imagine a company that introduces hundreds of new products each year (e.g., Rubbermaid), most of which are minor refinements to established product platforms. If customer preferences are stable and the technological environment is not changing rapidly, the most appropriate form of organization might well be a lightweight system, in which a project manager has responsibility for several projects in order to provide effective coordination within and between the many products. Where the requirements are well understood and the technical problems well defined, substantive leadership in developing these products may come effectively through the functional groups. In that circumstance, a lightweight team with an effective project coordinator may be able to achieve the required level of coherence and fit. Of course the company may have a few major products requiring a heavyweight team and heavyweight leadership, but for the bulk of the work a well-run lightweight setup may be satisfactory.

We have found that leadership and organization in most development projects fall along a spectrum between the lightweight and heavyweight modes. Strictly functional organizations and isolated teams are more often special cases. They appear primarily useful in exceptional conditions. Functional organizations are useful in environments where technical excellence is a norm, specialty is paramount, and where time and resources for methodical development are available. A good example is Kodak's Chem181 project. Project teams are useful in the opposite extreme, when a focused effort is required to develop a product or process that is a clear departure from established practice, requiring fundamentally new requirements, approaches, or capabilities. The FX15 compressor and DECstation 3100 are good examples.

## How Chaparral Steel Manages Multiple Development Structures

A company with only one approach to managing projects may find itself in a difficult situation, since it may confront many types of projects with very different requirements. In practice, development for most firms is likely to be characterized by a portfolio of ongoing projects, some large and complex, some smaller and less demanding, with others in between. Some might be "breakthrough" projects designed to chart a new commercial or technical course. The challenge, therefore, is to create the internal capability to manage multiple project types. Of the companies we studied, Chaparral Steel proved the most flexible.

The success of Chaparral Steel illustrates the advantage of building capability for several approaches to development. Chaparral has defined three types of projects: major advanced development, platform, and incremental. Projects of the first type might require expenditures of $3 million to $5 million over a period of three to five years; they are risky, but are intended to provide a breakthrough product or process. Platform projects might require $500,000 to $1 million in development expenses and take 12 to 24 months to execute; they are used to put into place a new capability or substantial upgrade from which new products or processes will spring. Incremental projects typically incur expenditures of $100,000 to $200,000, last a couple of months, and provide quick payback. At any point in time, Chaparral might have 40 or 50 development projects underway, of which no more than a couple would be major efforts, perhaps three to five platform projects, and the remainder incremental initiatives.

Regardless of the scope, each project at Chaparral is led by a single project leader. The choice of the person is made by top management, and is based on matching an individual's previous experience with the project scope and operating requirements. The role of the project leader is facilitated by Chaparral's culture and norms; the management of projects at Chaparral is based on a set of broadly communicated and continually refined principles, not on administrative or bureaucratic procedures. As a result, everybody is well aware of the company's expectations and norms with respect to effective project leadership and organization. Team members thus quickly rally to provide support to even the uninitiated project leader.

This is in part because the steel industry is very mature. There is a great wealth of research, and Chaparral's top executives are convinced that a radically new invention from the laboratory is unlikely but that innovations and significant advances will come from experimenting with real production processes. It makes sense to them, then, to conduct development projects out on the line, which when achieved have the advantage of already being compatible with the logic of the production facility. Furthermore, because the industry is so competitive, production processes must be incredibly efficient; out on the floor there is a real sense of responding to competitive pressure, and management wants its development people to absorb this ethic.

However, the team structure and leadership used for each of the three types of projects vary considerably. The incremental projects are almost all done by functional subgroups and are led by a project manager whose role is much like that of a lightweight coordinator. However, these projects do not fall prey to the usual lack of coordination that typifies the functional approach, as noted earlier, because projects are so common that everyone understands the role of the lightweight project coordinator and is supportive: they know, at some point, they may play that role and will want the same kind of treatment. Thus, the support and cooperation provided to lightweight project coordinators tends to be substantially greater than in many traditional functional organizations, and as a result Chaparral's project coordinators are ''heavier'' in their influence.

The platform projects are headed by heavyweight project leaders who have probably been a department manager and, following completion of the platform effort, will go back to being a department manager. The advanced development projects are put under the leadership of one of seven general foremen who typically report directly to the vice-president of manufacturing. These major projects start as advanced development efforts; once technical feasibility is proven they quickly become breakthrough projects, but with little or no change in team composition.

The mix of approaches has served Chaparral well. Depending on a new project's need for technical depth, coordination of tasks, level of systems integration, and the degree of breakthrough and new thinking required, Chaparral can pick an appropriate team structure, project leader, and overall management approach. Expectations of the needs for various projects have been established over more than a decade, and thus procedures and approaches as well as their governing principles are well known throughout the company.

## A VISION FOR PROJECT LEADERSHIP AND ORGANIZATION

Throughout this chapter we have attempted to establish a vision for project leadership and organization. Our vision hinges on a relationship between the functions of leadership and the characteristics of the surrounding organization. Our thesis is that in dynamic environments, the most effective development efforts are characterized by heavyweight project organizations with leaders capable of generating distinctive concepts as well as of catalyzing and coordinating the multitude of activities that lead to a successful project.

Building an organization that has that capacity for heavyweight organization, however, is not a simple task. Many companies have traditionally been organized by functions, which often have been deeply separated for years. For these firms, adopting the heavyweight approach is a radical departure, and the transition can be a substantial challenge. It is a challenge that must be met by senior management; meeting it, actually building outstanding development capability over a long period of time, is every bit as difficult and requires as much leadership as the creation of a string of outstanding new products. Here too the hallmark of outstanding leadership is the ability to see both the parts and the whole. From the perspective of senior management, the parts are the individual projects, while the whole is the total pattern of development capabilities that the evolving set of development projects creates. Senior management has an important role to play at both levels.

Although many senior managers equate leadership with intervention in the day-to-day details of individual projects, in fact such intervention is almost always counterproductive. As we saw in the case of the HP 150 project, senior managers often focus on the details of a project without the background to be effective. Furthermore, direct intervention in the details sends the organization a subtle (and sometimes not so subtle) message about where the real decision-making power lies. It tends to undercut the team and create confusion in the support organizations.

But senior management does have a crucial role to play in individual projects. Of course, there are times when projects get in trouble or where major investment decisions must be made. But apart from these exceptional situations, an effective development process needs senior managers that establish direction, set appropriate expectations, and create processes that support and equip project teams and project leaders. The analogy with the role of the leader of the heavyweight project is direct: to be effective the team needs an overall charter, a mission that clearly links the outcomes of the project to the strategic direction of the business. But the team also needs people with the right skills, methods for cross-functional integration in solving problems, and a process for establishing and reviewing milestones that connects the project to the realities of the business. All of this is the responsibility of senior management.

In a company with an effective heavyweight development process, senior managers neither design the product or process, create the marketing plan, nor solve the technical problems on individual projects. Instead they identify, select, educate, and develop leaders and teams. They establish strategic direction and build momentum behind good product and process ideas. They own the broad pattern of the development process, and watch over its application within the teams. And they connect these activities on individual projects—the parts—to the challenge of building heavyweight development capability in the organization as a whole. This means that not only do specific products get developed, but that the organization learns from its experience, changes and evolves what it does, and improves its development capability (see Chapter 2.)

For senior managers, effectively interacting with individual projects is hard enough; making the connections to ongoing learning and improvement is daunting. It requires ongoing change in most of what a company does, and the specific issues senior managers must face are difficult and complex. But because of its difficulty, companies that build heavyweight development capability over time reap significant advantage. The experience at Ford Motor Company in the 1980s illustrates how one company has confronted that challenge and the impact its efforts have had on development performance.

## Ford's Push Toward Heavyweight Project Organization

Ford's evolution in the 1980s illustrates many of the differences between lightweight and heavyweight project management, and captures both the potential and the challenges involved in achieving heavyweight project management.

In the 1970s and early 1980s, no official project manager role existed at Ford. Product concepts were the responsibility of the product planning department, and were strongly influenced by the entrenched views of senior management and chief engineers. The various engineering organizations were widely separated. Individual engineers had narrowly specialized roles and would often work on a number of different automobile projects at the same time. Development projects were steered by lightweight engineering coordinators, under the intermittent control of senior management through project reviews. These practices were reflected in excessively long lead times and in vehicles that often lacked integrity at the system level.

In the early 1980s, Ford faced a dismal future. Quality was far below competitive standards and market share was falling. The company's financial position was precarious and layoffs were ongoing. By the end of the decade, however, Ford had introduced a string of successful new products. Indeed, the Ford Explorer, which made its debut in the spring of 1990, may prove to be Ford's most successful product introduction ever. Despite the fact that it entered a down market, the four-door, four-wheel-drive sport utility vehicle has sold extremely well. Other new vehicles, such as the Lincoln Town Car, the Probe, and the Taurus, have also been notable market successes.

Behind these successes lies a decade of changes in Ford's management culture and its approach to product development. Under the leadership first of Phil Caldwell and then of Don Peterson, Ford's senior management embarked on a dramatic transformation of the company's character and its products. That transformation involved a focus on quality, employee involvement, and enhancing teamwork. Much important change took place in the company's manufacturing operations where Ford began a decade-long improvement in productivity and quality. But from the customer's standpoint, the proverbial "proof of the pudding" was in the new products the company would develop. In that regard, the development of the Taurus was pivotal. As a product, the Taurus was a family sedan with advanced aerodynamic styling and the ride and handling of a sophisticated European car. It offered a distinctive yet integrated package. As a development project, the Taurus was a crucial "vehicle" in bringing about change.

Traditional development at Ford was schedule driven, sequential in the way it organized activities, and punctuated by a series of detailed reviews that were highly procedural and bureaucratic. In developing the Taurus, Ford sought to break down barriers between functions by creating "team Taurus," the core of which included principals from all the major functions and activities involved in the creation of a new car. The development team was headed by the director of large car programs, and served to coordinate and integrate functions up through the senior management level.

The Taurus line of cars was very successful. But the new leadership at Ford had brought an attitude of continuous improvement. Thus, Ford executives recognized the need to build on the success of the Taurus and improve the process. And there was much to learn. Development of the Taurus, for example, took many years and many engineering hours, and Ford learned one major lesson: that integrated development, and in particular development that would reduce time to completion, requires more than a high-level project team under the direction of a single manager. While the vision of a highly integrated organization had been implanted in Ford by virtue of the Taurus program, much remained to be done to ensure the implementation of a structure that could develop integrated products consistently and efficiently. This goal required implementation of new practices at all levels of the company, from senior leaders to working-level engineers. It involved empowering project managers to make required decisions and giving them the opportunity to develop necessary skills. It also involved developing capabilities among working-level engineers in different departments so they could work together, joining different perspectives and cultures toward the efficient achievement of coherent results.

In order to cut lead time, improve quality, and bring products to market that were distinctive and attractive to customers, Ford launched what it called the "Concept-to-Customer" (or "C-to-C") process in the mid-1980s. To develop the process, senior management hand-picked a team of engineers and product planners. The C-to-C team took as its mission the creation of a new corporate architecture for product development. Its specific focus was to create a sequence of development activities and associated milestones that would result in a 48-month lead time on major new development programs, instead of the 60 months or more that was typical, while also improving product quality, attractiveness, and performance.

The C-to-C team was led by an experienced senior engineer, and included members from most of the important engineering groups as well as product planning and marketing. Through extensive interaction with senior functional managers, the group first sought to identify the overall structure of the current development process. They determined how the process worked, what the milestones were, and what procedures were used to make decisions. The C-to-C team then became the focal point for significant benchmarking. The team compared Ford to its major competitors and other companies outside the auto industry whose success in product development was well documented.

The benchmarking, as well as the intensive analysis of the internal process, revealed several opportunities for significant improvement. But the team also recognized the importance of establishing funda-

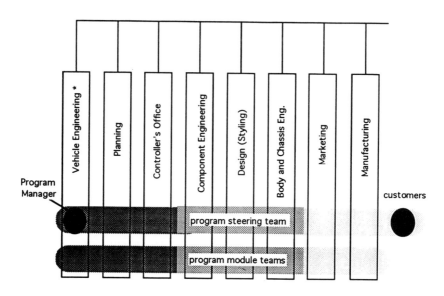

Program Manager

Vehicle Engineering *

Planning

Controller's Office

Component Engineering

Design (Styling)

Body and Chassis Eng.

Marketing

Manufacturing

customers

program steering team

program module teams

\* Includes vehicle packaging and system level functional testing.

**Figure 5.3.** The structure of Ford's development projects placed vehicle engineering, planning, and the controller's office under the direct influence of the program manager (conceptual guidance and direct access to working-level engineers). This is depicted with the darkly shaded area in the diagram. In engineering functions such as body, chassis, and components, the program manager's influence was less (primarily as referee and coordinator), but much stronger than in the past. There was moderate influence in marketing and manufacturing, but less than in the engineering functions. The overall leadership of the program was the responsibility of the program steering team, composed of managers from each of the functions and led by the program manager. Program module teams focused on specific components or subsystems (e.g., brakes, steering, seats) and involved working-level people from the functions.

mental principles for the creation of a new development architecture. Through a series of presentations and extensive discussion with the centralized development organization that initiated new vehicle programs at Ford, the group articulated and sought to create consensus around critical milestones, decision points, and criteria for decision making, as well as around patterns of responsibility and functional involvement.

Drawing in part on the recommendations of the C-to-C team, the central development organization went through a number of major changes to implement a more integrated development process. In particular, a system for formal project management was implemented in 1987. We witnessed the effectiveness and evolution of project management through the study of three projects: the 1988 Lincoln Continental, the 1989 Thunderbird/Cougar, and the 1992 Crown Victoria.

The evolution of the product development process is captured in the structure of Ford's development projects for early 1990 depicted in **Figure 5.3**. The core of each project, made up of vehicle engineering, development, planning, and the controller's office, was put under the direct influence of what Ford calls the program manager. In the Crown Victoria project, the entire team was co-located. Contact with other organizations was maintained principally at two levels. The Program Steering Team (PST), led by the program manager, was responsible for overall leadership, making the most crucial system-level decisions. The PST involved managers from all of the groups shown in **Figure 5.3**. Integration at lower levels of the project was ensured by the Program Module Teams (PMTs), which also had representatives from each function. Each PMT focused on one of the product's subsystems.

In the three car projects studied we noticed a considerable evolution toward a well-integrated development process. The earliest emphasis was on improving the efficiency and coherence of the development process by focusing on internal integration. The most marked improvements were found in the core team. The level of integration decreased somewhat as work moved away from the core, where engineers were not dedicated to one project. The PMTs had made a very significant difference, however, providing a focus for communication, discussion, and the resolution of issues surrounding a component or subsystem. However, true working-level integration had not yet been completely achieved, as age-old differences in culture and outlook sometimes clashed.

Recently, Ford has begun to focus on external integration. During some of the earlier car programs, the program leader and the project team did not always seem fully empowered by the company to develop their own view of what the vehicle concept should be. Extended negotiations took place between the project management team and top management, styling, and marketing. These discussions continued through a substantial part of the project, and did not always result in the creation of a precise and explicit concept. Ambiguities left in project objectives would sometimes inhibit the efficient resolution of complex multifunctional problems, contributing to project delays. By 1990, Ford had begun to target these problems, and was in the process of redefining the roles of program management and the project team to emphasize external integration.

Overall, the results of the Ford efforts have been quite positive. The Lincoln Continental was developed with about 25 percent fewer engineering hours than the average U.S. car program of the mid-1980s, and achieved a measure of market success. The Crown Victoria project was one of the first to be staffed by engineers with extensive previous experience in integrated development projects. The engineers had developed the capability to work with each other and with other functions, improving the efficiency and effectiveness of their interactions. This resulted in a well-integrated project that achieved improved coherence and customer fit, as shown by early market feedback.

By 1991, the implementation of heavyweight project leadership and heavyweight teams had progressed considerably. The drive for improvement was still continuing, however. In particular, the role of the program management organization as an effective mechanism for external integration was still being developed, focusing on early resolution of ambiguities in the concept and implementation of a new automobile.

## LEADING IN THE 1990s

Ford's effort to implement a heavyweight organization has been characterized by an impressive level of continuity, focus, and persistence. The company, spearheaded by senior management, is systematically identifying and implementing a number of consistent measures, processes, and procedures that is causing a gradual and constant evolution toward the heavyweight format. While the transition is not yet complete, tremendous change has already been achieved.

The interesting irony emphasized by Ford's evolution and the pattern of change in all the companies is that it takes the same evocative, dedicated, and persistent form of leadership to champion the organizational transformation as that which characterizes the project management structure it is trying to create. Changing a development organization is itself a development process, perhaps the most difficult, and the extent of success will be determined by the consistency and determination of the effort. There is much more here than coordinating or administering. In this context, to manage means to lead. Breaking down barriers, changing attitudes, designing new processes, and creating and empowering heavyweight project leaders requires an unmistakable purpose, a clear, persistent voice, and substantive action. It is a journey, not a destination, and the way is hard. But for those few who stay the course, the rewards are great.

## CHAPTER 6

# Ownership and Commitment

In each of the five companies, we found that the quality and level of effort expended on a development project—and thus the degree of success ultimately achieved—was tied directly to the extent of ownership and commitment exhibited by those involved. Unlike ongoing organizations, in which ownership and commitment occur within the functional groups on a long-term basis, development projects (which are by their very nature temporary) demand that individuals push themselves to the limit intellectually, socially, and physically. If they are not committed, or do not feel they own their work, they simply will not reach the level of effort required for outstanding success. The procedures by which the team works are also affected by the extent of ownership and commitment: conflict resolution, problem solving, communication are less effective if the people involved do not act with integrity, consistency, thoroughness, and genuine concern. Finally, the support a project receives from the rest of the company will also fall short if outside people do not feel that they, too, are important to its success and have a significant role in its completion.

Achieving the required ownership and commitment needed for development project success depends on people, not organization structure. Yet it cannot be dictated and ordered into existence; it must be built and inculcated over time, across projects, and at all levels of the organization. However, several mechanisms encourage, support, and reinforce such ownership and commitment. Many such mechanisms were identified in the projects we studied and are summarized in this chapter.

While both terms are used frequently in describing "people"-oriented organizations and successful development projects, they have a variety of meanings. As a starting point we have identified some widely accepted elements of definition. Ownership is the feeling of being able to make a difference and wanting to do so. It goes beyond duty in that a person or group begins to tie its identity to a project's outcome, thus putting forth extra effort to ensure its success. For example, owners invest while employees spend, and owners think of results, not budgets. Frequently ownership is used interchangeably with empowerment. Commitment is a sense of duty and resolve to follow through and achieve selected goals. It is a willingness to do what is needed to make a project successful, regardless of what that may require. Those who are committed change behavior to accomplish goals rather than stick to "conventional" behavior.

As just intimated, strong ownership and commitment have significance and impact at three levels. At the level of *individuals on the development project team,* ownership consists of feeling empowered and responsible for those activities that are an essential part of a successful development effort. These include not only the activities the individual performs directly, but also those influenced indirectly and performed by others. For individual team members, commitment involves linking their personal success, status, and esteem to accomplishing project goals. Ownership and commitment drive the emotional and intellectual energy individuals expend on the project, and the degree to which they view project success as critical to their career.

At the level of the *development project team,* strong ownership occurs when the team takes collective responsibility for all development activities—whether or not under their direct control—and feels it has the power to alter those activities as required for project success. Furthermore, the team is collectively committed to a shared set of goals that define project success. It feels empowered to modify, as needed, procedures and activities, including who does which tasks in what sequence to accomplish project goals. When especially strong, team members may come to value team success more highly than individual functional excellence or broad, company-wide interests.

Finally, at the *corporate level*—which includes both *senior management and support groups* such as test labs—strong ownership and commitment consists of having sufficient resolve and identity with project goals both to modify procedures and actions to support those goals, and to facilitate others to do likewise by empowering them (often by giving them more leeway to do what they consider essential for the project's success). In this way, the team's and the individual team member's efforts are supported to the fullest extent possible by the rest of the organization.

The interaction of ownership and commitment with development projects is sometimes clear, sometimes subtle. It is more effectively understood by looking at concrete cases, and so this chapter delves into many of the projects examined by the Vision Group. In doing so, we specify the nature of ownership and commitment and how they impact a development effort, expose the mechanisms that determine the degree to which they are achieved, examine a handful of issues that must be addressed even after the basics of these qualities are solidly in place in an organization, and suggest ways to improve ownership and commitment at all three levels.


## THE NATURE AND IMPORTANCE OF
## OWNERSHIP AND COMMITMENT

There are a number of characteristics that indicate the extent to which individuals, the project team, and the entire organization exhibit ownership of and commitment to the success of a development effort. These characteristics help define what ownership and commitment are and how an organization might determine the extent to which they are present for a given project. In addition, examining these basic characteristics can aid in understanding their impact and importance to development efforts.

To illustrate how an organization can build and enhance the characteristics that support ownership and commitment, and what the consequences can be if an organization fails to do so, let us take a brief look at two projects, and then refer to these as we examine each characteristic. The first project, Hewlett-Packard's DeskJet computer printer, illustrates how highly motivated people can pull off what may seem to be an impossible task. The second, Digital Equipment Corp.'s LANbridge 200 computer network, shows how the lack of ownership and commitment can foil even the best technical efforts.

*Hewlett-Packard's DeskJet printer.* By the mid-1980s, Hewlett-Packard's computer-printer division had developed a series of generations of printers that used ink-jet technology. Although several products had been technical successes, none had been strong commercial successes. Market acceptance had been poor; ink-jet printers had captured no more than 1 percent of the available printer market, repeatedly losing out to dot-matrix and laser printers. Revenues had peaked a few years earlier, and were sliding at an alarming rate. Furthermore, ink-jet technology served as the primary platform for the division's printer efforts.

Given the setting, the division general manager chose to put the entire organization in a precarious position: they would develop the new DeskJet printer and one other project as the only hopes for the future. The division general manager instilled a ''do-or-die'' mentality in team members, and the entire division, by repeatedly saying that ''anyone not working on DeskJet (or the other project) is simply rearranging chairs on the deck of the Titanic.''

Building on technology they had worked with for the previous five years, the technical people saw themselves as ''betting their careers'' on the DeskJet product. Unlike earlier projects, however, this time they viewed success as ''commercial success,'' not just technical demonstration. The project scope was expanded to ensure that substantial advances in print-head technology and in manufacturability occurred. A clear goal—near laser-quality printing for less than $1000 retail—focused these objectives into an easily measured result. Because of the division's precarious position, an extremely short product-development time of nine months was agreed to by all involved, and a project team representing all the essential organizational units was formed and physically moved to one site.

The project succeeded. The DeskJet quickly captured 5 percent of the available printer market. Consumer research showed that 95 percent of its users would recommend it to a friend, and it exceeded its original shipping rate projections by a factor of three. The division attributed much of its success to the high degree of ownership and commitment achieved within the development team and across the entire organization. Several lessons from this case emerged, which we will examine in a moment.

*Digital Equipment Corp.'s LANbridge 200.* The LANbridge 200 was intended to be a follow-on product to capitalize on DEC's remarkable success with its first-generation product, the LANbridge 100. The LANbridge 100 linked various local computer networks into one extended network. Because it was the first such product available for use with Ethernet networks, the LANbridge 100 had captured 60 percent of the market; the goal of the LANbridge 200 project was to continue DEC's leadership by offering enhanced features such as the ability to monitor and prioritize the flow of information between computers on the networks.

The LANbridge 200 was to be developed quickly to capitalize on DEC's initial market position and continue DEC's influence in defining features and standards for this important segment of the computer industry. An aggressive 13-month cycle from initiation to actual shipment of the final product was set.

In Digital fashion, the project was split among several groups, who tackled parts of the problem. However, the tight time frame was not met; the project took 11 months longer than originally planned. The long delay resulted from several factors. As part of its strategy to lead the market in networks, DEC's architecture group worked with a technical committee of the IEEE, the leading professional society, to develop industry-wide standards. As those evolved, the LANbridge 200's definition had to be modified and equipment adapted. In addition, a separate unit within DEC, over which the LANbridge 200 team had no authority, was charged with developing software; after months of delay the LANbridge 200 team finally canceled that software effort and instead upgraded an earlier program used with the LANbridge 100. A final delay occurred when team members visited key customer sites late in the project only to discover that certain missing functionalities were essential if the product was to be competitive in the marketplace. These functionalities had to be added at the eleventh hour.

Though the LANbridge 200 has sold acceptably in the marketplace, it did not achieve its objective of leveraging fully the success of the LANbridge 100.

Both the DeskJet and LANbridge projects, and the many other projects studied by the Vision Group, provide insight into several of the characteristics that affect ownership and commitment. These characteristics, which manifest themselves at the individual, team, and corporate level, are explained below.

## Characteristics That Affect Individual Performance[1]

*The power to make a difference.* One overwhelming characteristic of ownership and commitment underlies an individual's effort on a development project: the extent to which that individual feels he or she has the power to make a difference. When present, this characteristic enables people on a development team to assume responsibility for accomplishing the mission of the project and to have the confidence that their actions will influence the project's outcome. This was clearly the case for the DeskJet; a broad range of participants took the initiative to tackle substantial technical issues as well as organizational challenges. For the LANbridge 200 project, the primary technical contributors—design engineers—exhibited such exhilaration, but it was not shared by others on the team. For example, the marketing people felt they had information important to the success of the project, but because they had been made to feel they had second-tier status by the design engineers who ran the project, they felt they could not make a difference. After their recommendations were rebuffed early on, they no longer felt committed to the project, and weren't persistent in seeing to it that the implications of their information were addressed by changes in the product design. It was not until the team itself was nearing the end of the project and tested its product at actual customer sites that it discovered marketing indeed had been correct in its recommendations.

*Personal identification with project success.* A second characteristic of individual ownership and commitment is acceptance of project goals as the basis for performance evaluation. Rather than judging the quality and extent of one's contribution primarily by the way in which individual tasks are performed, the individual with strong ownership and commitment agrees explicitly and implicitly to be judged on the basis of project success, even though he or she may have very little or no impact on many of the activities essential to achieving project goals.

All people on a project need to feel ownership and commitment. Although some employees within the LANbridge 200 project were committed to their piece of the project, many did not take ownership of the project goals, which included acceptance of the product by customers. For example, while the design engineers did exhibit ownership and commitment, particularly to the product design, there was much less of it across the other functions of marketing, software development, and manufacturing—even for their own subset of activities.

Ironically, there is also a positive example in the LANbridge 200 project of the power of an individual who feels he can make a difference. It was the project manager who pushed the team, near the end, to visit key customers to get feedback on the product one month before its anticipated completion. At this point the product manager finally had sufficient control over the project; after discovering through the test sites the absence of desirable functions, he was able to slip the schedule by four months and use that time to correct obvious shortcomings.

## Characteristics That Affect Team Performance

There are several characteristics of ownership and commitment that manifest themselves at the team level.[2]

*Team members share a clear mission.* The most fundamental dynamic of a development team is the interaction of its members. Positive interaction begins if the people agree on and back the purposes and goals of the development effort. In the projects we studied, those with a clear mission, shared by all, generated substantially higher levels of ownership and commitment than those in which team members lacked a shared view.

A common vision is often most achievable if it comes from the team itself. Although corporate-level executives decided Hewlett-Packard's printer division had to attempt a do-or-die effort on ink-jet technology, it was the team that refined that broad mission into a specific goal—near laser-quality printing for less than $1,000. The full range of people involved—from team participants to others whose support was needed for success—agreed on the objective.

In contrast, the LANbridge 200 project lacked a clear, shared sense of mission. A couple of the groups, particularly the software group, appeared to lack any clear sense of purpose, even one of their own making.

*Team members feel a shared sense of responsibility and authority.* Strong ownership and commitment at the team level are also exhibited when there is a sense of shared responsibility and authority for the project, for the process of managing the project, and for the performance results of the project. This extends to the team the idea discussed earlier that an individual can make a difference. It also recognizes that collectively, such a team can reallocate tasks and add substantial value to the work of others.

In the DeskJet project, responsibility and authority were given to the team, and also supported clearly by the division general manager's repeated statements about the Titanic. The pressing sense that if the DeskJet did not succeed the entire division would be in jeopardy was clearly a motivating factor. While this "emergency" mentality is not necessarily healthy or even plausible for many projects, the shared commitment it invoked was real, and the project was better for it. A number of new procedures were also instituted that helped ensure a shared sense of responsibility. The team, with upper management, decided to prototype the printer every month in the factory. This forced the entire division—design, purchasing, marketing, and others whose efforts were needed to support the project—to come together. The practice not only ensured integration of various functions, but got division members used to meeting; they continued to contact each other directly in between prototyping intervals, which fostered a sense of commitment across the entire division.

We found that a shared sense of responsibility was fundamental to the success of projects at other companies, too. In Chaparral's Horizontal Caster project, to develop a new casting process for high-grade steel, this was fostered in several ways, including having the project carried out on the factory floor, and having the team understand it would operate the horizontal caster once the project was completed.

Chaparral's established norms, and the expectations of its employees, with regard to development projects, helped as well. The norm and the expectation at Chaparral are that project teams always have responsibility and authority for defining their projects, for the procedures used in the projects, and for the project's results. While every company we studied pursued this theme because of its impact on project success, Chaparral was most successful at achieving it consistently. The accomplishment appears to be due in a significant way to management's focus on this theme as a core principle in its philosophy. At Chaparral, ownership and commitment are fundamental tenets, and frequent and extensive use of teams operationalizes, refines, and renews these tenets on a daily basis. The lesson drawn from Chaparral is that the entire team, not just groups within it, must share a sense of responsibility and authority, and that the responsibility must extend well beyond simply meeting technical performance specifications, to the commercial success of the project and the procedures used for accomplishing that result.

*The team derives its identity from the project and its goals.* The third characteristic of strong ownership and commitment at the team level is that the intellectual and emotional identity for the team and its members is tied to the project and its outcome.

Although this characteristic is difficult to measure, its presence is most often indicated by a willingness on everyone's part to "go the extra mile" and to "do what it takes," rather than accepting the "fact" that traditional approaches, procedures, or personal perspectives prevent such efforts from being effective. Given the ambitious technical challenges in the horizontal caster project, for example, and the time schedule and market performance requirements targeted for DeskJet, neither of these two projects could have succeeded without a high level of identity and emotional involvement on the part of the whole team. Much of the shortfall of the LANbridge 200 project can be attributed to the absence of such identity. The leader for that project likened his "real job" to that of an engineering manager's, with functional and project management roles only secondary in importance. Achieving crucial emotional and intellectual identity under such conditions clearly would be difficult.

## Characteristics That Affect Corporate Support of Projects

At the corporate level, characteristics of strong ownership and commitment show up both among senior management and special support groups.[3]

*The entire company supports the project and its goals.* Just as all the members of a team must be committed to a project's success, the surrounding organization also has to buy into the objectives. This goes well beyond simply knowing the project mission and goals; the entire organization must cheer for and respond to requests for support of the effort. This perspective was captured by one person at Chaparral, who when commenting on the horizontal caster project said: "We can only blame ourselves if this project turns out to deliver less than the best and falls short of its purposes, potentials, and objectives." This characteristic also surrounded the DeskJet project, evidenced by the absence of "heroes" on the project and, instead, a sense of community success. On the LANbridge 200, many participants and subgroups felt that they did a good job on their piece of the program and should be recognized for that, even though the project could have achieved greater success.

*Recognition that corporate (or business unit) success depends on achieving project goals.* This entails that both management and the support groups see the overall success of the business and its goals as integrally linked to project success. When this occurs, the rest of the organization becomes willing to focus its energy and attention on making the team successful, with full confidence that success will create a win-win result for the entire organization. This also requires that the team recognize that its activities are not the only important ones of the corporation, and make requests in a balanced and reasoned fashion. On the DeskJet project this characteristic was reinforced by the frequent attention provided by the Division general manager and by the periodic prototyping pattern that involved all the support groups on a regular, reliable schedule. The total failure of the software group to provide its inputs to the LANbridge 200 project highlights the absence of this characteristic.

## ACHIEVING OWNERSHIP AND COMMITMENT

It is clear that ownership and commitment are necessary for a development project to succeed. The extent to which those characteristics associated with strong forms of these qualities are present determines in large part whether a project creates new competitive advantage. These characteristics and their links to individual team and corporate levels of ownership and commitment are summarized and illustrᵗed in **Table 6.1**. However, even having accepted the desirability of these characteristics, a tough question remains: How can high levels of ownership and commitment be achieved?

By their very nature, development projects require both unusual depth and unusual breadth. This entails integration across organizational units, disciplines, and technologies as well as between a development team and the larger organization. When working in a typical operating environment management often has the option of managing effort and exercising direct control over behavior, but this is not the case in a development environment. The most that managers can hope to do is to use indirect control to influence people's efforts, team procedures, and project outcomes. Thus, shaping and guiding

**Table 6.1**  Strong Ownership and Commitment at Three Levels

| Level and Definition | Key Characteristics | Examples |
| --- | --- | --- |
| *Individual Team Member* | | |
| • Empowered to direct key activities<br>• Personal status, identity, and esteem tied to project goals | Power to make a difference<br>Personal identification with project success | Assuming responsibility for tasks<br>Confidence that actions will influence outcomes<br>Enthusiasm and energy spent on the project<br>Persistence in making a difference |
| *Development Project Team* | | |
| • Responsible for all activities and procedures impacting results<br>• Collective agreement and pursuit of shared goals | Team members share a clear mission<br>Team members feel a shared sense of responsibility<br>Team derives its identity from the project and its goals | Concise, frequent statement of the mission<br>Willingness to help others succeed<br>Initiative and creative issue resolution<br>Recognizing the team as a central organizational unit |
| *Corporate (Management and Support)* | | |
| • Accommodating and encouraging modifications requested by the team<br>• Making the adjustments needed to achieve goals | Company-wide support of the project and its goals<br>Recognition that corporate success depends on achieving project goals | Sense of community<br>Willingness to aid and accommodate team requests<br>Linking business and project performance through plans and budgets<br>Structural choices—such as periodic prototyping—that encourage integrated support |

the degree of ownership and commitment become the essence of managing a development activity. These two qualities are the vehicles by which the required breadth of integration can be achieved. To the extent that ownership and commitment are limited or absent, management's ability to guide, pace, control, and lead is likely to be marginal or insufficient.

There are several different mechanisms that managers can use to achieve greater degrees of ownership and commitment, many of which we saw in action in the projects we studied.[4] This section examines these mechanisms, as they apply to the three levels we discussed earlier—the individual, development team, and corporate organization. While they can be used to create and enhance owner-ship and commitment, we also observed that a number of the same mechanisms could be misused, often inadvertently, to compromise a project. The subsequent section contrasts how ownership and commitment can be strengthened or unintentionally undermined. Management attention and action determine the outcome in each situation.

## Instilling Individual Ownership and Commitment

We observed a number of means for fostering individual ownership and commitment on development projects. The first was continuity in the personnel assignments of both individual team members and those providing key support functions. Often people were kept in their assignments not just for the duration of the development project, but as the project shifted into an operating mode.

Closely related to continuity of assignment was the linking of personal career progress and performance evaluation to an individual's performance on a development project. When used effectively, this mechanism tied closely the respect, status, rank, and subsequent assignments of an individual to the degree of success on recent projects. It did much to engender ownership and commitment on the part of individual participants in a project. On HP's DeskJet project there was no question that project success was central to future career opportunities, both in the technology functions and throughout the division. In some cases, we observed this mechanism in place with regard to the technical success of the project (and thus for engineers), but not for business success (and thus not for non-engineers). In such cases, technical and business success were decoupled and only the technical people developed a sense that they could (and should) make a difference. For most of the large companies, continuing assignment on a large project required a fundamental change in evaluating career paths, giving project completion and project results a more important role in individual advancement than past norms of ''a promotion every two or three years,'' irrespective of the status of the current project assignment.

Creating an understanding that superior product or process performance was expected resulted in recognition that a team's effort was part of the activity of a superior organization made up of people doing outstanding work. Often complementing this was the notion that respect for the individual would be based on recent, significant contributions to development activity. At Chaparral, where everyone in the organization participates in projects, this idea was firmly in evidence. At the other four firms, a similar norm existed, but primarily within the design engineering groups and much less so in other functions. Thus, in those firms, a greater burden fell on each development team to create such an expectation among its members.

To lighten the load, we observed that the most enthusiastic companies created a sense of excitement and fun surrounding project activity. Managers at Chaparral continually provided recognition and positive feedback to all those on development projects. In contrast, some of the smaller, less mainstream projects at other firms were clearly viewed by management as "out of sight, out of mind." The absence of excitement and fun was a significant demotivator to individuals, since all development efforts were viewed as requiring extra effort.

Incidentally, we also found that individuals often said they considered financial incentives as less important than nonfinancial ones, such as recognition by senior management and admiration from one's peers, or the promise of being placed on a project of even greater import in the future. Even when financial incentives did exist, they were only loosely tied to performance and in all cases were group, not individually, based.

Finally, we observed that a sense of individual power and responsibility was enhanced in companies that established an organization-wide norm of constant innovation, change, and improvement. In companies where such a norm existed, the entire organization saw projects as essential, and individual participants viewed both project results and changes in development procedures as part of a broader ongoing improvement effort. They recognized the cumulative nature of improvements in both operating activities and development projects, and were committed to a balance of the two. In contrast, some organizations viewed development projects as the only domain where significant progress could occur, with long periods of stability (and an absence of improvement) between projects and in development procedures. For such organizations, the momentum among individuals was for the status quo, and being assigned to a development project did not "automatically" change that momentum.

## Building Team Responsibility

Individual dedication is essential to a project, but it is not enough. An analogous sense of power and responsibility must exist on the part of the entire team. When fully developed, a team's ownership and commitment eclipses individual empowerment and causes the team to run with a project, obtain the best results, and develop the procedures by which those results are achieved.[5]

Many of the mechanisms used to build ownership and commitment at this second level require a careful balance between the initiatives taken up by a team and those of senior management. Such balance is needed so a project team receives support from the rest of the organization, is able to keep top management informed, and can build on longer term corporate strategies while still having the leeway it needs to set and achieve project objectives.

The mechanism that most often fostered team ownership early on in the projects we studied was the setting of clear, focused project goals that were tied directly to business purposes (see the three levels of guiding visions in Chapter 3). An important interchange was critical, though; while the initial statement and broad bounds of the goals were usually provided by top management, the project team would only own and commit to them if they were encouraged to translate those goals into specific statements that they could use unambiguously to guide their efforts. For example, division management at HP stipulated that the DeskJet project was to result in a commercial success that would build substantial sales and profits. The team then refined that to "DeskJet will deliver near laser-quality printing for less than $1000."

At Chaparral, all four projects had ongoing operating profit as their primary goal. However, it was not necessary for each of these development projects to have a specific numeric target for profit, since everybody in the organization—especially those on the project team—understood the basic economics and drivers of the company's profitability, and thus quickly and reliably related development activity to potential profit.

At Kodak, two of the four projects had clear business goals that were translated to specific agendas by the teams. The Chem 181 film-coating project, to develop an antistatic coating for microfilm, had a clearly stated goal for delivering a specific image sharpness, and the FunSaver camera, to produce the world's first single-use camera, had a clear goal of beating Fuji in U.S. market share. Although the other Kodak projects—the Factory of the Future and the Panda printer—had business goals, they were defined much less clearly and were not agreed to universally. As a result, they failed to generate significant ownership and commitment on the part of their development teams—to the detriment of each team's performance.

Of course, goals are sometimes too extreme, and if as a project moves on it becomes clear that goals are unrealistic, they must be changed. We found that making goals clear and measurable, and giving teams sufficient time at the outset to operationalize and commit to them—to take responsibility for achieving them—was more important than the fact that some goals were a real stretch. Ironically, this even proved to be problematic at times; in several cases senior management had to intervene to make such a change palatable to a team, because the team had generated such substantial ownership and commitment that it was unable to back off from its original goals without help.

An important aspect of making project goals measurable was to establish benchmarks external to the team doing the development. At Chaparral, each of the development projects had a clear ''best in the world'' objective and the team was provided with the resources needed to examine contenders worldwide, including visits to competitors or vendors. This ensured that each project had every chance of outperforming the efforts of other firms by learning from them and using them as an objective measure for comparison. During the horizontal caster project, for example, besides ongoing tracking of the efforts of other firms, the team twice made visits to all the horizontal casters in use worldwide.

While several other projects had goals that spoke of ''being the best in the world," many of them failed to generate ownership and commitment, because the term "best" was too generic, and because the team did not have the skills or resources to track, measure, and deliver the desired performance. In the case of DEC's RA90 project, to develop a high-density disk drive for computers, a clear goal was set for the team, but it related to technical, not business, performance. Furthermore, the goal was not revisited, revised, and adapted to reflect changes in the external market, which was changing rapidly due to competition between disk drive makers. Thus, while project goals generated substantial ownership and commitment early on, they lost much of their potential impact because they became dated, less relevant, and no longer credible.

A related mechanism for supporting empowerment at the team level is ensuring that project goals are complementary to business goals. An example of a project with narrow participation at the outset, that subsequently got much broader and stronger as project and business goals were aligned, was the Kodak FunSaver. While the shift from narrow to broad participation was triggered in part by the threat of Fuji, it also was enhanced by an organizational change. After floundering, the project was moved from the film division to the equipment division. The project suffered from lack of attention when it resided in the film division, because the people there saw the product as one that would cut into sales of regular film. Unless the camera could be made and sold for the same or greater profit margin than film generated, which it couldn't, the division had little motivation to pursue it. Further, the design of the camera required mechanical engineering, and the film division's strength lay in chemical engineering, so no requisitely skilled champion was there to push the project along. Finally, Kodak had so defined the jobs of people in the film division, all of which revolved around film-making, that handling a camera product was foreign, and apprehensiveness worked to limit commitment. Once the project was moved to the equipment division, it was pursued vigorously, because people there saw the product as a potentially large-volume seller, consistent with the division's mission, and understood the mechanical nature of the challenge.

For large projects, a mechanism that supported a shared sense of responsibility and authority was to define the scope of the work in a way that focused the team on doing a few things very effectively, rather than demanding they solve numerous problems simultaneously. Breaking a large project into subprojects, such as DEC did with the RA90 (separating development of the magnetic media, the disk-drive head, and the drive assembly) or Kodak did on the FunSaver (developing three different camera models as separate subprojects), enabled teams to see their way clear to progress. In Kodak's Factory of the Future project, there were too many goals that were not broken down into clearly defined subgroupings, making it difficult for the team to narrow the project to a scope they could own and commit to.

Another important mechanism for building team responsibility and empowerment was the physical co-location and full attention of team members. These provided a stronger sense of identity and ongoing problem solving, and resulted in broader outcomes. Dedication of the team members to a single project greatly facilitated the communication, sharing of concerns, and involvement in broader issues that helped the team quickly build its cohesion and identity.

A significant aspect of this staffing was including on the project team skills and abilities considered essential to project success, which strengthened the team's confidence that it could deliver expected results. Especially important were production people who would have to live with the results and yet were qualified to add value during the development process. The latter qualification was particularly crucial since it distinguished operating people who were viewed as "sitting in early" on the development effort to protect their own interests, from those who were there to serve as peers and add substantial value.

A major problem in Kodak's Factory of the Future project was that the line operators involved were seen as adjuncts or follow-on support, and not viewed as central to the initial development activities being conducted by design engineering. In contrast, on the DEC RA90 project, the Phoenix factory that was eventually to produce the magnetic media for the disk drive chose early on to send two of its people to Colorado Springs, the primary site of the project, for 18 months. While initially the two people might have been viewed as there to protect their division's interests, within a few months they developed a reputation for adding value to the entire project and created an increased sense of ownership and commitment on the part of the entire team.

Fundamental to the success of all the mechanisms mentioned above was giving teams freedom to act, and to bear the consequences of their actions, within the boundaries of the project and the team's responsibility as set by senior management. This is more than simple delegation. In the most successful projects, the teams accepted senior management's scope definitions and felt not only that they could take the actions needed for success, but that they were responsible for creating and managing development procedures as well. Effective use of this mechanism required balance and clear boundaries between the team's responsibilities and senior management's.

In all the Chaparral projects and in at least one project in each of the other four firms, such a balance was achieved. Top management felt in touch and up to speed throughout the project and the team felt appropriately in charge. However, on some projects, the team felt overly constrained, resulting in their failure to take initiative and responsibility. Other teams were given too much leeway, making it hard for top management to keep up to date, and resulting in the late intervention of top management after major mistakes had been made and significant time and resources lost.

It was at the team level of ownership and commitment that senior management's role was found to be most important. Senior management set the expectations and importance of individual projects—through their attention or lack of it. Similarly, it was senior management with whom the team "contracted" in agreeing to meet project goals and time lines. It was also senior management that gave the team the freedom to manage project activities as it saw fit, with senior management as a resource and periodic reviewer, not a judge and intervener. Finally, the team viewed senior management as the guarantor that their collective performance would be reflected equitably and appropriately in future career assignments and performance evaluations.

This relationship can be improved, or complicated, by the behavior of a project manager. A project manager can help bring together team members and senior management, but can also become an intermediary. And even if the project manager succeeds in bridging the gap, he or she is still responsible for generating team commitment if it is lacking. Management, for its part, can help the project manager succeed by making sure all employees understand the role a project manager must play. At Chaparral, so much work is organized into project teams that everyone understands and supports the responsibilities of a project manager, in part because many employees have served in that capacity, or know they someday will.

## Ensuring Support Throughout the Company[6]

In addition to individuals and the project team owning and committing to the success of a development project, for superior results the broader organization—including suppliers, support functions, and senior management—needs to achieve substantial ownership and commitment as well. That is, these other organizational units must feel empowered to direct their contributing activities and understand how they limit or enhance the project team's success. This is particularly important for two reasons. One is that, inevitably, a project team will not be able to do certain tasks alone or at all, and the effectiveness with which supporting organizations perform those tasks plays a critical role in project success. The other is that the timeliness with which such tasks are performed depends largely on the degree of ownership and commitment the broader organization develops for a project. However, this does not occur unless such groups are brought on board and made to feel they are vital to a project's success.

We observed a number of mechanisms that encouraged those not on the primary team to act in support of development projects. First among them was communicating a clear, measurable project goal across management and suppliers, and with support groups such as purchasing or sales, and outlining the contribution the project would make to overall business goals. As with the team, clarity and focus of goals helped. For example, when Fuji announced it would introduce a single-use camera in the United States, the distinct and measurable goal for Kodak's FunSaver project became beating Fuji in the U.S. market. The goal so crystallized the effort that it was easily and quickly communicated throughout a number of Kodak support organizations. Subsequently, getting cooperation in support work, which earlier had required considerable extra effort by the team, became much easier.

Building on a clear, measurable goal, a second mechanism that contributed to substantial ownership and commitment by the broader organization was active pursuit by the project team of broad participation by diverse groups. Rather than confining the majority of the responsibility, authority, and credit for development to an elite ensemble, bringing together a diverse group strengthened intellectual and emotional involvement. The broad involvement in the DEC RA90 project of diverse technical groups by dividing the effort into three subprojects promoted broad support. Care must be taken, however, not to dilute the guiding vision of a project; the Achilles heel of the RA90 was that, although each of the three subgroups had great ownership and commitment for their own tasks, none of them felt particularly responsible for the overall project; there wasn't even a dedicated project manager who had oversight of the work and could have attempted to tie the groups together.

One means by which project teams encouraged broader participation was by demonstrating their own level of commitment. For example, "betting the badge" conveyed to the broader organization that the team was fully committed and both needed and expected the help of others. Another was establishment by the team that the fundamental principle in the team's dealings with suppliers, support groups, and customers was mutual trust and respect. At Chaparral, violations of this principle have been made unacceptable through broad-based organizational norms. This is reinforced by the periodic assignment of project leadership to literally any part of the organization. In contrast, many problems in Kodak's Factory of the Future project could be traced to engineering's "knowing the answer" and not giving much "air time" or credibility to factory managers and operators.

When no overriding market or competitive pressure dictates strategic intent, broad-based support can be generated by frequent communication, review, and organizational discussion throughout a project's duration. This was achieved on the Kodak Chem 181 project by establishing two different steering committees, each with clear roles. One steering committee consisted of a broad set of management representatives; the other, a broad set of health and environmental specialists. The existence of the two committees meant they had to constantly interact, which caused employees in the various groups they represented to interact also, increasing project support and participation throughout the organization.

A variation of this mechanism used by Chaparral was to have line operators do the pre-project planning and analysis, conduct the project, and then be responsible for implementation. This of course required that career paths prepared operating people for such essential project tasks as organization and leadership. The failure to develop line people who knew how to add value and help manage the development process was a shortcoming in some of the firms we studied. Chaparral has gone well beyond providing a minimum cadre of team members and sought to make projects as common and natural as traditional operations management. The result has been that the vast majority of the organization is qualified and capable of playing a significant role in a development project. One of the things that distinguishes Chaparral from the other companies we studied is that it makes projects the rule rather than the exception. This not only provides a substantial pool of project participants but establishes a set of widely held norms and procedures, such as ways to track costs, request help, and measure performance, that require a minimum of special training and can be used effectively on a variety of projects.

Most of the other firms studied had difficulty finding a sufficient number of qualified people in marketing and production operations who could fully participate on development teams. As a result, teams were often made up largely of engineers; the non-engineering people were underrepresented, their opinions were undervalued, and their contributions were less than the project required. It was no surprise that many shortcomings might have been overcome had there been better-qualified and experienced contributors from the non-engineering functions. We concluded that part of the substantial ownership and commitment that permeated the engineering functions at places like HP, DEC, Kodak, and Ford could have been matched on the part of people from other functions had they felt as qualified and capable of managing and contributing to the project as their engineering counterparts. The willingness of key functional groups to create and apply such skills was an additional way the broader organization illustrated its commitment to development.

One of the approaches we observed for developing these critical skills among engineers seemed equally applicable to other employees. This was providing training and experience through graduated levels of assignment over a series of projects. In development engineering, it was not unusual for junior people to work on small projects and gradually be assigned to bigger projects and more responsible tasks. In marketing, production, purchasing, and other areas, that was not the general pattern. Rather, these functions seemed to consist of "specialists" who jumped into and out of different development teams, or generalists who could serve only as liaisons between the development teams and their department.

The better approach is to develop individuals who can add substantial value on the part of their function throughout the development effort and to then commit them to projects. The marketing group in many companies is a good example. Typically, marketing people make their input at the beginning of a project, then disappear until the project generates a physical product that can be tested or sold. By then, however, it is often too late for marketing people to make a difference, at least without seriously affecting the project's time line. Marketing can be much more useful if its people become part of the development team and stay with it for the duration. To generate commitment on the marketing people's part, management has to make it clear that it is part of a marketing person's job, and one that will affect his or her career path, to be of value throughout the entire development process. Management, then, has to be supportive, and train marketing people in ways to help during seemingly unrelated stages of the process, such as prototyping, and has to not move or promote marketing people out of a project while it is in progress.

A final mechanism that proved useful in developing broad-based ownership and commitment beyond the team level was evolving a set of organizational norms that valued fully integrated solutions to project goals as well as technical, specialist solutions. The efforts taken by the DeskJet team illustrate ways in which such norms can be achieved. Recognizing the value of the overall business results of a project, as well as the value of specific technical results, and achieving balance between them was a big part of this. DEC's RA90 project got unbalanced; by directing all attention to the three subprojects, the required systems skills and knowledge were never fully developed prior to introduction, and the operating organization later found itself with three disparate pieces to be integrated.

If nothing else, this corporate level of ownership and buy-in is important for one simple reason: as markets mature, the locus of competitive advantage invariably shifts from strict, technical performance to integrated systems solutions. This requires an operating organization that can influence and contribute to the team's solution, take over new products and processes without breaking stride, and capture, retain, and apply what is learned on one project to subsequent development efforts.

## INTEGRATING THE COMPONENTS OF OWNERSHIP AND COMMITMENT

The sheer number of mechanisms discussed above shows that managers can influence ownership and commitment in many ways. If they are not careful, however, managers can also misuse these mechanisms, often inadvertently, compromising a project. In addition, a number of day-to-day issues can add to the complexity and challenge of building ownership and commitment at the level of the individual, the project team, and the broader organization. This section addresses these issues, and suggests ways to avoid the underutilization or misuse of otherwise positive actions by describing two of the projects studied at Hewlett-Packard and the circumstances that led to strong levels of ownership and commitment on the one and only weak levels on the other. In fact, at each of the five companies, we were struck by the differences observed across projects and the management behaviors that contributed to those differences. The two projects are the DeskJet, a printer, and the HP150, a personal computer terminal.

### The DeskJet Printer

Based on management leadership at the division level and a systematic approach to focus attention and effort throughout the division, the DeskJet project adopted policies, procedures, and operating practices that resulted in strong ownership and commitment. At the level of individual development team members, it was understood that team assignments would last for the duration of the project—reassignments and transfers would wait until after project completion. In addition, project success was identified as a significant and necessary part of team member career paths; while assigned to this project, personal performance and recognition were largely project based. Finally, everyone on the development team was expected to provide innovative ideas and rewarded for doing so.

Individual ownership and commitment on the DeskJet were complemented with extensive support at the team level. Beginning with clear and bounded project goals and objectively measured performance standards, the team worked out with management respective roles and responsibilities. To keep the team small and facilitate physical co-location of individuals on the core team, management intentionally subdivided the project, giving the print head responsibility to another site. Finally, the team was staffed with the requisite skills for project success.

At the division level, strong ownership and commitment was reinforced by senior management defining and then sharing broadly and repeatedly the goals and strategy of the business, as well as this project's role and contribution to them. In addition, senior management has played an ongoing role by sharing and recognizing project status throughout the organization, supplying support and resources for training, and focusing the objectives and resources of specialized support groups on providing service to the development team. This last type of support was facilitated greatly by the adoption of monthly (periodic) prototyping. The result was mutual trust and respect, a sense of empowerment that extended down to the level of the individual contributor, and initial DeskJet success followed by a string of winning development efforts. **Table 6.2** summarizes some of the many mechanisms used by the Vancouver division to achieve these results.

Ford Motor Company's FX15 project to develop a compressor for an automotive air conditioner used almost all the mechanisms described for HP's DeskJet project. At the individual level, key design

**Table 6.2**  Mechanisms That Determine the Degree of Ownership and Commitment

| Levels and Mechanisms | HP DeskJet (strong) | HP150 (weak) |
|---|---|---|
| *Individual Level* | | |
| Staffing | Continuity throughout project | Continuity limited to engineers on core team |
| Performance criteria | Project based | Functionally based |
| Career opportunities | Project dependent | Project independent |
| Recognition | Project based | Task and division based |
| Innovation | Expected continually | Expected but risks not managed |
| *Team Level* | | |
| Project goals | Clear and bounded | Broad |
| Measurable standards | Externally defined | Internally based |
| Project size | Primarily within division | Large, cross-divisional |
| Proximity | Physical co-location | Dispersed except for core team |
| Membership | Essential tasks/skills | Dominant functions |
| Delegation | Empowered, with consequences | Responsibility without full authority |
| Management | Clear roles | Shifting roles |
| *Corporate Level* | | |
| Goals | Shared, fit with business | Conflicts |
| Project needs | Corporate support encouraged | We versus them |
| Basis of action | Trust and respect | Power and status |
| Project status | Widely shared | Not widely known |
| Training | Pervasive | Limited |

engineers were empowered to think boldly about competing with Nippon-Denso in the design and development of a new generation compressor. Early on, a clear sense of continuity in assignment, development performance as critical to individual performance, high expectations on project goals, and commitment to innovation were established among core team members. Many of these mechanisms were put in place precisely because of the critical competitive situation faced by Ford's climate control division in relation to Nippon-Denso.

At the team level, clear goals, ambitious targets, and a strong project focus were crucial in fostering outstanding ownership and commitment. With Nippon-Denso's next generation product as a clear target, the Ford division's business goals were tied directly to the success of the FX15 project. The project team and management jointly established ambitious goals that served to galvanize the team and were reinforced by decisions to dedicate and co-locate team members. Management took steps to ensure operating support from downstream units such as parts manufacturing and operations. Additionally, critical support activities such as testing and prototype building understood from senior management's direction and actions that the project was make or break for the division—the division's ticket to future production activities. Without it, the division was unlikely to become an in-house manufacturer of compressors. Thus at all three levels, strong ownership and commitment became realities on the FX15.

## The HP150 Project

In response to IBM's initial PC introduction in 1981, Hewlett-Packard adapted the follow-on project to its 120 terminal, the HP150, to be both a terminal and a PC product capable of running IBM's operating system, MS-DOS. This decision, made by HP's senior management group, was seen as a way to integrate technologies from several HP divisions into the HP150 "system." Unfortunately, HP had virtually no mechanisms in place to create ownership and commitment for such a cross-divisional development effort. HP's autonomous division practices unintentionally created a pattern of policies, procedures, and operating guidelines that undermined ownership and commitment on a project such as the 150.

The 150 represented HP's first entry into the computer marketplace, its first use of dealers as a distribution channel, its first attempt at building to inventory in a centralized warehousing structure, its first strong need to work closely with corporate procurement to ensure quality from suppliers, and its first introduction of design for manufacturability on a product that would be assembled worldwide. In retrospect, this represented an overwhelming set of largely new managerial complications.

Given the complexities of the project, strong leadership and commitment were clearly required. Unfortunately, although there was strong commitment on the part of the HP150 project team itself, leadership on the team as well as from senior management was lacking. The project manager was unable to maintain control over the project because his decisions were often overridden by his superiors. The corporate players were not close enough to the project to know all its intricacies, yet felt comfortable interfering. This left the project manager and the development team in the difficult position of having to respond to frequent changes in direction despite knowing that the new directions were misguided. There were too many cooks in the kitchen, each preparing a different recipe. Stated another way, the team did not feel fully empowered and, in response, modified its ownership and commitment.

The organizational environment was made more complex by the number of relationships that the team was expected to develop and maintain with other HP divisions. Keyboards and disk drives were particularly problematic.

Keyboard development was originally given to the Fort Collins, Colorado, division. The HP150 team required that the keyboard cost only $25 and that it have a quality advantage over other keyboards. The existing Fort Collins keyboard cost $100, and the general manager of the division did not believe that the team's request merited a high priority. Fort Collins' first priority was keyboards for its own products, which were workstations. No one pushed them, and keyboard design and manufacturing rapidly became a bottleneck to the HP150 project. Finally the keyboard was brought back by the primary team for a "crash design." It went through design, tooling development, and production ramp-up in six months. To give it flexibility, the team decided to use a unique but untested keycap print technology called sublimation printing, which made development all the more difficult.

The disk drive story was similar. The Greeley, Colorado, division had responsibility for disk drives in HP. This meant that they maintained control over the design, technology, pricing, and scheduling of the drives. The HP150 team was held captive by Greeley's demands. In looking out for its own well-being, the Greeley division leaders priced the new disk drive so they could make a reasonable profit on the HP150 "contract." This made it harder for the 150 team to achieve the expected margins.

Despite the internal let-down, the manufacturing people working on the 150 got off to a good start. This project was the division's first attempt at design for manufacturability. Manufacturing was brought into the design process early on and had some influence on design. A decision was made, for example, to limit complexity by limiting the number of different color screens that would be made available. Unfortunately, this decision was apparently made without any input from marketing; it turned out customers wanted more color options. Again, the 150 project required cross-functional ownership and commitment beyond the past patterns and practices then common at HP.

The most difficult task facing manufacturing was determining how to manage suppliers under conditions of great uncertainty. Their task was complicated by the need to work with a newly formed Corporate Procurement organization. Divisions were being asked to pool their supply requirements at a central location, from which HP expected to get additional leverage over suppliers by making large-volume purchases. Suppliers were understandably wary.

Marketing people, for their part, were not involved early on, thus no comprehensive marketing plan was developed and committed to. There was a plan for the HP150 as a terminal for the HP3000 computer, but when the emphasis shifted to a PC, few changes were made in the marketing strategy because no one recognized that the different set of users would want different configuration and because marketing's ownership of the PC version was very limited. **Table 6.2** summarizes the many mechanisms affecting ownership and commitment on the HP150 project and contrasts them with those on the HP DeskJet project.

The way in which the patterns of decisions and practices exhibited on the DeskJet and 150 projects influence the handling of ongoing challenges to ownership and commitment in development efforts provides insight as to why their cumulative effect is so substantial. A key concern is getting those who come to a project after it is well underway to feel an equal part of the team and share responsibility for its successful outcome. A variation of this same concern is getting commitment from individuals in support groups whose involvement in the project is only temporary. These challenges are difficult to address for at least two reasons: first, new arrivals have not taken part in resolving the original project definition and thus it is not "their" definition; second, relationships and interactions have already been established and newcomers are viewed, and view themselves, as outsiders.

On the DeskJet, division managers addressed this challenge head on by taking the time necessary to make sure that new people understood what was expected of them, and how their role was integral to the project's success. New people—especially those not on the core development team—were convinced that their roles were contributory, not just add-on. At the same time, the project leader and other managers took steps to make sure the longstanding members of the team also understood that new people's roles were crucial, and that it was part of the team's work to fully integrate them.

These measures helped, but in reality the DeskJet project addressed this challenge of late arrivals or temporary team members by minimizing its occurrence. For example, the division established the expectation that a team member would remain with the project until its completion, so that turnover caused by promotion was avoided. Furthermore, they trained team members, particularly those in marketing and manufacturing, in a sufficient breadth of activity and adopted periodic monthly prototyping so they could effectively contribute throughout the project's duration. They also minimized the number of individuals in support groups from whom a substantial commitment was required for the success of a project by involving the entire division in the project, broadening the skills and responsibilities of people on the team, and narrowing the set of tasks subcontracted to the print head group located at another site. When new people were assigned to the project in mid stream or existing participants took on an expanded role, the project leader spent substantial amounts of time bringing those people up to speed on the team's thinking, linking them to others on the team, and ensuring that communication paths were modified to include those people appropriately.

In sharp contrast, on the 150 project there were many complaints about the lack of ownership among latecomers to the team, especially those in other divisions, but little explicit action to change the situation. Scarce resources, competing projects, and alternative agendas, together with physical distances and limited contact, guaranteed a large number of part-timers. Since many subteams were not co-located, it was difficult for the project manager to sense who needed to be better integrated and to get around to visit each subgroup. Finally, with many people contributing to several projects, many they perceived as being higher priority, they focused naturally on their functional tasks rather than the 150 project as their point of reference. Little wonder that ownership and commitment to the 150 and its results seemed to stay at such low levels, in spite of what senior management considered its concern and involvement.

This comparison of the DeskJet and 150 projects at HP highlights three very important lessons regarding ownership and commitment. First, even within the same corporate organization, results can vary widely because the number of mechanisms and their application are so dependent on attention to detail throughout a project's duration and its full range of tasks. Second, ownership and commitment at one level—such as the core team on the 150—does not ensure equivalent ownership and commitment at other levels. For solid success, it must be achieved consistently at all three levels. Third, over time an organization can strengthen significantly its patterns and practices, enhancing its level of ownership and commitment across all projects. At HP, the DeskJet project—initiated four years after the 150 project— benefited significantly from the lessons learned and changes adopted by the corporation as a result of the 150 and several other projects. These same three lessons also had been learned by each of the other four companies we studied.

## POTENTIAL PROBLEMS FROM STRONG OWNERSHIP AND COMMITMENT

There were two types of situations observed in this study where having achieved strong ownership and commitment subsequently created its own set of problems and challenges. The first was where a project that had such buy-in needed to be terminated. While it would be wonderful if all projects could be completed successfully, that outcome is not realistic. Changes in priorities, available resources, competitor's moves, and technical developments sometimes make stopping a project the most appropriate course of action. But companies encountered an unavoidable problem when a project had to be stopped: disengaging team members from the project while still recognizing and rewarding their performance and the importance of ownership and commitment, so they would not be undermined on subsequent projects.

Two of the projects studied—the arc saw at Chaparral and the Factory of the Future at Kodak—were disbanded before completion, the former because of technical problems and the latter because of reprioritizing of business objectives. Two guidelines emerged from the disengagement process of these projects. First was helping the team recognize that senior management often must step in to make tough choices, without pointing fingers at individuals or the team. The more successful the team had been at generating ownership and commitment, the less likely it was that the team would be able to step back on their own and see the need for termination. Senior management had to accept that responsibility, and carry it out in a way that separated the need for such a decision from the substantial commitment that the team had demonstrated.

The second guideline was recognizing that the organization, the team, and individual contributors needed time to accept the inevitability of a decision to terminate a project. In both Chaparral and Kodak, this was done using a gradual phase out, which proved sufficient at Chaparral but only partially effective at Kodak. In the arc saw project, which had attempted to develop the industry's first electric-arc saw for cutting volumes of steel, a senior executive initially made the decision to move on to other options, but did not actually remove the experimental equipment from the production line where it had been located in parallel with other machines. This allowed a low level of experimentation to continue for a few months as the former development team identified and tried what they thought were solutions to the primary technical problems. After a few months, the senior executive removed the arc saw from the production line, but left it set up in a corner of the factory. Subsequently, the equipment was moved outside of the factory, but left on site, so it could be brought back should new solutions be identified.

In the Factory of the Future project, a major review was instigated by a group of managers who were concerned about the project's progress and direction. Over the ensuing few months, individual team members were reassigned and a target date for making a decision on the project's continuation was set. But by the time that date was reached, most team members had struggled too long over what to do with the project, and decided in defeat that the project should be terminated and replaced by a different project. In this case, additional input from senior management might have brought the issue to a head much sooner, saving considerable resources and smoothing reassignment to other projects. Kodak's approach adhered to the second guideline of giving team members time to adjust, but not to the first, of helping team members accept that senior management at times has to step in and close a project.

While the cost of not shutting down a project immediately can be substantial, and was in both of these cases, the damage done to ownership and commitment on subsequent projects would have "cost" the company even more if an immediate, irreversible shutdown had been dictated by senior management. The gradual release conveyed the notion that the original project was not necessarily in error, but rather that management was making a judgment that results were not forthcoming and other options needed to be pursued. Once the bulk of the organization agreed with that judgment and an alternative project was underway, it was possible to disengage team members without damaging their long-term ability to own and commit to future projects.

A second type of situation where having achieved strong ownership and commitment created another set of problems was where a project has been subdivided into subprojects to make it more manageable. While each subproject developed strong ownership and commitment, it appeared to work at the expense of ownership and control at the level of the overall project. The DEC RA90 project provides a classic example.

To get the required technical work accomplished, DEC senior management divided the effort into three subprojects—the media, heads, and drive assembly. Although all three had to be integrated to be able to call the entire project a success, much of the ownership and commitment was focused on the subprojects, since that was where it was initially required. Management clearly underestimated the importance and challenge of integrating the work of the three subteams and the need for ownership and commitment at that level. One senior manager described the RA90 effort as akin to three fully loaded freight trains, each going down its own track. Each train built up its own momentum, but collectively the trains did not arrive at the same time or even at the same station. By the time the need for total project ownership and commitment became apparent, the subteams felt such empowerment that management was unable to get them to shift their focus. Failure to gain ownership and commitment at the level of the total project was a major source of added cost and delays on the RA90.

The cases we examined made it clear that on large projects, dividing the effort into subprojects and managing the ongoing integration of them was essential to success. The trick was to ensure that ownership and commitment at one level (most often that of the subproject) did not come at the expense of achieving it at the higher level. We identified three guidelines helpful in addressing this issue. First, commitment at multiple levels must focus not only on technical purposes but also on business purposes. Each subteam, as well as the overall team, must understand how their activities tie into the major goals of the total project, with success on subproject goals linked directly to success on overall project goals. Second, each subteam needs to interact on a regular and credible basis with the other subteams, so that "current thinking" is shared and modifications that are required across subprojects occur in a timely manner. Third, appropriate management capacity must be committed at each level of the project in order to provide the attention, energy, and leadership needed to make mid-course corrections and maintain ongoing integration.


## HOW TO SMARTLY MANAGE THE PATH
## TO IMPROVEMENT[7]

On all 20 projects we studied, the individual teams and their companies were aware that they needed and wanted to enhance the ownership and commitment felt by all. Yet their effectiveness varied

**Table 6.3**  Stages of Ownership and Commitment at Three Organizational Levels

| Individuals | Project Team | Corporate Management and Support Groups |
|---|---|---|
| **Stage 1**  Do not believe individual efforts will impact project success; do not consider it appropriate to measure contribution in terms of project success; want their work judged independent of overall project | No mission, nor any attempt at one; all power resides in the functional organization and work within the function is done according to standard procedures; little team identity | Reacts to project needs only when someone complains or project is in trouble; business unit success is considered largely independent of project success |
| **Stage 2**  See their efforts impacting their own function's contribution, and want functional peers to judge their work | Each function has its own mission; function strives to do what is needed to achieve its agreed upon mission; function identifies with its subproject | Project response depends on workload and personality of team leader; varies widely; link between project results and business unit weak at best |
| **Stage 3**  Recognize interaction of their function with others, but want the help of others to be given extra credit; primary responsibility is success of their function's contribution | Clear mission stated, but not fully operationalized or accepted; functional subteams have power and control over their assigned tasks and their execution; strong team recognition but usually by functional subteam | Responds to requests when asked and given clear assignment; projects considered to be very important to business success but requires continued reminders as to why and how |
| **Stage 4**  Confident that their individual outcome will influence project success; committed to the entire set of project goals as their performance goals; function is thought of as a discipline that is available to contribute | Clear mission, shared and accepted by all because they helped develop it; shared authority and power over the project and how its work is done; team identity is stronger than functional identity during the project | Consistent, proactive support of the project mission; project success considered primary means of achieving personal and group goals; focused involvement early in details of project |

widely. Recognizing the current stage of ownership and commitment and adopting a handful of management actions seemed to explain the bulk of this variation (see **Table 6.3**).

In several instances we found a fundamental problem: management did not recognize that there were three levels of ownership and commitment that had to be watched over and that each needed to move to a more advanced stage. Without understanding that individual, team, and corporate dedication required different kinds of efforts, they could not put in place the mechanisms needed to ensure strong ownership and commitment.

A second action that greatly helped or hindered was the degree to which managers designed, staffed, and managed a project for the purpose of improving ownership and commitment. In the most successful settings, a senior manager knew when to slow down the initial definition of a project so the team could get on board, and when to push the team to move ahead rapidly. Numerous steps like this can be taken to improve ownership and commitment. In many of the projects we studied, serious trouble developed because management's shepherding, pacing, and building of the team's ownership and commitment was absent or lapsed at one or more critical junctures.

We found a related lesson on a broader level. Those firms most successful in generating ownership and commitment did so not just on a few key projects, but consistently across all projects. They established a set of corporate-wide norms, systems, and expectations that supported higher stages of ownership and commitment. Furthermore, they continually worked to weed out behaviors that hindered empowerment at all three levels. This did not mean abandoning historical strengths or adopting a set formula. Rather, the companies tailored the attributes of each project so that progress would be made in a manner consistent with the larger framework. For example, at DEC, HP, and Ford, engineering had long been the dominant function. The most successful efforts to improve ownership and commitment in these firms were done in ways that modified and complemented that dominance, rather than in ways that would threaten it. Since engineering was the function of highest leverage, actions such as co-locating development teams and making career changes in sync with project completions were done in the technical functions first. Subsequently, changes in the marketing and manufacturing functions that complemented those pursuits were undertaken.

This approach, of course, only succeeded when managers planned for it in advance. Such planning is another trait common to those firms that most successfully generated ownership and commitment. In these firms, senior management developed specific plans to build awareness within management and the ranks of the leverage that ownership and commitment can deliver. They familiarized their people with the various characteristics of ownership and commitment, and with the mechanisms available for improving these qualities. This resulted in a systematic effort that was broad-based in the organization, rather than localized efforts that focused only on "special" projects. There are steps managers can take to improve ownership and commitment, but managers have to plan how the steps will be pursued, and they have to promote the steps of the plan to everyone in the company. Chaparral is the epitome of this approach; the firm's top executives have made it clear that ownership and commitment form the basis for the corporate philosophy, and managers are continually making sure the setting they establish for work is in harmony with this philosophy.

When a project does not mesh with the philosophy, changes must be made, which leads to our final point. That is, in each of the companies that established the most successful settings, management was willing to change a wide variety of things, often simultaneously, in order to accomplish real, lasting improvements in ownership and commitment. Over an extended time horizon, virtually every system and procedure in these organizations becomes a candidate for change, if so doing aids this effort. Such sustained pursuit of the objective signals management's true priorities, and makes the difference between distinctive levels of ownership and commitment in development projects and traditional explanations of failure.

## CHAPTER 7

# Prototyping: Rapid Learning and Early Testing

$T$he competitive pressures of recent years have imposed severe demands on the marketplace. World-class products and processes must be completed in minimum time and provide the greatest possible value to customers through their features, quality, and lifetime costs.[1] Development projects are no longer endurance races; they are sprints. Companies who want to lead the way to the finish line must get up to full speed quickly and cannot afford any missteps.

In order to compete in this manner, a development team has to learn rapidly. The best development projects now rely on the integration of many functions and on concurrent engineering, and in these efforts prototypes are the key to learning, reduced mistakes, and increased system integrity.

Prototypes are one of the most powerful tools a development team can use to resolve important questions quickly and unambiguously. In addition, they provide a common understanding and integrating force for all members of the team, regardless of their differences in function and culture. Yet, far too often, companies do not create enough prototypes nor do they create them early enough to resolve important uncertainties. Furthermore, those that are made are often inadequate to prove out performance in production, compounding rather than solving problems. The traditional model of prototyping is not effective. A new view must be taken. Prototyping is no longer done to answer questions at phase review time; it is done to allow the team to progress swiftly and intelligently through the incremental steps of development. Prototypes are no longer the exclusive domain of the engineer-designer. They are the common language that knits together the development team, the company that supports the team, and the team's eventual customers.

Although prototype usage is not the sole determinant of product or process success, the projects studied by the Manufacturing Vision Group confirm the thesis that effective and timely use of prototypes is crucial. But readers must take a broad view; by prototypes, we mean not only the physical embodiments of the nearly final products often made by craftsmen before production begins, but a series of representations, from early mockups and computer simulations to subsystem models, system-level engineering, and production prototypes. The best products and most efficient processes we observed came from teams that effectively used a variety of prototypes at strategic junctures during development.

Conversely, many of the projects that fell short were marked by a lack of awareness of critical issues, issues that the teams could have anticipated and resolved with earlier, more frequent, and more judicious use of prototypes. Other teams failed to develop system-level prototypes, which led to late detection of difficult problems that were only resolved at added expense, product complexity, and much delay, detracting from the quality of the product and in some cases accounting significantly for the project's termination.

Hewlett-Packard's team that produced the successful DeskJet inkjet printer displayed exemplary use of prototypes. The team started with breadboards to confirm the technology; studied a series of rapidly constructed prototypes to check out form, fit, and function; and evolved to prototypes that were tested for customer reaction and served as the basis for final tool design, thereby optimizing the chances for smooth product launch. Prototypes provided a common basis for everyone's work, unifying the contributions of marketing, manufacturing, and design. For HP, smart prototyping was instrumental in the speedy realization of a breakthrough product.

We begin this chapter by examining how judicious use of prototyping can be employed to optimize development projects, and how it can be employed to reduce such critical factors as overall cost, time, and risk. We then look at the diverse range of prototypes available to development teams, consider which are appropriate at what stages of a project, and relate how they can be used as a vehicle for team integration. We examine a number of projects in which prototyping was pivotal to success—or failure—and derive some lessons from the outcomes. Finally, we reaffirm the challenge: a company will ultimately fail without excellence in the broad prototyping capabilities described here. The cost is high if it is not done, yet the opportunities are great when practiced well.

## REDUCING COST, TIME, AND RISK

Rapid learning decreases uncertainty; thus, the effectiveness of prototyping depends on three critical factors: the timing of prototypes throughout a development program; the scope, or completeness, of each prototype; and the quality, or fidelity, of the prototype, defined by whether it is made with the same materials, parts, and processes that will be used during the actual production of saleable goods.

### Timing of Prototypes: The Window of Opportunity

Timing plays an absolutely critical role in the development of new products. The design latitude essential to creating the best balance between the fundamental cost of a product, its competitive features, and its quality is only attainable in the early stage of the development process. As shown in **Figure 7.1**, the real window of opportunity is in the period preceding layout of the final concept. After that decision point, the changes that are possible can only have a marginal effect on the basic product. Most project managers we talked with agreed with the axiom that during the time spanning roughly the first 15 percent of a development project, about 85 percent of the ultimate cost of the product, including the use, maintenance, and disposal stages, will be set and committed (see **Figure 3.2**).[2] Hence rapid

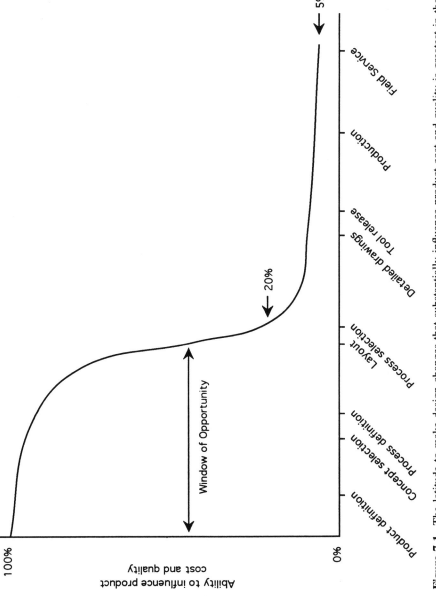

**Figure 7.1.** The latitude to make design changes that substantially influence product cost and quality is greatest in the early stage of a development project. The real window of opportunity is in the period preceding layout of the final concept. Early prototypes provide the most effective means for achieving the learning essential to sound decisions during this critical phase.

205

learning and the ability to make critical decisions early are essential for product success. Early prototypes provide one of the most effective means for achieving the learning essential to sound decisions.

Because substantial learning accompanies each prototype stage, it follows that early prototyping with subsequent updates at important junctures can provide several major benefits. These include a reduction in total development time, a reduction in the risk introduced by innovation, and the early detection of problems, which leads to the avoidance of expensive, late design changes.

Each prototyping stage provides new information and a major learning experience for the entire team. This is summed up graphically in **Figure 7.2**. The graph shows that a project with more frequent, high-quality prototypes provides earlier learning experiences that drive the project more rapidly toward convergence and thereby enhance the likelihood of sound decisions and ultimate project success.

## Limiting Risk with Early Prototypes

In competitive product lines, significant innovation is vital and must be achieved within very tight time schedules. But innovation compounds the risk of extended development time or even failure, which always comes with ventures into unfamiliar territory. Because of time pressures and reduced design flexibility, problems that crop up late in the development cycle have serious consequences. Ferreting out problems early, with a strategy of rapid prototyping, allows for corrections at the time of greatest project adaptability, thereby reducing risk.

This approach is used regularly at Chaparral Steel. Early prototyping of key elements and full-scale testing is a standard part of Chaparral's development practice, and it has been instrumental in elevating the small company into a leadership position in the steel industry. Similarly, early prototyping proved fundamental to success in many projects carried out by several of the companies we studied. For example, strategic use of prototypes made during Kodak's FunSaver project, to develop a disposable camera, provided invaluable insight into user reactions, which led to an innovative and refined product.

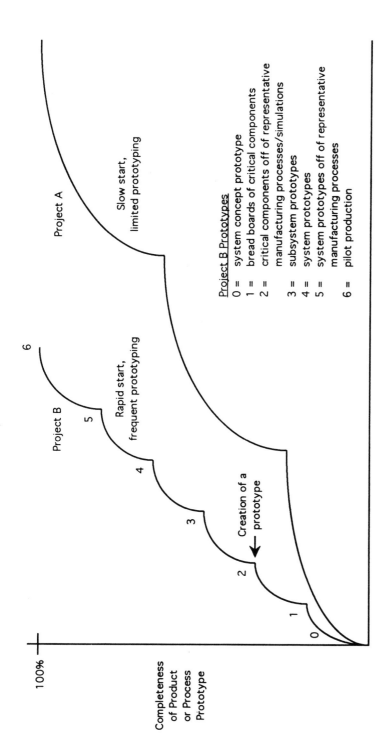

**Figure 7.2.** Because major learning accompanies each prototype made, a project that follows a course of frequent, early prototypes is driven more rapidly toward completion than a project characterized by only a few prototypes built at extended intervals. Early prototyping promotes a reduction in total development time, a reduction in the risk introduced by innovation, and the early detection of problems that leads to the avoidance of expensive, late design changes.

207

**Table 7.1**  Cost of Engineering Changes at Various Stages in
Development of Electromechanical Systems

| Stage | Description | Average Cost per Change |
|---|---|---|
| 1 | Predictive simulations | $4,000 or less |
| 2 | Testing, before product release | $20,000 |
| 3 | After production release | $100,000 |

For further information, see W. E. Dacey, "Concurrent Design for Product/Process," 4th Design for Manufacturability Conference, October 1990.

## Minimizing Late Design Changes

The process of development is by its nature a process of change. But when extensive design changes are introduced late in the development cycle they can undermine even the best of product visions, because they invariably upset the optimum balance between the features, cost, and quality required of a world-class product. In the long term, the negative consequences of late changes can only lead to costly, inferior products and can permanently pervade a company by creating a demoralized work force, poor productivity, and severely delayed schedules.[3]

Not only do the adverse consequences of change accumulate quickly with advancing phases of product development, but the cost of change also grows drastically. **Table 7.1** summarizes the exponential growth in the cost of implementing change as product development proceeds through its basic stages.

The quantity, timing, and quality of design changes constitute important measures of the effectiveness of product development programs. The impact of design-change patterns on product quality has been examined in independent studies.[4] An important insight from this work is shown in **Figure 7.3**. Striking differences are shown in both the time required for a development project to reach product launch and the rate of issuance of engineering changes. Simply put, if more changes are made early in the program due to prototyping, the total number of changes across the duration of the program are dramatically less, and the product can be launched much sooner.

A slow buildup in the rate of issuance of change notices stems from at least two sources. One source is a slow start to a project,

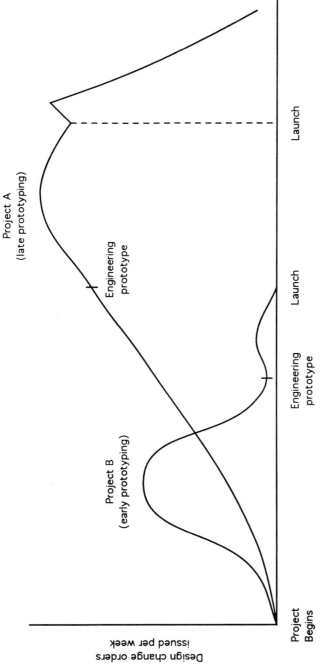

Design change orders
issued per week

Project Begins

Engineering prototype

Launch

Engineering prototype

Launch

Project A
(late prototyping)

Project B
(early prototyping)

Engineering prototype

**Figure 7.3.** If more changes are made early in a program due to prototyping, the total number of changes across the duration of the program is dramatically less, and the product is launched much sooner. This scenario is shown as curve B; the entire team is quickly brought to full strength and frequent models and prototypes are made, even if they are rough. Many projects typically have a slow buildup in the rate of issuance of change notices, as shown in curve A; the peak in engineering changes virtually coincides with product launch. Under the severe time pressure that this creates, first shipments may be made regardless of problems. Changes are then implemented at a furious pace even as shipments grow, invariably leading to products that will fall short of customer expectations. (Source: L. Sullivan, "The Seven Stages in Company-Wide Control," *Quality Progress*, May 1986.)

characterized by an insufficiently small staff and a lack of emphasis on error detection. The second source is a preoccupation on the part of the team with subsystem-level problems, and a turning of attention to system level issues only late in the cycle. In both patterns, the team size grows only after problems have been uncovered. In these substandard efforts the first truly representative models of a product are often only constructed on the actual production line, during the ramp-up-to-production stages. Major problems may be uncovered at this critical time: production parts that do not function in the same way as the hand-made models, system interactions that are uncovered for the first time, and unanticipated difficulties due to subtle effects.

This deficient scenario is reflected in **Figure 7.3** in the pattern for Project A. Note that the peak in engineering changes for such projects typically coincides with product launch. Under the severe time pressure to meet the product release plan, first shipments may be made on schedule regardless of problems. Changes are then implemented at a furious pace even as shipments grow. Clearly, this pattern invariably leads to products that at best do not meet world-class standards, and will likely fall short of customer expectations, jeopardizing sales, the whole product line, possibly even the company's future.

A case we studied was Ford's project to build the 1988 Lincoln Continental, a luxury car based on an existing Taurus platform. Late changes proved very costly. Early in the program styling considerations prevailed over engineering concerns. This led to a severely compacted front end that left minimal space for the engine cooling system. Extreme overheating problems under some conditions were discovered only late in the program. Since so much of the system was already committed by that time, and tooling was well underway, it was not possible to introduce the relatively simple modifications an ideal solution would have allowed. Furthermore, the time available for finding a viable solution was by then severely limited by the impending date for product launch. A delay would have threatened the entire program. With a solution urgently needed regardless of cost, a massive quick-fix program led to a complex, costly patchwork. It succeeded in cooling the engine, but detracted from the reliability, cost, and performance of the product. This marginal solution remains under the hood of each car, unalterable for the entire life of the product.

A superior approach to design changes is one in which rapid prototyping is used to flush out problems (**Figure 7.3**, Project B). In this scenario the entire project team is quickly brought to full strength. Firm goals are set early in the project, and system-level concepts are quickly defined as initial prototypes are built and tested. Early problem detection is achieved by the frequent modeling or construction of prototypes that are characterized by a reasonably high representativeness of parts and processes. The intent of such early prototyping is not to seek perfection but to gain essential knowledge.

To make rapid prototyping possible, development teams must be fully integrated from the beginning. If manufacturing people are so integrated, even the earliest prototypes can reflect the realities of production procedures. Early prototyping will require that management invest more money up front to reduce longer-term risk. The strategy emphasizes quick turn-around—which requires rapid prototypes to check out important ideas quickly and to avoid at a later stage the costly discovery that major redesign is necessary. To implement this strategy the team must enjoy priority access to prototyping resources such as simulation software, an extensive DFM database, and rapid prototyping facilities. Frequent early prototyping may even result in a later release of the final engineering drawings, but the ensuing development process, ramp-up to production, and early volume manufacturing will be much smoother so that in the end the product will get out the door faster and will have cost less to develop. Allowing more time to reach early milestones actually leads to a shorter time to delivery.

The rapid construction of many prototypes affords more opportunities to quickly identify and remedy problems. Rapid evaluation and prompt feedback by the entire organization is possible when multiple copies are made of prototypes at crucial stages of development. Thus marketing can assess competitive features and customer response, manufacturing can evaluate producibility and cost, while design checks function, system compatability, and reliability. Companies that followed such a scheme while limiting changes to essential issues were able to manage the process of change more effectively—that is, integrating changes into a uniform design and rapidly resolving conflict by judicious trade-offs.

With a comprehensive program of build, test, and refine, subsystems can be extensively developed with adequate assurance of full system compatibility. Companies that follow this strategy of early and rapid prototyping make more changes per week in the early stages of product development. Ideally, the rate of issuance of change orders reaches its peak roughly one-third of the way through the total development period, then rapidly decays to minor proportions about two-thirds through the cycle. In the wait-until-it's-perfect approach, design changes only begin to peak two-thirds of the way through a program, or even later, resulting in a crash effort to iron out problems during ramp-up and early production—a dangerous strategy.

An important aspect of the early-change pattern is that late changes are not only fewer, but different in nature. The pattern is indicative of a fundamental difference in the strategy by which development programs are executed. These kinds of late changes tend to be of relatively limited scope, and consist primarily of refinements of features that enhance manufacturing or reduce cost. Radical changes that might follow from late-breaking insights are deferred to the next product generation. This strategy is equally valid for processes as well as products; at Chaparral Steel, prototyping is done virtually every step along the way in developing a new process, and representativeness is ensured because the prototype processes are tried out right on operating production lines.

## Quality Prototypes That Improve Manufacturability

The development approaches observed by the Vision Group consistently demonstrated that the effectiveness of a project is strongly tied not only to the timing and frequency of prototypes, but to their quality as well. Quality of prototypes can be expressed in terms of two criteria: design representativeness, and process representativeness.

Design representativeness is a measure of how well the prototype reflects the detailed intent of the design. Process representativeness is a measure of the extent to which intended production processes are used or adequately considered in making the prototype. We observed two common problems that arose from the failure to execute quality prototypes, and both seriously impacted project timing and effectiveness.

The first problem stemmed from the failure to model the entire system in early studies, so that system-level concerns went ignored until a very late stage. Digital Equipment Corp.'s RA90 project, to develop a high-density disk drive for computers, fell prey to this oversight. The project hinged on the integration of three major subsystems, all of which required substantial innovation. Because of the initial intense focus on technology feasibility rather than product issues, prototypes were made only of each subsystem. There was no effort to create early system-level prototypes for the purpose of coordinating work across the three interdependent subsystems.

Any inclination to make system-level tests was further discouraged by slow feedback from each subsystem prototype step and prototype cycles that were out of synch with each other. For example, the thin-film head for reading the disk took over one year to fully develop and test, while the other subsystem prototypes typically took several months to complete. As a result, when the components were combined at the eleventh hour important problems were revealed. Because each group had emphasized local optimization, major effort was required to integrate the parts into a satisfactory product. This delayed the final delivery of the product, raised the internal costs of the program, and actually led to the compromise of several important features that could have been optimized had prototypes been used earlier to improve the integration of the subsystems.

A second type of problem arose from failures to build prototypes with the intended production processes. When prototypes are limited to laboratory mockups or are made in model shops that are isolated from the ultimate production organization, important learning is lost. It is one thing to make a very few accurate parts as required at a prototype stage. It is quite another when large-volume production is needed, involving very different tools, yields, quality, and levels of variability.

We found a general need to use prototyping as a learning basis for production processes, rather than solely for design feasibility. If this is pursued, the production process will be more efficient, less costly, and will require fewer changes during startup. What's more, we found that as programs shifted from the prototype phase to initial production, serious quality problems arose if the prototypes had not been used to check out production processes.

An apparently common problem was noted in several programs during the ramp-up to production—an initial inability of both in-house producers and key outside suppliers to match in production the quality they provided in prototypes. To avoid this problem, production-type manufacturing methods must be used or at least deliberately simulated in the manufacture of prototype parts. Furthermore, the parts should have been made with a high degree of conformance to original design intent.

Also involved in this difficulty was a general lack of attention to the tolerance question: How wide a range of feature variation can be tolerated without adversely affecting product quality? This problem is poorly understood by most engineers and is a common source of problems at product launch. Prototypes can contribute to understanding of tolerances before production begins. New developments in methodologies for addressing this problem using prototyping and computer modeling are also beginning to be implemented in the United States in limited applications. These are discussed a bit later in the chapter.

Failure to use prototype construction as a learning process for production led to several problems for both Ford and its suppliers during the FX-15 project, a major program to develop for the first time in-house a compressor for automobile air conditioners. Several problems complicated the effort. For example, although compressor castings machined in Ford's model shop revealed no dimensional problems, the first units made with production tools disclosed serious out-of-roundness. After much consternation it was discovered that during prototype construction the model-shop machinist had encountered and solved the problem by making some clever fixture innovations. But he failed to report them to the engineering organization. The out-of-roundness problem and the machinist's solution were unknown to the production planners until the production system went on line. The necessary backfitting that resulted was very time consuming and costly.

Similar problems arose during the FX-15 program when substandard quality was encountered with production-quantity oil seals produced by a key supplier. Defects were revealed only after the onset of widespread field failures. The problem was unanticipated because the quality of the part had been quite adequate in small prototype quantities. With volume production the seal quality seriously declined. Evidently, either the supplier was screening prototype parts to hide severe yield problems during the prototype phase, or the supplier was using a different manufacturing process than the one that would be needed for volume production.

Suppliers are just as likely to make prototypes that are not representative of actual manufacturing processes as are companies that make the final system. In the long run this will only hurt the final product, and vendors themselves should realize they are doing a disservice not only to their clients but to their own reputation. Companies must insist that vendors make their own prototypes using representative processes. Conformance to design drawings is not enough; parts should be made with the actual processes and tooling that will be used for volume production.

## Prototype Quality as a Harbinger of Product Quality

Even if companies use early, rapid prototyping to get a project off to a strong start, strategic use of full-system prototypes near the end of the development cycle remains critical. There is a strong relationship between the quality of the full-system confirmation prototype and the ultimate quality of the end product. The rate at which problems can be resolved during the short time left between final confirmation prototypes and production is very limited. The greater the number of problems remaining in the final prototype, the greater the likelihood that problems will persist when production begins.

The quality of a final prototype can be measured in terms of the number and character of design and production changes that follow.[5]

As illustrated in **Figure 7.4**, curve A represents a project that enters the final prototype stage with too many unresolved problems. Even with frantic effort at the end of the cycle, products that require major design changes after final prototyping will still be relatively deficient at product launch, placing the product at serious risk. Conversely, curve B indicates a project that has used multiple prototype cycles to reduce the unknowns as it goes into final engineering and production verification prototyping.

The coupling between high-quality prototypes and superior product development programs was demonstrated during Ford's Crown Victoria project. The new car was based on an existing car platform, but included a new modular engine and new suspension and handling systems. Once early problems in product differentiation and product definition were resolved, the program proceeded relatively smoothly. During the project, there was a keen awareness of the need to modify development practices to improve the quality of prototypes, to minimize late changes, and to institute new procedures to catch errors at a far earlier stage of the project than was common at Ford.

According to Ford employees, the project team produced the best prototypes ever seen at the company; they led to fewer late design changes and improved the level of manufacturing representativeness in the car design. A few prototypes were built on the production line at Ford's St. Thomas plant, interspersed with a current model being produced there. While providing a more accurate representation of the production process, this practice also gave the plant employees in-depth information about the upcoming product, enhancing production learning. The workers also developed numerous suggestions for improving the manufacturability of the car.

## Use of Structured Methodologies

Early prototypes provide an important basis for assessing whether the design concept can meet expectations, whether manufacturing, marketing, and design issues are reconciled, and whether the product will truly satisfy the intended customer. A relatively new structured methodology can help in this analysis. It is known by the acronym QFD, which stands for Quality Function Deployment (a better deno-

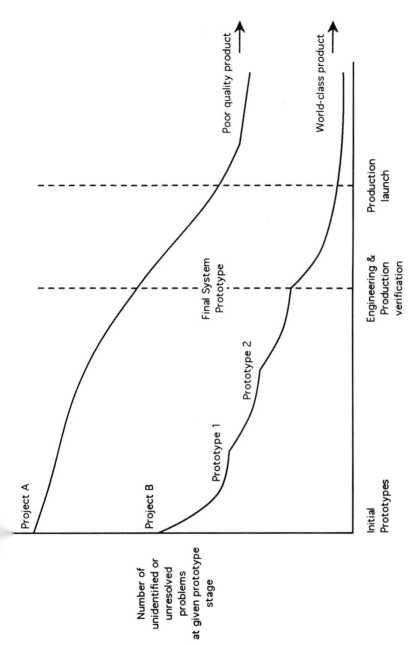

**Figure 7.4.** Prototypes are critical to resolving problems in the early stages of the project. Prototypes can be used to verify the totality of subsystems interactions and to demonstrate production-type tools and processes. A project with time constraints that seeks too many innovations or begins with high uncertainty can be expected to enter the final prototyping stage with more unresolved problems, as shown in curve A. Even with frantic effort at the end of the cycle, the product will require major design changes after final prototyping and will still be relatively deficient when production is launched. Conversely, as shown in curve B, a project based on limited, focused innovations and the implementation of proven technology begins with far fewer unresolved problems, leading to fewer surprises and less uncertainty. The rate of resolution of problems is rapid, and a final prototype of high quality can be achieved in minimum time.

217

tation might be Quality Focused Design).[6] QFD is used to relate intended customer needs to a product's technical features, design concepts, and manufacturing processes.

Usually, QFD is implemented using software programs employing a graphic matrix similar to a spreadsheet. Correlating desired customer attributes with required technical attributes helps to assure that the final product truly provides the intended features required for success. Although the use of QFD in the projects studied by the Vision Group was largely in an embryonic stage, the technique is being widely implemented in a number of programs at several companies. Ford and Hewlett-Packard have become particularly strong champions of the approach.

A second structured methodology receiving considerable attention concerns the issue of robustness in both product and process.[7] Robustness here relates to the extent to which the product design and manufacturing process are able to tolerate variability. The robust product functions well in spite of the inevitable variations in manufacturing processes and end use. The robust manufacturing process yields quality parts even though the properties of the incoming materials and the condition of the manufacturing equipment vary from day to day. Robustness is built into products and processes during development by systematic procedures for optimizing the design and processing parameters. Since robustness is a system attribute, it must be developed on prototype systems. Prototypes are the vehicle by which robustness is realized.

Robustness and QFD are just two of the structured methodologies devised by Japanese industry that are gradually being implemented in the United States. Ford has been the earliest champion of Taguchi methodologies and was instrumental in creating the American Supplier Institute, an organization dedicated to the dissemination of structured methods among Ford's suppliers.


## THE ROLES OF DIFFERENT PROTOTYPES

In the preceding section we argue that the quality of the final product depends on the effective use of prototypes at all stages of the development process. Although we use the word prototype rather generally, the precise nature of the prototype can vary widely according to the questions it is intended to answer. The most efficient way to obtain this diverse range of information is by appropriate use of a spectrum of prototypes, each tailored to a specific need (see **Figure 7.5**).

Actually, the best results are achieved when project teams use a variety of appropriate prototypes during different stages of development. The challenge is to understand the various prototype options, and when to employ them.

Most often, early prototypes are fashioned either as models, mockups, or computer simulations. As work proceeds, subsystem and full-system prototypes then follow. All the entities play important roles in the resolution of crucial questions, but each has different purposes. These are addressed in the text below, and are summarized in **Table 7.2**.

## Models and Mockups

Models and mockups constitute inexpensive and knowingly incomplete physical representations that are useful for focusing attention on a limited number of key features. They avoid the distractions and complexities of a complete system prototype. In automotive development, for example, clay models are the substantive medium for designing and quantitatively defining the body styling.

There are new and interesting innovations in model building directly from CAD data. One technique is called stereo-lithography.[8] In this process, solid plastic models are created directly from a computer design file. Under computer control, a laser beam traces out the part configuration, impinging on a surface of liquid plastic as it moves along. Under the laser action, the plastic solidifies. Layer after layer are built up, creating virtually any shape or contour directly from design data. Such models provide concept visualization in a form readily understood by all participants from top management to component suppliers. Stereo-lithographic models also serve as an excellent check on dimensional errors, which are a major source of design changes and delays in projects. Stereo-lithographic models have proven invaluable in facilitating cost-estimating and process

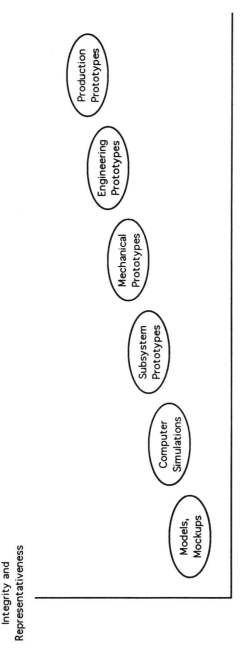

**Figure 7.5.** Prototypes take a variety of forms. Most early prototypes are fashioned as models, mockups, or computer simulations, and are useful in scoping out basic product characteristics even though their integrity, or completeness, is low. As work proceeds, subsystem and mechanical prototypes usually follow and represent more closely the end product. As ramp-up approaches, full-system engineering and production prototypes are called into action as a final check of systems integration.

**Table 7.2**  Purposes of Prototypes

*Models, Mockups, and Computer Simulations*

- Pre-project planning and product definition
- Concept clarification
- Common understanding of concept by entire development community
- Product assessment by focus groups
- Basis for cost-estimation and supplier bids

*Subsystem and Mechanical Prototypes*

- Concept selection
- Multifunctional team coordination
- Process selection and confirmation
- Integration of product and process
- Feasibility demonstration of component or subsystem
- Early problem identification
- Life testing, test of environmental robustness
- Change driver
- Dimensional checks

*Full-system Engineering and Production Prototypes*

- Test of system interactions
- Product schedule driver
- Multifunctional activities coordinator
- Predictor of ultimate product quality

---

planning. DEC and Ford are now actively using this methodology in development programs.

## Computer Simulations

The key to early realization of high-quality prototypes is the effective use of computational modeling that integrates past experience. These models are extremely versatile and flexible and permit rapid exploration of a wide range of conditions and concepts. Increasingly, the realization of high quality prototypes at an early stage is made possible with computer simulations.

With the advances in computer capabilities, electronic models today can provide attractive alternatives to physical prototypes. Computer models can often be used to provide accurate visualizations of design concepts, and yield accurate simulations of complex aspects of the performance of systems. Although such computer software is often costly to construct, once available in generic form, it can be applied to a range of development projects with benefits that accrue on a continuing basis. The future will undoubtedly see more computer-based "virtual prototyping."

The level of sophistication of computer simulations used in the projects we studied varied. Computer modeling was commonly used in developing electronic circuitry and software, as in HP's DeskJet project and Digital's DECstation 3100 project. Ford had major programs underway to address many difficult mechanical simulation problems. Ford's Crown Victoria program, for example, exploited computation power to an unprecedented degree to supplant traditional prototyping and testing. It resolved such difficult issues as optimum selection of metal thickness for critical parts, reduction in the transmission of noise and vibration, and enhancement of the crash-impact behavior of particular systems. The advantages to Ford proved great; the technique reduced the number of design changes and therefore cost. It also reduced the number of necessary crash tests of full prototypes, which are obviously very expensive since only one destructive test is possible for each prototype. Furthermore, earlier physical tests had proven more time consuming than simulations and provided less information.

### Subsystem Prototypes

Major development programs such as DEC's RA90 are often divided into several parallel efforts. Once system-level interactions and interdependencies are identified, this permits more efficient utilization of resources and reduces overall development time. The division of a product into sets of stand-alone subsystems also makes it possible to contain and focus risk posed by major innovations. As long as full-system checks are made at appropriate stages, the refinement of the product and detailed definition of parts design are best carried out with subsystem prototypes.

### Full-System Prototypes

Early prototyping of the full system was a significant factor in several projects. Where it was done effectively, it contributed heavily to ultimate success. Conversely, when done haphazardly or too late in the cycle it allowed significant system problems to go undetected. This occurred in several projects, particularly those in which unproven technology was fundamental to development. Where the total initial focus was on the feasibility of subsystems, and full-system prototyping was left to the end, serious complications arose.

Below, we look at several projects that succeeded or failed because of the use or misuse of prototypes.

## SUCCESSES AND FAILURES DUE TO PROTOTYPING

### Proper Implementation

Several of the projects we studied owed their smooth, timely, and cost-effective nature to effective prototyping. In these cases a variety of prototypes were used throughout the duration of the project, and regular feedback from one stage was applied to the next. The other key factor was that manufacturing people were included early; in some cases, as at Chaparral, they led the team's work.

*Horizontal caster and Pulpit Control system.* Chaparral took on both of these efforts with the aim of developing new processes. At Chaparral, prototyping is routinely carried out at the system level, and is largely done at full scale on the shop floor in a production environment. In this way, early prototype processes are representative of the company's manufacturing capabilities. Small project teams with strength and breadth in production are responsible for all dimensions of the programs, from fulfilling customer needs to process design and production.

Frequent prototype cycles provided quick feedback in both projects, led to rapid learning by production people, and fostered a large degree of innovation. Each project team did all its own prototyping, testing, and evaluation of results. The skilled and motivated team members exhibited great pride of ownership. Employees advanced concepts to maintain high, self-imposed standards while emphasizing practical aspects of the applications. By following such practices, Chaparral has compiled a remarkable record of successful innovations, including these two projects.

*FunSaver camera.* Kodak's FunSaver project, to develop a disposable camera, was driven by prototyping. Early prototyping was not difficult because the product was small and relatively inexpensive, and because critical issues related to user attitudes rather than infusion of new technology. Kodak's central development strategy was the rapid manufacture and testing of prototypes. Prototypes paced the rate of learning and the progress of product development. Rapid prototype design and manufacture was combined with extensive testing and feedback by Kodak employees who took home the interim designs and tried them for themselves. The FunSaver has been a success in the marketplace.

*DeskJet.* Hewlett-Packard's ink-jet printer project was estimated to require 75 percent invention and innovation, yet it was on a rapid development cycle of nine months. Hewlett-Packard used prototyping as a critical path learning tool to reduce uncertainty and integrate the project's elements, and periodic prototyping to pace this learning. Once the first prototype units were built, manufacturing took over the prototyping process. Each month, regardless of whether the product development organization was ready or not, manufacturing built 50 prototype units. Thus, rather than designers squeezing last-minute changes into prototypes and delaying the prototype, the regularity forced a better and more integrated prototype build.

## Poor Implementation

Opportunities for improved execution were found in a majority of the programs we studied. Unanticipated problems or oversights were often recognized late, significantly affecting the quality of the resulting product or process or the effectiveness of the team.

Too often, the misuse or lack of use of prototypes was triggered by pressures that encouraged a tendency to take risks, to assume that shortcuts were possible and that time, resources, and effort could be saved by not addressing important issues. During one of our interviews, a Ford engineer explained that the way he performed an instant check of the quality of a production prototype was by looking in the car's trunk to see how many of the parts had not fit and had been stowed away. In other cases the use of prototypes was not sufficiently rigorous, resulting from a total focus on design to the exclusion of production. While ultimately many such problems were resolved and the products reached the market, the effort was completed with a sacrifice in cost, timing, or quality, and the human scars that resulted often persisted into subsequent projects.

Failure to involve manufacturing early had a significant impact on several programs. This applied not only to in-house production, but equally to suppliers of key components. Even when manufacturing people were included, their involvement was at times too limited to be pro-active. For example, in several Ford car programs two representatives from manufacturing were present from the early stages. Their attention, however, was split among a half dozen programs, all at different stages of development. The two engineers referred to themselves as the "lone rangers." The input of manufacturing during the first two years of the car programs was thus relatively minor and reactive.

Several programs suffered from the temptation to introduce innovative, unproven technology too rapidly. Such programs bogged down when the full scope of the problems associated with the new technology finally surfaced, usually late in the program. This was shown schematically in **Figure 7.4**, where curve A represented the case of too much innovation for the project time line and resources allocated.

*FX-15 compressor.* This project was Ford's first in-house attempt to design an air-conditioning compressor for its cars. It illustrated several issues related to prototype use. Because the concept offered important benefits in product cost, size, and other competitive considerations, the project received great support and resources from upper management. But, by setting a rigid and early date for terminating production of the original air conditioner, management also imposed extremely intense pressures to see the project completed in the most optimistic time conceivable.

Many problems surfaced late in the allotted development time. Most resulted from the need to achieve a large number of major innovations in an extremely tight development schedule, which made shortcuts very tempting. In this environment, the risk of running into big problems was high, and they indeed arose.

To save time the team focused on subsystem development. No full-system tests of the compressor mounted on the targeted engine were made until late in the program. When finally the full complement of car and compressor were tested extensively, serious interactions between the two were revealed. The interactions produced unexpected noise, harshness, and vibrations that could not be fully resolved at that late stage. The result was a product that fell short of world-class quality.

*Factory of the Future.* This Kodak project was an ambitious effort to upgrade the capability of manufacturing to finish, cut, and package camera film. It required the participation of several disparate groups within the company. Each group introduced its own agenda of innovative but unproven technical solutions and sought to optimize the work to solve its own local problems. The program leaders took the risk that the individual subsystem technical solutions could be integrated into the system on the fly. Even where integration problems were recognized, their resolution was deferred under the presumption that they could be solved at a later time. Because of the multiplicity and diversity of the issues that had to be addressed, problems quickly accumulated and many were not confronted. Early mockups were incomplete and failed to give full technical demonstration, yet were viewed as having satisfied the proof of feasibility. This deficiency was further compounded by a severe time-lag between system prototype creation, testing, and performance analysis.

Driven by imprudent haste and overly ambitious goals, the groups never got together for a full technical demonstration, and never even required such a gathering. In this environment disciplined procedures were not enforced. Without a system-level prototype, major interface problems remained undetected and were only revealed piecemeal.

The project had too many loose ends that the team was not able to systematically solve within the time required, and new problems kept cropping up. In the end senior managers considered the issues too prohibitive and costly. They canceled the initial project and redefined a follow-on project with a narrower and more focused set of goals; the latter project was successful.

## IMPROVING YOUR USE OF PROTOTYPES

As we have seen, prototypes play a vital role in product development. They provide a basis for resolving crucial questions at virtually every phase of the development cycle. Effective use of prototypes that are representative of production not only forestalls negative consequences, it also provides opportunities to streamline manufacturing and improve learning throughout the company.

A general contention we took from our study is that the best project outcomes result from rapid implementation and early use of prototypes at key development stages, and that full-system prototypes must be pursued rigorously long before ramp-up begins. If you encounter problems early, you will have more time and options to fix them: you can change a design or retrofit a system. A supplier can remake a part. But if you encounter problems late, the solutions, if they can be reached at all, will inevitably add complexity, cost, and delay.

Managers who want to evaluate whether their company is making good use of prototypes, or who want to design a better approach for the future, should aim for the following qualities:

- Fast-start programs that get up to speed quickly by emphasizing early firming of the product definition and frequent, rapid prototyping.
- System-level prototypes that are used early to detect problems that may arise from subsystem interactions, and that are used to drive project coordination and integration.
- Prototypes that are representative of both products and processes.
- Supplier involvement in early design and in the development and use of representative processes.

- Error avoidance combined with early detection and elimination of errors.
- Prototypes manufactured by production methods so that process development goes hand in hand with product development.
- High quality, full-system confirmation prototypes.

CHAPTER 8

# Integration Within Projects

In 1988 management at Digital Equipment Corp. gave a small team in its Networks and Communications Group the opportunity to design the company's second-generation local area network bridge, a communications network that would link several computer networks. The first product had been a great success, commanding a dominant market share. On the team were people from manufacturing engineering, marketing, customer service engineering, and the lead group—design engineering.

At a meeting one morning an odd problem came up. Although difficulties with the guts of the hardware—a high-density circuit board—had been resolved, a debate broke out over whether the board should lie horizontal inside the equipment cabinet or be positioned vertically. Though the issue seemed simple enough, the questions it brought to light showed just how perplexing the problem was. If the board was to be readily accessible to service engineers in the field, then the vertical position would be better, and the posts that supported the board would have to be redesigned to meet reliability targets. If access wasn't a priority, the board could be positioned horizontally, a more reliable design.

The team got into quite a tangle. Who was to decide whether the box would be serviced in the field, or if it would be replaced so that repairs could be made at a DEC service facility? Who had intimate knowledge of how customers would use the box, where it would usually be located on customers' premises, and which field-service scenarios were best? Who determined the relative value of the stand-alone box versus field-service contracts, with respect to future sales? Would the solution to the problem be reached in an integrated fashion, drawing on the knowledge and experience of team members, or would the solution result from a series of handoffs between functional groups? Or would the answer come down from on high? Did the team have procedures and systems that facilitated integrated resolutions, or were the solutions embedded in the languages, systems, and methods of the separate functions? Would the same product database be used for design, manufacturing, purchasing, and field engineering?

As the complications from such a seemingly minor problem show, a key factor in a project's success is how the total investment of resources comes together in a new product or process. The elements of knowledge, materials, systems, and software must fit together coherently. Weak or missing elements diminish the quality of the outcome. An integrated effort during development increases the project's value, uniqueness, and success when the interactions and interrelationships among the elements achieve synergy, as the component parts achieve wholeness. Integration within development projects results in the whole being much more than the sum of the isolated parts.

Much of education in school and on the job involves breaking up problems into parts and then working on the parts; the focus is seldom on integration. Children learn at an early age that it is easier to build a toy house using similar blocks than with blocks of incongruent shapes and sizes. College students learn the calculus of differentiation first, because it is easier to perform than the calculus of integration, in which the missing constants determine the magnitude of the solution. Engineers and managers seem to learn the inherent skills of project management in an analogous fashion. Problem solving and learning skills appear to be most proficient when they are specialized and driven by the need for functional achievements; thus, a company's activities search for solutions of local optimization. However, these drivers arc counter to an integrating process that results in wholeness and total system solution. In short, success at designing or making the component parts is easier than integrating the elements and producing a total system solution. Success within subteams is easier than success across subteams. What's more, recognizing the failure of a collection of components to work together smoothly as a new product is easier than recognizing the failure of processes and procedures that create integration within the development project itself.

At a superficial level, integration might be seen as a set of formal systems, in which all team members recite the same design and execution goals, use the same timing charts, and follow routinized processes to manage the handoffs between upstream and downstream activities and the interfaces between functional groups. The projects examined by the Manufacturing Vision Group, however, suggest that integration within projects is much more. It has to do with the way work gets done, with perceived rewards and career paths, with the tools and methodologies that support a disciplined approach to problem solving, and with the role senior management is willing to play. Integration requires that the functional disciplines are applied in a fashion that leads both to success of the project and the glory of the disciplines. Integration means that all the required resources, both internal and external, are utilized in a timely manner that allows all to contribute and that overlapping efforts with concomitant communication and information contribute to the project's success. We found integration to be an overwhelmingly positive contributor to the success of development projects, especially for companies that operate in dynamic and highly competitive markets. Further, we found that integration is such a pervasive force it must be probed on multiple levels.

Why is integration such a key element to excellence in new product and process development? We found two answers:

1. The outcome of projects pursued using integrated processes is of greater value than those that lack integration. If a project team has all the necessary resources, the output of those resources is greater

when the elements work together throughout the project duration. The contribution of each element is of greater value because of the process of integration.

2. The outcome of a project is heavily biased by decisions reached during its early phases. Thus, all the resources that ultimately contribute to success must begin to contribute in these early stages, which is only possible when integration is utmost in everyone's minds.

How can you tell when you have an integrated development process? It is best measured in the way work gets done. This includes the individual and organizational skills that are used and valued, the way problems are articulated and solved, and the way decisions and approvals are made. Simply stated, to achieve optimum success a development team must solve a *system problem*. As subsystem solutions are reached they must be summed together. Integration, then, refers to the set of formal and informal processes that cause the necessary interactions, trade-offs, and synergies required to reach the total system solution.

In the first section of this chapter we present the advantages that integrated processes afford, and the problems that non-integrated processes routinely cause. The evidence is clear—integration results in better project outcomes. The following section goes inside some of the projects we examined, to show the extent to which they were integrated; it is often the case that certain aspects of a development project are integrated while others are not. An understanding of how to judge degrees of integration at different levels will help company managers analyze their own projects. The third section discusses three major factors that affect how well integration is achieved, factors that must be understood before a company works to improve integration. We then conclude with a number of actions that managers can take to enhance the integration of current and future projects.

## THE ADVANTAGES OF INTEGRATION

In the 20 projects we studied, we saw that technical objectives could be met through both integrated and non-integrated processes. However, the quality of solutions on a project-wide level (the degree to which goals were met in other critical areas such as development cycle time and cost) were substantially poorer when integrated processes were not achieved.

An integrated process is characterized by joint, proactive decision making among all functional units. Joint decision making means that experts from each function work as contributors of "disciplinary expertise," and not as defenders of their own divisions' agendas or their bosses' orders. An integrated process also causes team members to anticipate and manage problems and actively exploit opportunities for progress that exist at the interfaces between different technologies, subsystems, and value-added activities (see **Figure 8.1**).

The common result of an integrated effort, as we saw repeatedly, was a shortened development time. In some cases the number of engineering hours was reduced by one-quarter to one-third of the number spent on similar past projects. The quality of solutions was also enhanced, leading to the achievement of highly ambitious performance and quality goals that required pushing the limits of multiple technologies and organizational fronts simultaneously. By reducing unnecessary iterations and addressing conflicts before significant commitments were made, integration also worked to keep costs under control.[1]

The impact of these benefits was not limited to a particular project. Integration also provided longer term strategic benefits. Compressed cycle time and improved quality enabled several companies to mount rapid responses to new product announcements by competitors (as Kodak did with its single-use FunSaver camera), to make dramatic shifts in technological direction (as Digital did with its UNIX-based DECstation 3100 workstation), and to be the first to introduce high-margin products that were difficult for competitors to imitate (as was the case with Chaparral's new Microtuff 10 steel). Strong integration between design and manufacturing also enabled follow-on products to be brought to market almost immediately, as HP was able to do with the DeskJet printer. Hence, not only the product itself, but the entire family of products built on the initial platform, benefited significantly.

The extent to which integration must be reached for true success

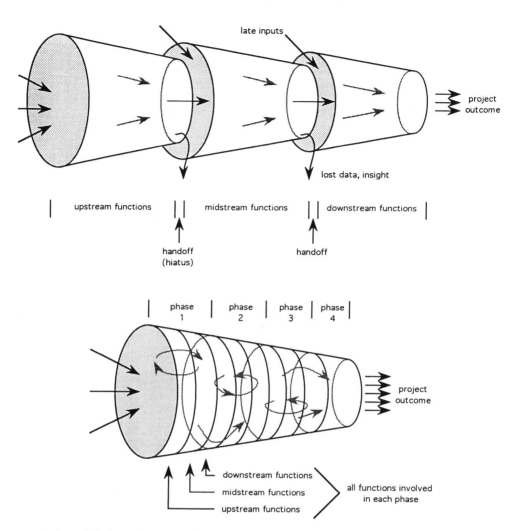

**Figure 8.1.** If project teams do not take steps to integrate all functions, the development process will proceed in a sequential fashion (top figure), with only a subset of the participants involved at various stages. This will result in one-way input from early groups to later ones, and in weak links between functions, both of which will work to lengthen time-to-completion and limit the range of possible positive outcomes. Sequential processes with handoffs often mean that critical information is lost and that new inputs that come in later have not been thought through by the team. If the team integrates all functions from the outset (bottom figure), strong ties and simultaneous give and take will result, leading to faster development and a wider array of positive outcomes. Inputs are examined, redirected, and iterated for consistency and congruency.

234

cannot be underestimated. Even projects that achieved integration between functions ran into difficulties on a more global, systems scale. For example, Ford achieved integration between the functional groups that worked on the FX15 project, undertaken to develop in-house for the first time a compressor for automobile air conditioners. But the project itself was not integrated with the rest of corporate development, which led to unforeseen technical problems after the compressor was built.

Driven by competitive pressure and unacceptable supplier actions, management charged Ford's Climate Control Division (CCD) with developing an air-conditioner compressor that would cost no more than 40 percent of existing models, and would be smaller and perform better. What's more, the project was to be completed in record time—cutting 18 months from the historical time line. The project would stretch almost every dimension of development performance.

An FX15 team was formed with 17 people who had experience in both design and manufacturing. All team members participated in the design phase. At an early stage, issues pertaining to manufacturability were addressed—manufacturing process alternatives were fully analyzed, potential cost savings were identified, and vendors were brought in. Although the integration of design and manufacturing, and the early involvement of all functions, including those to be carried out by outsiders, sounds obvious and prudent, this practice was not business as usual for Ford. Yet the company succeeded and the project benefited; it met all the goals for cost, size, and development time.

Nevertheless, the compressor caused severe vibrations when it was mated with the engine. Systems integration of the compressor with the entire vehicle did not take place until late in the project. Rectifying the vibration problem resulted in unnecessary cost and delay.

The systemic nature of integration must reach beyond physical systems. In many of the projects we studied, the linkage between technology development and marketing and sales almost always left something to be desired. With the exception of several projects at Chaparral Steel and Kodak's antistatic film-coating project, we found that a development team's integration with marketing, sales, and customers was often absent, too late, indirect, or inadequate. In technology-driven companies in particular, such as DEC and HP, input from marketing and other less technical sources was often disregarded or devalued by engineers who ran projects. The lack of such integration, its ambiguity, or its inconsistency plagued project definition in many cases. Interviews with managers indicated confusion, backtracking, and frenzy as changes were made even after production start-up. The impact of poor integration manifested itself in delays, budget overruns, production difficulties, and weak market positioning. One project was even aborted, and another had to be reintroduced with a new marketing approach. In a third case, the company actually fell further behind the technology curve of its competitors, even though an explicit goal of the project was to close the gap.[2]

Several of these problems showed up in DEC's attempt to develop a new workstation based on a UNIX operating system instead of the company's standard VMS system. Despite meeting highly ambitious technical objectives and a short development cycle time, market success was poor because of a lack of integration with applications-software development and sales. The project team, dominated by design engineers, viewed these as "downstream" activities that didn't have to be addressed until "later" in the project cycle.

When the workstation was introduced, only 20 software applications were available for it, even though market research had shown that customers would want scores of applications before spending the money for a new system. This contrasted with more than 500 applications for competitive workstations. The design engineers, almost all of whom had been trained in hardware development, had a prevailing attitude that a "hot box" crammed with superior hardware would be sufficient to generate interest among independent software developers who would scramble to write useful programs. Clearly, this view was wrong.

The internal sales force was also ignored. The sales force was well versed in products using the VMS operating system, but was ill equipped to sell workstations based on the UNIX operating system simply because the system was new. Salespeople received no training on the system until seven months after it was launched. When training was finally conducted, the trainees were mostly managers, not field sales agents. As a result, the sales force did not actively promote the product, because it did not feel comfortable with it and was not knowledgeable about it.

## JUDGING THE DEGREE OF INTEGRATION— AND NON-INTEGRATION

Before trying to undertake a more integrated approach to develop projects, managers must first understand how to judge the degrees of integration, and non-integration, that the company now routinely achieves. Integration takes place on multiple levels, and the extent to which integration is present is not always obvious. We observed five characteristics that differentiated integrated projects from non-integrated projects. Understanding these traits makes it possible to judge the degree of integration being achieved in a given project and to identify how to pursue better integration as new projects are begun. The five characteristics are: the nature of adjustment between the subgroups of a project team, the nature of linking mechanisms between subgroups, the assignment of responsibility for integration, the roles of downstream or less dominant subgroups, and mechanisms for conflict resolution. **Table 8.1** summarizes these characteristics.

### The Nature of Adjustment Between Subgroups

One of the first symptoms to look for when analyzing the degree of integration being achieved in a given project is the nature of adjustment between subgroups on the project team. When integrated procedures are in place, subgroups that represent separate functions are able to adjust to unanticipated problems and changes in direction in a coordinated and complementary way. The give and take between groups is two way and extensive; each group can exercise influence and be influenced by others. Indeed, each group comes to view such feedback as value-adding. This behavior occurs because the various groups have all started from the same point in time and with the same charter, and because as a team they have a chance to work together toward mutually beneficial solutions.

Several projects illustrated this type of adjustment. For example,

**Table 8.1** The Varying Characteristics of Integrated and Non-Integrated Processes

| Characteristics | Integrated Process | Non-integrated Process |
|---|---|---|
| Nature of adjustment | Contemporaneous<br>Non-recursive | Sequential |
| Linking mechanisms:<br>Early phase of project | Preproject planning<br>Goal setting<br>Coordination<br>Problem solving | Goal setting<br>Coordination |
| Intermediate phase | Problem solving<br>Continuity in people<br>Feedback and learning | Periodic reviews |
| Final phase | (linking has already<br>been completed) | Problem solving |
| Responsibility for<br>integration | Project team<br>Clear project leadership | Downstream unit or<br>special staff group |
| Roles of downstream<br>or less-dominant units | Active participation<br>Early information input | Information agents |
| Conflict resolution | Goal convergence<br>Lateral communication | Negotiation<br>Hierarchical authority |

early in the design of the Kodak FunSaver single-use camera, the manufacturing and mold-design subgroups provided inputs into critical plastic components that subsequently improved material yields, product quality, and the utilization of equipment. During Chaparral's Microtuff 10 alloy steel project, when management recognized that customers needed more technical support and that quality assurance people could provide it, they reallocated duties so that within a few months quality assurance became the primary customer contact point for both sales and service. In the HP DeskJet project the R&D manager created a manufacturing engineering group within R&D, prior to the start of the project. Once the project was underway, this group was spun off to manufacturing. The result was a very supportive, integrated interaction between R&D and manufacturing. The conversion to this integrated style was so effective and complete that at the end of the project the R&D engineers were lobbying for more manufacturing engineers.

When integration procedures are lacking, team members generally attend to issues in a sequential fashion and seldom involve the input of all subgroups. Information generally flows in one direction, from the upstream subgroup that starts its task early in the project to downstream groups that get involved later (see **Figure 8.1**). Furthermore, solutions tend to reflect the differing status of participants, following a pecking order from upstream to downstream groups or from more dominant to less dominant functions. Hence responses to problems tend to be unilateral and rigid rather than mutual and flexible.

This type of adjustment, or really the lack of adjustment, was observed in a number of projects. During DEC's RA90 disk drive project, the group working on the thin-film heads was reluctant to give prototypes to the team working on thin-film media because the heads were not yet "finished." This put off until late in the project the chance to uncover system-level issues—particularly those involving the interaction of the heads and media. The team missed out on the opportunity to uncover problems early and mutually find solutions. Predictably, problems between subsystems cropped up late, adding cost and delay.

## The Nature of Linking Mechanisms

To get a handle on the degree of integration and non-integration in development projects, managers can also analyze the mechanisms that link team subgroups and project activities. These include planning, goal setting, and problem solving—the coordinating schemes that drive the timing and sequencing of activities.

In non-integrated projects, the team relies on formal coordination mechanisms such as a top-down statement of goals to provide a common context and a schedule that subgroups strive to meet. Subgroups generally work on their own, frequently in separate locations. Interactions between subgroups during the intermediate phases of the project are sparse and often occur primarily in formal, pre-specified meetings to review progress. These represent the primary forums to formally identify and resolve potential conflicts between subgroups. Focus on system-wide issues generally does not take place until the last phase of the project when the subgroups have "completed" their individual assignments. Though useful, the formal methods and documentation often become too bureaucratic, severely restraining and substituting for the ad hoc communication that must take place to achieve integration. Integration in its best form implies a significant transfer of information and development of mutual understanding through informal processes and by a sense of having "walked the whole path together."

In integrated projects, system-level planning and problem solving by the entire team begins right from the start. This early attention not only addresses the comprehensive business aspects of the projects, but links the project and its purposes to the functional and business strategies of the company. System integration issues are addressed prior to and during the development of subsystems. Such problem solving generates policies, project goals, guidelines, and a shared language that form an overarching context within which all subgroups can work. Furthermore, we observed that integrated processes encouraged the effort to physically co-locate the key participants. This made day-to-day problem solving a natural phenomenon. For example, close contact between design and manufacturing engineers can result in innovative design decisions early in the cycle. Each function shapes the other.

This context is dynamic. It operates in real time and keeps pace with the learning and knowledge that is generated as the project progresses. For example, in HP's DeskJet project, design co-located with manufacturing to develop a new class of low-cost computer printers based on ink-jet print technology. Using frequent prototypes, the entire project team could evaluate, without delay, how subsystems would fit together as design and manufacturing developments were taking place.

## Responsibility for Integration

As suggested above, when a team works in an integrated fashion the team as a whole shares the responsibility and the authority for resolving system-level issues. However, the team will not be able to act in this way unless all the formal and informal actions and nuances emanating from senior management support it. The willingness of team members to accept system-level responsibility derives from a sense of ownership and commitment to the project's goals, and belief that each person's success will rise and fall with the success of the total project, not just their piece of it.

In non-integrated projects, a downstream function such as manufacturing frequently is left "holding the bag," because upstream subgroups think their job is done just because they've addressed their piece of the puzzle. Downstream units often find they must reconcile suboptimal choices caused by the team's lack of coordination. If this becomes too difficult, management sometimes forms a separate team to attack the problem by trying to integrate the subgroups after the fact. This can make matters even worse, because such a team, put together at the end of development, may not even overlap with members of the original team. The existence of tiger teams and special task forces at the end usually indicate that integration has been inadequate.

While all the projects we studied at Chaparral used integrated processes, we found a particularly clear lesson in the project to develop a new type of continuous caster for specialty steels. All the specialists, including mold designers, digital control experts, computer programmers, metallurgists, and operators viewed their responsibility similarly: to create an operating process that would produce high-quality specialty steels at significantly lower cost. Furthermore, even support groups, such as the melt shop and quality assurance, which produced sample batches of steel for the team and tested the resulting product, accepted significant responsibility for reaching project success.

The non-integrated handling of responsibility was apparent during Kodak's Factory of the Future project. Each of more than a half dozen subgroups had their own, isolated set of tasks and performance measures. The tunnel vision was so strong that even though each subgroup felt they had done an excellent job, they did not realize until after the initial project was disbanded how much their failure to have a common, integrated vision of project goals affected its outcome.

## The Role of Less Dominant Subgroups

Managers can pick up strong signals that indicate the degree of integration being achieved by stepping back and analyzing the different roles that subgroups take on. But the analysis must probe beneath the surface. For example, even in non-integrated teams representatives from less dominant (usually downstream) subgroups are often included in development steering committees. Purchasing, for example, may be brought in early to help figure out what parts should be used in a new product, based on availability from vendors. The issue, however, is more subtle than the physical representation of subgroups. It relates to the importance and weight attached to their roles. The less powerful functions often play a reactive role. They usually provide information or technical assistance, and act as liaisons who transfer information back to their functional areas. Their role is subservient—it is to support the implementation of directions formulated by the dominant members. As such, these people become primarily information agents.

In integrated teams all members participate in formulating the project's objectives, specs, and milestones. They not only contribute information but play active roles in arriving at the definition of technical parameters for the project, performing actual tasks, and solving the problems and conflicts. To the extent that downstream members participate in the identification of options up front, they enjoy a proactive role in "choosing" the constraints that the project will place on their function. Such teams also solicit participation by eventual customers and do not merely "hand off" the finished product to the sales force and field service. This interaction, in particular, is becoming ever more critical to success as customer service becomes more and more of a competitive tool.

Two projects in which less dominant subgroups followed non-integrated processes were the DeskJet printer project at HP and the LANbridge 200 network project at DEC. In both cases, marketing had valuable information on features required by customers and on quality characteristics. Marketing tried repeatedly to get them into the product design. However, in part because of their secondary status in the organization, their input was brushed aside when it was first offered. It was accepted only when the development engineers received the same input directly from unsatisfied test customers. A contrast can be found in the Kodak FunSaver project, where a traditionally less dominant subgroup—plastic mold design—took on a much stronger role in development, and significantly improved the performance of several key parts and thus the final product.[3]

## Mechanisms for Conflict Resolution

The fifth characteristic to look for when trying to determine the extent of integration taking place has to do with the mechanisms team members use to resolve conflicts. In non-integrated projects, team members often resort to formal negotiation or the hierarchy of power to resolve conflicts. Negotiation results in some degree of "give," which each person is willing to offer in return for some "take." While such bargaining may yield a common solution, the perspective it promotes is one in which people act to protect concerns of their function first, relegating the needs of the project to a secondary status. This does not create synergy. And when a dominant group exists within a company, it will almost always call the shots; the other groups simply accommodate them. Deferring problems to the hierarchy is no better; passing conflicts up the managerial ladder just adds delay and is likely to result in solutions that are politically acceptable yet not best for the project.

By fostering a sense of shared commitment to a project, integrated processes work to resolve conflicts by evoking a common goal, by leading people to seek resolution that benefits the project first and individual concerns second. Resolution also occurs more frequently and earlier, which helps avoid sweeping problems under the rug that are more difficult to resolve at a later stage (see **Figure 8.2**).

Two projects illustrate the nature of integrated conflict resolution. At Kodak, the antistatic film-coating project involved numerous environmental and employee health issues that were resolved through frequent, working-level interactions between operations and specialist groups. In the HP DeskJet printer effort, the project team employed monthly prototyping to focus communication between all subgroups on the fit between component modules and the problems that hin-

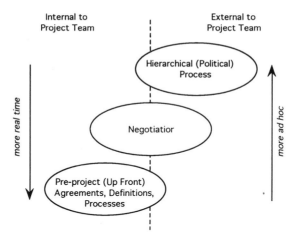

**Figure 8.2.** Influence of timing and organizational location on conflict resolution. The use of integrated processes allows conflicts to be resolved in real time because all the project's contributors own the plans. Less integrated approaches rely more on negotiation or political processes external to the team to resolve issues.

dered system integration. Prototyping served as a natural and less threatening vehicle for surfacing conflicts and centering attention on the needs of the product rather than the interests of specific functional groups.

In sharp contrast were the approaches in the DEC RA90 disk drive and Kodak Factory of the Future projects. On the RA90, the overall project was divided into three subtasks, carried out by groups at three locations separated by large distances and inadequate formal or informal processes for linking their outcomes. The result was that after the head, media, and drive subgroups finished their isolated tasks, more than a year was required just to make the product sufficiently robust for market introduction. At Kodak, much of the early and mid-term work revolved around the needs of the dominant function— equipment engineering. Many of the problems that caused the eventual cancellation of the project, however, concerned operations and distribution, which were largely ignored during these stages.

In using these five characteristics to analyze one's own company, "success" should not be allowed to blur the picture. We did find that non-integrated projects can result in successful products and processes. However, "success" was usually achieved at greater cost, a longer cycle time, and lower quality. We witnessed such results in many projects (see **Figure 8.3**). Indeed, only a few of the projects achieved full integration from concept to customer, yet for these success was truly impressive. Managers must also keep in mind that there are two levels of integration to examine; in most of the projects we studied companies found it easier to achieve technological integration (e.g., between design and manufacturing engineers) than it was to achieve integration between the technical specialties and business functions such as marketing or sales.

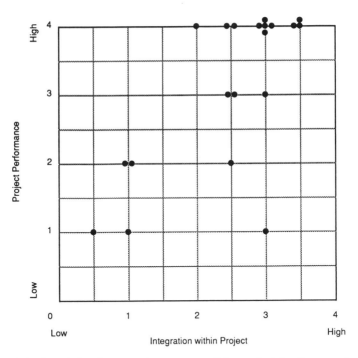

**Figure 8.3.** Correlation between the outcome of the project (performance) and the use of integration processes within the project. Integration within projects for large projects involves integration within subteams and also across teams.

# DRIVERS OF EFFECTIVE INTEGRATION

Having established the characteristics by which to judge the degree of integration, we now can examine the major factors that drive integration. It is important to note that the themes discussed in the earlier chapters of this book set the stage for how effective integration can be. Good guiding visions, leadership, prototyping, and so on help remove narrow and adversarial definitions of "turf" and lead to the formulation of proper incentives and coordination procedures needed for integration. They also affect the extent to which a coherent agenda is developed within a team and within the rest of the company that acts in support of the team.

We have identified three factors that strongly affect the quality of integration between team individuals and functions. These are the flow of communications, value-added translation, and task structuring. This section describes these three factors, how important they are to integration, and why they are difficult to achieve. Once these factors are understood, a company can then begin to take actions to improve integration.

## The Flow of Communications

Even when functions are represented in appropriate depth and breadth on a development team and are guided by a coherent vision, integration does not necessarily take place. It remains dependent on the flow of information to the appropriate people and on the communication skills of those people. How well people interact, mediate disagreements, listen to each other, and remain open to solutions all affect the flow of communications. Underlying these personal attributes are four larger factors that we determined are crucial to proper communication: functional specialization, organizational biases, difficulties with conflict resolution, and physical distance.

*Functional specialization.* Most firms we studied had a high degree of technical and functional specialization. While this has the critical advantage of disciplinary depth, it tended to foster rigid turf definitions that inhibited the open discussion of issues. Well-defined and well-guarded domains for decision making allowed people in different functions to preserve their control over particular categories of decisions, which essentially pre-empted legitimate negotiation with other constituents. In Kodak's FunSaver project, for example, sales and marketing maintained strong control over the initial choice of the product name, which it had decided would be "Fling." (The camera was meant for one-time use. The camera body and film would be sold as one inexpensive unit; once the film was exposed, it would be removed for developing and the body would be recycled.) Despite protests from Kodak's environmental engineers, who were highly sensitive to consumers' concern over new products that were expressly designed to be disposable, sales and marketing remained adamant over the name choice. Marketing only changed the name to FunSaver and approved the investment required to set up a recycling program well after product introduction, when other company-wide recycling initiatives were announced.

*Organizational biases.* Failure to keep an open mind due to functional specialization is often exacerbated by organizational biases embedded in operating policies and administrative systems, which raise the status of one technology or function over others. In many companies, engineering design dominates manufacturing; in others the ranking is reversed. It is not uncommon for a company to favor hardware groups over software groups, or electrical engineering over mechanical engineering. Such biases are dysfunctional and prevent certain groups from interacting on an equal footing. Problem solving is lopsided. As a consequence, inadequate consideration is given to the ideas, constraints, potential, and resource needs of the "secondary" functions.

*Conflict resolution.* When functional rivalry is not an issue, team members may still feel awkward about openly pointing out problems and differences in opinion. In the interest of getting along, the team may suppress potential problems. Even people on Kodak's Panda design team, who had worked together on a previous project, expressed reluctance to constructively challenge each others' premises. Team members felt that perhaps six months may have been lost because members were "too polite" with each other and let problems go too far and too long before they took the initiative to address them.

*Spatial distance.* Effective communication clearly depends on the frequency and form of interactions between team members. Integration requires frequent, real-time, and continuous exchanges. Meetings at specifically appointed intervals are a poor substitute for ongoing discussion. The location of team members at different sites, states, and even countries presents overwhelming logistical barriers. Distance also contributes to the problems of segregation and "we versus they" perceptions.

The issue of physical separation was not a major source of problems in the projects we studied, largely because it was explicitly attended to. For many projects, design and manufacturing team members were co-located. In most cases, however, marketing and sales were separated from the group, which did hamper interaction.

## Value-Added Translation

Even if information is transferred effectively, team members may not act on it. For example, if "touchy-feely" customer input from marketing is not translated into technical specifications, it is unlikely that design and manufacturing engineers will address it. Communication alone is not enough to foster integrated effort; product parameters, goals, and such must be more than conveyed—they must be put in terms that have meaning for each function, yet still create cohesion between functions. This takes considerable skill, and is an effort whose benefits are often undervalued.

Again, specialization tends to be the problem. Specialization fosters the development of languages, conceptual frameworks, and values unique to specific disciplines. Idiosyncratic languages and norms are useful for they establish a shared semantic space in which communication within a group can be more efficient and reliable. Unfortunately, specialized semantics also create severe obstacles in sharing information between groups. Team members also face a knowledge barrier. The scope of knowledge of each person tends to be deep but narrow due to specialized education and training and confined job responsibilities. Experts in a given discipline are often laypersons in others. Multiple local languages, knowledge bases, and cognitive schema hinder a team's ability to fully derive the implications of information coming from various subgroups.

When project teams we studied were largely composed of engineers, technical communication was the rule and it tended to be adequate for the conveyance of most information. On the other hand, teams composed of both technical and nontechnical people had a hard time interacting. These observations may explain the higher degree of integration we found between design and manufacturing but the poor integration between technical and marketing communities, as shown in **Figure 8.3**. However, to achieve true integration, to reach the total system solution required by a development project, translation between languages is necessary and unavoidable.

In many of the projects we examined, input from one function was often seen as vague, confusing, or simply irrelevant by other functions. Typical frustration was expressed in DEC's LANbridge 200 project, to design a communications system that would link several computer networks. Although in the early stages of the project marketing had strong and justifiable reservations regarding the direction of the product's design, it expressed its opinion through a sense of unease, indicating that "we have something wrong here." These objections were not articulated in a manner that would call into question specific parameters. As a result, the technology lagged "behind the power curve" of competitors until project goals were later accelerated—which required substantial extra effort and hurt product timing.

## Task Structuring

The clustering of activities in a development project and their assignment to individual groups also drives the degree of integration that can be achieved. The ways in which tasks are structured determines the flow of information between activities, the objectives of each group, the breadth and depth of group responsibilities, the scope of authority, and the bundling of resources and capabilities for addressing specific challenges. Since a project can be divided many different ways to create manageable tasks, the structure of the tasks and the interfaces between them remain key to successful outcomes.

Task structuring had a strong impact on Kodak's Factory of the Future project, undertaken to upgrade the capability and capacity of manufacturing to finish, cut, and package 35-mm film. The development effort was structured around existing functional units rather than around the major activities required to meet project goals. The functional units, in turn, defined problems in the ways that they were structured to create solutions. They were far less attuned to the challenges presented by the problems themselves. It is interesting that on a subsequent project undertaken to replace the Factory of the Future effort, a different task structure was chosen. Activities were organized to meet requirements that pertained to the factory floor and to film packaging, not to the division organizational chart. The latter project succeeded.

A similar lesson was learned at Ford. For decades Ford had split the work on new car programs among its standard functional groups, such as design, parts fabrication, and assembly. But it had begun a transition to dividing activities in a way that naturally addresses a project's problems. Because new car programs require the work of hundreds or even thousands of people, Ford came up with a structure that allowed the natural division of tasks and created a means for integrating the many subgroups. The groups are called Program Module Teams (PMT). Each team is made up of people from different functions who take on chunks of the car. For example, an instrument panel team would have people from planning, the controller's office, the in-house parts supplier, styling, vehicle engineering, and body engineering. Their job is to deliver a subsystem (the instrument panel) within the project parameters of function, quality, cost, and weight.

While this structure has improved the cross-functional coordination within each subsystem, Ford must evolve further. In recent projects there has been good coordination within PMTs, but not extensive integration between them. This higher level of integration has been handled through steering committees composed of leaders from each PMT. In the future, Ford hopes to integrate working people from each PMT into the steering committees to ensure extensive, coordinated problem solving.

We found an excellent example of how task structuring contributes to functional interaction in Kodak's FunSaver project. Because the camera body and its film had to be assembled in one step, and because the film, camera body, and package had to fit just right for proper use, Kodak emphasized integration of the subsystems from the start. The camera was divided into four main parts, each given to a product designer with final responsibility for the piece. Kodak then structured its Unigraphics computer-aided design/computer-aided manufacturing (CAD/CAM) system in a unique way that facilitated integration of the four parts.

For the first time, the CAD system was set up so that all the information needed by each product or tool designer for a specific part came from a single, central database. A designer would specify the shape of a particular part by creating a series of "objects"—points, lines, surfaces, and dimensions. All the objects for one part were grouped in one "layer," represented as both a collection of data and a three-dimensional graphic. Because of the integrated nature of the product's pieces, the design of a single part also entailed consideration of its fit with parts on one or more layers. To see how one part fit with another, an engineer could overlay the layers representing different parts.

Every engineer had access to the designs of all the parts, but only the designer assigned to a particular part could make changes to it. Nightly, all the changes made by each designer were uploaded to the central database. The following morning, everyone was able to download an updated model to their workstation. This gave all the engineers access to daily versions of the complete design. Team members could easily check how changes in parts made by other engineers affected their part. The team credited this approach with greatly reducing the development cycle time. The unique use of the CAD system was seen not so much as a productivity tool but as a communications tool that enabled cross-functional decision making to take place.

The experience of the FunSaver team shows how the structuring of tasks can be used to "force" a broader, more integrated perspective among team members. This perspective can be used to address the linkages between activities or eliminate certain interfaces. It also can be used to change the nature of the issues addressed by a team, the information set that is made available to team members, the control of subgroups over activities and outcomes, the performance measures by which individuals and subgroups are evaluated, and ultimately the skills of team members.[4]

## MECHANISMS FOR BETTER INTEGRATION

To this point we have established the characteristics by which to judge the degree of integration present on a project, and the major factors that determine how well integration can be achieved. This section presents actions that can be taken by management to facilitate integration. By comparing the measures used in all the projects examined by the Vision Group, we found five common actions that were fundamental to strong integration: co-location of team members, cross-training of team members, development of interpersonal communication skills, prototyping and simulation, and formal management protocols.

### Co-location

For many of the teams we studied, the first prerequisite was to locate team members from varied functional groups in one place. In the FunSaver project, designers moved into the manufacturing facility and shared offices with their manufacturing colleagues. Team members on Kodak's Panda printer project, who were keenly aware of the importance of interfaces between the hardware, software, and media components of the product, co-located in one building. The people on these and other teams said that co-location had many benefits; it enabled frequent interactions, quick feedback, bonding between members, mutual education, the substitution of an auditing mentality with cooperation, and an enhanced ability to conduct simultaneous engineering. In the HP Hornet project the division manager went so far as to move his desk into the middle of the team's space. His reason was that he wanted team members to be able to see when he was available not only so they would discuss questions with him, but so that they would not have to wait in line to do it.

Co-location, however, did not in and of itself generate interaction. To access the technical expertise of Kodak's Electronic Printing Division (EPD) needed for development of the Panda printer, for example, engineers from the Federal Systems Division (FSD) moved into EPD's design facility. Yet for almost 18 months members of EPD did not participate actively in the project. They served mostly as consultants. Later, when the division became strongly interested in the product for its own market, much of the design and development direction had already been shaped around FSD criteria. Co-location provided the opportunity for interchange but the requisite effort was not made.

At DEC, "virtual co-location" is used to supplement the benefits of physical co-location at certain stages of project development. Computer networks, information systems, and computer conferencing provide the infrastructure for real-time interactions and parallel problem solving. However, in no cases we examined were the electronic tools of virtual co-location used as the sole or primary mechanism for communication.

## Cross-Functional training

Even if a team can eliminate physical barriers, co-location will only lead to improved communication if team members can understand and appreciate the needs and challenges of each others' work. This requires cross-training. Serving on cross-functional teams is itself one way to achieve some degree of cross-training; rotating assigments between functional areas is another. In the Hewlett-Packard DeskJet project, for example, design engineers were encouraged to take on assignments in manufacturing. To provide an incentive to move to another function engineers were given a "ticket" that would allow them to return. The result was excellent integration between design and manufacturing.

In addition to being cross-trained, it is helpful to have experienced cross-functional team members and even better if team members have worked together previously.

Both Kodak's Panda printer and antistatic film-coating projects benefited from prior relationships between team members. Principals within each project had worked together on a prior, failed project. Memories of the mistakes were fresh in their minds and they articulated a strong desire not to make the same blunders again. Managers of the antistatic coating team felt that the earlier, failed project suffered from a lack of rigorous discipline and strong coordination; team members were at times either too standoffish or too polite to get down to brass tacks. This time around, they placed a high priority on achieving tight, meaningful project definitions. Similarly, leaders of the Panda project felt the earlier failure resulted from inadequate attention to the interface between three technologies: hardware, software, and print media. When the team was assembled, representatives from these three areas agreed to co-locate and were insistent on the need to approach design from a systems perspective in which interface difficulties would be given extensive attention.

Prior team interaction can help facilitate cross-training. Many of the team members in Ford's Crown Victoria program had participated on an earlier project. Because of that, engineering team members were slowly developing a much greater awareness of the project-wide cost implications of their decisions and were becoming more proficient at matching functional and financial objectives. The Crown Victoria program benefited significantly from thorough and accurate cost modeling implemented jointly by the engineers and the finance representatives.

Of course, prior exposure of team members to each other is not always possible. But if a company can create an ethic in which cross-functional exposure is a way of life, and can design it into the company's operating structure, employees will be much better able to cross-train when they do come together on a new effort. This practice underlies most activity at Chaparral Steel. To begin with, all employees at all levels and at all times participate in development projects. This fosters continuous and extensive interactions between individuals and functions. Also, employee evaluations are based on team, not functional, performance. As such, employees are more attuned to concerns pertaining to other functions on their team.

In addition, Chaparral provides training to team members in each others' activities, and generally rotates personnel among jobs so they can gain experience. Finally, Chaparral fosters hands-on experience in different functions by use of an interesting staffing policy: when an employee goes on leave, his or her duties are covered by other members of the team and no temporary replacement is sought. As a result, individuals learn how to operate in many diverse functions.

At its most basic level, cross-training enables team members to build trust and respect and to do so at earlier stages of a project. Cross-training also leads to more effective communication, empathy of team members for other functions, and constructive "give-and-take" interactions, and enables people from one function to "add value" to the tasks being performed by those from other functions.

## Team Building and Interpersonal Skills

Another action that widely led to strong integration was deliberate development of team-building skills. All team members on a development project perform important roles as information providers, knowledge consultants, problem-solvers, energizers, and ambassadors who articulate the constraints and capabilities of their respective functions. But to bring about integration, the contribution of team members must go beyond simply providing inputs; each person must constructively convert these inputs into operating parameters for the project as a whole. To do so, they must learn the language of different functions, build relationships with other team members, receive feedback in an open manner, and engage in give-and-take negotiations.

Integration places a premium on the skills of team members. The skills required exceed those of a technical nature. While technical expertise, reputation, and personal credibility often receive foremost consideration when staffing a new team, a person's interpersonal skills, particularly those relating to cross-functional communication and team building, are also critical and often are much more difficult to identify and evaluate.

How to develop the interpersonal skills needed for team building is often a matter of consternation to company managers. After Kodak had picked its team for the Factory of the Future project, for example, management tried to enhance team building by sending team members off-site on an "Outward Bound"-style sailing venture. Many of the employees who participated told us they thought it was the wrong format for teaching team building and was poorly timed. It took key people away at critical junctures early in the project and did not relate to the team's concerns, most of which were technical and all of which were specific to the project. They said they would have found it much more helpful to have received training on how to perform team tasks important to the project, not how to sail. Subsequent Outward Bound programs have incorporated project-specific activities as part of the experience.

Early on in Chaparral's Pulpit Controls project, management actually slowed work until all critical members of the team were on board. There was a maintenance manager whom management knew was central to the project who did not initially buy into the project concept; management spent time addressing his concerns before they allowed the team to proceed. Once convinced, the maintenance manager felt part of the team, and management's action served to boost the sense of importance given to team unity. Management also helped sustain the team's commitment and momentum by periodically sending it on visits to other steel plants and vendors to learn more about relevant technologies and operating practices.

Sometimes efforts to build team commitment must be undertaken on various levels if they are to work. On DEC's RA90 disk drive project, the group was divided into three development teams, to create respectively a new thin-film head for the drive, a new thin-film media, and a new mechanical drive system. Each subteam fostered a good level of team commitment by following such measures as having all team members participate in the selection and hiring of new members, having them attend classes on key technical topics, and traveling together to other sites to gain experience.

However, at the overall project level, where the three subteams were to integrate their results, there was no team building. There was not even a clear designation of who was responsible for integration, and none of the subgroups took it on themselves. Because of the lack of oversight and commitment to the ultimate goal, the subteams set out with different timetables and agendas; one employee described the effort as akin to three loaded freight trains, each going down its own track. Each train built up its own momentum, but collectively the trains did not arrive at the same time or initially even at the same station. Failure to develop effective integration at the level of the total project was a major source of added cost and delays.[5]

## Prototyping and Simulation

Of the companies we examined, Chaparral Steel demonstrated the highest degree of integration in its four projects, both in terms of development processes and outcome of specific projects. The single most important communications tool used by Chaparral's development teams was the "physical reality" of projects. That is, they would use prototypes to focus their discussion across functional differences. They would visit other facilities to benchmark their ideas, and use graphs and models of the concepts they were pursuing to communicate more effectively. In every case, the bulk of each development project was done on an actual production line. Improved communication between functional working teams revolved around the physical reality of what they were doing and what they needed— rapid movement from conceptualizations and generalizations to physical models or actual production systems. When the Arc Saw project, intended to develop the industry's first electric-arc saw for cutting production volumes of steel, did not generate the desired results, management did not remove the equipment from the facility, because they wanted to stimulate on-going tinkering and discussion. The physical reality focused communication on the substance of what team members were trying to accomplish, the specifics of how they were going to accomplish it, and the practical issues that would have to be addressed to achieve outstanding results.

Functional integration for Ford's Crown Victoria program was high and also benefited from physical reality. The prototyping operation, usually off in its own facility with its own equipment, was co-located with manufacturing. For the first time, verification prototypes were built on the production line during up-time. We stress the fact that not only were the people co-located, but the equipment with which they worked was centralized too. A planner could grab an engineer and pick up a financial control person on their way to look at a part on a car. The physical reality of the part would direct attention to the problems that needed to be solved and less so to the specific interests and stakes of the different people or functions.

For complex projects, communication may be stymied if there are many unknowns or when there is an information vacuum at the interface of technologies. To reduce these barriers, Kodak's Panda team members turned to such tools as mathematical modeling and simulation. During Ford's Crown Victoria program, extensive computer, clay modeling, and analytical constructs were used successfully at the system level to predict crashworthiness and noise-vibration-harshness characteristics. The team felt that the use of extended databases and modeling capabilities helped designers from different functions to interface more effectively.

Modeling and simulation often are used to improve the fidelity and bandwidth of communication between specializations, and they constitute an early form of prototyping. A few teams used CAD systems to help overcome interface issues between design and manufacturing. With appropriate software programs, for example, CAD can be used to verify whether load-bearing parts of a new product are strong enough and sufficiently stress or fatigue resistant. Other applications monitor qualities such as moldability and formability. Software can also estimate the cost of production, or specify the tool-cutting path for parts and stamping dies. At the same time, manufacturing engineers can enter the "dialogue" and provide feedback to design engineers before parameters are locked in. They can also get a head start on the design of tools and processes. In addition, CAD leads to faster development of future generations of a product by using existing platforms that are fully documented and accessible through the system.

The FunSaver project at Kodak illustrated a highly effective use of CAD. Geometries of the camera frame and other components were designed around the lens subsystem, the critical element. The entire design process was conducted using this approach, and design and manufacturing engineers worked jointly from a common database. A special protocol was developed by team members for labeling the timing and source of changes and determining when to purge prior design versions. The system was credited for the short development time of the product and the relatively trouble-free production start-up. Subsequently, two line extensions to the first product were begun within two weeks and took relatively few months to complete.

Though it can provide great leverage, we did not observe widespread use of CAD as a facilitator of integration. CAD was most often employed as an efficient drafting and design tool rather than one that facilitated cross-functional communication or provided for the evaluation of design with respect to manufacturability. The implementation of structured methodologies based on CAD capabilities, such as design for assembly or robust product design, appeared to be used only sporadically and in an ad hoc fashion. In fact, it appeared that an integrated process was a prerequisite for realizing the full potential of CAD, not the reverse. We would expect to see CAD used more extensively as more people learn how to leverage it to improve integration.[6]

## Management Protocols

Several companies we studied, in particular Ford and Kodak, adopted formal project management procedures to drive integration, and the teams that used the procedures said they did indeed contribute to integration. The procedures had different names and were modified to fit the needs of different types of projects, such as consumer products versus industrial processes. They were used to track progress through a series of stages that included concept development, technology demonstration, feasibility demonstration, successive iterations of design reviews, manufacturing review, and product launch.

Although the formal control of development activities is not new, its use as observed in this research is notable for a number of reasons. In the cases we studied, the carefully planned and more sophisticated protocols did much more than offer a highly organized procedure for coordinating activities; they reflected a new philosophy premised on the importance of integration and system integrity. They shifted the center of gravity from the traditional focus on technology development to the entire development process, from concept justification through commercialization and even product discontinuance. They also served to reduce and share risk and eliminate occasions for finger-pointing. In addition, they spread responsibility for success beyond the performance of the team, to funding sources and outside groups who had to provide proper support in order for all objectives to be met.

Though each company's procedures were different, there were common components. These included some way to clearly delineate each phase of development; a way to relate objectives, dominant issues, and activities to team composition; the types of analyses to be undertaken (such as market research); and the appropriate processes for deliberations (brainstorming, focus groups, or consensus gathering). In each scheme, the steps included measurable goals that enabled those involved to determine in an explicit and unambiguous manner whether or not the activities had adequately addressed the issues of that step. In some instances, the dates for completion of a future step were not set until the team passed the test of the current step. Whether a project would pass from one step to the next was determined by various people, often the project manager but in other cases by review committees or steering committees made up of senior managers.

The existence of management protocols did not in and of itself guarantee effective integration. Procedures were in place for Kodak's Panda project, for example, but they were not followed with rigorous discipline. Kodak had an established set of reviews for the project, but when the reviews turned up problems the project was allowed to continue anyway. The Panda project team reported that adherence to the process lacked intensity and commitment. Reviews were not rigorous, challenges were not raised, and difficulties did not receive the degree of scrutiny to the extent needed.

When used with discipline, management protocols can greatly aid integration. One manager described development efforts pursued after his company established protocols as a "well-choreographed ballet" versus the "hockey game" atmosphere that preceded it. Protocols can eliminate much back-tracking and improve the quality of decisions. Team members achieve a better understanding of each others' constraints and contributions. The focus of work is smoothly transferred in a seamless manner from one phase or function to another rather than being "thrown over the wall." Production start-up, in particular, becomes more efficient. Managers we spoke with also commented on how protocols fostered creativity and learning. For one project, team members estimated that strict adherence to protocols shortened the development cycle by as much as one-third.[7]

## AN INTEGRATED APPROACH TO ACHIEVING INTEGRATION

The fundamental lesson about integration that the Manufacturing Vision Group took away from the many projects it analyzed was that for integration to be truly effective, it must be pursued on multiple levels. Integration is required not only between functions and project phases, but also between different scientific disciplines, business units, and external parties.

While workable solutions can emerge from development processes that are integrated or non-integrated, the quality and efficiency of these outcomes differ markedly. Integrated projects generate solutions that are higher in quality and achieved with less cost and in less time. In a number of the cases we looked at, integration contributed to the attainment of highly aggressive technical and economic requirements. Integration also contributed to the achievement of strategic advantages, such as being the first to move to a new type of product or process, the setting of demanding hurdles that became more difficult for competitors to overcome, and establishing of strong defenses in response to new competitive offerings. Integration also benefited entire product families by providing a strong initial product platform and putting in place effective organizational communication processes that enabled follow-on products to be introduced almost immediately.

Despite these advantages, integrated processes were the exception rather than the rule. Overall, progress was further along with respect to the integration between design and manufacturing; linkages between technical development and other functions such as marketing and sales were almost always poor.

Though cross-functional teams were set up for a large number of the projects, corresponding development processes were not necessarily integrated in nature. In these cases, the cross-functional team achieved coordination but not integration, and thus the projects proceeded in a sequential manner between tasks and functional units. Information tended to flow from upstream to downstream functions, or from more dominant to less dominant functions. As such, the burden for integration often rested with the downstream units, or was passed on to specially created "SWAT" teams in more serious cases. Downstream activities often "lived" with constraints imposed by decisions made earlier on. Conflict resolutions tended to reflect the pecking order in the formal hierarchy or the preference of the dominant functions.

In contrast, integrated processes were characterized by joint decision making by all team members from the start of the projects. Both upstream and downstream units actively "chose" the constraints under which they would operate. The team's focus was anchored by the desired technical and economic performance of the end product. Integrated processes also enabled teams to be more aggressive in exploiting opportunities at the interfaces between technical groups, for example in trade-offs between software and hardware solutions, product design and field service, or chemical and mechanical subsystems. While integrated processes did utilize formal coordination mechanisms, they also benefited extensively from the real-time, spontaneous, informal interactions made possible by co-location of team members and other strategies. More important, these interactions helped build a shared language, common experiences, and trust, which enabled system integration issues to be addressed simultaneously with the development of functional policies.

While these actions are useful at the working level, their effectiveness is by-and-large circumscribed by the level of management's commitment to create the requisite capabilities and internal environment for achieving integration. The message for integration cannot be credible if the corporate culture endorses a mentality of first-class and second-class citizens. Major restructuring of tasks and sometimes complete functions is unlikely to happen unless it is initiated from the top. In the same vein, project management protocols are only effective if senior management is willing to commit to the financial and personal support of specific projects and to the accountability demanded by the process.

Team members' exposure to different functional and technical disciplines needs to go beyond training seminars to specific job and collaborative assignments designed to provide greater depth of knowledge and breadth of perspectives. Yet such moves must be part of carefully designed corporate-wide human resource policies that align the development of people and capabilities with the strategic directions of the firm. In some cases team members do not view the participation in cross-functional teams as their primary responsibility. The time they spend on such projects is tolerated as a necessary nuisance, while their performance on such teams often goes unrecognized. As such, evaluation and reward criteria can limit the extent to which employees support integration. Working-level integration can only be achieved through measures aimed at enhancing individual skills and knowledge, practices, and tools deployed at the project level, and the design of organizational systems and a culture that support such measures.

## CHAPTER 9

# An Opportunity for Leadership in Learning

It is a scene played out many times over in many companies: after a long and arduous process a new product is unveiled, the project team celebrates, manufacturing and sales crank up the commercial engine, and senior management smiles and anxiously awaits the market's response. It has been much the same in the Manufacturing Vision Group. We too have worked together as a team, have designed, prototyped, and developed our product (this book), and have been tempted to celebrate as the seven themes we derived from our study emerged in the form of seven completed chapters. But we also have been aware that even having finished the seven theme chapters, and the company histories that form the second half of the book, the "product" is incomplete. It is not that the seven themes are not the right ones; we believe they capture the driving forces of success in development. Indeed, our work together has convinced us of the power of these ideas. But it has also convinced us of the great challenge in actually putting these ideas into practice. The themes can only be effective to the extent they get implemented. Faster, better, more effective development will result from an understanding of these themes to the extent that the organization moves to action. And that effectiveness will only be deep and enduring to the extent that the action is coherent, creating a total pattern of development capability. Making this happen is in the first instance a matter of leadership, buttressed by a deep understanding of principles and the practical realities of bringing about change and improvement in the organization.

Thus, before we celebrated our product, we felt a need to make one final push. Our desire was to pull the seven themes together, to find their common roots, and to examine how to convert the themes into real action. To do that the senior executives in the Vision Group, in their own words, share here their perspectives and experience in a direct and personal way with the reader.

## To the Reader: The Voice of Practice

Okay, you've made it. You've read about the seven fundamental dynamics that drive the success or failure of development projects. So tomorrow morning, when you walk into work, you'll be ready to start making changes. Right?

Wrong. That's where we ourselves, the members of the Manufacturing Vision Group, thought we were late in 1991, as the deep probing into our own projects concluded and the seven themes common to all projects became clear. As those among us from the five companies got energized to charge back to our development teams and coworkers, we suddenly realized something was missing. True, we had seven aspects of our own projects that we could analyze—it gave us a way to examine our companies' strengths and weaknesses—and we had lessons we could apply to improve each of them. But we were missing the big picture. How did the themes come together? And *how* did we go about taking action on them?

We quickly realized these two questions were profound. If this three-year internal investigation was to be useful to us, and if the resulting book was to be useful to you the reader, the questions had to be answered. So in May 1992 we got together in a studio at Eastman Kodak in Rochester and held our own day-long panel discussion.

We re-discovered an important point: no one, not we the study participants nor you the reader, can simply take a lesson learned about a particular project at Chaparral or DEC or Ford or Hewlett-

Packard or Kodak and transfer it to their own projects without modification. We agreed that we indeed needed to understand the seven themes so we'd know what to look for back home, and that we needed to understand how a particular company dealt with a particular theme such as core capabilities or prototyping. But what we unearthed was this: each of us would have to *adapt* what we learned to our own company.

If, as you've been reading, you have been looking for some prescription, some magic bullet that will rocket your company to stardom, you will be disappointed. There is no formula. Once you complete the text you won't be ready to solve all your problems. But you certainly will be prepared to find your own solutions, and, we submit, you would not find them otherwise.

The point is that you cannot learn from Company X how to directly improve Company Y. But what you can learn from Company X are a whole lot of things you ought to take into consideration as you design your own solutions. You've got to go through a learning process about your company. You have to find a way to learn about how well your development efforts are working. You must understand your own development system—not just the flow charts or organizational structures you use, but the way in which your people actually work together. It is a living system, and to improve it requires a system solution. The hard part is that the system continually changes, and thus your solution must continually evolve as well.

How, you might ask, can you possibly design a moving solution to a moving problem? By figuring out how to learn about your company. That's what we realized at the panel discussion. Said Bill Hanson, from Digital Equipment Corp.: "One of our greatest problems as a company, and I think it applies to most companies out there, is that we are less of a learning organization than we used to be. We used to hold 'boot camp.' We'd all go off-site somewhere and sit down and discuss what was happening within our company. That's how we learned and how we made progress. We've stopped doing that. The value of this book is that it can be used as the focus for such a boot camp, right at the office. It is a platform for discussion, a catalyst for action."

To improve product development, to improve the very heart of the company, managers must rethink the way in which they view the various elements of their business. "You've really got to be rocked off the position that it's not necessary to continually learn about how your company works," said Hal Edmondson, from Hewlett-Packard. Once you open up your mind again and find a fresh way of thinking, you can use the seven theme chapters to help you initiate change.

This chapter presents that fresh way in which to think about your company. It lays out five insights that, once understood and embraced, will enable you to adapt the lessons in the seven theme chapters. The five insights, explained in detail as the chapter progresses, are the following.

1. Companies must continually learn about themselves and must use the process of learning as a competitive tool. The best way to learn about yourself is by examining your development projects, which are microcosms of what goes on in the entire organization.
2. Effective learning will not take place unless leaders in the company promote learning as everyone's primary responsibility.
3. Development projects may have two outcomes. The first and more apparent is a product or process. The second, and more elusive, is the opportunity to learn from the project's lessons and build capability within the organization. Thus development projects may become agents of change for a company.
4. A company's guiding visions, which exist at three levels—the project, the line of business, and the company—must support learning, leadership in learning, and the desire to leverage both outcomes of a development project.
5. Every strength is a weakness. Just as a core capability can become a core rigidity, internal learning and the leveraging of development projects can also inhibit your ability to change. This must be recognized and countered as your company evolves.

These five insights provide the context in which you can apply the seven themes to your company. Once you get your fellow employees to understand the importance of learning, how leadership is needed to create learning, how projects can be used as change agents to foster learning, how consensus in visions promotes learning, and how to confront the duality of learning as you move toward the future, you can begin to make changes.

Do not underestimate the degree to which you are going to have to adapt the lessons of this book. But know that you have at your disposal a broad and rich set of case studies on which to draw. The Manufacturing Vision Group examined five companies and 20 projects diverse enough to show the full range of development patterns encountered in industry. Companies in different markets will face different situations, different cultures, and different competitive challenges. The themes presented in this book will have to be translated, and that will be no simple task. But the framework established in this chapter will make an effective translation possible.

## LEARNING FROM DEVELOPMENT PROJECTS

All manufacturing companies are born from a development project. Some companies only get through one project and then go out of business. Those that persevere go on to a second project, then a third, and gradually build. Development projects are the essence of manufacturing firms. There may be times when projects are well down the life cycle and all the company is doing is producing and selling goods, but that won't hold true for long, especially in today's environment.

The best way to get a high resolution picture of the company is to delve deep into the heart of development. Development projects serve as a window on the essence of the firm, both its strengths and its weaknesses. They show where a company's opportunities lie and where its challenges are. Development projects, then, are the place in which to learn about the company and how people work together. And they are the place in which to instill the idea in employees that their primary goal is to learn.

Of the five companies in the Vision Group, Chaparral Steel most sees itself as a learning organization. The company's success proves what a powerful notion that is. "A company is a group of learners," said Chaparral's Dave Fournie. "At least, that's what it *should* be. If your people learn, then you as an organization will learn. The challenge is to figure out how people can learn, how as a group you face the unknown, how you stretch yourselves. This is the way you build a successful business.''

Indeed, the most successful projects we examined were those in which the development team operated in a learning environment. People learned from previous projects and advanced their skills. The learning, however, was not haphazard. "As an organizational phenomena, learning from development is not natural," said Kim Clark, from Harvard Business School. "You've learned something if the experience you gain on one project gives you new ways of working that are put into practice on the next project. But that doesn't happen on its own. You have to actually undertake a systematic effort to learn from development, put it into practice, and make it happen. You have to have a learning *process*."

Few companies do this, however. "Industry doesn't do much learning in a purposeful way," Edmondson declared. "It's coincidental, or anecdotal. It's not rigorous."

Much of the learning that does take place is piecemeal. People learn bits and fragments and carry them from project to project. Often, too, the learning is technical. Many people at manufacturing companies do a good job of advancing their knowledge in their discipline. But to learn about how people work together, about a company's capabilities, and to use that learning as a tool to continually improve competitiveness, someone has got to step back and ask what the development team, and the company in support of the team, did right and wrong. And they have to figure out what that all means and what should be changed. Once this is done, then senior managers can begin to answer fundamental competitive questions: Do we change people? Do we change process? Do we change methods? Do we change timing?

## The Difficulty of Learning How to Learn

The first step in learning how to learn about your company is to accept the idea that learning must be a process. We formed the Manufacturing Vision Group because we wanted our companies to be learning organizations so we could excel.

To be a learning organization, learning must take place on many levels. Just as expertise in specific functions does not result in effective, integrated development projects, learning in specific functions is not enough to move the company forward. A company's activities are broad-based and cross-organizational; therefore, the learning must be interdisciplinary.

There is a convenient way to think about the different levels of learning. Several earlier chapters address lessons found in the everyday work of development projects. Rapid prototyping, for example, is a better way to learn about your products as they are developed. Pushing the envelope is about learning how to advance a company's capabilities. This can be described as learning spelled with a "little l." Here, however, we are talking about creating a learning organization—creating a corporate environment in which line operators, managers, and senior executives continually seek to advance the firm's knowledge. This can be called learning spelled with a "Big L." The "little l" lessons are learned in project after project; the "Big L" lessons are learned by stepping back and examining the entire group of projects. If managers can create a system in which Big L learning occurs, then development efforts in particular and the company as a whole will advance smartly.

In reviewing the projects, the panel found great corporate inertia that inhibits Big L learning. "Many people think of learning as an inoculation. That attitude quickly becomes a rigidity," said Digital's Doug Braithwaite. "They think, 'Oh, I've got a BS. I've gone to college. It's over.' Or they think, 'I just need some additional training, then I'll be all set.' That attitude is quite pervasive."

What's needed instead is an attitude that learning must be continuous. When the Chaparral team was first formed to build a new horizontal caster used to make steel, for example, it visited every one of the existing horizontal casters worldwide, even though the casters were not being used in the way Chaparral intended. Five years into the project, after Chaparral had built prototypes and tried them on the production line, the development team, which still consisted of the same people who began the project, went abroad to revisit the same six sites, to see what progress had occurred and to verify how their own approach stacked up against the global state of the art. The team returned home to make further refinements, and by the end of the year the caster was operating around the clock.

"The same people revisited five years later!" Hanson remarked in awe. "Those words wouldn't exist at our company."

"And I'll bet in most companies that after five years, you wouldn't even know who the original project people were," added Chuck Holloway, from Stanford.

In this example, "little learning" refers to the technical advances the Chaparral team discovered during its visits. The "big learning" refers to the approach the team used. The team took for granted the need to benchmark its proposed system against the best, and to continue to verify the validity of its development against its competitors even after the project, to outsiders, seemed "finished."

To accomplish the cross-functional Big L learning you need perspective. It is management's job to figure out how to get that perspective. Ford's experience with its Concept-to-Customer (C-to-C) process provides a case in point. Recognizing the need for fundamental change, Ford's North American Car Product Development organization established a team to work exclusively on improving the development process. Although they were experienced in development, the team members had some distance from current projects and could focus on the challenge of learning and improving the process as a whole.

Clearly there are many ways to obtain perspective, but it was our feeling during the panel discussion that for people involved in a project, getting a complete perspective on the development process in that project is very difficult. For one thing, there is tremendous pressure in manufacturing organizations to move to the next activity. Projects are often late or behind, people are scrambling, money is tight. It's hard during all the commotion to carve out time and energy and resources to be able to step aside and reflect on what is being accomplished. You might begin by setting up a small group of people whose mission is to look at one project and ask: What did we learn? How does it relate to the previous projects we've undertaken? What was different? Did we do anything really well that we want to use to change the way in which we do future projects? Was there some hidden trait that now we can see that we want to make sure we avoid?

Get a small, systematic review going. Then you can begin to learn how to learn on a greater scale.

The focus must be kept at the system level, and the review group must be diverse. "If I'm a materials scientist and I'm in a room with other materials scientists, the perception will be that we can make a lot of progress learning about materials," said Kent Bowen, from MIT. "But when we try to look across disciplines, we'll become very ineffective."

## Learning as a Rigidity

As you start to understand how to learn about your company, you should realize that the learning process itself can become a rigidity. The managers instituting the C-to-C process at Ford foresaw this; they could have designed their C-to-C process, then rested, thinking they had found the answer to improving development. But they understood that implementation of this process was only the first step in an evolution toward better product development. An ongoing C-to-C team continues to assess and refine the process. This constant review motivates continual organizational change as Ford continually improves its teamwork.

In monitoring how well learning takes place, Ford and other companies in our study exposed several mechanisms that worked to prevent organizational learning. Some projects were indeed audited after their completion by a group from within the company. But the review was not systematic. Sometimes the reviewers were reluctant to shine light on problems because it would embarrass people and appear unfair. This perception has to be changed, and the way it can be changed is to establish the idea that learning from projects is a goal for everyone in the company. People should be made to feel that learning from within is a corporate asset that, if pursued objectively and openly, can become a core capability. Once employees understand this, then the review of failed projects will not carry a negative connotation.

Even when reviews were held and solutions to problems were designed, they often weren't implemented. "The company found a solution that worked," said Clark, "but then when you examined the next project, lo and behold, the solution hadn't been implemented. So management goes back and investigates some more. The solution never gets captured because the value placed on learning has not been institutionalized. Later, the people who go through the process of learning and designing a solution eventually get transferred. The next project comes around, the same mistakes are made, and new reviewers discover the same problems."

Two realizations at the corporate level can greatly assist managers in applying the lessons learned from one project to another. The first is to recognize that every development project affects the company in general, and every project should therefore have two distinct goals—to successfully develop the product and to advance the learning of the organization. By explicitly establishing this expectation, everyone in the company will begin to look for the transfer of lessons. Second, the desire to be a learning organization must be supported by guiding visions. If the visions that guide people in their daily work place a priority on learning, then people will slowly adopt the needed frame of mind.

## LEADERSHIP IN LEARNING

Even with proper project goals and visions, however, a company has little chance to become a learning organization if its senior managers do not promote the concept of learning. For this to occur, senior managers themselves must learn directly what is going on in the depths of the company. "If CEOs really want to know what their companies are all about," Bowen maintained, "they should come down and look into the development projects. They will gain much better understanding than they'll get from their high perch. When I looked at the different projects in the different divisions of Hewlett-Packard, I really began to see what made Hewlett-Packard tick. The same was true at Chaparral and DEC and Kodak and Ford. The power of this observation is that if there are aspects of the company that managers would like to change, the development project is the critical size element that they ought to start playing with. It has the right level of complexity, the right level of cross-functional interaction.''

However, most senior managers do not dig down into development projects. As a result, they do not have the level of understanding necessary to draw lessons from failures or successes. For example, Kodak's Factory of the Future project, undertaken during a time when the company was changing from a strictly functional to a more integrated organization, portrayed both the best and the worst of the old organization. The project was run by a group from engineering that had great depth of expertise and was willing to tackle very tough projects. Yet it was not as sensitive to the other parts of the company as it should have been; the group discounted the needs of others who would be affected by the project and lost sight of the original objectives as it got mired in technical detail. Had a senior manager been on the project group this would have been clear, and this higher level input could have helped remove the team's blinders. Once accomplished, the manager and the team leaders could have gone on to other projects and begun to transfer what they had learned. Instead, the lack of coordination and integration bogged down the project to the point of having to abandon it. In contrast, Kodak's antistatic film coating project embodied the best of the company's efforts to integrate. Managers took an interest in the project and began to get a clear view of how to transfer the positive lessons to other work.

In addition to neglect, senior managers are also guilty of thwarting learning, often not consciously. ''Most people in companies want to learn,'' Hanson noted. ''However, senior managers end up putting a whole bunch of roadblocks in place so it doesn't happen. All too often senior managers look down on a project only to declare whether it was successful or not. Maybe they look inside it a bit to see what made it succeed or fail. But what they don't do is analyze what their own role was. That role should be finding a way to put a learning process in place. Managers rarely look for this or even consider it. Meanwhile, they try to fix problems they don't fully understand, and do it by delegating, and end up putting roadblocks in place so the learning doesn't flow.''

For an organization to learn, its senior people have to think of themselves as leaders in learning. "I keep seeing a lot of managers out there, but not a lot of leaders," Bowen said.

Of course there will be different styles of leaders. Some will be more technically oriented, others more administrative. But in all cases senior managers must view their primary role as leadership. Said Clark: "If you are looking to the future, to creating things that are new, to pulling the whole picture together, then you cannot manage in the narrow sense of controlling, budgeting, planning, and directing. You must lead."

The first step in transforming oneself from a manager to a leader is to view your role as that of mentor, teacher, and coach, especially with respect to learning. However, managers must have a clear understanding of the company's guiding visions, and a strong sense of what goes on within development projects before they can teach and support.

And remember, as Fournie said, "Learning is not an isolated task. Learning must be continual and it has to change."

Few people view this role as their own responsibility. "I don't know if I can name very many of our people who know how Digital Equipment Corporation works, or are even concerned about it," Hanson mused. "And I would say the same applies at Ford and every other company on down the line. If everyone would just sit down and say, 'Wow, there is this organism here called Digital Equipment, and yeah I'm going to learn more about it every day, then people and functions will start to interrelate. Development will move forward. Communication will start to improve. The learning process will begin. Then, when I make a change over here, people will see how it impacts over there. As a group, we'll learn every year how to do our tasks better."

The requirement for senior management to have deep understanding of the substance of development activity, to really understand how projects operate, might be an anxious proposition for some. "It's a scary problem because a lot of managers get to where they are without that kind of understanding," Clark said. "If you're sitting there without that understanding, what do you do? This has some profound implications for senior management."

Part of the problem stems from the very premise that companies make about development projects: there is only one goal—the product or process. "If you're taught right from the very beginning that every project has two dimensions to it, that you don't simply measure the results but you also measure how you arrived at those results, then you'll be prepared to learn," said Hanson.

To bring senior managers to this new role, a company's top echelon must begin to change the environment within the company. One place to start is at the bottom. "I think back to some of the research done by Wick Skinner [professor emeritus from Harvard] on what happens to the young, bright graduates who spill out into the world and are ready to change it," Edmondson recalled. "He studied a group of graduates, and revisited them every year or two, and after ten years they looked like everybody else in the companies they had joined. They had conformed very nicely to what the stodgy managers had wanted them to conform to. Somehow we've got to figure out how to keep the old farts from trying to corrupt the fresh outlook of the newcomers. We've got to alter the career-pathing for people on teams and for project leaders. To prevent the bright young employees from being dulled, we've got to get their bosses into an evolving, learning situation as well."

## Better Support for Better Project Leaders

Another way to foster leadership is to make the job of project leader one that people want to pursue. There is a lot of personal risk associated with being a project leader, and a great deal of hard work. If you don't create the right atmosphere, people won't be lining up to take the position. That was certainly what we found at the companies we studied. People would turn down the opportunity, saying "No thank you. I don't need that heartache." One engineering manager at DEC, for example, spoke disdainfully about his concurrent role as project manager as "not my real job." He derived satisfaction and respect only from his engineering work.

Part of the "heartache" of being a project leader is that the job, by its nature, requires a person to be an agent for change. He or she must push the project team and the company to change in order to learn from and accomplish the project. Because they are pushing for change, which most people naturally resist, they often get burned out. Or, "They end up with a lot of arrows sticking out of their backs," Edmondson said.

Here is where some of the insights of this chapter come together. A leader must be a change agent, and to be a change agent, you have to create learning, demand learning, and you have to learn yourself. And somehow, you've got to get management to support that role. The reason so many change agents are shot at is because the organization is not moving ahead, or wishes it wasn't moving ahead. A leader who steps too far out in front without support from the top will pick up a lot of arrows from behind.

"We refer to it as architects or maintainers," Chaparral's Fournie said. "An architect causes change. A maintainer holds the status quo. That's the difference between a leader and a manager."

Surely, a forward-looking company wants to encourage people to become project leaders and change agents. A major issue that discourages people, however, is the typical company reward system. "In a small, hungry entrepreneurial company where the recognition and rewards for completing a project successfully are clear," said Stanford's Holloway, "people line up 20 deep for opportunities to manage development projects. Why don't the people line up at a large, established company? Because there are few potential rewards. Leading a new development project would be the most exciting job in the company if there was a reward system to back it up."


## PROJECTS ARE THE AGENTS OF CHANGE

To this point, we've established several strong premises: that to be competitive, companies must become learning organizations; that the best way to learn about the company is to focus on what happens in development projects; and that to capitalize on the learning you must have leaders who promote learning and an environment in which these leaders can excel.

But what is the best vehicle to implement what is being learned? Once again, it is the development project.

"It is clear from our investigation that projects are the best agents of renewal for the corporation," Hanson said. "That is a simple statement but it is extremely profound. I know we have missed that point at Digital. All the projects that we studied at our company were more important as agents for renewal than they were for the products that came from them."

"If CEOs and other top corporate people would just realize that the projects are the agents of renewal and the essence of the company," added Charles Farran, from Kodak, "then they would focus their attention very differently, and learning would be implemented."

The FX15 project at Ford's Climate Control Division (CCD), in which the division for the first time produced in-house a compressor for automobile air conditioners, was a good example of a case in which an organization did not have certain capabilities and used a project to create, in addition to the desired product, a whole set of capabilities that then became the basis for future product development. CCD used the project to integrate, for the first time, many different functions of the division—particularly design and manufacturing. The team members together defined the product's goals and vision. The attempt worked so well that the project became an agent for change throughout the division; when subsequent projects were initiated, teams were formed in the same manner, and cross-functional integration improved. It has now become a strength at Ford.

A great example on the negative side was Ford's project to develop the 1989 Thunderbird. Because it would require a new car platform and a new supercharged engine, the project had great potential to pull together various functions and create a new and increasingly important capability in the automobile business—the linking of advanced component development to product development. But senior management did not start the project with this new capability in mind. It didn't have a guiding vision that linked the two efforts. After the Vision Group reviewed the program, a number of senior people at Ford expressed surprise at the project's outcome, because they thought people understood that the connection should be made. But it wasn't because the people running the project had only one explicit objective and didn't see the larger issue. Ford did get a supercharger, but the process it used—ignoring technology developed in its research labs, myriad unexpected problems, multiple iterations on basic design, delays and cost overruns—was not one it would ever want to repeat.

Every project can serve as a positive change agent if it is managed as such. "The sad part about it," Hanson said, "is that, at DEC for example, there are thousands of projects going on. So the opportunity and the energy is there. But we as senior management haven't created a larger process that channels this energy forward."

The underlying point is that if you have the capability to do a wide range of projects in your company, then you have a very powerful advantage, a core capability, to create change. But if your organization has not thought of development projects as the primary agents of change, it will not be able to leverage that advantage.

Kodak made good use of a development effort as a change agent when it began its antistatic coating project. The project evolved from an evaluation by the line of business responsible for imaging products, which showed that some end-users of Kodak's microfilms thought the images on Kodak films were less sharp than those on films made by competitors. Kodak determined that actual image sharpness, as defined in standard tests, was no different, but Kodak's images were sometimes perceived as less sharp because the microfilm background appeared a bit darker. The slight darkening resulted from a coating placed on the film to reduce the attraction of dust. The perceived lack of sharpness could have led to potential loss of market share, so the business unit responsible for microfilms formed a team to develop a significantly clearer antistatic coating. As a result, Kodak created a superior microfilm, which captured added sales, and put into place a new capability to make clearer antistatic coatings.

Of course, trying to capitalize on both outcomes of projects does not come free. It takes extra time, extra effort, and probably extra money too. Unfortunately, too many companies do not see these investments as valuable.

"In our company, and I would guess in others, there is a tendency to specifically not use product development as a change agent," said HP's Edmondson, "because you're pushing some technical frontiers anyway, and you don't want to risk screwing it up by trying to effect organizational changes as well. Sure, managers sometimes recognize that when they've got a new product coming along they've got an opportunity for change, and maybe they'll throw a few things into the project. But these items are never given priority because people have an expectation boundary that limits any kind of change except technical change.''

Holloway addresses the point. ''Often senior managers and project leaders do realize they can build capability from a project, but they don't want to make any changes to attain that learning while the project is underway. They think they'll make the changes after the project is finished. Well, the project gets completed and then they move on. They don't want to take time to do the building during the project because it might foul up the project. Then they don't want to do it after the project is over because they think, 'What difference does it make now?' There are good intentions—'When we get through with this project we're going to get it right'—but then they're into the next project and they never get it right. What happens in the long run is that all the missed opportunities build up, and learning becomes impossible to pull off.''

Managers who do make the effort to develop new capability as a second project goal, however, must be careful not to view the projects as experiments in learning. Projects should not be regarded as a chance to ''try out'' something new. Learning and building capability must be integral to the work that takes place, and must be a continuum from one project to another.

It is important to recognize that building new capability means implementing new practices, skills, procedures, or methods that become an enduring part of the development system. That will only happen effectively in a project if the project itself is a good match for the capability you are trying to create. Consider, for example, Kodak's FunSaver project, in which engineers developed new capability in integrating design and manufacturing using an innovative CAD system. The system allowed design engineers and tooling engineers to interact at a very detailed level so that the design of the parts and that of the tooling to make the parts could be accomplished in a parallel, integrated fashion. That capability could have been developed in any number of projects, but the FunSaver project was particularly well suited: tooling was a crucial part of the project, short lead time was essential, the number of parts and tools was manageable so the team could achieve the focus necessary to learn and develop the new methods, and integration was recognized as a crucial element in the project's success.

Such a good match between product development and the building of capability does not happen by chance. Just as an effective project relies on good project planning, so the development of capabilities must be planned to make the right match. Thus, when establishing what we have called the project vision, the organization needs to focus explicitly on the opportunities that the project affords for building or strengthening the capabilities the organization needs.

## How to Be a Change Leader

If project leaders and project teams are to pursue learning to effect change, they must believe in this goal. It makes a big difference who decides that a team should create change. If an outside staff group tells them they should try something, or if a senior manager makes an edict that says change will occur, the team will not get behind it. The team must believe they can find a better way to work. For them to view learning as essential, they must have ownership of and commitment to this second purpose.

Senior managers can promote commitment by establishing an atmosphere in which everyone expects a second goal to be achieved. But most managers have low expectations for learning. Bowen confirmed this observation. "The questions from senior management that the people on the projects we studied always ran into were: How much did the product sell? Did it make any money? Short-term questions. Lots of people had pointed out things that they could have learned during their work, but their impression was that there was no room for that effort in the project. Nobody wanted it. Nobody gave them any time for it. Nobody upstairs cared."

Senior management must explicitly promote learning from development projects. "The people who should be most embarrassed reading this book are senior managers, because it was very clear in many of the projects what senior management wasn't doing," Hanson said. "They were depending on somebody else to say, 'This is what we learned on Project X. This is how the company should change.' They themselves should be looking at Project X and figuring out what was learned and what should be changing."

"That's just the thing that came through as we put together the chapter on pushing the envelope," added Holloway. "There's always a market push that causes you to pursue the first goal of a project, namely the product or process. Management is not going to let the team get too far off course on that. But for the second goal, there is no market out there, no external force. That's what senior management has to provide."

Certainly within the last several years there has been more thought and concern in business about trying to enhance a company's capabilities. There's been more independent discussion about emerging technologies and linking them to development programs, or using the programs as a way to gain knowledge of a new technology, even if financial guidelines say it doesn't make business sense. But a narrow financial perspective often gets in the way. It establishes a view in which people say: Everything new that you do to build capability will cost you something, so any amount of investment you make in the second goal of a project detracts from the money you have to reach the first goal. Senior managers are presumably wise enough to realize that the little bit extra invested in the second goal will provide a multiple return. But they often don't look at it that way. It is difficult to attach cash flows (especially cash flows that fit the guidelines of the capital budgeting process) to capabilities. As a result, senior managers see the costs, but not the returns; that's why they miss tremendous opportunities.

Hewlett-Packard demonstrated how to achieve both goals from a project, despite some financial worry, when it developed its Hornet spectrum analyzer. HP had traditionally made high-performance, high-cost analyzers, primarily for the military market, but by the mid-1980s Japanese competitors began to offer low-cost alternatives that were being scooped up by the burgeoning commercial market. It was against the nature of HP's engineers to remove or limit product features just to lower cost, but a new division general manager formed a task force to consider how to meet the development team's strict priorities—low cost first, then short development schedule, high quality, and then performance—the exact reverse of the usual order at HP. To facilitate the transfer of learning, the division general manager actually moved his desk into the Hornet development area. In the end, the Hornet product sold very well, and HP began to learn how to customize high-end products to the more modest commercial market.

How do you justify investments in learning and capabilities? Chaparral's Fournie said you have to take the long view. "One year the amount of money that we lost was exactly the amount of money we spent on development projects. So we could have taken the view that, had we not pursued development, we would have had a break-even year. But we knew that, to be in the market position we wanted to be in two years down the road, we had to do the projects, even if the finances were bad. You have to believe that even if a project will not make money, it will ultimately be worth it. You cannot take a financial-department view. Half our projects would never get off the ground if we did that."

Many companies, in reading this, might be tempted to formulate some loose financial justification for the second goal of development projects. At Ford, for example, there is a separation between advanced "research" projects, for which having a financially attractive goal is not a requirement, and "implementation" projects, where a financial payoff is required. But this causes an insidious problem, according to Richard Billington, from Ford. "We'll work on an interesting project down in the research phase, but we won't transfer it to the implementation phase because it may not make commercial sense."

A similar mindset exists at Hewlett-Packard, according to Edmondson. "Our step improvements are timed from a periodicity standpoint to our financial statements. There are some improvements you pursue if they will pay for themselves within a year, some within a quarter. But you only do as much as you can pay for. Most of our changes have not held up because of this criteria."

This mindset must be overcome. At Chaparral, it has been. The sense at Chaparral is to build capabilities that are important and to justify them on strategic, operational impact. There is no narrow dollar and cents analysis that misses the forest for the trees and leads to inaction. Said Fournie: "The acid test is, would you hock your house for this project or not? And if you would, then likely you should do the project, even if it doesn't look like it makes financial sense. You need to be more creative about how you pick projects, how you structure projects, how you sequence projects, and how you evaluate projects. That's how we get at the second purpose."

## DESIGNING THE RIGHT GUIDING VISIONS

The impetus to learn, the desire to lead people in learning, and the formulation of goals that include learning, will have much greater profiles if they become an integral part of a company's guiding visions. If the three levels of visions—project, line of business, and corporate—work together to promote and support learning in an integrated way, it is far more likely that your company will become a learning organization.

The great difficulty we observed with respect to guiding visions was how to create them and how to make them complementary. It is not easy, and it certainly is not something that can simply be assigned as an overnight task.

What tends to happen at companies that realize they need visions, according to Ford's Billington, is that a senior manager says to a group of supervisors, "Okay, starting tomorrow I want to hear a vision statement from you for each of your projects." What will result are clichéd statements that people won't buy. Everyone will think "Boy, that was a dumb idea." For visions to have any impact, if they are to be accepted by employees, they must come from within. They must bubble up collectively from each project team, each line of business group, and each set of senior managers.

Words are important, and the way in which you state guiding visions is important, because you want to create a vision in the heads of the people who take action on a daily basis. You want people to have something in their mind when they're trying to decide whether to build a unit that can be serviced in the field or that must come back to the shop for repair, for example. It's important to articulate the visions in a way that is meaningful to people. However, the visions must be based on substance, substance that comes from every level of the company.

As different groups of people struggle to come up with visions, senior management must see to it that the visions complement each other. They should be interlocking. Maybe you'll need a two-day, off-site retreat at the outset of a project, with all the team members there to debate the project's goals and the customers' needs. As they do so, the vision for the project may emerge.

Meanwhile, at the senior level, managers cannot just run off and develop a corporate vision. "I think almost every company represented on this panel has a corporate vision," Billington said. "But that hasn't helped us, because the visions are independent of everything else. For the individual working away on a development project the corporate visions are too far up there, they're too disconnected."

So what should come first, the corporate vision at the top, or the project vision at the bottom? Maybe the line-of-business visions are needed to connect the two? These are the wrong questions.

"It doesn't matter where you start," said Edmondson, who hit on the key point to creating visions. "What's vital is that the process at all three levels is iterative, iterative within each level and iterative between the levels. As long as you keep going around the loop and addressing the last piece of added thought, you'll get the visions together."

At Chaparral, for example, what has emerged as the corporate vision is a simple but powerful statement. Said Fournie: "Our overall vision is to be the lowest-cost producer of steel products. That's the first level; it's simple and it's clear. So then what happens is, say we find that a competitor in a particular line of business is beginning to approach us on cost. That automatically signals that our line of business had better start a project to figure out how to reduce cost further. So they ask themselves, 'Well, what are the possibilities?' That might spawn a new project. Or senior management might wonder if they can manage production differently, or perhaps educate people differently. Then we'll try it."

The first reason for iteration is to improve communication, to make sure everyone understands what is being sought. The second reason is to test how practical goals and visions are. For example, Chaparral may articulate its vision of being the lowest-cost producer of all steels it makes. Each line of business and project team will take its shot at it. But if a few years go by and one of the lines of business has tried several projects that haven't achieved their goal, then senior management may need to rethink what it wants to do. Perhaps there isn't any raw material within 3000 miles that is inexpensive enough. So Chaparral might decide to open a new plant closer to low-cost suppliers. Or perhaps it will decide that the line of business is not one it will pursue any longer.

The other important point about iteration is that it needs to be continual. If you don't keep regenerating and renewing visions, if you don't recognize needed changes in the visions, then the visions will not convey the right messages to people. The visions will become rigidities. The same will occur if as they evolve the three visions don't continue to fit with each other. This is why creating visions cannot be viewed as isolated tasks.

Here again is where senior managers must take the lead. They must routinely test the three visions to see if they continue to fit together. If the visions don't fit, then managers must intervene.

### Creating Visions That Fit Together

Simply "fitting together" is not enough, however. The visions must have a substantive connection, said Steve Wheelwright from Harvard, who moderated the panel discussion. "What is powerful about the Chaparral vision," he said, "is that you can see the threads connected all the way down to the smallest project. If you go there and ask people, 'What's your vision on this project?' they'll tie it right back up to the corporate vision. That shows there is enough substance in the way people define and articulate the corporate and line-of-business visions that there are hooks that people can tie into when they think about their little project way down in the organization."

To test for substantive connections, senior managers have to "listen to the system." Managers can convince themselves they have three levels of visions that fit together. But the system—the people who interact with each other day in and day out—can reject them. Even if the visions tie together, they may not be accepted.

It is clear when the system accepts visions. Said Kodak's Farran: "One of our best continuously operating areas is the color-negative paper area. Several years back people at different levels of that line of business spent a lot of time together establishing project visions and line of business visions. What they were really doing was interconnecting their visions. Now everyone in that area knows every day just what to do, how the decisions should be made, and they've dramatically improved customer satisfaction and cut manufacturing costs."

It is also clear when the system—the people—who have to actually work in support of the visions are buying into them. Holloway described the evidence this way. "There are two aspects to visions— their content, and their intensity. For example, in HP's DeskJet project, the team created a vision that said, on the content side, 'We want a near laser-quality printer for under $1000.' But the intensity side, which came from senior management, was 'If you don't do it, you're out of business.' It took the two of those together to get everyone's attention. If you only had one of them, you wouldn't have had the same product in the same time frame. What they had really done was to connect the project vision to the business vision."

Often conflicts in projects arise from incomplete business visions. Tensions mount because the visions for projects within a line of business are inconsistent. Iteration is needed not only between project, line of business, and corporate visions, but between project visions themselves. Does one project in a line of business fit into a stream of projects or is it an orphan?

There is also the question of finding the best fit for a project. Kodak's FunSaver project, to develop a single-use camera, was first attempted by the film division, where it fit for production reasons, but did not fit for market reasons. The division saw the camera as an item that would cannibalize film sales. Later, when the equipment division took on the project, suddenly the goals fit both for production and for marketing.

Without iteration, visions can also be created that are flawed from the start. A vision needs to be well debated and tested for "reasonableness," said Ford's Billington. "In our project to develop the 1991.5 Crown Victoria, for example, the team generated a vision that the car would be a step-up product for existing Taurus owners. In reality it turned out that wasn't really a workable proposition. The Taurus owners rejected the Crown Victoria as being too big and too unwieldy. Also, when they looked inside the car, they didn't see the features and convenience items that were in the Taurus. They thought, 'This is a step down, not a step up.' "

"But," asked Harvard's Clark, "was the vision flawed, or was the execution flawed?"

"The vision really," Billington answered. "Part of having a vision fit and be consistent is having it fit the market."

"There is another way to see this problem, however," Clark continued. "It could have been that the process of creating the vision was wrong. In Ford's product-line planning process, there was a decision made that Ford needed a car that would replace the current Crown Victoria, which meant it would fit into a certain price range, a certain kind of size.

"Then what happened was some guys got elected to decide what this thing was actually going to be. They detailed out the vision. They even began to do a product concept, even though there was still no project vision the way we have defined it. Then the guys got the idea to create a step up from the Taurus. But that's not where the vision started.

"The other way to have done it was to say, 'Gee, you know, we've hooked all these Taurus buyers; we must have sold a million, two million Tauruses. Boy, wouldn't it be nice if we could figure out a car that would take them up the market a little bit?' It would be a little more attractive and it would catch some owners whose incomes are growing and so forth. And then you would have come at Ford's goals from a very different angle. You might have gone off and done one project that would simply create a more modern Crown Victoria.

And you might have thought separately about what an upscale Taurus buyer would really like. That would have been a different project and a very different product.''

## EVERY STRENGTH IS A WEAKNESS

The last insight that managers must understand is that every one of the themes discussed earlier in this book will, if pursued, bring your company strength. But they can also work against you in the long run if you don't continue to apply and change them. There is a duality to each theme.

The concept is the same as that explained in the chapter on core capabilities—that your very strength may inhibit your ability to change. Ford, for example, built over time the core capability of vehicle architecture that depended on steel-bodied construction. Ford developed a strong capability in this technical approach. But now, to stay competitive, Ford has begun to develop new concepts such as spaceframe construction. However, there is inertia in the organization that makes change difficult; there is an entire manufacturing system geared around the traditional way of constructing a vehicle. The change to spaceframe construction would ripple through the whole company.

Part of the challenge in adapting and changing the application of themes derives from their nature—they are pervasive. The reason that rapid prototyping, a good system for generating empowerment, or strong methods for integrating project teams can be used as such strong capabilities is that they really permeate all aspects of a company.

"To me," said Digital's Hanson, "every strength is also a weakness. We've certainly had such an experience, for example when we began converting from our historic VMS computer architecture to the new UNIX architecture. You can't be afraid to look at a strength and ask 'What's the down side to this? How might it also limit us?' It doesn't necessarily mean you're going to change anything, but you need both perspectives."

Part of the difficulty in avoiding a rigidity lies in timing. Even if you see that a strength is turning into a rigidity and you want to initiate change, part of the company will be relying on that strength to make money, even though another part of the company might be ready to move ahead with the change. How, then, do you tackle the impending rigidity?

Use a development project as a change agent.

For example, in HP's DeskJet project the team confronted a real rigidity: R&D had become so dominant that manufacturing had taken on lower status in the organization, and was not listened to. "The interesting thing was that the rigidity wasn't broken by the manufacturing people on the team," Holloway noted. "The R&D engineers broke it, because they saw the rigidity. They said 'We understand that if we're going to be competitive with this new printer we're going to have to do better in manufacturing.' So they started a new, miniature Manufacturing Engineering organization within their team. They got it up to speed and integrated it with the manufacturing guys. They created a new capability, and broke a rigidity."

Every strength, no matter how seemingly far removed from development, can become a rigidity. Billington gave an example. "Years ago there was a man named Ed Lundy who was Ford's vice president of finance. He established an outstanding financial system, probably one of the finest around. But that very strength is almost a weakness for the company now, because that group and the perception of that group carry more weight than they should. So Lundy's very success has finally become a problem for the company."

The seven themes are so pervasive—they cut across systems, technology, values, and organizational structures—that change will have to take subtle forms. At Ford, for example, changing the finance system will be more than a matter of changing what the finance people do. It will involve changing the way their systems influence other people's systems and procedures, and the bias that it gives to other people as they think about budgets and other financial aspects of their work.

The trick in preventing a strength from becoming a rigidity is not to force change, but be prepared to implement change. Said Hanson: "Senior management should sit down and say, 'Yeah, at this moment in time these are our core capabilities.' Then they should ask themselves 'At what point do these begin to be restrictive to us?' Maybe they are an engineering-driven company. That's great and that's exciting. But they can also try to understand what the down sides of that can be. Then they should look at some specific projects. Perhaps they'll find they have disenfranchised some people. Then they can put some corrective steps in place in the next project." A good example was the DECstation 3100 project at DEC, to develop a new workstation. The vision was to create a new "hot box" of hardware. Hardware development had been one of the company's longstanding core capabilities. And that is still a strength. But what did they learn from the project? That they needed a "hot solution" instead of a hot box; their focus on hardware caused a lack of attention to software, which hurt sales.

"You can overwork the search for rigidities, however," Hanson concluded. "Just look at your strengths, and be open to the possibility that rigidities might lie within them. Have it at the back of your mind."

"Otherwise," quipped Clark, "you can imagine, with horror, coming to work one day and finding the Capabilities and Rigidities Committee."

"That would scare the hell out of me!" Hanson replied.


## A TIME FOR ACTION

At the panel discussion, we also admitted, perhaps for the first time, our own anxiety about what we'd learned. We were ready to go back to our companies and prod for change. That, you probably well know, is a frightful notion. Everyone has a fear of making mistakes. A new employee right out of school is expected to make mistakes, and the hope is he or she will learn from them. But more seasoned employees often reach a point in which they become afraid of making mistakes; everything must be right before they do something. As a result, the learning quits.

We have to overcome that fear. Fear of failure just causes paralysis. So go organize a boot camp, if that's what you feel would work, or send this book around to the key leaders in the company, then set aside a few days to discuss it. Consider the insights presented here, and use them to create your own framework in which you can begin to discover how the seven key dynamics of development work in your company. Learn from what you uncover, adapt some of the solutions presented in this book, and design more of your own. But above all, once you've undertaken the exercise, remember that it is not a one-shot deal. The self-examination must take place again and again. The learning must be continual, and the leadership for learning must never waver.

The Panel

| Richard Billington | Manager, Cross-car-line Planning | Ford Motor Co. |
|---|---|---|
| Doug Braithwaite | Program Manager for Manufacturing Research (now retired) | Digital Equipment Corp. |
| Hal Edmondson | Vice President, Special Projects (now retired) | Hewlett-Packard Co. |
| Charles Farran | Director, Product Commercialization, for the Imaging Group | Eastman Kodak Co. |
| David Fournie | Vice-President, Operations | Chaparral Steel |
| William Hanson | Vice-President | Digital Equipment Corp. |
| Kent Bowen | Ford Professor of Engineering | Massachusetts Institute of Technology |
| Kim Clark | Harry E. Figgie Jr. Professor | Harvard Business School |
| Chuck Holloway | Kleiner Perkins Caufield & Byers Professor of Management | Stanford University Graduate School of Business |
| Steve Wheelwright | Class of 1949 Professor | Harvard Business School |

# Chaparral Steel Company

Chaparral Steel is a steel minimill in Midlothian, Texas (near Dallas). Begun in 1975, it is a relative newcomer to an old and battled industry, but Chaparral has rapidly grown to become the tenth largest steel producer in the United States. In 1991 it had sales exceeding $400 million and employed 930.

The company makes primarily bars and beams from scrap metal. Junked cars and industrial scraps are hauled in by truck or train and shredded. The fist-size chunks of steel are then melted in electric furnaces, and are cast and rolled using a variety of processes into a range of end products (see **Figure 10.1**).

Chaparral's competitive strategy has remained straightforward since it was voiced in 1975. At that time, overseas makers were steadily capturing U.S. market share. CEO Gordon Forward noted that it cost $30 a ton for overseas makers to ship steel to the United States. It would be Chaparral's goal to reduce its labor costs to less than $30 a ton, so, as Forward said, "even if other countries paid their workers nothing, they would still not be able to undersell Chaparral in the U.S. market." The strategy persists today in a more generic form—Chaparral strives to be the world's lowest-cost producer of quality steels. Because labor rates in much of the world are substantially less than those in the United States, Chaparral relies on a

**Figure 10.1.** Photograph of horizontal continuous caster (bottom) with tundish and ladle (above). Note the flow of hot metal from vertical to horizontal as it proceeds through the caster. (Reprinted by permission of Chaparral Steel Co.)

294

singular mechanism to fulfill its strategy: lowering the labor content of a ton of steel by continually pushing processes and equipment to their limits.

Many executives in the industry believe that processing practices are very mature. The conventional wisdom is that there is little opportunity to gain much competitive advantage by improving processes; therefore companies focus on increasing volume or offering a broad product line. But Chaparral has proven that a motivated workforce operating in a very unconventional corporate environment can indeed make major advances in processing. The company's employees are almost four times as productive as average U.S. steel workers and more than twice as productive as their Japanese counterparts. Chaparral has repeatedly reduced what were thought to be rock-bottom prices in various markets by cutting their own costs through innovation.

Chaparral has also increased market penetration by raising the quality of its products. The approach of most large, integrated steel producers that want to produce higher quality steel has been to install more sophisticated and expensive equipment. Chaparral cannot afford such investment. Furthermore, CEO Forward and Chaparral's small team of top managers believe the better path is to continually make process improvements with existing or improved equipment and occasionally develop whole new processes as a basis for entry into new product segments. The large number of incremental changes combined with occasional major changes add up over time to greater production efficiency and better products.

This approach means that Chaparral conducts numerous development projects, often simultaneously. The majority are small in scope and all are staffed with line operators from the shop floor. Using production people to run development projects has several advantages. At a minimum, Chaparral avoids the problem of having isolated research or engineering groups gear up new methods only to throw them over the wall to manufacturing. More to the point, it results in new processes that can be brought into practice quickly and seamlessly, since the projects are run by the same people who will operate the processes once they begin to be used to produce saleable goods. Furthermore, operating people keep their eye on what works and has a strong payback in the marketplace.

The other unusual aspect of development projects at Chaparral is that they are undertaken in an environment that may best be described as a working laboratory. First, most development is conducted on active production lines, so direct feedback relating to the impact of innovation is obtained. Second, projects may be headed by employees from any area. Virtually every employee will be a project manager at some time. This generates solid, genuine support for team leaders, since everyone knows that at some point they will want the same support when it's their turn to lead. It also eliminates biases and control by any one group.

Gordon Forward's personal philosophy adds to the skunkworks atmosphere. He believes that a company made of well-rounded generalists is better equipped to make incremental improvements than one made up of specialized experts. Thus Chaparral trains workers to be proficient in many cross-functional areas. Production workers are trained in maintenance, and vice versa. Not a single person has ever been laid off because of lack of work. Production workers have helped build new production equipment and rolling mills. Security guards routinely enter safety and quality control data into computers between making their rounds. Several years ago, members of quality control took over sales of specialty steels because customers wanted access to their technical problem-solving knowledge; Chaparral trained them in such far-out skills as how to set up credit for buyers. There is no personnel department; foremen are responsible for hiring, benefits, and training their people. And of course, everyone is a stockholder with a corporate-wide profit-sharing plan.

Although these measures may run counter to many commonly held principles of management, the net result is a company in which process development is continuous and new projects are undertaken by all. Anyone can initiate a project, and that person often will become the project manager. Once begun, projects are not held to formal financial or managerial reviews. They are monitored continuously by managers who keep abreast of weekly or even daily progress through direct conversations with project managers, foremen, and line operators. Chaparral seeks to "push responsibility to the lowest competent level and to make the lowest level competent."

Chaparral's approach to project management has received much attention. Skeptics point out that the company has so far been able to operate on such a flexible basis because it is still young and relatively small. Though the company has grown dramatically while most U.S. steel makers have been facing cutbacks, its development philosophy will be challenged by tough tests yet to come. Its parent company, Texas Industries, a vertically integrated firm involved in cement, concrete, aggregate materials, and real estate, is strapped for cash, and may not be able to help fund further expansion. Also, Chaparral, until this point located at one site, will face a geographic challenge: to better serve its markets it has decided it must open facilities in other locations, and this will test its ability to transplant its unusual environment.

## The Chaparral Case Studies

Two of the Chaparral projects studied by the Manufacturing Vision Group involved the creation of new processes, another one a new process and a new product, and the fourth a new product. All were conducted in the 1980s, and all give insight into Chaparral's heavy reliance on innovation and continuous improvement as its means for competing. A brief summation of the cases follows.

*Horizontal caster.* Before this project, all carbon-steel makers used a so-called vertical casting process. A horizontal caster would enable Chaparral, a minimill, to compete in cost and quality in new speciality products with the large integrated steel conglomerates in the market for carbon steels and low-alloy forging-quality steels. The project resulted in the first such caster of its size in the world and allowed the company to enter a whole new product segment.

*Pulpit controls.* The electric-arc furnaces used by Chaparral to melt scrap were initially controlled with analog instrumentation. To improve process control and efficiency, even though the analog controls had several years of useful life remaining, the company developed digital controls, despite some internal resistance, and again ended up with a significant improvement in operating performance.

*Microtuff 10 steel.* This was one of the company's new product efforts, a very high-quality forging steel. Though present sales are limited in tonnage, they far exceed original projections and the product's successful introduction has established Chaparral as a high-tech innovator and product technology leader.

*Arc saw.* This project was an attempt to use intense electrical arcs instead of saw blades to cut steel beams. An arc saw for steel (which becomes magnetized when electric current passes through it) had never been done on the scale or throughput required for mass production. The project did not result in a successful arc saw, but holds two very interesting lessons, one negative, one positive.

Each case description is divided into three sections. The first describes the competitive environment in which the project was undertaken and the strategic planning that led to its undertaking. The second describes the execution of the project itself. The third section describes how well the development team performed relative to project goals, and the lessons that were learned about product and process development.

## HORIZONTAL CASTER

### Competitive Environment and Product Strategy

Steel minimills are built around a process known as vertical continuous casting. The scrap metal, once melted, is poured into a vertical caster, and emerges as long rectangular billets that are hot rolled into end products such as bars, angles, rounds, or beams (see **Figure 10.2**). Minimills achieve economies that are competitive with large integrated steel companies because they use scrap and avoid the expensive steps of converting iron ore to steel, casting ingots, and reheating ingots in order to hot roll them. However, not all grades of steel can be produced from scrap using vertical casters; achieving the highest grade of some alloy steels is difficult because not all impurities from the scrap are purged and because the nozzle of the vertical caster can become clogged.

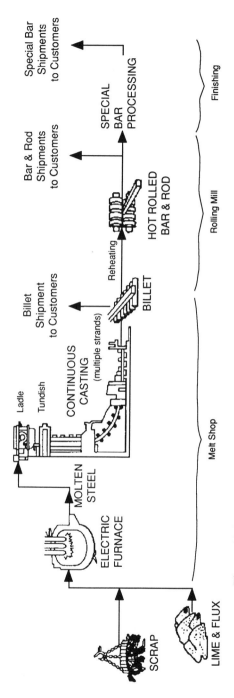

**Figure 10.2** Steel minimills such as Chaparral use scrap metal as raw material. The scrap is melted in an electric arc furnace. The molten material is then poured into the holding vessel of either a traditional vertical caster or the newer horizontal caster. As it flows through the caster it is cooled and solidified into a continuous billet and cut to the desired length. The billet is then hot rolled on a mill into its final shape, be it a round bar, angle, or I-beam.

Chaparral decided in the early 1980s that if it was to grow beyond the conventional limits of a minimill, it needed to compete with the large steel companies in high-quality steel markets. After looking around for a process that would allow it to do so, it decided to develop the first horizontal caster for production volumes of high-grade alloy steel. A horizontal caster would enable residual impurities to be controlled during casting, and would avoid the problem of clogging.

Horizontal casters were being used at about half a dozen sites around the world for casting aluminum, copper, and high-alloy specialty steel. Experiments had been done to develop a large-scale caster for high-grade carbon steel, but none had been successful. Although Chaparral figured development might take two or three years and cost several million dollars, it never developed a formal return-on-investment analysis. Development of the horizontal caster was justified on a strategic basis because it would expand the marketable grades of steel offered by the company, put it in direct competition with the large steel makers, and be significantly cheaper than the production processes used by competitors.

It is typical of Chaparral to not worry about a formal ROI before undertaking a project. Although rough budgets, cost estimates, and paybacks are calculated, the small and closely knit group of top managers and operations people has sufficient knowledge to recognize when to take the next logical step to initiate improvement of process capability. General budgets are developed and project teams try to stay within them, but the first goal is to achieve highly profitable technical success. As might be expected, a number of projects go over budget, but others come in lower than expected. This is partly because of Chaparral's extensive profit-sharing plan. As one walks through the plant one sees monthly profit statements posted on bulletin boards. Employees understand that money saved on operations will end up in their pockets, so they do not spend frivolously.

## Project Execution

By 1984 Chaparral was ready to begin the horizontal caster development. Its project team, consisting of line operators, had visited the other horizontal caster sites around the world, surveyed various equipment suppliers, and drafted their own concept for a horizontal caster for carbon steel alloys. In the spring the team let a contract to Steel Casting Engineering in California, a supplier that had developed a concept of its own. Chaparral sent team members there to help in developing a prototype caster, but results were disappointing. After 10 weeks Chaparral personnel returned to Texas.

In hindsight the team should have recognized that Steel Casting Engineering would run into problems, because it had no experience working with steel casting. It had been working with aluminum and copper, which become molten at 600°C and 1000°C, respectively. Steel melts at 1500°C, a temperature so much higher that it creates numerous additional engineering and technical challenges.

By the fall of 1984 Chaparral had arranged with the supplier to move the prototype caster to its melt shop in Midlothian and to take full responsibility for its further development. By mid-1985 it had five operators who were making steel in occasional trial runs. Later that year the team added a plasma torch to help maintain a constant high temperature in the holding vessel and made numerous small modifications.

Over the next two years Chaparral purchased and modified equipment for additional iterations of the pilot line. By mid-1988 a full-fledged production line was ready to begin, staffed by one foreman and a crew of eight. The first four casts ran successfully, but then the team "lost the recipe" and could not reproduce the early runs. The line was redesigned once again, and parameters were varied one at a time to uncover how each affected the repeatability of the process. Trial runs based on customer orders were successfully begun in early 1989.

Later in the year the operating team, built around the same people who had developed the caster, revisited the six horizontal caster sites worldwide that they had visited five years earlier to see what progress had been made and to verify how their own approach stacked up against the global state of the art. They returned to make further refinements, and by the end of the year the caster was operating profitably around the clock.

By April 1990, after even further refinements to improve efficiency in cooling the billets and eliminate microcracks in end products, production had increased from two to three "heats" (batches) a shift. Supporting engineers were finally removed from the project and line operators took over complete operation. The same year, drive units and controls on the horizontal caster were upgraded to further improve efficiency.

## Project Outcome and Lessons Learned

Chaparral produced some 300,000 tons of high-grade steel with the horizontal caster in 1990. Indeed, the steel is even more free from impurities than expected, and Chaparral believes the product is of a quality higher than that achieved with more expensive processes at the large firms. Chaparral has gained a competitive advantage in what is a new market for the company; it is the only minimill capable of producing the highest quality steels. The company has also broadened the skills of its operators, who are now proficient at both vertical and horizontal casting.

Just the same, the project cost much more in time and money than originally expected. It took six years and $5 million in capital investment before commercially viable steel was produced. The caster did not expand the company's overall capacity significantly, either, both because it represents only 5 percent to 15 percent of total output, and because it did not increase furnace melting or rolling mill capacity. However, it allowed 300,000 tons of lower priced output to be replaced by a substantially higher priced product.

Chaparral learned it could not rely on equipment vendors to provide manufacturing insight into what was a completely new process. It had to develop the expertise within its own people, by educating them and through extensive field research of related processes. Furthermore, it took repeated refinements to improve efficiency and quality to make the process competitive, and these were only possible once the caster had been placed in its proper position on the production floor in Midlothian.

The success of Chaparral's team can also be expressed in the language of the concepts presented in the early chapters of this book. Once the team determined that no supplier could produce high-quality steel with a horizontal caster, it bought into the vision that it could gain a competitive advantage if it could develop such a process. This meant pushing Chaparral's processing technology envelope to advance the state of the art. Lacking a strong outside vendor, the team turned to two of the company's core capabilities—its ability to train its own people and its skill in making continuous process improvements—to push that envelope. In turn, the project advanced the knowledge and skills of the team, further strengthening Chaparral's core capabilities.

## FURNACE PULPIT CONTROLS

### Competitive Environment and Product Strategy

All the scrap that comes to Chaparral has to be melted in one of two electric-arc furnaces, denoted furnace A and furnace B. Each "melt" takes between 40 and 60 minutes. By 1986, the controls and motor drives on furnace A were no longer state of the art. Management modernized them in order to raise them to the level of the equipment on the newer furnace B, to reduce the maintenance on furnace A, and to further increase the quality and efficiency of furnace A.

Although arc melting is simple in principle, efficient operation requires careful control of the process. Heat is supplied by running intense current through large carbon electrodes that are inserted into the furnace. During melting, the electrodes are slowly consumed, and as they become shorter they must be fed into the melting mass. If the electrodes are not fed in far enough, heating is slow and nonuniform. If the electrodes are fed in too far, the current is shorted, causing severe strain on the power transformers that supply electricity, excessive wear on the electrodes, and a lower melting efficiency. Optimal operation of the furnace requires precise movement of the electrodes and tight control in all other aspects of furnace operation.

### Project Execution

In December 1986, after the plan to upgrade had been put in place, a furnace maintenance engineer who was attending a trade show in

Dallas learned about a unique control system being used at Hylsa, a steel mill in Monterrey, Mexico. Chaparral's furnaces used analog electronics, but after further investigation the engineer became convinced that Chaparral could adapt and expand Hylsa's system to create a full-scale digital control and operating system as well as digital controlled motor drives for moving the electrodes.

The engineer developed a conceptual system in 1987. At the same time, Chaparral asked two major equipment suppliers to propose upgrades for furnace A. They both returned with analog systems. Prodding by the maintenance engineer, however, persuaded management to visit the Hylsa facility before letting a contract. But the visit was put off, because the maintenance supervisor was skeptical about digital controls; he considered the new technology unproven, did not want his staff to have to learn a whole new technology, and personally preferred a sophisticated analog system.

Nonetheless, management allowed the engineer to take a small team of operators to Hylsa. After the trip, everyone on the team was convinced digital technology was the way to go. They convinced others to look into digital controls, and a growing consensus developed in favor of the approach. This persuaded the supervisor and top management to agree to try it.

Because Chaparral did not have sufficient in-house computer expertise, it contracted with AMI, a Mexican software firm of former Hylsa employees, to help develop the system. AMI personnel, plus other construction contractors such as electricians, came to Midlothian to join the development team, which would install the new system during the summer shutdown of 1988. A new control room was built in time for the shutdown, and it took only four weeks after the shutdown ended to bring the system up to full production (see **Figure 10.3**). Subsequently, digital controls have replaced analog controls elsewhere at Chaparral.

## Project Outcome and Lessons Learned

The results were dramatic. Not only did the system save wear and tear on the electrodes and power system, it also moved the electrodes so smoothly and uniformly that scrap could be melted without con-

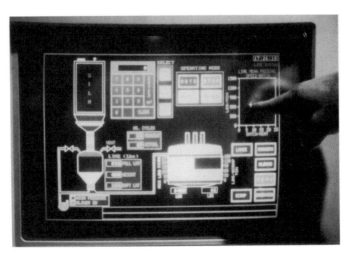

**Figure 10.3.** View of Chaparral's (a) pulpit controls with melt furnace in background; (b) close-up of an example process control screen on monitor. (Reprinted by permission of Chaparral Steel Co.)

stant supervision by operators, who previously had to make continual adjustments during the duration of every melt. This freed them to focus on other variables and apply additional diagnostics during melts, allowing for a better understanding of the dynamics of the process and enabling them to adjust the system for even more efficient operation.

By fall the system had proved so beneficial that management decided to upgrade the controls on furnace B in the same manner, even though they were relatively new. This was accomplished by the following summer.

Originally estimated at $1 million, the furnace A project overran budget substantially, costing almost twice the planned sum. Although Chaparral has not calculated specific cost savings, operators have catalogued less maintenance, reduced downtime, cut electrode consumption, and achieved greater process control. They feel subjectively that the system is simpler to use and more efficient, and that the project easily paid for itself, particularly now that digital controls are installed on both furnaces.

Furthermore, the successful outcome has sparked an upgrade to digital controls and drives throughout the company. The technology has been added to portions of the casters and is being considered for the rolling mills.

In addition to the cost overrun, the other negative of the project was that it could have been completed more quickly were it not for the resistance of the maintenance supervisor. Had management been sold on the engineer's concept earlier, the project would have been completed faster. To some degree Chaparral suffered from the same problem as many others—the lower the status of the person developing a major new idea, the less likely people are to give it prompt, full consideration. The engineer in this case had to campaign hard and long for his proposal.

Just the same, the fact that the supervisor's initial resistance did not kill the engineer's idea is telling. The unfolding of the project is an excellent example of how an employee with relatively low status can make an idea work in the Chaparral system, which would have simply been impossible in many other companies. Because Chaparral undertakes projects once there is consensus, the engineer knew he had to build support if he thought the idea worthwhile, rather than make a suggestion and let it go at that. And because employees there have respect for each other, the supervisor took seriously the opinions of those who were coming into agreement, and he himself then "signed up" for the trial.

Like the horizontal caster, the pulpit controls project was a good example of pushing the envelope. Chaparral once again designed a custom system, and became the first steel company to create and install a complete digital control system and drives on its arc furnaces.

## MICROTUFF 10 STEEL

### Competitive Environment and Product Strategy

The Microtuff 10 case is the one of the four studied at Chaparral that primarily involved development of a new product, rather than a new process. The project was a major psychological undertaking because Chaparral's strength had been in process innovation, not new products.

Chaparral's original ware was steel bars used to reinforce concrete (rebar), which is a relatively low-margin item. As early as 1979 the company began to market "special bar quality" (SBQ) steel, with certain chemical compositions and three to five times fewer impurities that together give it better mechanical properties. By the mid-1980s Chaparral had 200 customers for SBQ steel (who in turn made final consumer products), but most bought only small quantities. To enhance Chaparral's reputation as a technical leader and a major producer of SBQ steel, and consolidate its customer base and then develop a position as a majority supplier to those customers, the vice-president for quality decided to take charge of a project to develop a new "forging steel" and establish Chaparral as a technical leader in that field.

Forging steels are SBQ steels that have a high degree of "toughness," meaning they are not prone to fracture when mechanically stressed and can be heated and hammered into complex shapes for such products as carpentry tools, scissors, or even automobile parts. Because they possess both strength and toughness, they command premium prices. Strength for forging steels comes via a process called microalloying—the introduction of small quantities of elements such as titanium, vanadium, or niobium. Toughness comes from thermally treating the material under specific conditions, so the end product does not fracture as easily as common steel when it is forged. Hence the compound name of Microtuff.

## Project Execution

Though at the time Chaparral had no specific project in mind, it decided in 1986 to enhance its image as a technical leader by co-sponsoring with the Colorado School of Mines a conference on microalloy forging steels. Chaparral sponsored a book of the proceedings and sent free copies to all its customers. The real advantage, however, was that Chaparral learned a great deal about how to produce top-quality forging steels in the course of inviting and reviewing technical papers and by participating in the conference, which brought together technical experts who otherwise would not have convened.

By 1987 the vice-president of quality and others in his department felt they had learned enough to develop a new forging steel of their own. The goal was a product that had improved toughness. They asked operators on the production line to alter the chemical composition of a few batches of steel, to obtain a few pounds of new SBQ material to study.

Because this process affected an entire production batch, making it suitable only for reinforcing bar, the few pounds of study material came at a high opportunity cost—approximately $10,000. Several subsequent test lots were made. The resulting steel was tested and found to be better than the standard SBQ steel. Initially it was sold to customers at the routine SBQ price, since Chaparral had no grounds for charging more.

Carrying out development on actual production lines is the preferred method at Chaparral. Developing Microtuff 10 in a laboratory-style operation would have saved considerable money in materials, because small lots could have been used instead of the much greater tonnage of production-scale lots required by the equipment on the line. However, Chaparral believes that maintaining a separate lab-oriented melt shop would cost more. More important, Chaparral conducts development using actual production processes and lot sizes because it allows them to get full-scale production experience, avoiding the problem of spending extensive time and money for small-scale trials only to find later that there are major or even insurmountable problems in scaling up processing. Chaparral also avoids additional prototyping steps that would otherwise be needed to prove the feasibility of production.

By late 1987 the quality people had identified what they thought was the best alloy composition and thermal treatment. The new product was tougher, and costs were very much in line with those on regular SBQ products. But at this point, customers had not yet recognized the value of the higher quality Microtuff 10.

Over the next several months the quality group held several more test production runs, costing more than $100,000, before the Microtuff 10 became a formal development project. Again, no elaborate ROI was calculated, and extensive approvals were not needed for the project budget to proceed. The manager of the project simply was responsible for controlling costs and informing senior management when expenditures were becoming "significant."

Chaparral's next task was to encourage customers to perform production trials of end products using the Microtuff 10 steel. Chaparral had found that quenching (cooling in water) right on the forging line gave Microtuff 10 even better performance and eliminated additional steps in the traditional heat treat-forging process. Because customers were not equipped with machinery that could quench without the need for reheating, Chaparral designed portable quenchers and loaned a demonstration unit to customers so they could see the benefits of this new product (and process) (see **Figure 10.4**). Customers discovered both production cost savings and quality improvements as they ran tests, leading them to install their own on-line quenching and to purchase primarily from Chaparral. Since it had been the quality people and line engineers who had developed the new steel and the new process for its quenching, they took over the job of marketing it from

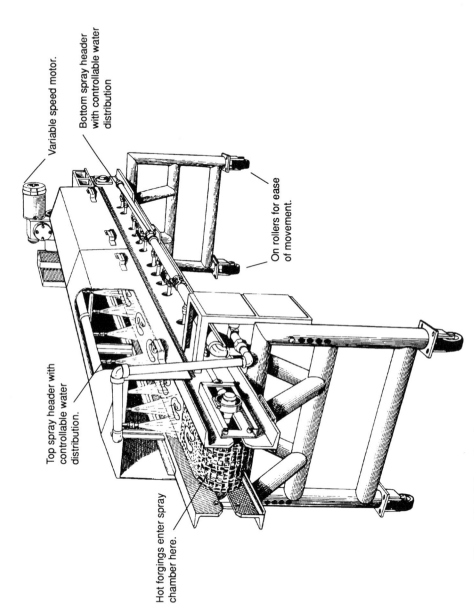

Variable speed motor.

Bottom spray header with controllable water distribution

On rollers for ease of movement.

Top spray header with controllable water distribution.

Hot forgings enter spray chamber here.

**Figure 10.4** Schematic of portable quencher developed for customers to test their use of Micro-tuff 10 for forged products. (Reprinted by permission of Chaparral Steel Co.)

310

the regular marketing staff, which did not know as much about the metallurgy of the material or the process. This further enhanced the sales of Microtuff 10, because customers appreciated and made use of Chaparral's technical expertise.

## Project Outcome and Lessons Learned

By the summer of 1988 a new group of users had developed. Chaparral priced the steel at cost plus a mark-up, rather than push for a premium price to expand profits, in order to penetrate the market and build the company's technical image by more pervasive use of its Microtuff 10 product.

The total project cost was several hundred thousand dollars. In 1991, total annual sales were approximately 5000 tons a year, a tiny percentage of Chaparral's 1.5 million tons of output. Thus revenue is small, and may never grow extensively because customers have to meet many regulations and standards that prevent them from making extensive changes in their processes, which the Microtuff on-line quenching requires. But management sees much of the product's value in building Chaparral's image as a high-tech steel company.

The project points out several interesting marketing lessons. First, the sales force learned that getting customers to adopt a new product that requires them to alter their own processes takes a significant selling job. The salespeople had to bring in technical service people and offer loaned equipment to get customers to agree to try the product. This leads to the second point, that technical people can be effective marketers when the explanation of a new product's virtues requires extensive understanding of the science behind the product and of how it will alter the customer's processes. Finally, the image enhancement that Chaparral has since enjoyed proves that technical leadership can be marketed as a significant advantage.

## ARC SAW

By 1984 Chaparral's product line had expanded considerably, and the company was growing rapidly. That year internal projections indicated that orders for I-beams with wide flanges up to 24 inches across would grow by 300,000 to 400,000 tons. The capacity at Chaparral's mill for beams would have to be expanded; it was limited in part by the throughput of the band saws used to cut and square the ends of beams. In addition, band sawing, which was done off line, was already producing $3.5 million in scrap each year, which was growing intolerable.

Although cold saws—similar to tabletop circular saws used to cut wood—were commercially available to handle this problem, they were very expensive, running about $3.5 million each, and they required extensive maintenance and more space than was readily available on Chaparral's line. Chaparral sought to find another solution.

Investigation revealed that the aerospace industry was using arc saws to cut stainless steel. These "saws" produce an intensely hot electric arc that melts through steel to cut it. Although the aerospace companies had used arc saws to cut some very sophisticated and hard materials, they had never tried to cut sections wider than 8 inches. Nor had anyone ever used arc saws to cut through anything near the volume of material that Chaparral would need.

But Chaparral was determined to try, so in 1985 it commissioned a demonstration project at the plant of one of the suppliers of arc saws for the aerospace industry. The vendor designed a custom saw to meet Chaparral's width and throughput requirements, but it soon became evident that realistic tests would not be possible at the vendor's site. The vendor had neither the electrical equipment and power levels needed to operate the large system nor the space. Chaparral decided to bring the saw back to Midlothian and insert it into the beam line during the 1986 summer shutdown, since the equipment had been designed to fit the specs of the line.

While the arc saw was being tested and developed on line, band saws were set up in a parallel stream, so throughput was not hampered by problems with the arc saw. Also, if the arc saw, which was being tested on production pieces coming down the line, made cuts that were unsatisfactory, the piece would be transferred over to the band saw and a good cut would be made.

The arc saw ran into several problems. The one causing the most consternation was magnetic arc blow. This is the movement of the arc to one side or the other off the cut line, due to the very strong magnetic fields generated by the intense current in the arc and the magnetic fields induced in the steel itself by the arc. The problem was so intractable that by mid-1987 management had to step in to stop development. The project team had gotten so caught up in the work that they were losing sight of the cost and time they were spending on it.

However, management did not remove the arc saw from the line. It was left in place for an entire year so that the team, the vendor, or others who wanted to continue to tinker with it could do so. Because the band saws were running in parallel, the idle arc saw merely consumed floor space but did not slow down production. After the 12 months, however, management removed the arc saw and purchased a cold saw to put in its place.

The arc-saw project cost on the order of $1.5 million. In retrospect, Chaparral learned two major lessons. The first was that one cannot stray too far from one's area of expertise and still depend entirely on the in-house staff. The project required sophisticated knowledge and understanding of physics and electromagnetics, which are neither common disciplines in the steel industry nor strengths of Chaparral. While the company's usual approach of educating its employees to tackle any necessary problems is laudable, in this case it was perhaps a fault. Their employees' education was not sufficient to drive this project at the level of sophistication required. Even when Chaparral brought in a consultant who was well versed in the basic physics behind arc sawing, it was unable to make the progress needed. The second major lesson learned was the need to accurately assess the supplier's knowledge and the degree to which a supplier could adequately prototype Chaparral's production environment. Chaparral management believes that given the amount of new knowledge needed in this case (which was significantly underestimated), they should have done much more preliminary investigation before having a production scale unit built and installed.

An interesting managerial aspect of the project involved the way in which the project was ended. Management did not simply yank the project when it felt time was up; it left the arc saw in place so the team could continue to experiment with it. Management recognized that the team and other individuals from the vendor and elsewhere in the company needed time to accept the inevitability of a decision to terminate the project. And they wanted to send a message that it was okay to fail if a team gives a project its best effort. Because development projects are so common and fundamental to Chaparral's progress, an abrupt ending to a failed project could be a disincentive for employees to commit to and take ownership of future projects, especially ones in which the risk for failure is high. Though it cost extra time and money to allow people to continue to experiment with the saw, management felt it was well worth it to save the team dedication and risk-taking so vital to its success.

## CHAPTER 11

# Digital Equipment Corporation

Digital Equipment Corporation is one of the world's leading manufacturers of networked computer systems, software, and services, and is a leader in the integration of computer systems from disparate vendors. The company, usually referred to as "Digital" by its employees and "DEC" by the computer and financial industries, opened its doors in 1957 in a pre-Civil War woolen mill in Maynard, Massachusetts. In the 1960s, founder (and chairman until 1992) Ken Olsen quickly established DEC as the creator of the minicomputer industry. Today DEC designs, manufactures, and services a full range of desktop, client/server, production, and mainframe hardware and software systems for local and worldwide enterprisewide computing. As another major round of restructuring occurred in the computer industry in the early 1990s, DEC began the decade with an employment level of 120,000 people at 1200 sales, service, manufacturing, and engineering sites in 83 countries. A major element in DEC's competitive strength is the distributed nature of its manufacturing organization, spread across 52 sites in 12 countries. Sales now surpass $13 billion, more than half of which are outside the United States.

## DEC's Competitive Position, Culture, and Modus Operandi

DEC's present strategy in developing computer products was established more than a decade ago. It was motivated by the role that computing played within DEC itself. The strategy is based on three visions: that pervasive, consistent networking be available to any employee, that computing power be distributed among all employees, and that all products be interoperable, so that any software application could be written just once and could then be deployed on any system within the company, regardless of its size. Thus DEC's products reflect a high priority on networking, distributed computing, and software compatibility.

This philosophy of access, power, and networking for all people in an organization also underlies the structure of the company. There is a corporate staff that oversees broad functional units such as engineering, manufacturing, marketing, sales, and field service. Other senior managers oversee the operations contained within major geographic areas, such as the United States, Europe, and the Pacific Rim. The structure within the broad functional units, however, is loose and distributed. People are organized in a matrixed manner; employees interact with other employees on all professional levels, cutting across many areas of responsibility and many chains of command. People talk on a first-name basis with anyone they think can help them and go wherever they think they need to go to get their job done. Most managers have both technical and business responsibility, and report to both a corporate officer and a geographic one. The matrix organization is goal-oriented and depends on trust, communication, and teamwork. As a result, most employees function as independent consultants on every level, interacting across functions as necessary to accomplish a given task.

Historically, the company has competed on the basis of product innovation. The corporate staff has given managers of product and process development considerable freedom to define their own methods. Corporate management has relied on skilled people who have a great deal of autonomy, and in return expected a high level of hard work and achievement from everyone, trusting them to give their best effort to any job. It is a strongly held corporate belief that individual discipline should be self-generated. People are encouraged to develop technical skills, breadth of knowledge, and expertise in a specific area. Promotions are based not only on technical performance but also on a person's ability to get a job done and shoulder the responsibility that goes with that job. In fact, a string of successful product developments has traditionally been *the* way to ensure a spectacular career. The ultimate recognition for technical leaders is promotion to corporate consulting engineer. These 20 intellectual architects of DEC's technology agendas are recognized with some equivalency to senior officers and appear in the annual report.

The business result of this culture has been a continuous string of innovative products. The down side has been that products are sometimes of uneven quality, and have often been developed along unpredictable schedules at relatively high costs. During periods from the mid-1970s to the mid-1980s, members of a product development team essentially determined their own conventions and work ethic as the company grew and decentralized. The company offered limited central support, so development depended on loosely coordinated efforts at the project level. By the mid-1980s, however, the computer industry had gotten intensely competitive, and DEC became increasingly concerned with improving the company's performance. Senior managers began to pay more attention to process issues. By 1988 the company achieved remarkable improvements in integration, quality, and productivity, but gains were offset by dynamic and fast-moving competitive pressures that were redefining the whole computer industry. The rise of the low-cost personal computer, efficient competitors, the growing complexity of software, continued shortages of skilled personnel, and customer demands for ever-higher quality, increased customization, lower prices, and faster delivery made it imperative for DEC to exert greater control over its development of products and process.

In 1992, founder Ken Olsen and several other longtime senior managers left DEC. Under the new chairman, Robert Palmer, there are experiments in organizational structures as the company responds to competitive challenges in the computer industry. Today, managers continue to face what has become a classic dilemma—a tug of war between individual autonomy and corporate standards. On the one hand, too much emphasis on control stifles creativity, innovation, and the ability to initiate change, the very qualities that had bolstered DEC to global leadership in the 1970s and 1980s. On the other hand, too much independence creates problems in controlling development costs, quality, and long-term service.

Faced with the very significant changes in their marketplace, DEC's corporate officers resolved in the 1980s to improve the quality and competitiveness of products while finding ways to reduce costs and decrease time-to-market by better managing the balance between freedom and control, and between specialization and integration. Part of the strategy has been to respond more to customer needs instead of relying on a myopic drive toward higher technology to solve problems. For example, while the current market is calling for new software that is technically more complex, it is also calling for software that is more reliable and easy to use. This requires better coordination and control among disparate development groups at DEC. Communication between teams has become increasingly important, a difficult challenge since many employees are used to working on teams that operate independently. Customers have also started to pay more attention to software costs, because these are beginning to exceed the cost of hardware for many applications.

Basic to these efforts is a push at DEC to leverage the skills of its engineers by creatively eliminating redundant work. In both hardware and software development an integrated approach is leading to better tools and practices for each phase of the development process. As the projects that are detailed later in this chapter reveal, however, it is far easier to conceive an efficient development strategy than to implement and sustain one in a long-standing, highly "culturized" organization facing the explosive competitive demands of a dynamic industry.

## DEC's Development Process

Of course, DEC remains committed to the spirit of invention, the tradition of scientific experimentation, hard work, and the value of learning. The corporate culture is one of entrepreneurial indepen-

**Table 11.1** DEC's Phase Review Process

| Phase Scope | Goals |
|---|---|
| 0  Strategy and requirements | Concept definition; plans that outline manufacturing, customer service, marketing, and sales |
| 1  Planning and preliminary design | Functional specifications; engineering plan; plan of record |
| 2  Implementation and design | Design development and completion |
| 3  Qualification | Design verification |
| 4  Production, sales, and service | Ramp-up and sustain manufacturing, marketing, customer service, and engineering support |
| 5  Product retirement | End of manufacturing; phase-out plans; system for continued customer service |

dence and encourages each employee to take ownership of his or her piece of a project. Throughout all the changes of the 1980s, the product development model has remained mostly decentralized and continues to be dominated by non-standardized processes, focusing instead on serving a variety of customer needs with versatile, insightful, and dedicated product development engineers. (There have been, however, major change initiatives in the past two years.)

Just the same, the hand-wringing of the 1980s made it clear that senior management had to inject a measure of consistency in the way development projects were conceived, run, reviewed, and coordinated. The outcome was the formal and corporate-wide application of a Phase Review Process defined in the late 1970s. The process is an operational guideline for managing products throughout their life cycle. It provides a common framework for the planning, measurement, and implementation of innovation, and is designed to help development teams deliver quality products to DEC's customers. The process encourages and facilitates effective collaboration among functional groups, and improves the discipline, communication, and predictability required for an effective product creation and delivery process.

The process organizes work performed in the normal course of doing business and identifies six key phases during a product's life cycle, from concept definition to product retirement (see **Table 11.1**). The amount of time spent in each phase is totally dependent on the internal processes created and used by each development team. The phase review process itself does not impose any time constraints.

Ideas for new development projects can and do come from employees at every level within DEC. Employees have authority to conduct research or advanced R&D before they propose a formal project. At some point when an employee or group of employees feel they know enough to begin development of a specific product or process, they then propose a project to senior management. If management agrees the effort should proceed, it chooses a project manager (typically the head of the group who made the proposal) and a group of senior managers to act as advisors to the project. The project manager then selects people from all the various functions for his team. Senior management assigns a finance manager to work with the team in preparing a business plan and other product planning activities. He or she will continue to coordinate finance activities across all team functions for the duration of the project.The team then fleshes out the product concept and formulates a detailed business plan. This work constitutes the first two phases of the review process. At this stage senior management decides if it will commit funds to the entire project.

If the project is a go, the team itself becomes responsible for full implementation of the phase review process. Each team member is responsible for soliciting input from his or her function and communicating project status to that function on an ongoing basis. This creates a pro-active approach to life-cycle management and allows the team to resolve issues that could negatively impact product introduction or retirement. As a project proceeds, however, an advisory group will review the work of the team at the end of each phase.

In the current economy, as life cycles become more complex and time-competitive, the phase review process has become an essential tool for minimizing the uncertainties associated with bringing a product to market, and even in planning when to retire a product. The process is now used throughout the company as the primary product life-cycle management tool. The process establishes, confirms, and documents several important aspects of development work: that there is corporate visibility to products under development, that new products fit with DEC's product strategy, that new products are viable and are being pursued with well-integrated plans, and that new projects reflect sound investment decisions.

In practice, however, the phase reviews can turn out to be loose and overly subjective, causing managers, the development team, and customers to complain of budget and schedule overruns as well as high maintenance costs stemming from design, programming, and other errors. These problems suggest that the phase review process either falls short of providing adequate management control, or is simply not taken seriously. Senior management continues to try to instill the rigorous self-review that the process is intended to invoke, while still trying to protect the creative freedom that is the cornerstone of the company. This struggle is evident in several of the projects that were studied by the Manufacturing Vision Group.

## The DEC Case Studies

As this chapter proceeds, the four projects studied by the Vision group are presented in chronological order, beginning in the late 1970s. In this way, readers will be able to see how DEC's people tried to retain the strengths derived from autonomy while attempting to work toward better project integration and consistency. A brief summation of the projects follows.

*RA90 disk drive.* This project was undertaken in 1979 to develop a high-density disk drive for computers. It was divided into three subprojects that progressed in parallel but without coordination, which in the end proved troublesome. It represents the kinds of integration problems that were beyond the scope of the review process as practiced and managed at DEC at the time.

*LANbridge 200.* This product, a communications network that would link several computer networks, was a follow-on to an earlier product. Because the new team had the remnant experience from the team that developed the first product, work proceeded in an integrated fashion. Key customer requirements, however, were not identified until late in the project, which in turn caused the product to be introduced seven months late.

*DECstation 3100.* Facing competitive pressure, DEC launched this project to develop a new workstation based on a UNIX operating system, instead of the company's standard VMS system. It was a technical success completed in record time, but sold less than intended because of a lack of applications software.

*CDA software.* As DEC's line of office workstations expanded, the company perceived a need to develop an overreaching computer architecture to link desktop publishing products and other desktop applications, including word processing, spreadsheets, and graphics applications. The compound document architecture (CDA) software was the solution.

Each case description is divided into three sections. The first describes the competitive environment in which the project was undertaken and the strategic planning that led to its undertaking. The second describes the execution of the project itself. The third section describes how well the development team performed relative to project goals, and the lessons that were learned about product development.

## RA90 DISK DRIVE

### Competitive Environment and Product Strategy

Since it began, DEC has developed and manufactured central processing units for computers. During the 1970s, however, an internal reevaluation of corporate strategy expanded the company's identity; DEC would become a broad-based provider of information systems. To fulfill this new vision, DEC needed a full range of leading edge, high-performance equipment, including high-density storage devices.

Storage technology in the late 1970s was well understood and embraced by all the key computer makers. Forward-looking researchers, though, foresaw a dramatic revolution predicated on the integration of two innovative technologies: thin-film magnetic storage media and thin-film heads for reading the media. In 1978 IBM announced a new storage system—the IBM 3390—that merged these new technologies.

At the time of the announcement, DEC was perhaps 10 years behind the major storage companies in producing hardware. DEC's experience was limited to experiments on thin-film media. A skunkworks project begun in 1979 by a small team of relatively inexperienced engineers was exploring new applications of the media. In June 1981, a prototype process for making thin-film heads was demonstrated a single time. The engineers, however, still could not determine if the result was repeatable.

During the same time, DEC engineers were developing a digital storage architecture, a generic standard for the hardware and software for DEC's computer storage systems. The architecture promised a significant competitive advantage, because it would enable a user to introduce new storage devices into a system without changing a line of storage code. This would give DEC significant flexibility and enable easy interchange of storage products. Parts of the architecture had already been laid out.

Hearing the projections about high-density storage and seeing the progress on the digital architecture, several engineering managers decided a project should commence that would make DEC a major player in the emerging market. Thus the RA90 was begun. The project was not seen as a short-term effort, nor as a task undertaken simply to meet minimum standards of customers. The managers and later the development team sought to generate the knowledge and skills necessary to make DEC a leading competitor in high-density storage systems.

Key engineers determined from study of the industry that DEC would have to develop state-of-the-art technology internally. Purchasing complete storage systems or components externally would neither give DEC a competitive advantage nor leverage DEC's nascent digital architecture. Purchasing technology from IBM or Fujitsu, the other storage leader at the time, would also not offer DEC a competitive advantage.

## Project Execution

For such a grassroots initiative to succeed, a person with significant technical credibility would have to shepherd the project through the company and build support among corporate management. In 1981 an experienced engineer in storage systems was hired and appointed the high-end disk-drive engineering manager, and a team was formed. The team was to combine the digital architecture being developed with DEC's manufacturing capability for 14-inch-diameter plated drives, which had recently been built. Team members were also to keep an eye toward 9-inch drives, which DEC was already piloting in two versions.

Success would require four significant innovations: the thin-film media and the process to manufacture it, the thin-film head and process to make it, a new electromechanical drive system, and a new assembly process. To enhance innovation the project was split into three parallel efforts at three distinct sites. Drives would be developed and manufactured in Colorado, media in Arizona, and thin-film heads in Massachusetts.

Though the future need for such technology had been determined by senior management, project definition was left to the team, which also made decisions on all changes. The product's initial definition emerged very early. The RA90 was to be shipped in 1986 as a 9-inch disk drive. It would have 1 gigabyte of capacity, and would cost roughly $2500 (see **Figure 11.1**).

Some of these goals were founded in the results of an earlier research team, which had determined that by the mid-1980s DEC could build a 9-inch drive for $2.50 a megabyte (which would then sell for about $10 a megabyte). At the time disk drives cost $10 a megabyte to make, and sold for $40 a megabyte, but based on existing technological performance trends the group expected the price to be cut by one-quarter at market introduction.

The RA90 goal of 1 gigabyte of capacity translated into a storage density of 30 million bits per square inch. This measure was based on the technology curve for the best products in the industry. The skunkworks project that had been underway enabled the team to

**Figure 11.1.** An exploded view of the RA90's key elements, including the thin-film media disk and read/write heads. (Reprinted by permission of Digital Equipment Corporation.)

shoot for this very aggressive goal; without it a significantly more conservative number would have been adopted.

In early 1983, after work had begun, two key engineering managers visited Japanese competitors. They reported that Fujitsu planned high-density drives that would achieve 45 million bits per square inch. When the RA90 team members heard this, they increased their own goal to 45 million bits per square inch, and a drive with 1.2 gigabytes of capacity. They slipped the schedule by six months to accommodate the work they thought would be needed, advancing the delivery schedule to mid-1986. Since the goal was tougher and the drive would be denser, the expected cost also increased. Moreover, manufacturing determined that they could not build the RA90 for $2500 but rather $3000. On hearing the new goals, they revised the figure again to $3500. Even though this meant the cost per megabyte would increase from $2.50 to $3.00, it did not cause real concern because the cost goals were still very aggressive compared to leading edge developers.

The new density goal was well above the technology curve. Fujitsu was taking the position that its work would alter the curve. In matching its objective to Fujitsu's, the RA90 team conceded a completion date that would be one year following Fujitsu's theoretical shipment date. DEC accepted its inability to match Fujitsu's date because the new product would be so far beyond anything else available that sales would not suffer.

Shooting for the extremely aggressive density goal, however, provoked some unfortunate decisions. Based on the depth of the organization, DEC's experience in manufacturing, and the team's own ability to conduct such a project, the team faced considerable risk. It was also obvious that so much rested on the heads and disks that failure in either could destroy the entire program; if either failed, DEC would not have a high-density disk drive. No fallback position existed and no one else produced the necessary parts for the open market. The project was so unique that the team was totally dependent on its own capabilities.

As development progressed a series of roadblocks unfolded. Once the RA90 team decided to raise the density goal, the ensuing delay forced management to ask for an interim project. The existing storage system, the RA81, would not maintain DEC's market position for the years that would pass before the RA90 would be available. In turn, subsequent demands for work on the interim project, the RA82, compromised the RA90's schedule.

In the middle of 1984 the team began receiving 14-inch plated disks for testing. As a rule the disks failed. Only then did the team realize that DEC was still not capable of manufacturing thin-film media disks. By the time the disk plating was resolved both the RA82 and RA90 were another year late.

At this point the subteam working on the disk drive turned down the wrong path. Two possible avenues existed for developing the servo system (the electronics that position the head and keep it on track). Traditional systems were based on analog technology that was well known in the storage industry. A small concurrent research team at DEC was developing a digital servo system that would save circuit-board space and enhance several performance measures. The new system looked promising enough that the RA90 team committed itself to using the technology. Resources were assigned to the digital program and the analog one was cut. The digital servo system may well have been perfected quickly, but the chief engineer who had designed the experimental system left DEC. With no qualified replacement available, servo development stopped. A year later the engineer returned and continued development from the same point he had left off. The servo delay prevented the full testing of the drive's mechanical design until early 1986. The tests uncovered problems with the drive actuator, but it was too late to make many mechanical design changes.

Soon after another issue arose: whether or not to shorten the rotary arm that moved the head. Shortening the arm would help meet the "seek specification"—the time it took the head to find data—but would delay the project an additional six months and cost manufacturing a significant amount of money. In mid-1986 the team decided to continue with the current design, allowing the desired seek time to slide from 16 milliseconds to 18 milliseconds. The team would phase in speed improvements at a later date.

## Project Outcome and Lessons Learned

The RA90 was finally shipped in early 1988, two years later than the original target. Ultimately, the team could not pack 45 million bits of data per square inch; it had to go with 40 million bits. The capacity remained at the elevated level of 1.2 gigabits. Originally projected to cost $2500, the final box cost $5000. The good news for DEC, however, was that Fujitsu could not deliver what it had predicted either, and the window of opportunity was still there.

The silver lining in the project was that even though the effort took longer and fell short of some technical goals, those goals were so aggressive that the RA90 still emerged as a significant step forward; the density of 40 million bits surpassed the state of the art, which had risen to 30 million bits by this time. The product was innovative enough that it made DEC a major player in the high-density storage market. Sales were somewhat slower than expected because of a variety of changes in the tumultuous computer industry, the crucial one being that the industry was moving toward 5.25-inch and smaller form factor drives. But follow-on products such as the RA91 and 5.25-inch products based on thin-film head and thin film media did sell well.

The key to the RA90's success was the presence of strong intellectual leadership from engineering early in the project. A critical weakness was the inaccurate market assessment of product competition and market size. Although engineers examined Fujitsu's projections early in the project, the team made no ongoing analysis of Fujitsu's progress or that of other companies.

The team also lacked a consistent, overall project strategy. Three subgroups worked pretty much in isolation, leading to major integration problems once the work was convened as a single project. Part of the problem was that no single manager took responsibility for the overall project and scheduling during the early years. The project manager served essentially as a communications coordinator, not as a driver. Indeed it would have been unlikely that a project manager could have acted in any stronger fashion, since it was uncommon for subgroups to respond to an "outside" manager who tried to exert control. The organization failed to understand how the issues being faced by one group would affect the work in another. For example, although everyone was aware that to test the new media the new heads would be needed, people developing the new heads needed the new media to test their own work. There was no appreciation of how a partially completed unit from one group could have aided work by another group. Each subgroup proceeded down its own path at its own pace.

Even so, the RA90 project exhibited some strengths in project management. All project members understood clearly that the strategic intent was to lay a strong foundation for future high-density storage products. The RA90 was never seen as a single product, but as the platform for an evolving line of business. Therefore, DEC management was willing to invest heavily in the development of skills and critical processes necessary for high-quality manufacturing. Team members were inspired to redefine the state of the art even if it meant delaying product introduction, which in the long run put DEC in a stronger competitive position. The project cost approximately $1 billion to complete, including the construction of a new automated plant. The skills, groundwork, early products, market position, and manufacturing flexibility in place made DEC a leading producer of high-density disk drives by the end of the 1980s.

## LANBRIDGE 200

### Competitive Environment and Product Strategy

The LANbridge 200 was initially envisioned by DEC's Network and Communications group as a follow-on product to the earlier, extremely successful LANbridge 100. A local area network (LAN) bridge connects multiple computer networks within a limited area, so information and programs can be exchanged between systems. The LANbridge 100 had been a big surprise success, introduced during the early days of office networking. It operated using a communications protocol called Ethernet, a proprietary technology developed by DEC, Intel, and Xerox and dominated by a DEC-defined standard.

Nonetheless, the LANbridge 100 could not be expanded and only functioned over a very limited distance. Moreover, the software embodied in it inhibited flexibility and was not extensive enough for the changing and growing demands of network users. It was time for an expanded product.

After the LANbridge 100 was introduced nearly all the development team members moved on to other projects, taking their expertise with them. One of the motivations in beginning the LANbridge 200 project was the desire to grow a new team capable of building a second-generation product for the same market. The team convened in 1985 was relatively small, but had a clear goal: to introduce into what was thought to be a stable external market a new LANbridge, using technologies developed within DEC. Included would be two new technologies emerging from DEC research groups: repeaters, which enabled data to be sent at greater distances from computer to computer, and long fiber-optic links between computers.

## Project Execution

The new team began less than a year after the LANbridge 100 was released. Because there were still few knowledgeable and experienced customers, most of the specific ideas for the 200's design and functionality came from DEC's internal technical leadership.

While the 200 was being defined, the Network and Communications' group management was developing an alternative strategy for the next local area network, called FDDI. This strategy involved the upgrading of Ethernet with such technology as high-performance fiber optics with repeaters and remote bridges. Simultaneously, DEC's upper management was stressing the value of partnerships with outside vendors. The network group consequently decided to not develop remote bridges internally, but form a partnership with Vitalink, a competitor that had just released a successful remote bridge.

The partnership never got off the ground, and was canceled some months later. Management considered canceling the 200 project too, but decided to continue after an independent DEC team introduced a LAN monitor that met with clear market success. By incorporating the monitor technology into the bridge project, the 200 could still be successful. The decision to continue the 200 project was thus based purely on business grounds, on the assumption that the monitor would lead to a new bridge that could be sold for sufficient profit.

In July 1987 the 200 team held its first formal project review, proposing a 13-month schedule to first revenue ship. At the time most people felt that 13 months was an achievable goal. The 200 was considered just another bridge with the inclusion of a monitor. Not everyone on the team, however, felt so confident. Some believed that the 13-month deadline was too short and was chosen primarily to persuade management to approve the project.

During the initial review a few significant risks were identified. The largest rested in the development of new software to replace the inflexible software used with the LANbridge 100. The team would have to depend on a separate DEC software group. Eight months into development the team realized the software group was far behind schedule; the software group's priorities did not coincide with the needs of the LANbridge team. After extensive delays, the LANbridge project manager decided to take control over the software work; the team itself would modify and improve significantly the software written for the LANbridge 100.

Even at this point the design team still had no clear concept of the features customers wanted since customer data was unavailable due to the newness of the networking business. The functionality developed was therefore based solely on the design engineers' perspectives of future customer demands and DEC's overall perspective on the market's direction.

Unfortunately for the team, the external environment was changing. In the mid-1980s the emergence of workstations popularized a network protocol called TCP/IP, developed by competitor Sun Microsystems. It was based on the UNIX operating system, an alternative to DEC's VMS operating system. In contrast, most people at DEC had a naive belief that those who made networks in the computer industry would simply adopt the next generation of DEC's network communications architecture, which was based on Ethernet, not TCP/IP. DEC engineers had hoped they would drive the Open Systems Interconnect (OSI) protocol, which would fuel the workstation boom. Some of those hopes were predicated on the belief that DEC would have a significantly larger piece of the workstation market than it did.

Few foresaw the fantastic growth of new competitors such as Sun Microsystems. In addition, the engineers assumed that DEC would participate more fully in the UNIX market and would therefore have more influence over that segment. Finally, although OSI products from various vendors were projected to be shipped in 1987 or 1988, they never reached the market until late 1990. Based on all these incorrect assumptions, the LANbridge 200 project became unravelled in March 1989.

The emergence of TCP/IP at this juncture had a very detrimental effect on proprietary, inflexible bridges. Suddenly, network products capable only of bridging and not of the more flexible functions that were available with TCP/IP became a major liability, instead of an asset, for customers with large heterogeneous networks. The only solution was to add capability to bridges using such devices as routers and filters. The 200 project had to be held up for three more months so filters could be added.

DEC's marketing, product management, and field personnel had already expressed the need for filtering for nearly a year. Customers had requested filtering when competitors, including Vitalink, began to include it in their bridges. The difficulty for the DEC team was in deciding which of the competitors' features to include in the 200. Some even felt that customers did not need the features; they thought Vitalink, at least, included them simply as a means for differentiating their product.

To get an answer, the marketing people and the project manager convinced the engineers to visit key customers to get direct feedback, even though there were only five months left before the intended shipping date. After the visits the design engineers clearly understood the seriousness of the problem: DEC's network systems model was evolving too slowly. Ideally, the engineers would have preferred to put TCP/IP routing into the 200, but the product was already getting somewhat dated technologically. The final decision was to ship the 200 as a filtering bridge, with some missing features, so as to not hold it up further and risk the possibility that the technology would be completely outdated and uncompetitive. If nothing else, the team could keep its pulse on the market by shipping the product as it was.

Manufacturing learned of the LANbridge 200 project in July 1987.

According to early designs, the electronics board needed six interconnect layers; soon thereafter, though, designers called for a board with eight layers, and for the use of surface-mount technology, a relatively new and improved method for securing integrated circuits to the circuit board. This meant that both the LAN product and the manufacturing process were new to manufacturing. No one on the team clearly understood the implications of using surface mounting; it led to several significant design and manufacturing problems.

Manufacturing conducted several prototype runs for a total of 60 to 70 boards. All the prototypes were built on the same line used for general production. Assembling the prototypes at the manufacturing plant had definite advantages. Manufacturing engineers learned a great deal about the manufacturing process even though not all of the same equipment was used for actual production. Following the prototypes the pilot builds went fairly smoothly.

### Project Outcome and Lessons Learned

In the end, it took 24 months instead of 13 before the first shipments were made. All the slippage was attributable to factors external to the development team. This included the time required to write new software and improve functionality following the visits to key customers. Nonetheless, product introduction went smoothly, and the LANbridge 200 has sold reasonably well.

Even though the team's problems were largely caused by outside factors, these could have been foreseen and prevented. That they were not can in part be attributed to the inexperience of the team. Software development within hardware development teams was not a strong capability of DEC's, yet the team trusted the software group to come through and exerted little oversight. Marketing did not speak up strongly enough in calling for customer visits until late in the program. Inexperience may also have been the reason the team did poor benchmarking of the evolving network industry and the emerging technology from competitors. Had the team been more in tune with current events, it could have responded more quickly to the changing market.

# DECSTATION 3100

## Competitive Environment and Product Strategy

As the prior case study indicates, the computer workstation market was growing and changing rapidly by the mid-1980s. Although DEC had a strong position with its line of VAX products, which ran on the company's proprietary VMS operating system, there was a groundswell of interest in products that used the increasingly popular UNIX operating system.

By early 1988, as the price/performance curve for UNIX workstations began to diverge from that for VMS workstations, customers began to pressure DEC's salespeople for a powerful UNIX product. One senior sales manager, in particular, pursued the possibility of quickly developing a UNIX workstation for engineering users. Variously described as "dynamic" and "one of the best speakers ever," this person was able to elevate the need for the new workstation to the highest levels of DEC management. Recognizing that the demand was not only to develop a competitive workstation but to build one very quickly, DEC management in May 1988 canceled an internal effort to develop a UNIX/RISC-based workstation and decided to follow an alternative path; a new team would piece together a workstation in nine months using state-of-the-shelf components (see **Figure 11.2**).

The team was assembled at DEC's engineering facility in Palo Alto, California; manufacturing would be done at DEC's Albuquerque, New Mexico, plant. The team, which from the start integrated all the relevant functions such as manufacturing, marketing, and sales, established two rigorous objectives that would have to be achieved if the newly dubbed DECstation 3100 was to make an impact. First, the machine would have to be competitive with any prospective workstation scheduled for release in 1989. Second, it would have to break the $1000/MIP barrier, then the threshold of the best price-to-performance measure for such machines (MIP stands for million instructions per second, a rating of computational speed). Management imposed a time-to-market deadline of nine months; first revenue ship for the DECstation 3100 would take place in January 1989.

**Figure 11.2.** The DECstation 3100. (Reprinted by permission of Digital Equipment Corporation.)

## Project Execution

To meet the deadline, the Palo Alto team recommended to management that it use a central processing computer chip developed by MIPS Co. Almost always, DEC would develop its own processing units, but adoption of this cutting-edge chip would significantly reduced overall development time. Management agreed. DEC's exploration with MIPS ultimately brought in not only the specific technology for the workstation, but was the first step in building a long-term, cooperative relationship with this firm.

Despite management support, many within DEC doubted the project's likelihood of success. In a firm in the Maynard, Massachusetts, area, accustomed to developing a central processing unit internally over a two-year period, pursuit of the nine-month goal seemed to invite excessive risk. Furthermore, the chosen development site, Palo Alto, was relatively new and lacked a proven track record. To improve its chances, the Palo Alto team imposed as a decision filter the limitation of using a single circuit board in the workstation. This provided a clear guideline for development and served to discourage engineers from including as many new ''gadgets'' as possible; if a feature could not be implemented on this single board, it would not be included in the workstation. The designers also insisted that design developments not adversely affect either the time-to-market or the price/performance objective.

The project managers decided early that everyone involved had to be physically located at a single site to meet the schedule. A complete Ultrix operating team was sent out. Regular trips back and forth or even virtual co-location through computer networking and teleconferencing would not satisfy the constant demands for communication required by such a project. Consequently, during the first few months the development staff was supplemented with people brought in both from DEC's headquarters in Maynard and outside DEC. The seasoned Maynard engineers and managers brought experience and expertise to the Palo Alto center. Before assigned to go west, however, each one was screened to ensure he or she would be compatible with the ''California culture'' and capable of handling the demands of the rapid development process, which included daily deadlines and a 24-hour-per-day, 7-day-per-week schedule. The perception of team leaders was that development projects at DEC took too long and were too costly. People with a fresh attitude would be needed.

Indeed, throughout the project design managers in Palo Alto showed a sense of pride in being part of a counter-culture group within DEC. There was a perception of Palo Alto versus ''DEC

East," evident in discussions with team members, and it served both as a rally cry and a motivator.

Palo Alto engineers spent three months designing the initial layout and framework for the DECstation 3100. Design efforts were assisted by a relatively new, UNIX-compatible computer-aided design tool (called the "WRL tool") recently developed by DEC's California research labs. The engineers chose this tool over the available VMS-compatible computer-aided design tools widely used throughout the company. Significant difficulties were later encountered during production because outputs from the new design tool differed from VMS outputs and manufacturing technicians were not fully acquainted with the WRL tool's distinctive characteristics. In addition, the WRL tool could not transmit data directly to the manufacturing equipment, necessitating downloading, translation, and reloading of all design information in the manufacturing plant. On the other hand, if the WRL tool had not been used, the product would not have been introduced on time. The WRL tool has proven valuable in all follow-up products, even though it remained difficult to use as a real time-to-market aid.

Members of the Palo Alto group visited the Albuquerque plant in early June 1988 to explain the new product. Soon after, the manufacturing group sent an engineer to Palo Alto to gather more information. This initial visit was the first of a stream of trips from Albuquerque to Palo Alto.

Largely because of the intense time pressure, a decision was made to conduct all development and testing within a small radius of Palo Alto. Two manufacturing technicians set up a small storeroom and supply center in the neighborhood to assemble the kits that would be needed for building prototypes. The prototypes were built at a local assembly house rather than at Albuquerque. To achieve rapid prototype turnarounds, the team paid top dollar for full use of the assembly house's lines; total process time from layout release to a physical board was only 10 days, allowing design to continue virtually without delay. Rapid prototyping provided engineers with immediate feedback on their progress and highlighted areas that needed focused attention.

The first prototype was built in July at the local assembly house.

Ideally, three prototypes for a project of this type would have been built—one each for design verification, process verification, and production development. But the design team conducted two additional prototype steps, to ferret out and fix system bugs not corrected in the first two prototypes and perfect variant designs that would enable production and shipment of the workstation overseas. In early October manufacturing received its initial opportunity to build the DEC station 3100, this the third prototype, with only three months before ramp-up to first revenue ship. Two manufacturing technicians were moved to engineering to help with prototype development and facilitate technology transfer back to manufacturing. Ultimately, 10 manufacturing representatives moved to Palo Alto, assuming a variety of roles. The first workstation was shipped in January.

The rapid time-to-market goal entailed significant modification to existing DEC development policies. The corporate-wide phase review process used to identify risks, coordinate activities, and gauge progress was altered by combining various steps. The team honored the spirit of the phase-review process but not the actual structure; the process was seen by team members as an internal guideline for critical activities as opposed to a tool for external control over product development. Over the entire period only two major corporate reviews were conducted, fewer than normal for a significant program. The first review, in September 1988, involved corporate management and all major players in the DECstation 3100's design and manufacturing. They reviewed the technical, business, and manufacturing plans and the potential risks and opportunities. As a result of the review, major funding was allocated, participants committed to the production time schedule, and manufacturing signed off on the project. The second major review was held in December, one month before first revenue ship. It was used to evaluate overall product quality and readiness for product announcement and ramp-up to full production. The design and manufacturing groups received very positive feedback from this review and felt for the first time that all of DEC was completely behind their efforts.

Other DEC procedures, such as price approval, component qualification, and field testing also had to be significantly modified. The traditional price approval mechanism, for example, would have taken more then three months, nearly a third of the total project cycle. The design team kept work for both parts qualification and field testing within the Palo Alto vicinity and, as much as possible, out of DEC's East Coast corporate pipeline, which the team felt operated too inflexibly along the typical two-year development cycle. Reliance on state-of-the-shelf components enabled the team to minimize qualification time. To gather information for product qualification, testing was begun on early prototypes and continued through early non-revenue shipments. A "wrecking crew" was also created, comprising 25 senior engineers at the design site who were not connected with the project. Each person was given an early model of the DEC station 3100, and agreed to use it daily for three months in an effort to uncover problems. The top 15 problem finders would each receive a 3100. The wrecking crew logged 50,000 hours on the systems prior to revenue shipments and constituted a doubling of the number of software experts intimately involved with the project. Some 785 bugs were identified, including such things as the feel of the keyboard and specific software and hardware interaction problems. Wrecking crews are now used on all workstation products, and have become part of the culture.

Because this was the first joint project between Palo Alto and Albuquerque, it took some time to build trust and respect between design and manufacturing, and the two-way communication needed for design-for-manufacturability. Initially, the co-location of manufacturing people at Palo Alto was viewed more as a form of assistance for design and as a tool for technology transfer to manufacturing than as a source of manufacturing input into design. Over the life of the project a positive relationship between manufacturing and design was built. At the close of the project one key member of the manufacturing team observed that "Whereas design ignored 80 percent of what we said in the beginning, they now at least listen to 80 percent of what we say even though they may not accept our suggestions."

Development of the DECstation 3100 entailed two critical steps for manufacturing: the introduction of surface-mount technology and the education of technicians in the use of a new diagnostic program for a UNIX-based workstation. After design presented the workstation plans to manufacturing in July 1988, an order was placed for new surface-mount equipment. Though it arrived only weeks before ramp-up, the equipment was successfully brought up for production. The development of the new diagnostics program and education of the technicians in its use, on the other hand, proved to be a critical deficiency in the technology transfer to manufacturing. Recognizing a clear lack of UNIX experience and knowledge at the plant, manufacturing had requested early that design engineers visit Albuquerque to conduct training programs. That little training had been conducted by ramp-up was due both to the design engineers' lack of appreciation for how important diagnostic development was and manufacturing's inability to communicate just how critical education was. Ramp-up remains a problem today—manufacturing skills are not matching the needs of high-quality, quick-introduction products and processes.

As a result, the ramp-up to production was both slow and difficult. To complicate matters, the final design was not formalized until three days before first revenue ship. To ease production and distribution, the design and manufacturing groups limited potential workstation configurations to 30. This compared to nearly 1000 permutations for some earlier DEC workstations. The limitation enabled manufacturing to introduce a new distribution system in which a large proportion of the workstations were build to stock and were later sent to customers off the shelf.

### Project Outcome and Lessons Learned

Overall, the DECstation 3100 project was viewed as a success. The team met all pivotal goals, including the nine-month development cycle and the desired price/performance ratio. The DECstation performed well in comparison to other workstations introduced in 1989.

These successes notwithstanding, the DECstation 3100 had significant difficulty penetrating the market because of a single but clear oversight—a notable lack of software applications. Only 20 applications had been developed when the product was introduced. Users of competing workstations could choose from more than 500. Concern over the breadth of applications, although raised early in the project, was not adequately addressed. The team (engineering, marketing, and sales) naively felt—after much discussion—that a "hot box" would still sell without applications. Even when the workstation was near completion, the team did nothing to expand the applications set; the team sent the first workstations coming off the line to key customers, not to software developers who could have developed new programs. Within a few months, the team knew this was not the case, and the problem has since been remedied—there are now more than 3000 available applications. But once again, lack of applications software development and market study proved to be weaknesses at DEC.

A second marketing challenge arose because the DECstation 3100 was the sole UNIX-based workstation in the VMS world. From a compatibility point of view the DECstation team had made a remarkable breakthrough—at this point in the evolution of the computer industry, it was rare that computers with different operating systems could even communicate, much less work together. Unfortunately, DEC's sales representatives, who were familiar with the VMS operating system and the company's long line of VAX products, did not understand the intricacies of the UNIX-based system and did not sufficiently push its sale. Part of the problem was that the salespeople received little training on the 3100 until seven months after first revenue ship. When the training was finally conducted, most of the participants were managers and not field sales engineers. The 3100 team quickly learned that this product required a totally different sales approach from past DEC products.

Since that time, many needed adjustments have been made in the applications and sales program for DEC's line of UNIX-based workstations. Follow-on products, such as the DECstation 5000 series (which was developed with the same rapid product development/time-to-market approach) have been both technological and market successes.

## CDA SOFTWARE

### Competitive Environment and Product Strategy

As the case study of the DECstation 3100 workstation suggests, DEC was having some trouble cracking the office personal computer and workstation market in the late 1980s. Prior to 1987, efforts tended to lack focus. A number of people who had seen the writing on the wall realized that DEC was not going to enter the office through sales of personal computers; DEC's entree, it became apparent, was through workstations. By 1987 industry initiatives involving dumb terminals linked to minicomputers were being superseded by development of powerful workstations like the 3100. If workstations were to be DEC's niche in office products, then the company had to develop a package of basic office applications for them, including competitive word-processing programs, a set of business programs such as spreadsheets, and other common programs such as electronic mail and graphics.

Inspired by the strong push to develop a new standard for workstations, DEC's engineers and marketing people wanted to go beyond developing office applications and create an industry standard for high-level desktop publishing, which would incorporate all the basic office applications. In addition, reaching the market before IBM, which was rumored to be developing an overall architecture for its desktop publishing software, would give DEC an ''architectural foothold'' with customers in the office systems market.

DEC had already experimented with DECwindows, software that used window formats to present programs on the screen. Today this is common on most computers. However, what was needed to expand this software was an overall architecture that would allow office applications software to work within the DECwindows system. In essence DEC needed to create an overall desktop architecture using DECwindows to present various applications such as text or graphics that would be developed both by DEC and independent vendors. This Compound Document Architecture (CDA), as it came to be called, would also be capable of converting data between multiple applications; for example, a table drafted in one program could be translated and presented as graphics by another program. And the architecture would have to work on both VMS and UNIX machines (see **Figure 11.3**).

Prior to the CDA project most of DEC's attempts in desktop publishing had failed. One reason appeared to be conflicts within the development teams, including an incompatibility among team mem-

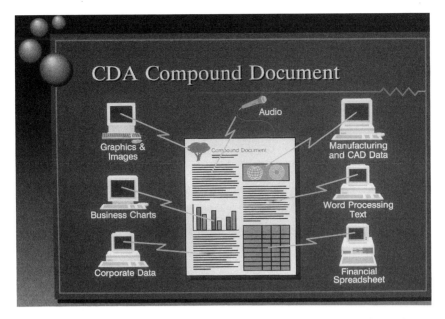

**Figure 11.3.** A schematic illustration of the integration of multiple software inputs in a single architecture.

bers who often came from divergent backgrounds. Some people had worked previously in personal computer development while others came from high-end publishing. This conflict impeded the resolution of trade-offs between ease of use and sophistication of functions. The conflicts festered because management's attention was scattered among a variety of projects, and because involvement of the key architect of the joint software/hardware efforts ended as a result of a 1985 car accident in which he was severely injured.

## Project Execution

To get the ball rolling again, DEC formed a Core Applications Group in October 1986. The group would devise the compound document architecture through the integration of four independent project teams. One of the four teams was to adapt DECwindows to work within the CDA framework. The other three teams were to develop specific applications packages for DECwindows: DECwrite, a word processing package; DECdecision, a business package; and CDA

Toolkit, a set of useful programs such as a graphics editor, file translator, and other aids that would enhance the use of the total system for applications development.

Because DEC's history in applications software development was not stellar, the company hired an outside person to oversee the Core Applications Group. He brought experience in integrating such software efforts, but sensed this charge would be a hard one to fill. "No one in DEC believed that we could do applications," he had said.

Luckily the Core Applications Group was not starting from scratch. The concept of a compound document architecture had remained in the backs of several individuals' minds, and some very basic development had already taken place. As part of development, CDA had to take into consideration several international software and communications standards, DEC's internal standards for software interfaces, and *de facto* standards created by the market dominance of such high-volume applications as WordPerfect and Lotus 123. CDA would also push beyond existing standards for the movement and integration of data between programs, leveraging DEC's networking strength.

The manager of the core applications group was viewed as the technology leader. He set priorities and solved problems, served as tie-breaker and task-driver, and had to think from one month to one year ahead. Product managers for each of the applications groups wrote business plans, worked with marketing, and chose the software compilers that would be used during development. They had no "heavy role," however, until the point of shipping, at which time they coordinated with manufacturing, secured pricing approval, and so forth. Product managers met weekly with the group manager. The managers for DECwrite, DECdecision, and CDA Toolkit met often during the early stages of design but less and less frequently as their products developed. Unfortunately, the central architect did not remain in the core group; he was moved to other projects mid-stream. Technical leadership and overall program coordination were thus strongest during the early phases of the project. As work continued, the level of intergroup contact diminished, resulting in problems toward the end of the program when the individual applications needed to be integrated into a single overall package.

Work was further complicated because early on, top management informed the core group leader that the majority of the desktop applications could not be internally developed, due to financial considerations. They would be written by independent software vendors. As a result early versions of the CDA specifications were released to key vendors, prompting a simultaneous public announcement of DEC's intent to garner public support for the CDA architecture.

Before discussing the final integration of the projects, a brief look at the work in the three applications groups is warranted.

*DECwrite.* The development of early DEC word processing programs, which were having a tough time, led to the creation in mid-1986 of two task forces, one to seek outside technology to solve problems and one to evaluate existing internal work. When the task forces reported their conclusions in December 1986, the two existing word-processing development programs were canceled and an entirely new project begun. Ultimately, the DECwrite project leader advised the business unit manager to buy developed code from Frame, a five-person company. His reasons were that Frame's product was up to date, was not "overblown" in complexity, and used a small amount of code. The Frame product was technically sufficient and compact enough to be altered. On the negative side, the code was undocumented and had been developed for a workstation made by competitor Sun Microsystems.

The DECwrite team received 60,000 lines of code from Frame in May 1987. Working with unlimited telephone access and a week-long visit from a Frame developer, the team began using and adapting the code. Approximately 30 percent to 40 percent of the work consisted of adding new functionality, with the remainder dedicated to customizing the code to DEC's specific needs.

The benefits of buying code were twofold. First, much of the code was highly "polished," saving DEC's developers several months. Second, it reduced ambiguity, since developers could simply refer to the finished product to answer design questions. In addition, Frame's code could be easily translated between VMS and UNIX machines. Also, the purchase infused the team with momentum and self-confidence.

*DECdecision.* Work on specifications for DECdecision was begun in the summer of 1986. Through August 1987 the team focused on designing and prototyping the software, which was to function as the primary spreadsheet and chart-making application within DECwindows. DECdecision included code from many other projects, both successes and failures. The key challenge was to improve the functionality of the applications and make sure they would be compatible with the DECwindows scheme and CDA framework.

Team members gathered market information for DECdecision from a number of sources. They talked to customers of an earlier product, met with visiting consultants, engaged in data gathering at trade shows, and evaluated competing products. The team examined, for example, various spreadsheet programs for the Apple Macintosh to evaluate ease of use. One software manager developed a systematic comparison of spreadsheets and word-processing programs and employed factor analysis to examine the most popular and common features.

*CDA Toolkit.* In addition to building the CDA architecture the core applications group was charged with drafting the CDA Toolkit programs, which among other things would be used by software engineers to build applications at customer sites. Subsequent CDA development was difficult because the project manager inherited a disorganized team of 33 people collected from canceled projects who had suffered under both full-time and part-time supervisors.

Responsibility for CDA Toolkit rested with three people: a "guru" who worked on high-level problems; a data architect who documented the guru's work; and a consulting engineer brought in to help rectify specific problems. The consulting engineer, because of his ability to solve problems, became the primary designer.

## Project Outcome and Lessons Learned

DECwindows, modified to operate under the CDA framework, was shipped for external field tests in October 1987. The entire package, including DECwrite, DECdecision, and the CDA Toolkit went with it. By this time the CDA system had already been tested internally;

about 10 development groups had used it as part of their own projects. For example, an engineer developing a graphics program—DECpaint—had used CDA and thus the CDA Toolkit because it was convenient.

External field testing took place at numerous Fortune 100 companies and other concerns. Many reviewers proved useful. For example, a member of the Coast Guard who had been particularly thorough and hard to please not only commented on things that didn't work but made valuable suggestions for alterations.

Notwithstanding, internal field testing was the most critical. The team estimated 90 percent of the bugs in DECdecision were found by this means. Through an internal computer conferencing system for employees (Notesfiles), developers received a great deal of valuable feedback from some 150 sites that had been supplied with DECdecision software kits. For engineers, the on-line files provided "living specs" that enabled them to keep apprised of what others were doing to the code.

Development progressed very well within the independent subprojects. The challenge was in integrating the three applications projects into one coherent package. Early efforts were problematical, however. One key engineer felt that difficulties in integration were due primarily to resource constraints. One of the two central architecture engineers, for example, had never taken the time to codify specifications; he believed that giving CDA project members the building blocks was sufficient, and that the process for putting these together was intuitively obvious. There was no lower level specification or description for how these building blocks were to be aggregated. This lack of exact specification, and the operational use of such generic terms as integration and interoperability instead of specific plans for meshing the programs, led each subteam to interpret early decisions in accordance with their own needs. Beginning in late 1987 a technical team composed of people from each group began to meet weekly to resolve the issues complicating integration of the whole package.

The product release dates were relative, but all had to be available for concurrent release; DECdecision was to be out in the quarter that followed the release of DECwindows, which occurred in December 1988. Initially, DECdecision had not even been tied to DECwindows, and in the end came out four months late, within two quarters of DECwindows. Because the project was intended to fill an unoccupied market niche, it was important that the entire package reach the market before competitors' products. The planned ship date for DECwrite, in April 1989, was altered some due to slippage in the schedule of a DECwindows, but the slippage did not prove troublesome. In the end, DEC won this battle with IBM as IBM's MODCA product, the DEC competitor, is no longer being pushed.

Overall, the DECdecision team got extremely good feedback; the DECwindows package was well liked. Today, computers using the compound document architecture can handle graphics, text, and images; soon they will be able to accommodate 3-D images and voice. The CDA architecture provided for an effective interchange of information between a set of highly competitive applications that worked within the DECwindows environment. Complications that arose were due primarily to the attempt to create in one fell swoop a broad desktop publishing environment and set of applications. The CDA project leader said work would have progressed more smoothly had the group been able to first focus on creating a seamless system for interchanging information between applications, leaving development of specific applications programs for later.

CHAPTER 12

# Eastman Kodak Company

With the slogan "You press the button, we do the rest," George Eastman in 1888 put the first simple camera into the hands of the American public and set in motion what would become the world's most successful producer of photographic products. Today, Eastman Kodak Co. of Rochester, New York, manufactures and markets products as diverse as pharmaceuticals, office copiers, specialty chemicals, polymers, and imaging materials for the health, business, and professional markets. With sales approaching $20 billion, Kodak ranks as the eleventh largest exporter of U.S. goods, doing business in over 150 countries and employing more than 130,000 people world wide.

The manufacturing capability of Eastman Kodak in Rochester is devoted primarily to imaging products and is split between two sites known as Kodak Park and the Elmgrove Plant. Kodak Park is the company's largest manufacturing facility and one of the biggest integrated manufacturing sites in the Unites States. Its 20,000 employees are devoted to imaging consumables—some 980 different types of film, 270 kinds of photographic paper, and 900 chemical formulations. The Elmgrove plant produces hardware such as cameras, photographic processing equipment, plain-paper copiers, and medical diagnostics equipment. Each of the four development projects studied by the Manufacturing Vision Group took place at one of these two sites.

## Kodak's Competitive Position, Culture, and Modus Operandi

For nearly 100 years prior to 1985, the Rochester facilities operated under a highly centralized, functional structure that served the company well as it focused on the growing photographic business. Roots for this structure can be found in George Eastman's early experiences with the inconsistent quality of materials supplied by vendors. He determined that the only way to control the consistency of his products was to vertically integrate supply and manufacturing, which in turn led to centralizing the research, manufacturing, sales, and marketing functions. Another factor that contributed to centralization was the invention of continuous film-base casting machines and high-speed emulsion coating techniques; these required very sophisticated ongoing technical support for Kodak to produce the high-volume, high-quality, low-cost products desired by customers. Basically, most of Kodak's photographic products were thought of as variations in formulations that utilized a common, capital-intensive manufacturing process. Driven by this capital intensity, the research and central engineering functions evolved as the key product and process leaders, with functions such as manufacturing, sales, and marketing playing supportive roles.

Historically, the undertaking of new photographic products typically involved technology innovations from Kodak's Research Laboratories. The innovations were turned into product concepts that were proposed for corporate approval via a technology demonstration phase. At this juncture, business strategy set the guidelines that drove product and process requirements. Due to the enormous capital investment in the common film-casting and coating process, a key technical challenge was to ensure that laboratory formulations could be scaled up and made compatible with manufacturing processes that were already in place. This process was not always as smooth, quick, or successful as desired. In addition, the central engineering and development group was charged with designing and developing downstream finishing and packaging equipment. The engineering and design challenges were further complicated because most of the photographic media products had to be manufactured in complete darkness or substantially reduced lighting conditions.

During the implementation of development projects, it was common to test many generations of product, to verify and evolve the manufacturability of design. Various customer try-outs would also take place (usually using a vertical slice of company employees) to determine product performance characteristics under typical usage conditions. These "total systems tests" included not only the media produced at Kodak Park but also hardware (cameras and such) produced at the Elmgrove plant. Once the system testing had been successfully completed, full-scale manufacturing would be initiated at both sites. Although a gross oversimplification, this process was largely sequential, in which one functional group passed the results of its efforts "over the wall" to the next group in the chain. Integration was provided by a corporate project coordinator.

## Kodak's Model for Product Development

This deeply ingrained approach to development began to change in the mid-1980s. For decades the unrivaled leader in the photographic industry, Kodak was confronted with new competition. Not only were the number of competing companies increasing, they were growing and becoming more aggressive. While some of them attempted to compete on a broad scale, others were attacking focused markets by responding faster to specific customer desires, or by raising quality or lowering cost.

As Kodak began to face competition in traditional silver halide technology (the chemical basis for its film products), digital electronics also began to emerge. To sustain a viable future, Kodak realized it had to maintain a strong silver halide base and also develop a strong foundation in the hybridization of traditional technology with digital electronics. Kodak's senior management, cognizant of the trend since the early 1980s, decided the historic organization had to change, because the functional structure rendered decision-making slow and made it difficult for the company to nimbly focus on multiple, segmented groups of customers. Kodak restructured the centralized management into the line-of-business (LOB) format, which culminated in 1991 with the formation of three core business sectors: Imaging (products such as film and cameras), Chemicals (products for the photographic and other markets), and Health (products such as diagnostics media and equipment, and drugs). In restructuring, management saw that the success of the company would depend not only on the three sectors, but also on new ways to develop products within the LOB structure and on methods for integrating platforms across the LOBs to leverage Kodak's technical and manufacturing strengths. The transition has been gradual, and is still taking place.

This new emphasis has changed the company's approach to development projects. Under the old functional system, the choice of product and process features and functions tended to be directed by the technical disciplines. Project leaders were drawn mainly from people with functional expertise. Representation from support groups was added when required. However, as the line-of-business structure became recognized, it was expected that issues such as customer focus, responsiveness, quality, and cost would be addressed more effectively.

Of necessity, the execution of projects also had to evolve to support the LOB structure. To be fully effective, the LOB structure had to have a project development process capable of recognizing and utilizing efficiently the broad technical, manufacturing, and marketing strengths of the company. Kodak came up with the Manufacturing Assurance Process, or MAP (also called the "phases and gates" process) to assure that manufacturing, marketing, and engineering people are on the same team early in the project cycle to enhance project appropriateness and execution. Though the development and formalization of MAP had begun prior to the LOB reorganization, its strengths have been particularly valuable to the LOB structure.

Because development projects in the line-of-business scheme would be taking place independently in many organizations, the MAP process attempts to assure that manufacturing, marketing, and engineering people are all committed to focusing on customer needs, enhancing integration of project subgroups, improving manufacturability, and streamlining decision-making. MAP is meant to improve the

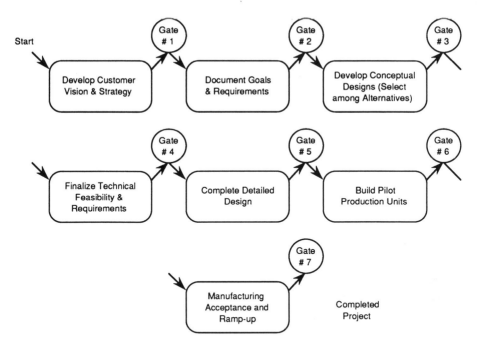

**Figure 12.1.** So that projects are executed in a somewhat uniform manner, development teams at Kodak follow the Manufacturing Assurance Process (MAP). The process consists of seven phases, separated by gates. Each gate consists of three parts: verification by a "gatekeeper" that key questions and issues have been addressed, a formal management review that must be passed before the project can continue, and the establishment of specific criteria and milestones for the next phase, which are agreed to by the project team and management (the "stakeholders") before work proceeds. Theoretically, commitment is not made to a downstream phase until the gate that precedes it has been passed.

planning and execution of development projects while leaving room for flexible procedures and adaptation to particular circumstances. MAP is still not being used universally throughout Kodak because of the sheer size of the company, the inertia of old practices, and the need for training, but management intends for it to become ubiquitous and it appears to be on its way.

As shown in **Figure 12.1**, MAP divides development projects into phases. Between each phase is a "gate." The gate consists of two parts: a formal management review that must be passed before the project can continue, and the establishment of specific criteria and milestones for the next phase, which are agreed to by the project team and management before work on that phase proceeds. Theoretically, no commitments are made to a downstream phase until the gate that precedes it has been passed.

Development activities in Kodak's three major sectors have many similarities, but are also flavored by the unique needs, culture, and dominant disciplines of those sectors. Thus the health care sector is influenced by the evolution of health care economics; the photographic chemicals sector is influenced by environmental and material handling concerns, among others. Kodak continues to evolve in its new development mode while also seeking to leverage the unique capabilities of each sector in a synergistic manner. To fully leverage the line-of-business structure, there is a particular need in the future to strengthen the cross-functional integration between the sectors as a means of achieving common objectives that support the corporation's strategic intent not only within a sector but also between sectors.

Underlying this is the premise that success in equipment design and manufacturing can best be achieved through a unified network of partnerships between lines of business. Each line of business will naturally develop core strengths, which a given partnership can leverage. While the lines of business will have overall responsibility for specific programs, they will rely heavily on the skills supplied by their own people as well as other core areas in their development programs. Although senior management feels Kodak will always be a technology-driven company, the line-of-business direction will necessitate that future projects be more heavily influenced by areas other than functional R&D units, such as marketing, manufacturing, and field support, in order to achieve the customer focus required.

## The Kodak Case Studies

The four development projects examined by the Manufacturing Vision Group all took place while Kodak was converting from the centralized, functional organization to the line-of-business structure. Two projects involved new products, and two new processes. They also, deliberately, represented varying degrees of success. Because Kodak was in transition, the projects point to many interesting differences between the old and new organizations and the MAP approaches to development. A brief summation of the cases follows.

*Factory of the Future.* This project was initiated to upgrade and expand the capacity of Kodak's factories that cut, spool, and package 35-mm consumer films (activities referred to as ''finishing''). It was begun early in the conversion from a functional structure to the line-of-business structure.

*Antistatic film coating.* To improve sales, this project was undertaken to develop a new, clear, antistatic coating for microfilm, to prevent the film from attracting dust while maximizing the perceived sharpness of the images on the film as seen by the end-user. It made use of off-the-shelf but state-of-the-art technology. The project was fully executed under the line-of-business structure using the MAP development approach.

*FunSaver camera.* This project was begun to design and produce a single-use camera. In this scheme the film is packaged in a simple, inexpensive plastic camera body. Once pictures were taken, the consumer would hand in the whole assembly to a photofinisher. The film would be processed and the body would be discarded or recycled. The design was based in part on existing design knowledge but was done on a unique CAD/CAM system to shorten the lead time to manufacture.

*Panda printer.* Panda was to be a thermal printer that could output large-format, color images of extremely high quality from digital data. Such a product was needed by the U.S. Department of Defense and top-of-the-line industrial and professional concerns. It was one of Kodak's first attempts to integrate divisions from different lines of business and merge both government and consumer product specifications.

Each case description is divided into three sections. The first describes the competitive environment in which the project was undertaken and the strategic planning that led to its undertaking. The second explains the execution of the project itself. The third section describes how well the development team performed relative to project goals and the lessons that were learned about product and process development.

## FACTORY OF THE FUTURE

### Competitive Environment and Product Strategy

In 1984, approximately a year prior to the LOB restructuring, Kodak's Film Manufacturing division manager and the central Engineering & Design division manager agreed that substantial production capacity would have to be added by 1990 for the cutting, perforating, and packaging of 35-mm consumer films. The equipment required for this "finish" step is sophisticated, automated, and high-speed in nature. Equipment design and the flow of work is extremely complicated. Because the film at this point is sensitive to light, the entire finishing process, which occurs on a large scale, must be carried out in darkroom or near-darkroom conditions. Equipment design, building, installation, and debugging were the responsibility of the Engineering Division at Kodak Park.

Based on benchmarking information, the two managers also agreed that future cost and quality considerations dictated new approaches to finishing. Historically, finishing had received less management attention than production of the wide, master rolls of film (the "raw" film) that were then sliced, cut, and packaged in canisters (see **Figure 12.2**). This project was thus seen by the Engineering division's mechanical design group as an exciting opportunity. As a result, the division embarked on a "skunkworks" program to provide a quantum leap in finishing technology.

### Project Execution

As that more ambitious goal was adopted, the work became known as the Factory of the Future (FOF) project. Eventually the effort was staffed with more than 100 full-time representatives from five Kodak

**Figure 12.2.** One step in finishing film is to slit wide rolls of coated film into smaller format sizes, such as 35 mm. (Reprinted by permission of Eastman Kodak Company, 1992.)

organizations (Manufacturing, Engineering & Design, Maintenance, Quality Assurance, and Marketing). However, the majority of people on the team came from one group—central Engineering & Design—whose primary focus was production equipment for loading film into canisters. During the 1970s and early 1980s, Engineering & Design had spent considerable time and effort exploring options for how such equipment might be improved. They viewed the FOF project as their one and only chance to apply a host of new techniques.

The project team proposed to design and build a prototype Factory of the Future within $1\frac{1}{2}$ years. An economic evaluation indicated the project would add enough capacity to generate a significant increase in cash flow, while also incorporating several highly desirable technical innovations, such as the ability in some areas to work under white light, instead of darkroom-like conditions. At the same time that the FOF was being proposed, part of the team also discussed an alternative system using conventional and commercially available equipment. Cost and milestone charts for a conventional expansion were prepared for base-case comparison purposes.

As work began, it soon became apparent that the prototype system would be at least one year late, with no firm date as to when production capacity would be available. This came about in part because too many engineers were trying to cram too much new technology into the project. As the team began to lay out in detail what would have to be done to turn all the new technical ideas into reality, they realized basic innovation would have to occur before complete development of the FOF could take place. In parallel, those in operations, distribution, and sales began raising questions about increasing variety and flexibility—concerns not being given primary emphasis by the equipment designers. Nonetheless the team pushed ahead. As equipment began to be designed, engineers were confronted with numerous problematical interactions between equipment modules and operator stations. That extensive redesign would be needed was becoming all too obvious as the team struggled to balance the needs of operational flexibility, materials handling, work flows, and new technology.

In retrospect the engineers in the core group that led the team had become overly determined to push the processing envelope, without fully appreciating the effects on the total manufacturing system, especially considering so much of the technology was unproven. Within the next six months the team established a new production start-up date, which would be the early part of the third year from program inception.

### Project Outcome and Lessons Learned

By this time the manufacturing unit was making the transition to the line-of-business structure. The original manufacturing manager had retired, and the new line-of-business management requested a full review of costs, resources, and schedules to ensure compatibility with future plans. Sales of film continued to increase during this period, putting additional pressure on the technical community to end their development efforts and "build their machines," for better or worse.

A thorough evaluation revealed the obvious—the project had ballooned too far. It would require a significant increase in expenditures, and would take an additional two years before production capacity would come on line, putting that threshold five years from the start of program. This prompted management to cancel the project.

The FOF work was not abandoned, however; the positive parts of the program were corralled and redirected, and were fit under an alternative model for expanding capacity using conventional technology. This time the project was not led by engineering, but by the line-of-business production, marketing, and sales people who were focused on creating an operation that provided the flexibility and variety in packaging that was being demanded by the market. This project succeeded and added substantial capacity.

The FOF project had consumed on the order of $800,000 in equipment prototyping and the time of 110 people for more than a year during its peak. It had also delayed expansion by a few years. The Achilles heel of the project had to do with the lack of a clear guiding vision shared by all participants. In this case, Engineering & Design was focused on squeezing in as much advanced technology as possible, since large capital expansions such as this one did not come along very often, perhaps once a decade or even longer. Manufacturing, however, saw the project as a chance to become a "world-class manufacturer" by improving materials handling, work flows, employment practices, and systems. For them, FOF was a broad-ranging improvement effort with new equipment playing an important complementary, not central, role.

For the sales and marketing group (the "Business Unit"), the project was an opportunity to improve the flexibility and responsiveness of film packaging, thereby reducing substantially the need to annually repackage, for specialty markets, tens of millions of rolls of film coming out of the factory. This flexibility was required to address the needs of different distribution channels and the variety of packing materials and designs increasingly demanded by customers. The financial group, along with much of senior management, viewed the FOF project primarily as a way to add capacity to meet demand. Any improvements in the production process were desirable although secondary, as long as they were not too expensive and did not delay or alter the traditional capital budgeting procedures followed in adding capacity for a large volume product.

Finally, the lack of a common vision was exacerbated by the leadership void that was created when the Film Manufacturing manager retired and the new line-of-business structure came into play. If the MAP system had been in place, it might have provided some checks and balances as the project began to outrun itself, but it was not yet firmly established.


## ANTISTATIC FILM COATING

### Competitive Environment and Product Strategy

For years Eastman Kodak has been the leading manufacturer of micrographic films, used for archiving information. Known to most people as the "slides" put into microfiche machines found in libraries, the majority of users are people working at banks and insurance companies who store and retrieve information. Micrographic films are based on black and white silver halide technology, one of Kodak's most mature technologies.

Historically, new micrographic film products and technical advances took place at a measured pace. The product line was supported by a small, stable development and manufacturing staff that was integrated into a larger manufacturing and development organization. The antistatic film project began in late 1985, about the same time the new line-of-business structure was put in place.

The project evolved from the line of business's evaluation (done primarily by field sales) of customer needs and the changing competitive environment. Studies showed that some end-users thought the images on films made by Kodak were less sharp than those on films made by competitors. It was determined that actual image sharpness, as defined in standard tests, was no different, but Kodak's images were sometimes perceived as less sharp because the microfilm background appeared a bit darker. The slight darkening resulted from a coating placed on the film to reduce the attraction of dust due to

**Figure 12.3.** Microfilm images are stored in cartridges for automated access by special reader equipment. (Reprinted by permission of Eastman Kodak Company, 1992.)

static build-up and decrease the possible degradation of the film (see **Figure 12.3**).

## Project Execution

Obviously, the perceived lack of sharpness could lead to potential loss of market share. The Business Imaging Systems division, the unit responsible for the product within the imaging line of business, formed a team to develop a significantly clearer antistatic coating. The team was headed by a business manager who represented the business unit's interests and an engineering manager who represented the chemical and manufacturing groups. Because of advances made by competitors, the two managers decided they would have to formulate a new coating, incorporate it into the manufacturing process, and be making new films in little over a year, a very ambitious schedule.

Given the magnitude of the effort, management instructed the team to use the recently refined Manufacturing Assurance Process as a means to break the complex goals into specific program stages and tasks. MAP brought focus to the activity, a way to communicate progress, and a means for sharing with various managers the risks undertaken to achieve timeline compression.

As an initial step, a program concept document was drafted, in which project "musts" were stated. Then the team evaluated various antistatic technologies and identified a recent invention from Kodak Pathé, a unit in France, as the solution to the problem. The new formulation would give state-of-the-art antistatic protection needed to reduce the tendency of the film to attract dust, and would optimize clarity of images on the film. Because clear and agreed on performance specifications were established early in the project, the team was able to demonstrate the technology in just a few months. Progress through the other MAP stages, such as design reviews and manufacturing readiness review, proceeded at a brisk pace because management from the development, manufacturing, and business communities were brought together at the milestone review meetings and were informed as to what was needed to keep the program on schedule. This was effective because the review meetings required that the uncertainties and risks be made visible in a structured way, and that the consequences be assessed by all groups with a hand in the project before the next step was allowed to proceed.

### Project Outcome and Lessons Learned

As a result of this process the improved films were completed on time (14 months after initiation) without compromising health and safety. (In any product that uses chemical formulations, the health and safety of workers and end-users is always a concern and often requires changes in design or manufacturing processes that can delay projects.) All critical milestones were met in a timely fashion, and all production quality, performance, and cost goals were met or exceeded. Most important, the new micrographic films were well received in the marketplace. Not only has Kodak retained its past market share, but the new product has generated incremental new business.

The antistatic film project succeeded for several reasons. First was a simple and well-defined vision, espoused through strong leadership from both the business manager and the engineering manager. Implementation under the tight time schedule was possible because all the requisite players were integrated early into the team. The health and safety group, for example, was involved from the beginning, and their concerns were addressed continuously during design. Often this particular group is not brought in until the tail end of a project, and then identifies issues that require redesign.

Team members also felt ownership and commitment to the project because they as a group set the technical and business specifications of the effort. In addition, the group was able to reach consensus quickly because many on the team had years of experience and long-term working relationships with each other. Finally, the team used MAP effectively to gauge its progress, keep management on board, and periodically refocus its resources and efforts.

## FUNSAVER CAMERA

### Competitive Environment and Product Strategy

Looking to expand its product line in the mid-1980s, Kodak's camera design engineering group proposed to camera and film management an intriguing new product—a single-use 35-mm camera. It would be targeted at individuals who did not regularly take pictures but wanted to capture a certain event as well as those who suddenly found themselves without their regular camera. The camera, initially dubbed the Fling 35 and later renamed the FunSaver 35, would be a simple plastic housing and 35-mm lens packaged around a single roll of film (see **Figure 12.4**). It would be sold retail for between $13 and $18 at tourist havens such as Disneyland and Sea World, at department stores, and at airports. After taking pictures the customer would return the entire camera to a photofinisher who would remove the film,

**Figure 12.4.** The Kodak Fling 35 camera (later renamed the FunSaver), introduced in 1989, was the company's first single-use camera. (Reprinted by permission of Eastman Kodak Company, 1992.)

process it, and discard the frame and lens (later on recycling of the bodies began). The FunSaver would be designed as a platform on which two subsequent variations would be developed—the Weekend 35, an underwater camera, and the Stretch 35, a camera with a wide-angle lens for panoramic shots.

Although the proposal was considered by senior management, it went nowhere for several years because there was no clear consensus on the need for such a product. Management feared it might simply cannibalize regular film sales and result in inferior photographs. That changed early in 1987 when Fuji, a major competitor, indicated it intended to market in the United States a disposable 35-mm camera it had introduced in Japan.

### Project Execution

Though Kodak had made a name for itself earlier in this century by introducing a succession of camera products, it had gotten out of the 35-mm camera market in the late 1960s. Kodak found it more profit-able to concentrate on the easy-to-use camera market—cameras that used the so-called "110" or "126" film formats. For the 35-mm market, corporate strategy was to focus on volume film sales, though Kodak did again begin in the late 1970s to produce a limited number of 35-mm cameras. Although the FunSaver was a niche camera product, senior management placed it under the direction of the film manufacturing division instead of the camera division, because they viewed the FunSaver as a "sales premium" film product, not a low-end camera product. Initially, market strategy and plans reflected this view.

Unfortunately, the concept languished for months in this setting. People in the film division were concerned that the camera would cut into mass market sales of film. Because each division reported its financial health separately, as in most large companies, the film division felt the FunSaver could actually detract from its profitability; at a minimum it would be a distraction to development, manufacturing, and sales people. The film division had no incentive to push the project.

The camera division, however, saw the FunSaver as an opportunity to expand its 35-mm product line. Division managers lobbied senior management for the project, pointing out that if the project was allowed to lie around Kodak could lose market position. Some senior managers were still not convinced, but data showed that sales of the Fuji camera in Japan were encouraging. So management gave the camera division responsibility for the concept. As it did so, the focus changed from that of a "sales premium" film product to the profitable manufacture of an inexpensive, high-quality single-use camera. This switch to a niche market, however, was still at odds with Kodak's historical mass marketing strategies and capabilities. Marketing needed to learn to build niche strategies and support specialized sales infrastructures to make this product fully successful.

There were still some starts and stops in pursuing the concept, because various cost-benefit analyses questioned whether the product would make money. In addition, the transfer of the product concept and existing knowledge was cumbersome; the two divisions, though only six miles apart, had a hard time communicating smoothly. But the camera organization had firm convictions regarding the concept and kept it alive through various management reviews.

The new project team, wholly within the camera division, was organized to develop both product design and manufacturing under one project manager, and used elements of the MAP process. They also decided to co-locate design and manufacturing engineers. To meet product objectives in quality and cost the new team agreed to use geometries and parts, such as the lens and viewfinder, that had already been developed for other 35-mm camera research projects. The key to rapid and efficient design, though, was the application of CAD/CAM (computer-aided design/computer-aided manufacturing), which was new to Kodak. The project manager was a strong believer in the technology and convinced that manufacturability was the key to success.

The team first chose upgraded internal software that allowed CAD/CAM to be used with three-dimensional modeling, instead of two-dimensional modeling. It then customized the system to make it more user friendly and altered design procedures to create a totally "paperless" and integrated system. Each designer responsible for a particular part of the camera could work on his or her element, then insert the updated drawing in the proper three-dimensional "layer" of the product, on top of and beneath other layers from other designers, to ensure the "fit and function" of all elements. Each evening every designer's work would be uploaded to a central computer. The next morning the new composite design would be downloaded so all designers and engineers could see the effects of their combined efforts. Although only the original designer could alter the drawing of his or her part, each person could critique any drawing and request changes. This parallel processing of information and immediate feedback fostered strong and effective communication, a common design platform, and quality verification. In addition, manufacturing "prototyping" using the three-dimensional CAM technology and simulation tools reduced overall program time significantly.

## Project Outcome and Lessons Learned

The FunSaver reached the public in 1988 and was a hit. It was competitive with Fuji's camera, and tens of millions have since been sold. Its success also prompted Kodak to follow up with the two other products originally considered, the Weekend 35 and the Stretch 35. By 1991 Kodak was adding production capacity for all three products and initiating development of a second-generation design that included a built-in flash.

The project presented Kodak with several lessons, some negative and some positive. Fundamentally, it showed that ultimately a development project must fit into the corporate business strategy and that all those working on the project need to understand and support that fit. Clearly the film division did not fully support the project, because it seemed to contradict its own goals. The camera division, however, understood the niche strategy and its team members got behind the project. An additional lesson was that a strong project manager helps in promulgating and sustaining the strategic vision; there was no champion in the film manufacturing division, but there was in the camera division.

Furthermore, the project showed that all units that are accountable for any step in the development of a new product should participate in its definition and planning. Management simply gave the original project to the film division, which then did not support it. The camera division sought the work, and then redefined the project of its own accord. On the positive side, the FunSaver project showed in a somewhat unusual way how technology can be used to improve the integration of a development team. The CAD/CAM system fostered a high degree of interaction among a varied group of designers—mechanical, industrial, tooling, and manufacturing—working in a distributed environment. The use of the system also enabled Kodak to rapidly introduce the two follow-on products, which were derived from the same CAD/CAM base and were developed using the same procedures.

## PANDA PRINTER

### Competitive Environment and Product Strategy

The Panda project was initiated in late 1986 by Kodak's Federal Systems division in response to inquiries from the federal government for a computer printer that could convert digital data into large color images (more than 100 square inches). The primary application was for the creation of hard copy from computer graphics programs used by the U.S. Department of Defense. Since conventional laser printing technology would not be sufficient, Kodak decided to perfect a thermal imaging process it had recently developed for a small-to-medium-format printer called the 6500. Initially, this was to be a feasibility demonstration.

The thermal imaging process is similar to that used by commercial printing presses—preformed dyes are transfered through a web to paper or film. The transfer is controlled by the amount of heat applied to a linear-array printing head (see **Figure 12.5**). Fitting the attributes of a printing press into a desk-size computer printing unit posed several technical challenges. Chief among them were great precision in the movement of the material to be printed on, conversion of non-uniform heads designed for the 6500, and the integration of hardware with the thermal imaging media and electronics.

### Project Execution

Though the Federal Systems division did not have firsthand expertise in thermal printing technology, it had developed some of the technologies required for Panda during materials research and processing innovation for various applications in other areas. To execute this project, people on the team realized they would need to alter the normal development process to ensure the coalescing of this knowledge. Many on the team were drawn from the 6500 project and they knew their main technical challenge would be integration. This focus was maintained throughout the project.

As work began, another Kodak division, the Electronic Products division (EPD), took an interest in the effort. Managers there thought commercial companies might also find great use for such a printer. EPD wanted to monitor the early work, and suggested it co-locate some of its own development engineers with the Federal Systems team. The government group resisted, however, because it did not want its work to be unduly influenced by commercial considerations. The Federal division worked quite differently from others at Kodak;

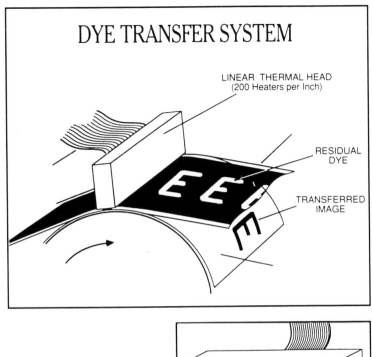

# DYE TRANSFER SYSTEM

LINEAR THERMAL HEAD
(200 Heaters per Inch)

RESIDUAL
DYE

TRANSFERRED
IMAGE

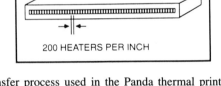

200 HEATERS PER INCH

**Figure 12.5.** Schematic of dye transfer process used in the Panda thermal printer. Pinpoints of heat are applied to dyes coated on a ribbon-like material. The heated dye transfers to a receiver material and an image is formed. (Reprinted by permission of Eastman Kodak Company, 1992.)

because products were developed to solve specific problems posed by government buyers, performance of its products took first priority, with cost and manufacturability concerns a distant second and third.

As EPD managers pondered the product, they became increasingly convinced that there was a real commercial market for it, and they made their case to corporate management. The senior people agreed with EPD's analysis, and worked out an agreement with the Federal division to add EPD people to the project and co-locate them at the EPD site. By this time work on the project had been underway for almost a year, and early prototype demonstrations were about to take place. A significant effort would be required to redesign the product based on commercial needs, namely that priorities would be placed in the following order: quality, cost, performance, and manufacturability. The merging of government and commercial specs was additionally difficult since potential customers had not been well identified. No one knew clearly what commercial customers would want, so redesigns further altered the product specs as the team explored its buyers. This in turn muddied the marketing strategy. Confusion developed over whether the product would be marketed directly or through value-added resellers. In the end the resellers were chosen, but the extended confusion left the resellers providing less-than-desired support and lead times.

## Project Outcome and Lessons Learned

The Panda printer was finally delivered to both the government and commercial markets in January 1990. Although the product was a technical success, total project costs and timelines missed their targets by substantial amounts; development took almost four years and required more than $12 million. This exceeded original budgets by more than 60 percent and was caused in large part by the project missing the original Federal division introduction goal by two years. While the product has been quite well received by customers in both markets, its production costs are high for a commercial product and its late introduction allowed competitors to come close to its performance.

The Panda project raised several organizational lessons for Kodak. At the fundamental level the project suffered from a lack of a strong vision, which was manifested in the weak business case made for the project. Though difficult, the product could have been developed successfully for both government and commercial markets if detailed and rigorous specifications had been drawn up to satisfy both. At first there were detailed design criteria for the government buyers, but these were compromised when commercial requirements were added. In turn, the commercial specs kept changing because customer desires were not well understood; engineers made their best guesses on specs until they learned more.

The vision broke down further due to lack of a strong leader. Since it resided in the Federal division, the project was pursued in a corporate research lab environment. It was typical in the division for project leadership to ebb and flow as dictated by technical circumstances; as a new problem came up, a new person from within the group who could solve the problem took over, until the next problem and person appeared. While this was tolerable for a government contract, in which performance dominated concerns over price, it was not effective in meeting commercial needs. Throughout its duration the project was essentially technology driven, developing only a limited knowledge of commercial customers and business case implications.

In terms of team structure, many of the key technical people had worked together previously but on projects not driven by budgets, timelines, and defined check points. Although the team agreed to follow the MAP system, it was used largely in name only, and not with careful discipline. Just the same, most of the engineers involved had a strong sense of ownership over the project. As a result, project execution did focus on ultimate goals, although near-term goals did not guide resource distribution and problem solving, which might have held down costs and eliminated some time. Assessment of the project was guided more by team optimism than any particular milestone.

## CHAPTER 13

# Ford Motor Company

$\mathbf{F}$ew companies can lay claim to a more noteworthy record of significant advances in manufacturing and mass production than the one started by Henry Ford in 1902. Driven by a vision of a light, simple, low-priced motor vehicle, Ford launched his company in a converted wagon shop in Detroit to assemble the first Model A.

As his company grew, Ford embarked on a project to design a car that could be made in great volume at modest cost. The result was the famous Model T. The "car that put the world on wheels" would become a classic; more than 15 million were sold. In 1908, the same year the Model T was introduced, Ford embarked on a novel experiment at the company's Piquette Avenue plant in Detroit: workmen pulled an automotive chassis along two rails while others connected necessary components. It was the first crude attempt at a moving assembly line.

Though the Ford Motor Co. has produced more than 200 million motor vehicles since its founding—including such classics as the Thunderbird, Mustang, Lincoln Continental, and Taurus—the company has also succeeded in other businesses, including electronics, glass, plastics, climate-control systems, electrical and fuel-handling products, service and replacement parts, vehicle leasing and rental, and land development. Other ventures have not fared as well; Ford has withdrawn from or limited its involvement in consumer electronics and household goods, satellite and defense systems, steel production, and agricultural and industrial equipment.

## Ford's Competitive Position, Culture, and Modus Operandi

Today Ford is one of the world's largest industrial corporations, with revenues of $95 billion. It concentrates its energies in two powerful arms: an Automotive Group and a Financial Services Group. Together these core businesses employ approximately 370,000 men and women.

Ford's top executives expect the financial services group to contribute approximately 30 percent of the company's earnings during normal business times and buttress the automotive group during cyclical downturns in auto sales. It consists of Ford Motor Credit Co., Associates Corporation of North America, First Nationwide Financial Corp., and United States Leasing International Inc.

The automotive group is responsible for the lion's share of corporate revenues. It faces an incredible challenge each time Ford decides to develop a new car. Automobiles are among the most complicated products made. Their development is mastered by a very few organizations around the world. A car project requires thousands of individual contributions from engineers, managers, designers, line operators, and specialists from marketing, purchasing, and finance.

Though a complex undertaking, the development of a new car can be divided into basic segments. The first is the concept development stage, in which business strategy and intent are translated into a description and specifications for the automobile. These guide the group charged with developing the car. The descriptions are then implemented in drawings and clay models that capture the car's interior and exterior styling. These guide different engineering groups, which develop designs for the ensemble of subsystems that make up the automobile. A central group of program managers and engineers then brings together all the drawings, models, and subsystems to ensure they fit in a coherent system. Process engineers work with design engineers to ensure the feasibility of the various components and develop specific manufacturing processes. The product and process designs are tested in various generations of prototypes. After a pilot stage (the "functional build") in which the assembly process is verified, mass production is finally begun at the manufacturing locations.

Though straightforward in concept, this development process is fraught with difficulty. And just getting through it is not enough. It must be efficient and effective if the company is to survive. Although the global auto industry has become conditioned to cyclical market swings, some companies are notably better at readjusting to these swings than others. Those that have adapted have made strong gains in market share. There is no dispute that the cycles are getting shorter and that the auto industry is today characterized by almost constant turmoil. There is widespread recognition that competition from somewhere in the world will overwhelm a stagnant company. This has forced extensive changes in the way auto companies develop new products.

Ford's automotive group learned this lesson late. Its competitive position had begun to decline in the 1970s, and by the end of the decade Ford faced major layoffs, empty hallways, and a real possibility of going under. Management knew it had to make a radical change in product development in order to revive the company's image and reverse the slide. The plan was to offer a different kind of car. This required that the car be developed in a different way. The executives bet the company on a single new model—the Ford Taurus. Luckily for them, the car sold extremely well, and subsequent models have saved Ford from disaster. Today Ford, like General Motors and Chrysler, is struggling against ever-tougher global competition, but it has a position from which to fight.

## Ford's Development Process

The Taurus, first sold in 1986, demonstrated Ford's ability to design an automobile with advanced styling and superior engineering. The styling themes established a new trend in the industry. The tight handling characteristics established a new standard for a best-selling American sedan. Boasting coherence in design and integrity in concept, the Taurus quickly became one of the most successful cars in the world.

It also marked a permanent change in Ford's approach to product development. Instead of organizing development projects along traditional lines of functional expertise, Ford used integrated teams of people from various functions. The Taurus was but a first step, though; integration was achieved at the level of senior management only. Management knew it would have to push integration down further. The rising competition from overseas manufacturers also clearly demanded that Ford become more responsive to rapidly changing customer demands and more flexible in offering a broader product line to serve an increasingly segmented market. This required that Ford develop cars with shorter lead times and with greater engineering productivity. Even with Taurus, the company's development approach lacked speed and efficiency; the Taurus program spanned seven years. The typical development time for a new car would have to be reduced from an average of six years to four, and the required number of engineering hours decreased substantially.

To address these challenges, senior management convened a special group of experts from within Ford, as the Taurus came to market. The "Concept-to-Customer" (C-to-C) team developed an aggressive new series of concepts, guidelines, and milestones for product development. Some of the basic tenets were that

- Senior management review of a development program should be driven by substantive milestones rather than by calendar schedules.
- Suppliers of production parts should be responsible for the prototypes of those parts; they may subcontract production of prototypes, but the production suppliers remain responsible for quality, performance, cost, and delivery.
- Parts used to manufacture pilot vehicles should be made with production tools.

Over the course of several months the C-to-C team defined the major development milestones as well as critical sequences of activities and patterns of responsibility required to ensure efficient and effective product development. This architecture culminated in the "Concept-to-Customer" process (see **Figure 13.1**). It was a macro paradigm for product development, and introduced as an official *modus operandi* in 1987. It would be supported by a number of new measures such as simultaneous engineering, early manufacturing input, improved prototyping, and the benchmarking of development and manufacturing processes against the best in the world. These measures, in turn, would be made possible by a number of new practices ranging from the very "hard," such as shortening the testing queue, to the very "soft," such as co-locating project teams and empowering employees to make decisions.

The implementation of the C-to-C process was the first step in an evolution toward better product development. An ongoing C-to-C team continues to assess and refine the process. Underlying the process is a conviction that strong cross-functional interaction and involvement throughout all the steps of a development project is needed to eliminate significant engineering changes and rework occasioned by poor communication and lack of shared understanding. Implementation of the C-to-C process motivates continual organizational change as Ford seeks to formalize and improve its team structures.

### The Ford Case Studies

The four projects studied by the Vision Group took place during the decade of the 1980s and during various stages of Ford's evolution (see **Figure 13.2**). The projects included three car development programs and one component program. They are presented in chronological order, to show how Ford broke from a functional approach to development to one characterized by integrated teams. The progression also shows a transition from lightweight to heavyweight project managers (for more, see the chapter Organization and Leadership). A brief summation of the cases follows.

*1988 Lincoln Continental (FN9).* This was Ford's first attempt to build a luxury car on the new Taurus platform. It required major suspension system modifications, and was the first implementation of a 3.8-liter engine in a transverse configuration. The Continental was

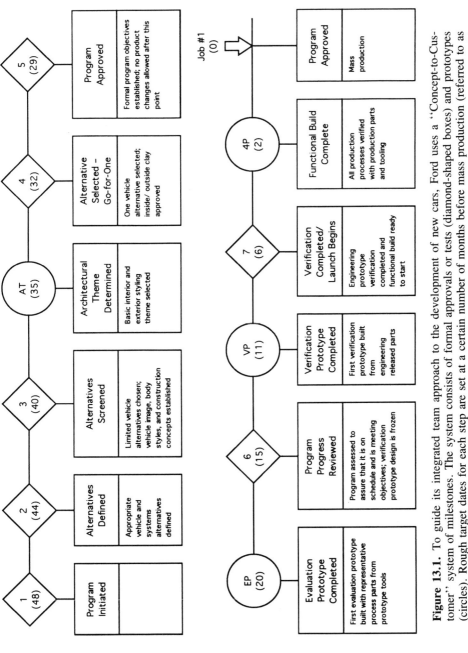

**Figure 13.1.** To guide its integrated team approach to the development of new cars, Ford uses a "Concept-to-Customer" system of milestones. The system consists of formal approvals or tests (diamond-shaped boxes) and prototypes (circles). Rough target dates for each step are set at a certain number of months before mass production (referred to as Job #1) is to begin. For example, a final choice of alternative designs should be made at Step 4, which occurs 32 months before mass production. The "functional build," a pilot stage in which the assembly process is verified, should begin six months before production, and should be completed with two months to go.

377

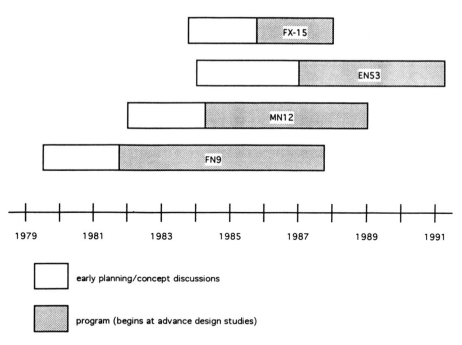

FX-15

EN53

MN12

FN9

1979    1981    1983    1985    1987    1989    1991

☐ early planning/concept discussions

▨ program (begins at advance design studies)

**Figure 13.2.** The four projects studied by the Manufacturing Vision Group spanned Ford's evolution toward integrated product development teams. The transition from projects organized along functional boundaries to those organized by teams peaked in 1986 and 1987.

begun in the old, functional mode, and though it was finished after the C-to-C process had been initiated, it still relied on old procedures. Spanning the transition caused some difficulties, but the car was successful.

*1989 Thunderbird/Cougar (MN12).* This generation of the Thunderbird was built on a new car platform that included a novel supercharged engine. It was the first project begun as lessons from the Taurus program were being codified, and Ford tried to complete it under the new system. It therefore suffered from growing pains.

*1991.5 Crown Victoria/Grand Marquis (EN53).* The Crown Victoria was built on a modified platform. It was the second vehicle to use a new engine based on an innovative modular design. The project was the first to be launched under the full C-to-C system, and shows the great benefits of the approach.

*FX15 Air-Conditioning Compressor.* This project represented the first time Ford tried to design in-house a compressor for automobile air-conditioning systems. The compressor was developed by Ford's Climate Control Division, which is run as a separate company and does not use the C-to-C system. However, the division did try several new methods on this product development, including concurrent engineering. The compressor was a success and so were many of the new techniques.

Each case description is divided into three sections. The first describes the competitive environment in which the project was undertaken and the strategic planning that led to its undertaking. The second describes the execution of the project itself. The third section describes how well the development team performed relative to project goals and the lessons that were learned about product development.

## 1988 LINCOLN CONTINENTAL (FN9)

### Competitive Environment and Product Strategy

For years the Lincoln Continental was a strong seller for Ford. It was a classic American luxury car—big, with a plush interior and large engine. But as the 1980s began the Big Three U.S. makers began to lose ground to Japan and Europe in the luxury market. The overseas cars were as plush, but they were smaller, more fuel efficient, and handled better. What's more, the ad campaigns from overseas makers, which promoted these so-called contemporary features, were striking a chord with consumers. Ford decided to contemporize its line of big cars, and thus the Continental FN9 Program.

### Project Execution

Though the Continental program was begun in 1982, before the onset of the C-to-C process, it was one of the first at Ford to be run by a program manager who had broad responsibilities. It was also one of the first to try to integrate people across traditional functional boundaries because many of the members of the program had participated in the early development of the Taurus and had learned the benefits of that trend-setting experience.

It is evident from discussions with the program manager that Ford had moved significantly along the road toward a heavyweight system in a relatively short time. Significant steps were taken to give the program manager and subordinate product managers authority and responsibility for product planning, and to provide them with the means to carry out a strong leadership role. Unlike in earlier development projects, the program manager was responsible for concept proposals, product planning, coordinating activities inside and outside the development group, and setting and meeting lead times, as well as specification and performance targets.

Though progressive, the program manager role did not include oversight of decisions traditionally made by the marketing and manufacturing functions. And, unfortunately, consistency in playing out the role was compromised because the original program manager was moved elsewhere and replaced in 1984, two years into the work.

## Project Outcome and Lessons Learned

Despite difficulties, the Continental emerged as a distinctive, trend-setting car, which created a new segment of the automobile market: ''Contemporary Luxury'' (see **Figure 13.3**). The program was successful in that it produced a vehicle with good market performance in about 25 percent fewer engineering hours than the average U.S. car program of the era. The lead time to market was about average, compared with other U.S. projects. When compared with similar Japanese projects, however, the program used about half a million more engineering hours and took considerably longer, on the order of a year. Though the car was competitive in the marketplace, the development program was still not competitive in time, staff, and cost.

Several factors were singled out as contributing to unnecessary cost and delay. In the early stages of the program there was a series of stops and starts related to styling issues. In the later stages, the program was characterized by delayed prototypes and flurries of engineering change-orders. These difficulties may have been partly rooted

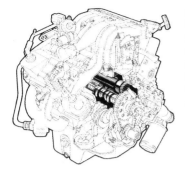

Continental's 3.8-liter
V-6 engine employs
advanced engineering
to provide luxurious
driving smoothness
and energetic response
without wasteful
inefficiency.*

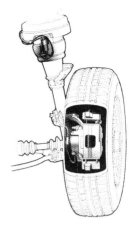

Continental's computer-
managed suspension
system can change from
a soft to firm damping
rate in milliseconds
based on inputs from
sensors in the brakes,
suspension and engine.

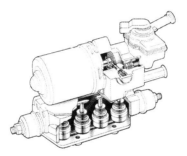

Hydraulic controls within
Continental's anti-lock brake
system precisely regulate
fluid pressure levels at
each brake based on input
from electronic sensors.
This computer-managed system can apply brakes
up to ten times per second.

**Figure 13.3.** Lincoln Continental advertising, stressing the idea of "contemporary luxury" and translating the product concept into a final design. (Reprinted by permission of Ford Motor Co.)

in the imperfect integration of marketing, design, engineering, and manufacturing. Ford had moved significantly toward cross-functional integration through better teamwork and coordination, but not far enough, because the success of integration depends on the extent to which it penetrates to the detailed working level.

The design and development of the Continental's body panels and the dies used for their manufacture provide a good example of the insufficient level of integration achieved on the project. The principal coordinating mechanism for the people charged with this work was the "structures meeting." Body-panel engineers and stamping engineers met to review progress in panel construction and the creation of stamping dies. What is now apparent, however, is that the individuals actually doing the design of body panels and the individuals designing the tools never interacted. True integrated engineering would have required face-to-face contact, a greater depth of understanding of each others' tasks and responsibilities, stronger attitudes of collaboration and cooperation, and strengthened bonds of trust between body designers, body panel engineers, and the designers and developers of tools and dies, but this was not achieved. The structures meeting may have been a useful coordinating mechanism, but it was not an effective substitute for true integration at the working level.

A second cause for some of the difficulties in this program can be found in the creation and use of prototypes. Early mechanical prototypes were of suboptimal quality; they were not made using parts representative of actual manufacturing techniques, because this approach was deemed too expensive. (Such avoidance was common in the industry, and was not originally seen as a problem.) Therefore, the first representative models were delivered only 20 months before mass production was to begin. These prototypes uncovered some serious problems that the earlier ones had not revealed, but by this time it was very late in the program. Prototypes also were not used extensively to prove out the production process. They could have provided a good opportunity to test the integrated team approach on the entire production system.

## 1989 THUNDERBIRD/COUGAR

### Competitive Environment and Product Strategy

As it did for the 1988 Continental, the impetus to redesign the 1989 Thunderbird came in response to a change in direction in the marketplace, this time from Europe. The new Thunderbird was to be Ford's supercharged car—not a sports car but a small, sophisticated, high-performance road car, a growing niche strongly held by BMW.

The Thunderbird was built on an entirely new platform, which included a supercharged engine that was novel for Ford (see **Figure**

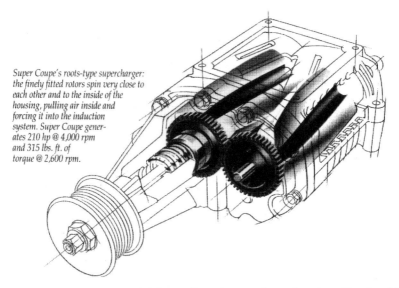

*Super Coupe's roots-type supercharger: the finely fitted rotors spin very close to each other and to the inside of the housing, pulling air inside and forcing it into the induction system. Super Coupe generates 210 hp @ 4,000 rpm and 315 lbs. ft. of torque @ 2,600 rpm.*

**Figure 13.4.** The Thunderbird Super Coupe's supercharged engine. (Reprinted by permission of Ford Motor Co.)

**13.4**). The program met its target date and its functional objectives, and the car was critically acclaimed in the press. However, the program failed to meet important internal targets, including weight, cost, and investment. As a result, the program has been perceived internally as problematic. Moreover, the excessive weight and cost have hurt the car's market penetration.

## Project Execution

The Thunderbird program was one of the first to make extensive use of teams. Within the engineering organization teams were formed to develop both components and subsystems. Higher level teams were also formed to coordinate the vehicle at the systems level and to provide strategic direction.

From the beginning, work on the supercharged engine was placed under a single project manager. The engine design was a radical departure, coming directly from an advanced technology group, and so Ford decided it would need a strong leader to see that it was successfully commercialized. Detailed work for the rest of the program, however, was split among traditional functional groups—the old management model at Ford. About halfway through the program, as the C-to-C process was finalized, formal program management was introduced. A program manager was selected and put in charge of the entire Thunderbird project.

Unfortunately, this good intention came too late. Before the program manager was chosen, there was no leadership at the system level. Once the program manager was instated, he was not able to articulate sufficiently or communicate deeply enough the product concept and the strategic direction of the program. He lacked full power because he was put in charge after the work had progressed significantly and was not fully behind the program's vision since he had no hand in creating it. As a result, local teams tended to focus on local objectives without strong overall guidance. The effort lacked the high level of integration and strong champion that characterize outstanding development projects. At a fundamental level, the traditional functional organization asserted itself throughout the program. The absence of strong conceptual leadership was compounded by a lack of continuity: the supercharged-engine program had four different managers during its lifetime and the managers from product planning who initially championed the new car did not remain involved in the program's later stages.

A basic premise repeated frequently in this book is that companies that use integrated teams are better able to develop integrated products than companies organized along functional lines. Good evidence for this was seen in the Thunderbird project, which was initially organized by function. The thrust of functional specialization is to obtain depth of expertise and competence in specific aspects of the product. This created two kinds of problems at Ford. First, the highly specialized organization meant that a large number of people were required for the program. This made communication and integration difficult. Second, because it was so large, a significant amount of turnover and instability occurred within the specialized structure; Ford employs thousands of engineers who work on limited parts of cars, say door locks, or steering columns. To gain experience, many of these engineers stay in a job for only a year or so and then move to another part of the car. As a result, at any given time many of the specialized jobs may be filled by people without depth of expertise. The seriousness of the problem this creates is difficult to judge, but there were several indications in the Thunderbird program of gaps in experience. One example is afforded by the engine, which had to be redesigned late in the cycle. It appeared that many of the problems that caused the redesign of the engine were understood by people in the advanced technical group, but that knowledge was not shared by the development team. Strong links between the advanced research and engineering groups and the development team—separate functions—were not established.

## Project Outcome and Lessons Learned

The Thunderbird effort can be viewed as a transition project. It did not follow Ford's traditional norms and procedures. It was one of the first projects that attempted fundamental change at the roots of the development team—the working-level engineers. On the other hand, the new C-to-C process had not yet taken hold. New working-level practices had not yet been established. Engineers had not yet learned how to execute cross-functional integration effectively and efficiently. While the car suffered because of the transition, the program was a valuable learning experience for Ford. It was clear that all the necessary skills and capabilities for integrated teamwork were indeed present. The problem was in finding ways to bring these skills to bear in the right place and at the right time. The crucial issues were clear direction, commitment, and effective allocation of human resources.

Some part of the failure to meet cost and weight objectives was also rooted in problems with the program's guiding vision. In the midst of the program, engineers working on the car seemed to develop an approach that might be described as "world-class vehicle with best-in-class parts." Indeed the target vehicle appears to have been one that would match the BMW 5 series. But the strategy called for a vehicle that was priced for a domestic specialty segment. In short, Ford was trying to make a BMW that could sell for $15,000. The goals of exceptional quality and low price were too far apart. This inherent problem only got worse as people attempted to translate the strategy down into working-level details. Designers tried to match the quality of BMW-class parts and overran cost goals. Or they tried to meet cost goals, and quality expectations were not met.

The inability to meet internal targets is an important feature of this program. At the most basic level it resulted in part from lack of commitment to the project goals. The early planning documents in 1984 projected the cost, investment, and weight for the vehicle. However, there was widespread disbelief of these numbers; engineers who saw the technical goals said there was no way they could be met for the intended low price and therefore never got behind the project. This also surfaced in the form of reluctance to make difficult choices to redefine the design as the project progressed so it could meet cost, weight, and investment objectives. It is worth noting, however, that redesign efforts subsequent to product launch identified some significant cost and weight savings. These problems underscore the lack of a clear process—well understood and accepted by people in the organization—at the concept development stage.

It is interesting that the Continental, which preceded the Thunderbird, appears to have had a more integrated outcome. The teamwork was better on the earlier program. What happened? Did Ford go backward?

A reasonable conclusion is that the Continental project benefited from better institutional memory and more holdover personnel from the Taurus program, which pioneered the team concept at Ford. Personnel on the Thunderbird project had far less experience with the team concept and workings. And the Continental project was completed under Ford's old system which, regardless of its faults, was well understood.

The lesson to be learned is that the first use of empowered teams may be such a learning experience that it takes a second project to fully realize its benefits. This lesson comes home in the next case study, on the 1991 Crown Victoria. The project team for this car was derived from a team originally formed for the new 1990 Town Car. The Town Car effort, not studied by the Vision Group, had some of the team and integration problems of the Thunderbird program. But the second time around, with the Crown Victoria, both the program manager (the same one who led the Town Car work) and the team were able to get beyond the basic problems of how to put the team concept into play, and they began to use its attributes to their advantage.

## 1991.5 CROWN VICTORIA/GRAND MARQUIS

### Competitive Environment and Product Strategy

The market strategy that prompted this development program was interesting and unusual. Ford had no obvious reason to change its Crown Victoria; the car sold extremely well. Detailed research in the mid-1980s had shown the average age of people who bought the car was high (early 60s) and increasing. The design of certain aspects of the car had been changed incrementally to reflect this: gauges were made bigger and auditory signals such as the click on blinker lights were made louder.

Further study, however, showed that this market, though important, was shrinking. It also illustrated a growing gap in Ford's product line; as the Crown Victoria was engineered for an aging buyer, nothing was left that specifically addressed middle-aged consumers. Ford had plenty of cars for young families, in particular the Taurus, but it needed a model to serve as a middle step before buyers were ready for the grand sedan of their golden years. Thus Ford decided to split the product line. It would develop two cars that would be built from the same platform—a Crown Victoria dedicated to older customers and a Grand Marquis for those who still had children to cart around.

### Project Execution

The development of a stable and accepted concept for the new product line was a long and difficult process. The platform was born as a compromise between an updated version of the old Crown Victoria platform and a scaling up of the Taurus platform. These two concepts were quite different. The Crown Victoria had traditional styling and a plush ride, and was a rear-wheel-drive vehicle. The Taurus was a progressive, tight-handling automobile with front-wheel drive. As such, there were several independent visions for the new concept: the styling vision, the program management vision, the senior management vision, the North American Automotive Operations marketing staff vision (the Crown Victoria crowd), and the Ford/Mercury marketing vision (the Taurus crowd).

As a result, the new concept went through a number of revisions as the conceptual models created by the various groups converged over time. Though some concept uncertainties lingered long into the development process, consensus was attained through frequent meetings at the insistence of the program manager who, for the first time at Ford, was operating in a true heavyweight mode.

The new program was characterized by several significant innovations in the development process, which resulted in earlier identification of design and feasibility problems. For example, Ford instituted a Mazda procedure of key design checkpoints, which prompted review of the compatibility and feasibility of parts while designs were still on paper. Computer-aided engineering was used extensively to model system characteristics; this uncovered problems related to crash-worthiness and interior noise and vibration early in the development cycle. Cost management practices were improved. Quality Function Deployment analysis was introduced to a limited extent. A new change-control process was instituted that reduced the number of design changes and sped up the implementation of those that were necessary through better coordination of disparate groups. Finally, the quality of evaluation prototypes was outstanding, and a few prototype vehicles were built on the actual production line in the St. Thomas, Ontario, assembly plant.

### Project Outcome and Lessons Learned

The Crown Victoria/Grand Marquis program was one of the more successful and well-executed efforts at Ford. In the beginning there was slow marketplace acceptance; however, that grew to a resounding success (e.g., it is the car of choice for police officers across the country). The program made strong progress in the development of team management capabilities within Ford's engineering groups, as well as progress in creating representative prototypes and early process prove-out. It also reflected thorough and accurate cost-modeling practices, which were implemented jointly by the engineers and the finance representatives throughout the development program. The program represented a large number of significant improvements over previous programs in both efficiency and effectiveness.

The program was also one of the first to engage a majority of engineers with extensive program management experience. In contrast with the Thunderbird project, most of the Crown Victoria/Grand Marquis engineers had already worked together on integrated teams. Team members had become experienced in eliminating coordination and communication problems. Moreover, the core members of the program team (the program manager, vehicle and development engineers, and finance representatives) were co-located for tighter interaction. Ford was continuing to build momentum in developing the engineering and managerial capabilities necessary for effective integrated program management.

Additional progress is still possible. While improved over previous programs, the representation of manufacturing engineers in the Crown Victoria/Grand Marquis program was very limited until about 20 months before mass production began. Feasibility engineers were remote from the plant, and their input was often called into question. Though the planning and engineering managers stayed on through the entire project, there were three different program managers.

## FX15 AIR-CONDITIONING COMPRESSOR

### Competitive Environment and Product Strategy

The FX15 project was born out of an odd competitive situation. Previously, Ford had licensed compressor technology and contracted with one of its manufacturing plants for the system's manufacture. Its latest deal had been a license from Nippondenso. But shortly after Ford paid its license fee, Nippondenso unveiled a new and improved air-conditioning compressor.

Ford was outraged. Senior management decided it would develop its own compressor, in part to get control over the hardware and in part to show up Nippondenso by developing an even better product. It gave the project to the Climate Control Division (CCD), which, angered by Nippondenso's deceit, pursued it with great enthusiasm and strong management support.

## Project Execution

The project's objectives were very aggressive, both in product specifications and demands on the design process. The product was engineered by a co-located group of design and manufacturing engineers. The team consisted of 17 people, and was led at the technical level by an engineer who had a lot of design expertise in compressors. He was a dominant source of creativity in the project. There was a project manager, too, who had worked as a design engineer and then as a production manager on the FS6, the last compressor made by CCD. The rest of the team included designers, engineers, machining specialists, a quality-control person, assembly people, a plant engineer, and a material-handling specialist. It was well rounded and represented extensive manufacturing and design experience. This led to a design that incorporated aggressive performance and packaging goals as well as significant advances in manufacturability (see **Figure 13.5**).

The level of internal coordination and teamwork was outstanding. The aggressive targets were made feasible by good cross-functional integration during the design work. Before establishing a production process for the FX15, the process used to manufacture the FS6 was fully analyzed and potential cost savings were identified. Competitive products and alternate processes were benchmarked. Vendors were carefully selected for their capabilities and cost. Several design improvements reflected close attention to manufacturability issues. For example, the new design had self-aligning cylinders: the product was loosely assembled, then tightened as the cylinders were moved up and down, to provide the best alignment.

## Project Outcome and Lessons Learned

The FX15 project was revolutionary for CCD. Since it was the first internal development of a compressor, the project was also an experi-

**Figure 13.5.** Cutaway of Ford's FX15 compressor with center shaft exposed. (Reprinted by permission of Ford Motor Co.)

ment. It achieved commendable goals of cost, size, and performance. The project demonstrated a number of the advantages of the joint design/manufacturing team. The product was indeed easier to manufacture than the FS6, and was considerably cheaper.

However, the project also had a few problems. The design stage went very fast, especially considering its ambitious goals. The various technical dimensions of the project were also accelerated. In retrospect, the program may have been a bit too aggressive, because the product was launched with poor noise and vibration characteristics, and testing failed to find a crucial weakness that caused very high warranty expenditures. Given the extensive pressure and the novelty of the project, it is perhaps not surprising that a few things simply fell through the cracks.

Overall, the FX15 project was a tremendous learning experience for Ford. It marshaled the efforts of design and manufacturing in a truly integrated manner. The FX15 team went to the Connorsville manufacturing plant two times a month to meet with individual component teams and swap ideas. While the project's objectives were perhaps too ambitious, many of the lessons learned will undoubtedly be used in the future. For one thing, the concept behind the FX15 was clear and stable from the very early stages of the development process. Thus the program had a very clear direction. On the other hand, the compressor could have been better were it not for a lack of input and buy-in from its customer, Ford's Car Product Development division, which makes Ford's cars. The division was potentially a very useful source of feedback, but was greatly underutilized.

The commitment of the Connorsville plant was also very impressive. While running beyond full-rated capacity, at three shifts per day, seven days a week, plant management pulled out some of its best people so they could participate in the development of the FX15. The plant makes only compressors, and its management and staff believed that if it did not succeed on the FX15 the plant might have to shut down because Ford would throw up its hands and simply begin to buy compressors from vendors. Keeping the plant open was considered especially critical because the unemployment rate in the area had reached 13 percent. Plant managers put together teams made up of both salaried and hourly personnel to oversee the manufacture of every component, and to generate new ideas on the production of the entire unit.

## CHAPTER 14

# Hewlett-Packard Company

The study of product development at Hewlett-Packard is extremely compelling, because in the last five years the huge corporation has made a radical shift in the way it pursues development projects. For decades the company was organized into highly structured and completely autonomous divisions. Project development was always contained within a division. The methods by which one division pursued projects, however, were often completely different from those used by another, although one relationship was always common to them: design engineers ran the show, and marketing, manufacturing, and other groups in each divisions were left to adapt to whatever the engineers settled on.

Since 1985, however, HP has begun a number of projects that for the first time have attempted to integrate these groups, with both tumultuous failures and grand successes. The four projects at HP studied by the Manufacturing Vision Group were chosen to show both how development projects were pursued differently between divisions in the "old HP" and how the general tenets of those projects have changed markedly in the "new HP" that is trying to integrate functions. The comparisons are quite dramatic.

## HP's Competitive Position, Culture, and Modus Operandi

Hewlett-Packard is an international manufacturer of instrumentation and computer products. The company's 12,000 products and services are used in industry, business, engineering, science, medicine, and education in approximately 100 countries. HP employed about 98,000 people and earned revenues of $13.2 billion in its 1990 fiscal year.

HP was founded in 1939 by Bill Hewlett and Dave Packard. It began as a provider of electronic instrumentation and diversified over the years into computers and computer peripherals. The wide diversity—from gas chromatographs to disk drives and minicomputers—places the company in a unique position: Its instrumentation designs leverage its computer expertise, and collectively all product lines can take advantage of common manufacturing and distribution processes. The tie that binds these diverse products is the manipulation of information: acquiring it, displaying it, analyzing it, communicating it, storing it, and making it manageable.

An important aspect of the company's culture is derived from the organizational form that was put in place by Hewlett and Packard as the company grew. They chose a model in which individual divisions were created to serve specific product lines. Each division stood on its own as an autonomous entity and contained its own marketing, manufacturing, R&D (engineering), finance, and personnel functions. Only the sales organization was more centralized for management and administrative purposes.

The division general managers, with perhaps 1000 to 2000 employees each, operated on a simple incentive system: they were expected to make a profit on their product lines. Included in this was the expectation by a division that if it was to develop a component for another division, it would "sell" it to them at a profit.

This system was steadfastly maintained, even when it resulted in several divisions inventing similar or competing products and despite the fact that some manufacturing processes, such as printed circuit-board assembly, were replicated and maintained throughout the organization as many as 45 times. While this was wasteful, the company was willing to suffer the waste because the set-up allowed R&D people to stay close to production processes, which they felt was critical. Projects were managed loosely, and relied for cohesion on the excitement of members of a project team, who were made to feel they were doing something new, either for the world or at least within HP, and were making a key contribution to the company.

A company-wide profit sharing program available to all employees tended to foster a sense of belonging to the larger organization and counteracted divisionalism. It continues today. There are other present-day aspects of the "HP Way" that Hewlett and Packard put into place. The atmosphere is a collegial one; although individual (rather than team, in many cases) performance is highly regarded, individuals are not set up to compete with one another. Respect for the individual is a fundamental value. Engineering prowess is typically the source of the respect. HP is well known as a company for which good engineers aspire to work. Entering engineers know that they can expect a fair amount of freedom to perform their work, and that they will be rewarded with ever more interesting projects if they perform creatively and well. Individual engineers within HP do not generally feel that their jobs are at risk if they fail. Those who succeed, however, are clearly provided with more advancement opportunities. Thus, there is strong incentive to succeed.

The divisional structure remained intact through 1985. Since then, significant shifts have occurred in the company's direction, organization, and culture. Due to a much greater growth rate in computers, information products overtook instruments as the company's primary product type. In addition, because the computer market has become fiercely competitive in recent years, much of the company's business—particularly in the peripherals arena—is now based on low-cost, high-volume consumer products. This strategy is a radical departure from the high-margin, highly technical product mix that dominated for decades. Exacerbating everything is the fact that HP has simply become a very large company.

HP has undergone some substantial organizational transformations in the past five years. The organization established in 1990 attempts to preserve some of the good aspects of the traditional structure while allowing the company to be more nimble in responding to market

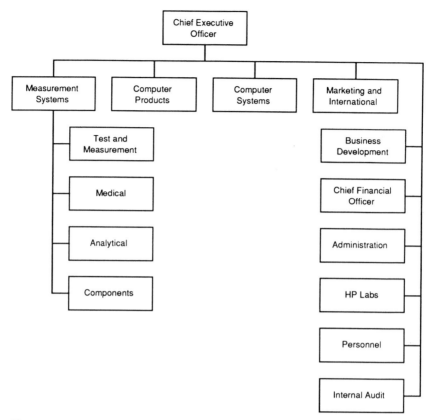

**Figure 14.1.** Organization of Hewlett-Packard (1990) into three major business sectors.

pressures (see **Figure 14.1**). The company now comprises three sectors: one focuses on the traditional instrumentation business (Test and Measurement Systems), one on the high volume, low-cost, dealer-distributed peripherals and personal computer products (Computer Products), and one on direct-sales minicomputer and networking products (Computer Systems).

Because each sector needed to operate in a unique business environment, three substantially different organizational structures evolved. The instrumentation sector continues to use autonomous divisions. Computer Products combines a divisional structure with some cross-divisional product lines. Computer Systems is organized by function, with manufacturing, marketing, R&D, and sales reporting to the vice-president of the operation. New product development is clearly very different in each setting. The projects studied illustrate some of these differences.

## HP's Model for Product Development

R&D engineers traditionally have enjoyed the highest status at HP. Until as recently as 1984, R&D engineers were actually paid on higher pay curves than manufacturing engineers. While such differences are receding, there are still battles waged to break down functional barriers. It is only in the last year, for example, that the corporate-wide R&D Council and Manufacturing Council, each consisting of senior members of their respective functions, have begun to meet together to address common issues. The councils set broad policy and determine the strategy of how corporate-level resources will be spent.

An important aspect of R&D's superior position has been the approach that was used for product development. R&D engineers developed new product ideas by understanding the needs of fellow engineers who sat at the "next bench." In the early instrumentation days the approach worked well, because these engineers did accurately represent the end-users in other engineering companies, which was HP's initial market. As HP grew, the number of internal customers became large enough to represent a reasonable market, and so the next-bench syndrome continued. Once products were developed, however, they were "thrown over the wall" to manufacturing and marketing. Manufacturing was then stuck with performing heroic deeds in figuring out how to make the products, and marketing was stuck with finding ways to sell them to the outside world.

In recent years, particularly with the increased focus on computer products, the "next-bench" approach has worked less and less well. New product development teams have had to learn to actually study and analyze customer requirements from outside the company. Marketing has played an increasingly important role, and has had to develop a new set of skills for market research. Increased emphasis on product cost and quality has also drawn R&D and manufacturing closer together as serious attempts are made to "design for manufact-urability." This shifting balance of power in the organization is also seen in the series of cases in this chapter. In the Logic Analyzer case, for example, the old "next bench" approach is quite apparent. In the DeskJet case, the new evolving organization appears. Project teams are also now much more managed; the old, loose style that relied largely on enthusiasm has given way to more conscious pursuit of many of the themes discussed in this book, such as ownership and commitment, and cross-functional integration.

Despite some of the changes described in this chapter, HP remains largely a technology-driven company. Its success over the years has been based on its ability to develop new technologies and then bring them to market. New technologies are developed in numerous places around the company. HP Labs, a centralized research group in Palo Alto, California, has primary responsibility for "basic" research. It is funded with a fixed percentage of the company-wide R&D budget. The Circuit Technology Group spans the company, and has responsi-bility for conducting research into integrated circuits and printed cir-cuit boards. Divisions maintain responsibility for developing techno-logies specific to their product lines.

There is a longstanding tradition within HP, started by Hewlett and Packard, of performing annual product and technology reviews, and the existence of these influences the procedures by which project teams perform their work. Corporate executives used to get to each division once a year to review programs, see the up-and-coming new products, discourage overlap between divisions, and get a feel for which employees were destined for promotion. As the company has grown, the executives simply have not been able to get around as much, or go as deep, resulting in less contact between senior officers and junior people.

To maintain some consistency, and simplify the task of keeping senior management informed, HP has instituted a corporate-wide phase review structure. It consists of seven phases that in a general way guide the development, sale, and support of a product, from the initial idea to its retirement from the marketplace (see **Figure 14.2**). Before a team leaves one phase for the next, a review is conducted

| | Phase 0 | 1 | 2 | 3 | 4 | 5 | 6 |
|---|---|---|---|---|---|---|---|
| Phase Name | Requirements/plan | Study/define | Specify/design | Develop/test | User test/ramp up | Enhance/support | Maturity |
| Objective | Define market, customer needs, competitors | Define a product | Agree on detailed design and functional plans | Design, prototype, and test product | Test integrated system and support products | Ongoing product support | Revise or replace product |
| Deliverables | Analysis of customer needs and system requirements | System specifications, development schedule | Cross-functional plans for design, manufacturing, and marketing | [tk] | Functional sign-off, ship to market, field preparations | Verify return-on-investment | Plans for discontinuance and compatibility of third-party products |
| Management Commitments at Phase End | Business plan | Development funds | Funds for functional plans | Final price, performance parameters, availability | Customer shipments, enhancement, support | Customer support | System migration |

**Figure 14.2.** Phases of product initiation, development, sale, and retirement at Hewlett-Packard.

by management. The review serves as a formal ''go-ahead'' from senior management to move to the next step and also improves communication between divisions and between project teams and senior management, though some in the company feel it may also constrain or slow development in some cases. The seven phases will be referred to throughout the chapter, and are as follows.

The first phase, the *requirements/plan phase,* emphasizes clear definition of target markets, complete characterization of customer and user needs, and understanding of competitor activities. The output of this first phase is a clear specification of the product or system to be developed. The *study/define phase* creates more detail; specific functional specifications are spelled out and resources and schedules are established for the project. During the *specify/design phase,* all the functional plans are made firm, including those for quality assurance, manufacturing, product support, and marketing.

During the *develop/test phase,* physical products are developed. In addition to functioning, tested system components, the output of this phase includes updated quality, manufacturing, support, and marketing plans. The *user test/ramp-up phase* focuses on testing the fully integrated system and support products and demonstrating that the system can be supported in the field. The product is then introduced to the marketplace and shipments commence. During the *enhance/ support phase,* field and factory support requirements are met, and a return on investment is calculated for the product. Finally, in the *maturity phase,* the responsible organizations plan discontinuance and how to ensure customer satisfaction, the migration of customers, and the compatibility of third-party enhancement products such as software.

In general, Hewlett-Packard is conservative when it comes to taking risks. Business risk and technological risk are typically identified separately. The company is accustomed to investing in technology development and does so at HP Labs. The divisions, then, can minimize technological risk by using technologies from the Labs or other sources, and focus on applications. Business risk is minimized by developing products for known markets and committing to product introduction only late in the development process.

These days the timely completion and introduction of products has become much more important. Consequently development projects have changed. It used to be that a development team could change every aspect of a developing product at one time and take five years to get it to market. Today, in the face of aggressive competition, quick time to market has become essential, and development teams are trying to limit their focus to a few critical items per project.

## The HP Development Projects

As a group the four products studied span a period of 20 years. The first case—the Logic Analyzer—provides insight into how development projects were pursued in the "old HP." The second case is about the Hornet, a similar product (both are instruments) that was developed as HP began to make the transition to its "new" structure. The last two cases—the HP150 and the DeskJet—also make for good comparison; they were organized in a way that attempted to bridge old functional boundaries, and they were similar in nature (both were low-cost, high-volume computer products distributed through dealer channels), but the first fell short of its goals while the second took its market niche by storm. A brief summation of the cases follows.

*Logic Analyzer.* The Logic Analyzer was an instrument developed in the early 1970s in HP's traditional development setting.

*Hornet.* The Hornet is an instrument that was targeted to reduce encroachment by competitors at the low end of the spectrum analyzer market. Creating a low-cost instrument required breaking some well-entrenched product development concepts. The effort, undertaken in the "new HP," provides a good contrast to the Logic Analyzer.

*HP150.* The HP150 was the company's first formal attempt to enter the personal computer market. Unfortunately the strategy was not fully developed. This project makes clear the difficulties in integrating development across a diverse set of autonomous divisions.

*DeskJet.* The DeskJet is a very successful printer for computers. The development effort put forth to get it to market very quickly and at low cost is one HP is particularly proud of. It illustrates HP's recent attempts to integrate manufacturing, marketing, and R&D.

Each case description is divided into three sections. The first describes the competitive environment in which the project was undertaken and the strategic planning that led to its undertaking. The second describes the execution of the project itself. The third section describes how well the development team performed relative to project goals and the lessons that were learned about product development.


## LOGIC ANALYZER

### Competitive Environment and Product Strategy

This case is set much more in distant history than the others. It describes the transition of HP's oscilloscope (scope) business from a focus on analog applications, which had accounted for the entirety of the market for years, to digital applications, which were emerging as the electronics industry moved to digital design. It provides some meaningful insight into HP's history that is useful in understanding the company's current situation. More important, it provides a real-life example of a fundamental business principle: know your customer's real needs.

The case takes place in the early 1970s. At that time, HP had been in the scope business for nearly 20 years. It held from 10 to 20 percent of the market, but the business was not very profitable. Tektronix, of Beaverton, Oregon, was the primary competitor, holding most of the market share and making significant profit.

Tektronix and HP were both early entrants into the instrumentation field. Tektronix specialized in oscilloscopes and HP in all other types of electronic test equipment. Both produced high-quality products and each enjoyed a substantial part of the market they served and the attendant high profitability. The companies were roughly the same size at the time. In order to have a more complete line, HP got into the scope business in the late 1950s. The Colorado Springs Division was formed to develop and manufacture oscilloscopes as its main product line. Corporate management at HP glibly felt that they would soon dominate the scope business. But Tektronix proved a worthy competitor. The attempt by HP to "out-invent" Tektronix was ineffective. Although HP engineers had many excellent, creative ideas, they never resulted in products that took much market share. Tektronix spent several times as much money as HP on R&D and thus was able to both create its own good ideas and copy HP's new product successes. Trying to outdo Tektronix put enormous pressure on the Colorado Springs Division's profit margin.

In the mid-1960s mainframe and minicomputer manufacturers were using more and more scopes in their work. Computers began to employ digital technology but the scopes that both HP and Tektronix provided were designed to measure analog characteristics. Old habits die hard, though, and the new digital engineers continued to use equipment designed for analog applications.

Customers didn't exactly suffer in silence, though. They did keep asking for better performance. However, it is significant that they continued to define their needs in terms of analog scope specifications. In turn, HP and Tektronix sales and marketing people continued to inquire about new product specifications in terms of the existing analog product line. Not surprisingly, customers answered by talking in terms of a next-generation analog scope. It wasn't until HP's R&D engineers happened to ask what problems customers were trying to solve that a new vision emerged as to what computer test equipment should be.

This vision led HP's R&D people to start experimenting with prototypes that were more in tune with the digital applications. A small team set out to learn the technology. Although they made progress, they were not able to simulate a computer environment due to a lack of appropriate test tools. Their managers were slow to appreciate the contribution their "new thinking" could make to the industry and unwilling to devote adequate resources to the new "dream." They were reluctant in part because they couldn't comprehend the full power of the new approach. In their mind, the traditional scope must still have been doing the job—after all IBM bought thousands of them a year.

The corporate research funds available to the division were based on profitability, and since the difficult battle with Tektronix sapped much of the division's profits, R&D funds were at a premium. Division management was reluctant to divert any of these scarce research funds from traditional scope programs. Competing with Tektronix was imposing enough without splintering off money for a risky project. In 1970 the effort was cut back, and the team leader was stripped of his rank and most of his people. He left to pursue other interests, while a few of his compatriots continued on in a mini-skunkworks fashion.

Gradually over a two-year period, division management came to see the opportunity presented by the digital logic analyzer (see **Figure 14.3**). They began to see the opportunity to beat Tektronix to the punch in a new marketplace (luckily for HP no one at Tektronix had yet seen the potential for the technology either), and the profit potential that usually accompanies a successful technical innovation, which would provide much needed relief for the beleaguered division.

In 1972 division management decided to pursue the digital analyzer again, but in a formal way. It brought back the team leader and offered him an adequate staff. Management pulled out all the stops. Their greatest fear was that Tektronix would come to the same realization and once again swamp them with substantial product development resources. (As it turned out, that did not happen and HP got a four- or five-year head start.)

In September the team announced a test product with several attributes that matched well the needs of the digital electronics industry. The project team was galvanized, and committed to ship a product in one year, which they did. Soon after, though, digital analyzer customers began to complain; the team had compromised their specifications because of the short cycle time. The marketplace evidently didn't treat this as a major failure, though, because the product kept selling. Customers seemed willing to view the instrument as a powerful dream that was not yet complete.

Eighteen months later a next-generation product was introduced. Tektronix missed its mark when it introduced a product that had only two of the four key functions offered by HP. Seeing the success,

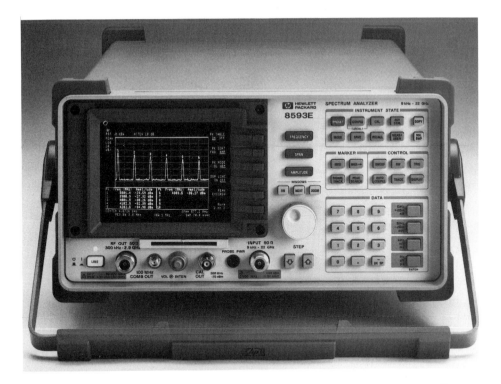

**Figure 14.3.** Illustration of HP Logic Analyzer, a plug-in model to the top oscilloscope. (Reprinted by permission of Hewlett-Packard Co.)

CEO Young offered the division the opportunity to broadly expand its efforts into digital instrumentation, which it did. The focus became a full-fledged digital analyzer product line.

## Project Execution

This project was initially pursued in a skunkworks environment. Marketing and manufacturing were not part of the team. The entire effort was driven by engineering, as were most HP development efforts at the time.

The technology needed for a new breed of digital test equipment was not particularly difficult. Digital components were available from the computer industry and Colorado Springs engineers were familiar with how to make digital circuitry work. By far the greatest difficulty came in trying to determine exactly what features these new oscilloscopes should have. The HP sales force, which usually could be called on to interpret customer's needs, was of no help because they could not break free from thinking about analog scopes. The customers themselves proved to be of little help because of the mental baggage they carried regarding traditional scopes. Thus the product definition was unclear.

Ultimately, years later, both the customers and the field engineers became more adept at describing customer measurement problems. But in the early days the division relied on their own imagination and the then-famous "Japanese digital watch approach," which in essence was "Let's invent something we think will work, put it on the market, and see if it sells."

The sales people (who, recall, worked from a central location) had been quite competent at selling traditional products. But they were not up to speed on the new technology. This hurt because they were not emotionally behind the sale of the new analyzer since they didn't understand it. Had they been on the team from the start they would have. This disinterest was aggravated by the feeling that once the product was produced, it was "thrown over the wall," meaning engineering knocked it out and left sales standing there figuring out how to sell it.

They did not, however, do a very good job of opening their minds to this new technology either. Thus, the division was faced with essentially propping up the sales force with extensive support and training. The additional resources needed for this were above and beyond the normal costs of development, and put added strain on the financial expectations of the fledgling product line.


## Project Outcome and Lessons Learned

Because it was basically sound, the product line continued to sell, even with its initial shortcomings. By 1980 there were more than 600 people working on it in Colorado Springs, and it accounted for 40 percent of the division's sales and 67 percent of its profit.

Marketing and sales were gradually converted and began to contribute substantially to the understanding of customer needs and formulating of new product suggestions. The customers, too, became more familiar with the power of the product line and many soon became repeat customers. The profitability of this new product line turned out to be substantial and was able to relieve a lot of the profit pressure felt at Colorado Springs.

In retrospect, HP has learned a number of lessons, particularly in comparing this early development effort with later ones. There were indeed clear design concepts, and clear objectives for market penetration, profitability, and time to market, all of which gave the effort form and direction. Although the difficulties were great, they were addressed head on by a small band who had been early believers. It didn't take long before the new technique was recognized as a true breakthrough in instrumentation thinking. By the middle and late 1970s the product line was staffed with extremely capable people who approached their job with an enthusiasm and dedication approaching religious zeal.

But HP learned that when structuring a new product line or a new business strategy it is best to force yourself to answer the question "How can I best help my customers be successful?" Don't ask yourself how you can sell more existing product or how you can modify the existing product to meet customer needs. Go directly to the basic reason for the product—the problem the customer is trying to solve. At first HP and Tektronix tried to soup up an analog scope to handle digital work. The breakthrough only occurred, though, when HP engineers asked how the scope was to be used and then proceeded from scratch to design a product specifically for that application.

The lesson is not to let your customer define directly the next generation of your product; they will undoubtedly do it in terms of your existing product line. Your customer's problems are uniquely his or her problems and that's all he or she should be expected to describe to you. It is your job to imaginatively determine how to solve those problems. Of course it's necessary once you've arrived at a feature set to test these on the customer, but that is a follow-on step.

# HORNET

## Competitive Environment and Product Strategy

The Signal Analysis Division (SAD), located in Rohnert Park, California, produces spectrum-analysis devices used in testing and analyzing radio-frequency and microwave signals. Hewlett-Packard was a pioneer in this product line, and still supports products sold over 20 years ago. For many years, the company held 80 to 90 percent of the market share. It still dominates with a 50 percent share worldwide.

In the mid-1980s Japanese competitors such as Anritsu and Advantest began to capture market share in the low end of the market. They competed not on features but on price, often by imitating existing products. They also introduced many of their products in Europe where HP had less penetration. It was in response to this threat that the Hornet product was conceived in February 1985 and introduced in September 1986, a record development time of 18 months.

Product quality and performance are the traditional bases on which the Signal Analysis Division (SAD) had competed. Known in the marketplace as technological leaders, HP could always be counted on to generate state-of-the-art products. Tektronix and a number of smaller niche competitors played a similar game aimed largely at U.S. military communication and aerospace applications.

The price-inelastic military market had begun shrinking, and the commercial market had begun expanding, primarily at the lower end. Makers of telecommunications products, ranging from microwave transmitters to satellite communications and cable TV equipment, were using more and more spectrum analyzers in design, production, and maintenance applications. Although there was increasing awareness in the division by the mid-1980s that the marketplace was changing, and that the Japanese threat was becoming more intense, R&D engineers were reluctant to remove or limit product features just to lower cost.

A low-cost spectrum analyzer did exist in the R&D lab, but it had made little progress toward the marketplace. The turning point in the division's thinking occurred when a new division general manager was named. He was very concerned about encroachment by the competition and formed a task force to consider the feasibility of developing a low-cost product. His concern was heightened when the R&D section manager returned from a visit to a customer in Italy. The customer had given him a tour of the local plant, and showed him a "high-priced" HP spectrum analyzer next to a "low-priced" Japanese product.

The two managers chose as the project manager a prominent R&D engineer who had been the lead engineer on the two most successful products in the division. He was "between projects" at the time, and himself had begun to think about lower cost products. Marketing also predicted that a lower cost product was needed, that there would be a significant dip in division revenues without one, and that the Japanese competitors, if allowed to dominate the low end, would continue to move up the product line toward the higher end products where HP still reigned supreme.

## Project Execution

A product development team was put together from within the division. The team's priorities were very clear and were set in this order of importance: low cost, short development schedule, high quality, and then performance. This was the exact reverse of the usual order in HP. To set the cost objective, the division general manager decided that the market required a product that sold for less than $10,000. Later this was revised down to between $7000 and $8000.

Setting the introduction date at only 18 months away required that they design and manufacture the product correctly the first time. The schedule was remarkable considering it was half that of the usual HP project. But the group thought they had a 75 percent probability of making it.

There were no critical technology hurdles the project team would have to overcome, although they wanted to change the way in which the display technology was designed in order to reduce cost. Systems technologies would be the key to low cost more so than components. The team thought of its challenge as "leveraging" existing technology to quickly put together a low-cost instrument. The project manager's experience with an earlier product from which Hornet was derived was invaluable in smoothing this integration. In addition to the primary objectives, the team also wanted to have three months of inventory on hand at introduction, and wanted to remove all need for product tuning and adjustment during production.

The team, and the division, treated Hornet as an experimental effort, or a "skunkworks." The general feeling was that if Hornet failed, the division could simply go on making higher cost, higher performance analyzers. Strong support was shown by senior management; to evidence it, the division general manager actually moved his desk into the Hornet development area. He felt that by doing so he could shorten the introduction cycle time by being readily available to help resolve problems as they arose.

The operation of this project showed improvement over those in the past, but it was still uneven. For years at the signal analysis division, R&D was considered the function at the top of the heap. Although this project showed more interaction between marketing and R&D than had past projects, the relationship between R&D and manufacturing was not well developed.

Marketing was more of a full partner than it had been allowed to be on past projects, though, partly because they helped extensively with early identification of the need for the product. They were no longer in a position, in this case, of just trying to sell whatever R&D delivered. While they did not use formal or particularly sophisticated techniques for market assessment, both marketing and engineering personnel made customer visits together. Also, for the first time in the division's history, marketing did an initial price study. R&D, however, maintained responsibility for product definition and did not involve the marketing organization directly in this process. There seemed to be ongoing problems with R&D's view of marketing's status and credibility. The R&D engineers were convinced that they knew the market requirements and were the ones who decided that if they missed a feature or two it would not be too costly in the long run. Rapid introduction of a follow-on product would catch "mistakes" made on Hornet, they reasoned. This was the best strategy, they decided, because they did not want any delay that would result in more lost market share.

At the time, the manufacturing organization at SAD was still treated as a service group that was required to deliver products, and not provide a competitive advantage. The status of the group is now increasing as more emphasis is placed on development of new, low-cost manufacturing processes, but involvement in the Hornet project was minimal. Purchasing was not involved in the design process at all.

The manufacturing engineers that were assigned to the Hornet project were only part time, and were not added to the team until after the develop/test phase was begun. As such, the lead manufacturing engineer also had responsibility for $800,000 in shipments of another product. As a result, almost no design for manufacturability was done and the transfer to production and the production ramp was complicated, inefficient, and stressful to people in the plant.

The project team decided to reduce the number of prototype cycles on this project, because a typical cycle at HP lasted six months. Even though management scheduled two prototype cycles, the team planned for only one. Manufacturing, rather than R&D, did the prototype build. With six units built and two days of testing, the team decided to go with only one prototype cycle, greatly reducing development time.

## Project Outcome and Lessons Learned

The Hornet exceeded sales expectations, and was considered by SAD to be a very successful product (see **Figure 14.4**). That in part was because, despite its attitude, R&D did listen to feedback it got from marketing about what customers wanted and how competitors were positioning products. The Hornet met the stringent cost goals that were set for it, and was priced under $10,000 as marketing suggested. Further, the product was completed on schedule in September 1986, a record 18-month development time, largely because R&D used mostly off-the-shelf parts and manufacturing ran an effective prototyping program.

The Hornet design was robust enough that it could be used as a platform for the development of follow-on products, although it took another 27 months before the first new model was introduced. Lack

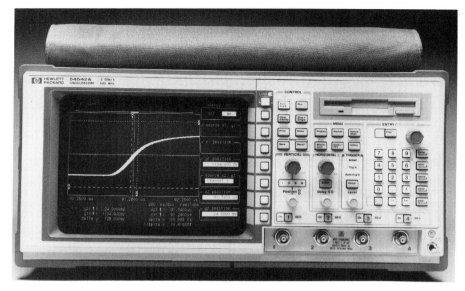

**Figure 14.4.** The Hornet. (Reprinted by permission of Hewlett-Packard Co.)

of resources and a long concept phase, during which an attempt was made to gather feedback from the market on Hornet and to investigate new technologies, lengthened this time.

The greatest "failure" of the project in most people's minds was the lack of early involvement of manufacturing. Late involvement caused a long and painful manufacturing ramp. From this experience, the division developed a stronger sense of the requirements of managing a product on a tight time schedule. They have set up various ways to transfer what they learned to current and future projects, including a training course for new project managers. With these mechanisms in place, they continue to improve the integration of R&D and manufacturing on each development project.

R&D learned a management lessons of its own—not to veer from the course once you're certain what that is. Design changes were minimized during development; there was only one major change, and that was passed through quickly and deliberately.

To strengthen the team's commitment, the general manager of the division made a nice move, literally, when he positioned his desk in with the team. This also heightened the profile the project had in the rest of the division. While forceful in the beginning, he later tried to stay out of the way; he wanted the team to believe they could replicate the effort without significant input from the top.

The division has learned these and other lessons extremely well. Prior to Hornet, it was not unheard of for a development project to take five or even eight years. Now the division completes new development projects routinely in 20 months.

## HP150

### Competitive Environment and Product Strategy

In the early 1980s the personal computer industry was still very much in its infancy. Apple Computer and a few others were selling products, but IBM had not yet entered the game. There were no industry standards, and the market's size and technical requirements were not well understood. Hewlett-Packard had experience in related markets ranging from minicomputers and terminals to calculators and peripherals. It was from this base that HP decided to enter the PC business.

As previously noted, Hewlett-Packard's historical structure was best characterized as a collection of autonomous divisions focused on product lines. This was to become a particular problem for the HP150.

During this period HP was figuring out how to address the growing computation marketplace. It decided to attack on four fronts, using four divisions: hand-held calculators from Corvallis, Oregon; desktop calculators and computers (which later became workstations) from Fort Collins, Colorado; personal computers from Sunnyvale, California; and minicomputers from Cupertino, California. Because divisions were largely autonomous, however, overlapping projects arose, and HP decided it had to sort out the work. The sorting was still going on as the HP150 began to be developed. This created a background of uncertainty as to the product's charter, though it didn't directly impact anyone on the HP150 team.

The company was already developing the HP120, a terminal for the HP3000 minicomputer. The charter for the HP150 defined the product as a follow-on to the HP120. But given the need to address the emerging PC market, corporate executives and division leaders decided to try to squeeze into the HP150 terminal enough computing power so it could also perform as a PC and capable of running the MS-DOS operating system being developed at IBM. To compete as a PC, the HP150 would also have to have a small footprint, and use technologies residing in other HP divisions (see **Figure 14.5**). HP didn't know whether this would be something customers would want, but it had to do something, fast.

The real challenges in developing the HP150 were as much managerial as technical. The basic technology strategy was to think of the HP150 as a system, to access technologies developed elsewhere in HP, and to integrate them to create the final product. While this sounded intellectually compelling, HP had virtually no mechanisms in place at the time to do cross-divisional product development.

Furthermore, the HP150 represented HP's first entry into the consumer marketplace, its first use of dealers as a distribution channel, its first attempt at building to inventory in a centralized warehousing structure, its first strong need to work closely with corporate procurement to ensure quality from suppliers, and its first introduction of design for manufacturability on a product that would be assembled worldwide. In retrospect, this represented an overwhelming set of largely new managerial complications.

### Project Execution

Given the complexities the project began with, strong leadership and commitment were clearly required. Unfortunately, although there was strong commitment on the part of the HP150 project team itself, leadership from senior management was inconsistent or came in bursts.

Throughout HP, R&D engineers felt very secure in their jobs. In this division, the general sentiment was that minicomputers were on their way out and that the PC market was just opening. The major concern on the part of the R&D engineers seemed to be that the projects on which they were working would never come to fruition.

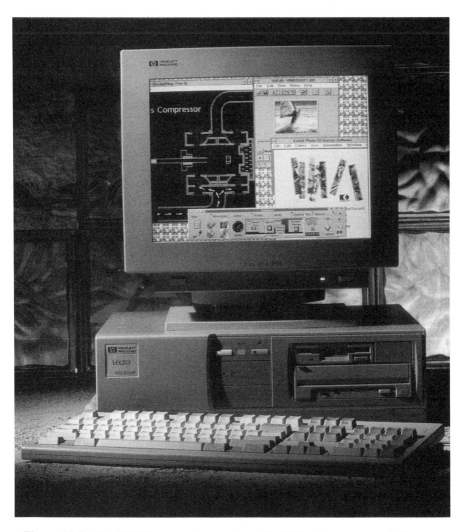

**Figure 14.5.** The HP150 personal computer, with HPTouch, supports a full range of peripherals, including the new HP 7475 plotter. (Reprinted by permission of Hewlett-Packard Co.)

For many of them this turned out to be true. Of 120 R&D engineers there at the time, only 20 were working on the HP150, and they were the only 20 that saw their project brought to market.

A greater problem was the lack of clear leadership, or of a consistent champion in upper management, for the HP150 project. The project manager was unable to maintain control over the project, as his decisions were often overridden by his superiors. The corporate players, however, were not close enough to the project to know all its intricacies but nevertheless intervened. This left the project manager, and the development team, in the difficult position of having to respond to decisions they had no part in making and which in some cases they disagreed with. There were too many cooks who had power to make changes.

The organizational environment was made more complex by the number of relationships that the team was expected to develop and maintain with other HP divisions. Keyboards and disk drives were particularly problematic.

Keyboard development was originally given to the Fort Collins, Colorado, division. The HP150 team required that the keyboard cost only $25 and that it have a quality advantage over other keyboards. The existing Fort Collins keyboard cost $100, and the general manager of the division did not believe that the POCD request merited a high priority. Fort Collins' first priority was keyboards for its own products, which were workstations. No one pushed them, and keyboard design and manufacturing rapidly became a bottleneck to the HP150 project. Finally the keyboard was brought back to POCD for a "crash design." It went through design, tooling development, and production ramp-up in six months. To give it flexibility, the team decided to use a unique but untested keycap print technology called sublimation printing, which made development all the more difficult.

The disk drive story was similar. The Greeley, Colorado, division had responsibility for disk drives in HP. This meant that they maintained control over the design, technology, pricing, and scheduling of the drives. The HP150 team was required to buy from Greeley but had no leverage. In looking out for its own well-being, the Greeley division leaders did not see the HP150 as a profitable opportunity. Rather than rising to the challenge of providing a new, cost-effective drive, they simply modified an existing one. This made it harder for the HP150 team to achieve the expected margins.

The lesson in both cases is a simple one. In the "old HP," divisions expected to set their own priorities. If a particular project came along on which it didn't look as if a good profit could be made, or if a project's demands were contrary to the division's own priorities, the product was left to languish. In this environment it would have been easier to achieve commitment to system components if they were farmed out to suppliers; while divisions may have seen themselves as secondary services to one another, suppliers would have seen service as their primary mission.

Despite the internal let-down, the manufacturing people got off to a good start. This project was the division's first attempt at design for manufacturability. Manufacturing was brought into the design process early on, and did have some influence on design. The most difficult task that manufacturing faced was determining how to manage suppliers under conditions of great uncertainty. Their task was complicated by the need to work with a newly formed Corporate Procurement organization. Divisions were being asked to pool their supply requirements at a central location, from which HP expected to get additional leverage over suppliers by making large volume purchases. Suppliers were understandably wary.

Marketing people, for their part, were not involved early on, thus no comprehensive marketing plan was developed. There was a plan for the HP150 as a terminal for the HP3000, but when the focus changed to a PC midstream, few changes were made in the marketing strategy.

Finally, six months before the product was to be introduced, senior management decided it would be more effective to distribute it through a dealer network. This was a first for HP, which had always sold direct, and required building a new distribution system, one HP had no prior experience with and did poorly with during the HP150's lifetime. The company did learn many lessons from this dealer experience and has subsequently turned the dealer channel into a valuable resource.


## Project Outcome and Lessons Learned

As a personal computer the HP150 never became profitable and was unable to gain market share against IBM. There were a number of lessons about product development that HP learned from the experience. Clearly the biggest problem was lack of a consistent guiding vision. First the HP150 was a terminal, then it was a PC attempting to satisfy a set of moving targets. In fairness to those directing the project, the PC market was not well defined, but the effect on the project was very detrimental. This was complicated by what might be termed too much ownership at the top and too little at the team level. There were too many people who had strong views and power over the project. Inevitably, the project got pulled in many directions.

A strong lesson was also learned in regard to pushing envelopes: don't push too many at once. POCD ended up instigating several major managerial and organizational changes all at the same time. Too much was attempted. This was the first endeavor to truly integrate marketing, manufacturing, and R&D, and the first try at a distribution channel that used dealers. In addition, this was the first major project that required the team to rely heavily on technologies from sister divisions, a formidable challenge given the company's history of autonomy.

Nonetheless, integration between the functional areas was improved over prior projects. The project served to uncover the barriers to making cross-divisional integration work, and was worth it on this ground alone. If nothing else, it opened everyone's eyes at HP to problems of cooperation across divisions. It has since become clear that this model does not lead to the best results for the company as a whole.

# DESKJET

## Competitive Environment and Product Strategy

The DeskJet project was undertaken at HP's Vancouver Division late in 1985. The division had been formed in 1979 to manufacture and market impact printers. By the early 1980s impact printers, so called because a lettering device strikes a page, had become the prevalent printers used with computers. By 1985, prototype ink-jet printers began to appear, but they made few inroads; they offered better resolution and more flexibility in type style, but were more costly, not particularly reliable, and at the time required special paper. Soon after, laser printers hit the market. They offered much better resolution still and took over as the quality leaders, even though they cost considerably more. Ink-jets were further crowded by dot-matrix printers, which had some similar attributes but gained more widespread acceptance. Vancouver's original charter evolved to include development of printers that used an HP-proprietary ink-jet technology.

Prior to 1982, HP, DEC, and IBM all sold their own peripherals with their computer equipment. In that year, however, Japanese companies began to create an "independent" printer market and by 1985 Epson alone owned the general purpose low-end market with an 80 percent market share. Vancouver's revenues had peaked and were dropping significantly each year. In November 1985, after a full review of HP's printer line, the Vancouver division received and endorsed a new charter from group management: concentrate on a printer for the low-end personal and office market.

The Vancouver division responded by shifting all its resources to two new product development efforts: DeskJet and RuggedWriter, a variant (see **Figure 14.6**). Quickly the division placed all its bets on one machine; the strategy was to create a niche between low-priced, low-quality impact printers and higher priced, high-quality laser printers by creating an ink-jet with resolution close to that of laser printers, but at a price so much lower that it would wipe out sales of impact printers and dot-matrix printers for general computer use.

HP was confident it could reach this target because ink-jet technology was invented at HP Labs. Both the Vancouver division R&D manager and the DeskJet project manager were ink-jet technology champions and had devoted several years to its application. In addition, the DeskJet project team had experimented with inkjet technology for three years. Thus, the division felt it was well positioned to take advantage of the technology. Significant development was still required, however, to make the product meet laser-quality standards and low cost.

Product life cycles in the low-end printer business are short, averaging two years. The DeskJet was intended as a "base hit" rather than a "home run" on the path to a longer term low-end printer strategy. The division expected to be ready with a follow-on product within 15 months.

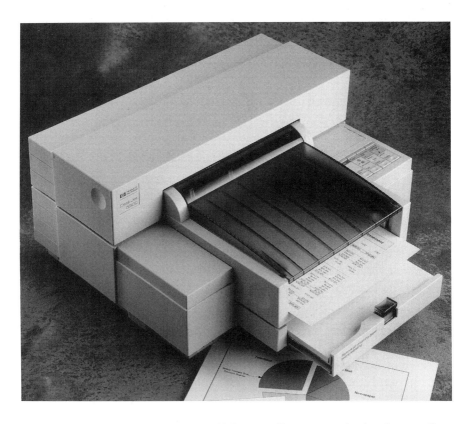

**Figure 14.6.** The DeskJet printer, which uses office paper and prints laser-quality output with 300 dots-per-inch (dpi) resolution for text and graphics. (Reprinted by permission of Hewlett-Packard Co.)

HP's senior management made it clear the division's future was riding on the ink-jet printer. But they stipulated only that Vancouver find a way to get solidly back into the market, and allowed the project team to set particular goals. The team picked a specific objective that was easily understood throughout the division: develop a laser-quality printer for under $1000 retail. The division manager maintained focus by reminding the team that "If you are not working on DeskJet (or RuggedWriter), then you are just rearranging the deck chairs on the Titanic."

## Project Execution

The DeskJet goal established some difficult challenges. First, the print head, the key component, would require major development. The team estimated that the effort required 75 percent invention, 15 percent design, and 10 percent communication. Complicating matters further, the print head was to be developed and manufactured by the InkJet Components Operation in Corvallis, Oregon, some two hours away from Vancouver by car. The rest of the technology would be developed at Vancouver. Because the team worried about the print head effort being off-site, it made an explicit decision early on to lower risk by taking on additional design tasks at Vancouver to relieve as much burden as possible from the print-head effort.

The second challenge was to design for manufacturability, to cut cost. The team decided the best way to do this was to minimize the total number of parts in the printer, to simplify assembly, parts handling, and purchasing, so manufacturing and suppliers had to be involved early.

Finally, the team was challenged because it had little experience in the high-volume, dealer-oriented marketplace in which the DeskJet would be sold. Competition was much fiercer in this arena than HP was used to, and the DeskJet was positioned to fundamentally change the low-end printing market. Winning was expected to take from 5 to 10 years, requiring strong initial understanding of the potential market along with well-executed follow-up efforts. The task was a tough one, particularly because the marketing team was inexperienced. All these challenges added up to a need for team members to work in a more tightly linked cross-functional mode than any of them had experienced in the past. All functional areas—marketing, manufacturing, R&D, and suppliers—played new roles.

Early in the effort, marketing obtained user preference data and analyzed it statistically to determine product feature requirements. A Portland-based market research firm was used throughout the project to conduct focus groups as the product evolved. Use of the same firm throughout the project allowed the firm to become very familiar with the product and offer useful insights in interpreting customer feedback.

"Mall studies," unheard of in HP prior to DeskJet, were performed as well. Unfortunately, the mall studies would have saved more time and effort had their results been heeded. Early on, the marketing people suggested these studies because the DeskJet was meant for the average computer user. They went to shopping malls to ask potential customers what they thought about proposed features. When marketing brought back twenty suggestions for important changes that would be necessary to ensure success, the R&D engineers heeded only four. Later, as the product took final shape, marketing became insistent that the design engineers go to the malls to hear from the future customers' own lips what was wanted. The engineers reluctantly went, mostly because the idea was novel. After direct exposure to the same information they had rejected earlier, the designers made 16 of the other changes originally requested, but it cost time and money because so many changes had to be made and the design was so near completion.

Early involvement of manufacturing on the DeskJet project was also critical. The R&D manager understood this and established, within the R&D budget, a manufacturing engineering group assigned solely to this product. From the start this group worked in R&D, and only later moved to manufacturing. Also, as early as the study/design phase review, the materials engineers had compiled a materials checklist, which by its presence alone began to focus the team on cost, especially in its interactions with suppliers. Later, during the develop/test phase, manufacturing engineers got tooling designed and released to build early test units. In a traditional setting, R&D would have skimped on spending for tooling and let manufacturing pick up the slack once the product was further developed.

The DeskJet team was also strict with itself during prototype stages, which significantly shortened the time to introduction. Once the first prototype units were built—nine months before product release—manufacturing took over the prototyping process. Each month, regardless of whether R&D was "ready" or not, manufacturing built 50 prototype units. This was a psychological change within HP; typically, design engineers controlled the prototyping schedule, and would allow themselves to squeeze as many last-minute changes as possible into a prototype before it was run to see the outcome. But in this case manufacturing was in control and simply didn't allow this to happen. Thus manufacturing (and marketing) could reliably use the prototyping process for their needs, and not have to succumb to the whims of the designers that more often than not muddled the usefulness of individual prototype cycles.

Suppliers played an important role too. One of the decisions that the team had to make was how many parts to contract for before the final design had been approved. To meet the extremely short time to introduction, and with materials lead times of three to six months, they decided they had to buy about one-third of the parts before R&D released its final design. But early integration of the team led to good success; they ended up ordering $1.5 million of parts early in the process, but only had to write off about $50,000. To help technical communication and feedback between all parties, the team set cost goals prior to meeting with the vendors, and then placed engineers in key suppliers' facilities during both the design and product ramp-up phases.

Integration of all aspects of the product by the team was well done. When the DeskJet project was started, the manufacturing and marketing people were moved into the lab to sit with the R&D engineers. This resulted in strong integration among the three functional teams, a tactic not normally pursued in HP, where R&D engineers usually pushed on alone. In fact, R&D's top priority was to get more resources for the manufacturing group. The R&D section manager played a dual role of not only managing the R&D engineers, but as a "first among equals" with his manufacturing and marketing counterparts. This meant that he wanted all the team members to view each others as equals, while still realizing that R&D played the lead role. The clear product charter, and a history of working together on an earlier project, made it possible for the three functions to reach quick decisions as the project progressed.

The team produced a well-integrated product because its members were located together for the duration, and they themselves were an integrated bunch. There were about 30 R&D engineers, 20 manufacturing engineers, 4 marketing people, 2 quality persons, and 1 financial person. While the numbers may seem unbalanced, they were more integrated than in most HP projects; this was further helped because the decision-making body—the core group within the team—consisted of one person from each function.

## Project Outcome and Lessons Learned

The DeskJet was highly successful. The share of the market held by ink-jet printers rose from 1 percent to 5 percent due to sales of the DeskJet alone. Some 95 percent of DeskJet users said they would recommend the machine to a friend. The project team met the very tight 22-month development schedule, introducing the product in September 1987 as planned. The product then proceeded to exceed shipping rate expectations by a factor of three. The only user need that the DeskJet failed to meet was for a permanent (non-water-soluble) ink.

The DeskJet team learned two primary design and manufacturing lessons. First, they realized in hindsight that the design for manufacturability objective of minimizing the total number of parts in the printer caused more trouble than it was worth. Casting of the printer's plastic main deck became so complex in an attempt to integrate so many different components that it was difficult to tool and manufacture. The team agreed that it would have been less expensive to have had a few more parts. The second lesson had to do with handling the steep production ramp. Because order volume was three times higher than expected, reaching steady-state production was difficult. Tooling wore more rapidly than expected and manufacturing engineers were pulled away from future development projects to manage DeskJet production.

Overall, the DeskJet project has many positive lessons for product development, and many that echo the themes identified in the earlier chapters of this book. Certainly the DeskJet is a great example of how to use a rigid (periodic) prototyping schedule to drive the development schedule. If design changes came from R&D in time to meet a prototype cycle, they were incorporated. If they were not ready, the run ensued anyway. This forced the design engineers to maintain a certain pace of development. It also provided manufacturing with much needed "practice" for its ultimate job. And it supplied a fairly large number of prototype units so marketing could conduct field tests and QA could run its tests.

Managing the pieces of the project so the team could push the envelope on the key component was also done well. The print head was the key to success; if it could deliver near laser-quality images, the product would be a hit. Simply developing a print head that could do this was a major step forward, so the team took other burdens off the head subteam. One burden that was lifted, for example, was the usual requirement that the print head work quickly, so the machine would print quickly. The team modified other parts of the machine to speed delivery, so the print head could work more slowly, which enabled it to make a sharper image.

One striking aspect of the team was its drive and energy. The sense that the entire Vancouver division's fate rested on the project's success or failure created considerable ownership of and commitment to the project by the team members and the rest of the company. The fact that many team members were new to the division also made some difference in the extent to which the message of fatality was believed. There was a real eagerness within the group to "stand up and be counted." Plus, they were entering a market they had not yet penetrated, which helped keep them focused.

The DeskJet also is one of the earliest examples in HP's history of strong integration between traditional functions. Marketing, manufacturing, and design people were all part of the project from the beginning. And despite the early problem of getting the design engineers to listen to the results of the mall studies, they did end up meeting customers and making changes, which would not have happened otherwise had marketing not been on the team from the outset. Since that incident, other HP teams have listened much more closely to their marketing people.

Finally, there was a rare and compelling harmony between senior management and the team with respect to the so-called guiding vision of the effort. Senior management made a strong statement—that the division had better steal back market share—but it allowed the division to translate that into product particulars: an ink-jet printer with laser-quality output for less than $1000. The two groups galvanized their goals without stepping on each other's toes.

# Notes

## Chapter 2

Material in this chapter is adapted from Dorothy Leonerd-Barton, "Core Capabilities and Core Rigidities: A Paradox in Managing New Product Developments." *Strategic Management Journal, 13,* 1992, Summer Special Issue.

1. See, for example, C. K. Prahalad and G. Hamel, "The Core Competence of the Corporation," *Harvard Business Review, 68* (3), 1990, pp. 79–91.

2. See H. Itami with T. Roehl, *Mobilizing Invisible Assets* (Cambridge, MA: Harvard University Press, 1987).

3. See, for example, M. Hitt and R. D. Ireland, "Corporate Distinctive Competence, Strategy, Industry and Performance," *Strategic Management Journal, 6,* 1985, pp. 273–293; and R. H. Hayes, S. C. Wheelwright, and K. B. Clark, *Dynamic Manufacturing* (New York: The Free Press, 1988).

4. See R. P. Rumelt, *Strategy, Structure and Economic Performance* (Harvard Business School Classics, Boston: Harvard Business School Press, 1974; 1986).

5. See R. H. Hayes, "Strategic Planning—Forward in Reverse?," *Harvard Business Review,* November–December 1985, pp. 111–119.

6. See, for example, D. Teece, G. Pisano, and A. Shuen, "Firm Capabilities, Resources, and the Concept of Strategy" (Consortium on Competitiveness and Cooperation Working Paper 90–9, University of California at Berkeley, Center for Research in Management, Berkeley, CA, 1990).

7. For a discussion of values in general, see E. Schein, "Coming to a New Awareness of Organizational Culture," *Sloan Management Review,* Winter 1984, pp. 3–16.

8. See R. Rosenthal and D. Rubin, "Interpersonal Expectancy Effects: The First 345 Studies," *The Behavioral and Brain Sciences, 3,* 1978, pp. 377–415.

9. Kurt Levin is credited with originating this idea, which has since been widely imitated.

10. For an extensive treatment of how small departures from traditional can inspire eventual large-scale change, see R. Kanter, *The Change Masters: Innovation for Productivity in the American Corporation* (New York: Simon and Schuster, 1983).

## Chapter 3

1. For a discussion of corporation-wide guiding visions, see G. Hamel and C. K. Prahalad, "Strategic Intent," *Harvard Business Review,* 67 (3), 1989, pp. 63–76.

2. For a discussion of "emergent" strategies that grow out of pragmatic management behavior, see Henry Mintzberg and J. A. Waters, "Of Strategies, Deliberate and Emergent," *Strategic Management Journal, 6,* 1985, pp. 257–272.

3. See Kim B. Clark and Takahiro Fujimoto, "The Power of Product Integrity," *Harvard Business Review, 68* (6), November–December 1990, pp. 107–118.

4. For a discussion of lead users helping product development, see Eric von Hippel, *The Sources of Innovation* (New York: Oxford University Press, 1988).

5. For further discussion of this dilemma, see Dorothy Leonard-Barton, Edith Wilson, and John Doyle, "Commercializing Technology: Imaginative Understanding of User Needs," Harvard Business School Working Paper #93–053.

6. For a primer on scenario-building, see P. Schwartz, *The Art of the Long View* (New York: Doubleday, 1991).

## Chapter 4

Bralla, James G. (Ed.). (1986). *Handbook of Product Design for Manufacturing.* New York: McGraw-Hill.

Chryssolouris, George. (1992). *Manufacturing Systems: Theory and Practice.* New York: Springer-Verlag.

Compton, W. Dale (Ed.). (1988). *Design and Analysis of Integrated Manufacturing Systems.* Washington, DC: National Academy Press.

Corbett, John, Dooner, Mike, Meleka, John, and Pym, Christopher. (1991). *Design for Manufacture.* Reading, MA: Addison-Wesley.

Crawford, C. Merle. (1991). *New Products Management,* 3rd edition. Homewood, IL: Irwin.

Cross, Nigel. (1989). *Engineering Design Methods.* New York: John Wiley.

Ettlie, John E., and Stoll, Henry W. (1990). *Managing the Design-Manufacturing Process.* New York: McGraw-Hill.

Girifalco, Louis A. (1991). *Dynamics of Technological Change.* New York: Van Nostrand Reinhold.

Heim, Joseph A., and Compton, W. Dale (Eds.). (1992). *Manufacturing Systems: Foundations of World Class Practice.* Washington, DC: National Academy of Engineering.

National Research Council. (1991). *Improving Engineering Design: Designing for Competitive Advantage.* Washgington, DC: National Academy Press.

National Research Council. (1991). *The Competitive Edge: Research Priorities for U.S. Manufacturing*. Washington, DC: National Academy Press.

Noori, Hamid. (1990). *Managing the Dynamics of New Technology*. Englewood Cliffs, NJ: Prentice-Hall.

Norman, Donald A. (1988). *The Design of Everyday Things*. New York: Doubleday.

Pugh, Stuart. (1991). *Total Design*. Reading, MA: Addison-Wesley.

Trucks, H.E. (1974). *Designing for Economical Production*. Dearborn, MI: Society of Manufacturing Engineers.

Vincent, Geoff. (1989). *Managing New Product Development*. New York: Van Nostrand Reinhold.

Viswanadham, N., and Narahari, Y. (1992). *Performance Modeling of Automated Manufacturing Systems*. Englewood Cliffs, NJ: Prentice-Hall.

## Chapter 5

1. See Takahiro Fujimoto, Marco Iansiti, and Kim B. Clark, "External Integration in Product Development," Harvard Business School Working Paper 92–025.

2. See, for example, Paul R. Lawrence and Jay W. Lorsch, *Organization and Environment* (Homewood, IL: Richard D. Erwin, 1967).

3. See also T. J. Allen, *Managing the Flow of Technology* (Cambridge: MIT Press, 1977); T. J. Allen, M. L. Tushman, and D. M. S. Lee, "R&D Performance as a Function of Internal Communication, Project Management, and the Nature of Work," *IEEE Transactions on Engineering Management,* EM-27 (1), February 1980; and T. J. Allen and O. Hauptman, "The Influence of Communication Technologies on Organizational Structure," *Communication Research,* 15 (5), October 1987, pp. 575–578.

4. See also Eric von Hippel, *The Sources of Innovation* (New York: Oxford University Press, 1988).

5. See Michael L. Tushman, "Special Boundary Roles in the Innovation Process," *Administrative Science Quarterly,* 22, December 1977, pp. 587–605.

## Chapter 6

1. For additional discussion of the factors that affect individual performance, see Rosabeth Moss Kanter, "When 1,000 Flowers Bloom: Structural, Collective, and Social Conditions for Innovation in Organizations," *Research and Organizational Behavior,* 10 (1988), pp. 169–211.

2. An excellent discussion of the characteristics that affect team performance can be found in J. Richard Hackman (Ed.), *Groups That Work (and Those That Don't)* (San Francisco: Jossey Bass, 1990). Hackman's work details studies of several teams in seven organizational settings and identifies the conditions necessary for effective teamwork. See also Paul R. Lawrence and Jay W. Lorsch, *Organization and Environment* (Homewood, IL: Richard D. Irwin, 1967), and Thomas J. Allen and Oscar Hauptman, "The Influence of Communication Technologies on Organizational Structure," *Communication Research,* 14 (5), October 1987, pp. 575–578.

3. An in-depth discussion of the characteristics that affect corporate support of

teams and their projects is contained in Richard Walton, *Up and Running* (Boston: Harvard Business School Press, 1989); see especially Chapter 4, "Promoting Organizational Commitment and Competence." See also "Building Development Capability," Chapter 12 in Steven C. Wheelwright and Kim B. Clark, *Revolutionizing Product Development* (New York: Free Press, 1992).

4. A thorough explanation of the ways in which ownership and commitment can be achieved is found in John P. Kotter and James L. Heskett, *Corporate Culture and Performance* (New York: The Free Press, 1992); see especially Chapter 8, "Leaders in Action," and Chapter 11, "On the Role of Top Management." See also "People Make it Happen," Chapter 9 in Robert H. Hayes, Steven C. Wheelwright, and Kim B. Clark, *Dynamic Manufacturing* (New York: The Free Press, 1988); and "Mobilizing People," Chapter 11 in James L. Heskett, W. Earl Sasser, Jr., and Christopher Hart, *Service Breakthroughs* (New York: The Free Press, 1990).

5. An excellent discussion of how team level commitment and ownership can be developed is found in Kim B. Clark and Takahiro Fujimoto, *Product Development Performance* (Boston: Harvard Business School Press, 1991); see especially Chapter 9, "Leadership and Organization: The Heavyweight Product Manager." See also Chapter 8, "Organizing and Leading Product Teams," in Wheelwright and Clark.

6. For additional reading on organizational change and methods for gaining support for such change throughout the organization, see Michael Beer, Russell Eisendstat, and Bert Spector, *The Critical Path to Corporate Renewal* (Boston: Harvard Business School Press, 1990). See also the section on "Conclusions: Creating More Effective Work Groups and Organizations" in Hackman (Ed.), *Groups That Work*.

7. In addition to the references cited above, the reader interested in managing the improvement path might examine Chapter 9, "Implications for Pratical Affairs," in Lawrence and Lorsch, *Organization and Environment*. See also Chapters 2 and 11, "The Concept of a Development Strategy" and "Learning from Development Projects," in Wheelwright and Clark, *Revolutionizing Product Development*.


## Chapter 7

Some of this material has recently appeared in P. Barkin and M. Iansiti, *Concurrent Engineering: Research and Application*, Vol. 1, 1993, pp. 125–134.

1. See, for example, Clark and Fujimoto, *Product Development Performance*.

2. This widely cited statistic can be found, for example, In Daniel W. Whitney, "Manufacturing by Design," *Harvard Business Review*, July–August 1988, pp. 83–91.

3. An insightful, critical benchmark study of prototype roles is presented in B. Bebb, "What We Have Learned About Roles in Achieving World-Class Engineering Design Quality," Proceedings, Design Productivity International Conference, February 3–9, 1991, Honolulu, Hawaii, sponsored by University of Missouri-Rolla.

4. See L. Sullivan, "The Seven Stages in Company-Wide Control," *Quality Progress*, May 1986.

5. The original concept was suggested by J. Fox, "Design Quality and Reliability Through Technology Readiness," Publication 89 DPC003, Design Engineering Center, University of Missouri, Rolla, MO 65401.

6. For an excellent overview, see J. R. Hauser and D. Clausing, "The House of Quality," *Harvard Business Review,* May–June 1988, pp. 63–73.

7. For more details, see G. Taguchi, "Off-Line and On-Line Quality Control Systems," *Proceedings of the International Meeting on Quality Control,* B4, 1978, pp. 1–5.

8. Representative of current thinking is D.K. Medler, "Stereolithography and Concurrent Engineering," *Concurrent Engineering,* 1 (4), July–August 1991, pp. 5–10.

## Chapter 8

1. For further reading on the benefits of and practices leading to fast innovation, refer to George Stalk and Thomas Hout, *Competing Against Time* (New York: The Free Press, 1990), Chapter 4—"Time and Innovation."

2. Discussion on managing the marketing interface can be referred to Stephen Rosenthal, *Effective Product Design and Development* (Homewood, IL: Business One Irwin, 1992), Chapter 12—"Key Linkages with Other Businesses."

3. For further discussion of the cross-functional tensions faced by project members, see Philip Thomas, *Getting Competitive: Middle Managers and the Cycle Time Ethic* (New York: McGraw-Hill, 1992), Chapter 5—"The Andy Problem."

4. For further discussion on work structuring, see Stalk and Hout, *Competing Against Time,* Chapter 6—"Re-designing the Organization for Time." See also Gary Rummler and Alan Brache, *How to Manage the White Space on the Organization Chart* (San Francisco, CA: Jossey Bass, 1990), Chapter 10—"Improving and Managing the Processes of the Organization."

5. For more extensive discussion on effective teams, see Bob Harper and Ann Harper, *Succeeding as a Self-Directed Work Team* (Croton-on-Hudson, NY: MW Corporation, 1992).

6. Chapter 6, "Selecting and Using Design Technologies," from Rosenthal, *Effective Product Design and Development,* provides a set of criteria to guide the evaluation and use of design tools.

7. An excellent presentation of project management protocol in the form of phases and gates is provided in Chapter 2, "Structuring the Work: Phases, Gates and Simultaneous Engineering," from Rosenthal, *Effective Product Design and Development.*

# Index

DECstation 3100, 73–74
Lincoln Continental, 74
"pocket rocket," 72
project, 64–71
 alignment with line-of-business vision,
  67–68
 DECstation 3100, 64–66
 DeskJet, 70
 LANbridge 200, 70

Heavyweight project leaders
 guiding visions, 147
 roles, 146
 traits, 145–146, 148
Hewlett-Packard Corporation, 393–425
 DeskJet, 11, 401–402, 418–425
  development project as agent of change,
   54
  fit with customer expectations, 136–138
  ownership and commitment, 168–169,
   188–191
  project definition, 420
  project guiding vision, 70
  prototyping, 422–423
 Hornet spectrum analyzer, 11, 401, 408–
  413
  learning from a development project,
   282–283
  pushing the envelope, 111
 HP150, 11, 401, 413–418
  fit with customer expectations, 136–138
  misalignment of core capabilities, 33
  ownership and commitment, 191–195
  project definition, 414
 logic analyzer, 11, 401, 402–407
  misreading state-of-the-art envelopes, 94
  pushing the envelope, 110–111
 phase review structure, 398–400
 successful implementation of prototyping,
  224

Incentive systems, 42, 177–179
Integration, 229–263
 Chaparral Steel Company, 241
 coherence, 133
 communication, 246–248
 conflict resolution, 243–244, 247–248
 with corporate development goals
  FX15 air-conditioning compressor, 235
 cross-functional training, 253–255
 Eastman Kodak Company, 241
 Ford Motor Company, 381–382
 judging degree of, 237–245
 lack of, in DECstation 3100, 236–237
 management protocols, 259–261
 ownership and commitment, 241

project vision, 65
prototyping, 257–259
 of subgroups, 237–239
 system-level responsibility, 240–241
 task structuring
  Factory of the Future, 250
  Ford Motor Company, 250–251
  FunSaver, 251–252

Learning
 becoming a learning organization, 270–
  272
 as core rigidity, 272–273
 as dynamic process, 266–267
 guiding vision, 64, 284–289
 organizational, 52
 project leadership, 273–277
 as project outcome
  Hornet spectrum analyzer, 282–283

Manufacturing Vision Group
 organization, 6, 24
MAP, 9, 54, 352–354, 362

"Next bench" design, 50, 82, 103–104,
 397–398

Organization
 dedicated system, 128, 143
 functional system, 127, 139–141, 143
 heavyweight system, 127–128, 142
  Ford Motor Company, 158–163, 380
 lightweight system, 127, 141–142
 matching with project leadership, 151–154
  Chaparral Steel Company, 154–156
 specialization, 131–132
Ownership and commitment, 165–201
 at the corporate level, 167
 DeskJet printer project, 168–169
 development of, 184–188
 fostered by guiding visions, 179
 guiding vision, 64
 at the individual level, 166
 integrating the components, 188–195
  DeskJet, 188–191, 193–195
  HP150, 191–195
 LANbridge 200, 169–171
 managing subprojects
  RA90 disk drive, 197–198
 potential problems
  arc saw, 196
  Factory of the Future, 196
 at the project team level, 166–167, 281

Perpetual enterprise machine, 14–17
Project definition, 57–58